MELVILLE'S

BILLY BUDD AND THE CRITICS

SECOND EDITION

MELVILLE'S
BILLY BUDD AND THE CRITICS

SECOND EDITION

edited by

WILLIAM T. STAFFORD

Purdue University

Wadsworth Publishing Company, Inc., Belmont, California

10262

for Fran, Lindy, Jocy, Katy, and Kisu

SECOND PRINTING: | *January 1969*

L.C. Cat. Card No.: 68–11208

Printed in the United States of America

Preface to the Second Edition

This revised edition of *Melville's Billy Budd and the Critics* brings to the student and the scholar the latest addition—both textual and critical—to the continually developing literary history of Melville's most widely read tale. It also provides for the first time the complete text of the highly acclaimed dramatic adaptation by Louis O. Coxe and Robert Chapman. With, therefore, the most authoritative text of the story (that prepared by Professors Harrison Hayford and Merton M. Sealts, Jr., for the University of Chicago Press in 1962), with the dramatic version, and with representative samplings of the most recent kinds of criticism of the tale, the student has available for him here both the requisite primary material and samples of and guides to the most recent secondary material.

This edition contains a number of other new features. This editor's essay-review (in 1962) of the new Chicago edition is reprinted here in full. Also, since much of the criticism of the tale before 1962 made wide interpretive use of the Freeman edition, the controversial "Preface" to that edition is included. The text of the play, moreover, is followed by a note by the playwrights themselves, explaining their interest in and use of the story as source material for their adaptation.

The five sections of criticism included in the first edition are all retained but are supplemented with three different kinds of recent critical attention to the story: a notable example of historical scholarship, in which the actual Articles of War, in contrast to the fictive ones given such a prominent part in the story, are examined; a very brief explication of the thematic function performed by contrasting the role of Red Whiskers (on *The Rights of Man*) to that of Claggart (on the *Bellipotent*); and, finally, a recent, extensive, over-all view of the tale and its critical history up to 1965. The study questions and theme topics have been extensively revised and extended; and the annotated bibliography of studies of *Billy Budd* has been brought up to date.

Evidence attesting to the continued vitality and dramatic relevance of *Billy Budd, Sailor* is around one everywhere—from the Peter Ustinov production of the movie adaptation (in which he starred and which he also directed) to the more than forty additional critical articles that have been written about the tale since the first edition of this volume, in 1961. Perhaps, however, the Preface to that first edition (also here reprinted) is preface enough to the larger significance embodied in the tale itself, its various adaptations, and its expanding critical history.

Instructions about editorial method in that first Preface apply as well here.

W. T. S.

Preface to the First Edition

Melville's *Billy Budd* is an instructive example of American fiction. First, it is more *novella* than novel, more the long tale than the novel as we traditionally think of it—as are so many of our most celebrated works of fiction: James's *The Turn of the Screw,* Crane's *The Red Badge of Courage,* Fitzgerald's *The Great Gatsby,* Katherine Anne Porter's *Pale Horse, Pale Rider,* Faulkner's *The Bear,* to name only a few. Like many of them also, *Billy Budd* joins simplicity of action with complexity of meaning, its surface directness oddly at ease with the moral obliqueness within. It is instructive, finally, in that uniqueness with which major works of any important writer reflect his abiding interests and major themes. No serious student of Melville can ignore *Billy Budd* and pretend to any thorough knowledge of his literary achievement. By similar token, *Billy Budd* is literally a comment on all of Melville's preceding works, just as they are in a sense meaningful preparation for *Billy Budd.* This tale, then, is an ideal introduction to fiction generally, to American fiction specifically, and to the other works of Melville. And when we remember that the tale has been adapted into a highly praised play, a celebrated opera, and a television drama, it may also be, through the study of those works, an ideal introduction to some of the other arts.

The criticism written about *Billy Budd* is equally instructive. No important school of modern critical thought is without representation in this criticism. A study of it therefore becomes a study of modern literary criticism since the early 1920s, when the tale was first published. As a consequence, I have attempted to arrange this criticism in a way that reflects both the development and the variety of that widespread attention. The first section, for example, contains brief, early notices, all written during the 1920s. The second section joins the first extensive analysis that was made of the tale (in 1933) with a diametrically opposed point of view made by a critic in 1959. The question of whether or not *Billy Budd* is a testament—and, if so, what kind of testament—dominated criticism of the tale until recently. The third section is composed of five different readings—a biographical reading, a social reading, a mythic-psychoanalytical reading, and two aesthetic readings—each embodying and operating from a different critical premise and yet each also representing in one sense a total interpretation of the tale. The fourth section is composed of studies of sources and parallels. And the fifth section is an examination of some of the special critical problems posed by the tale. The book concludes with an extensive list of questions and topics for discussion and papers and a checklist of additional studies of *Billy Budd.*

v

Such an arrangement, I believe, will make this volume useful for a wide variety of purposes. It can be used as a source book in composition courses for both brief and long documented papers. For schools with large library holdings in literary criticism, the checklist provides directions to ample additional studies of the tale. For schools with limited holdings, the collection of criticism within the volume is extensive enough to indicate the various approaches that have been made and that can be made to the story. The book, it is therefore hoped, will also be useful for introductory classes in literature and criticism, for classes in American literature generally, and in the American novel and short story.

For the convenience of the student, page references to the original sources of the critical articles are given in raised numbers between brackets. The number before the diagonal (/) indicates the end of the original page; the number after it signals the beginning of a new page. Whenever a page of text in its original form ended with a divided word, I have ignored the division and placed the page reference at the end of the completed word. The articles have been as accurately reproduced as possible, with the exception of occasional footnotes that have been dropped and the remaining ones renumbered, and with the exception of an occasional creation or substitution of a title. In the case of the latter, a footnote states the original title.

Finally, I would like to express my appreciation to the various authors and publishers whose works are collected here; to Harrison Hayford of Northwestern University for advice about the text and checklist; to my colleague Maurice Beebe, who, as general editor of this series, has helped me with a variety of problems too numerous to list; and to two other Purdue colleagues, William Braswell and Allen Hayman, who have allowed me to borrow from their excellent collections of studies about Melville more times than I like to remember.

W. T. S.

Contents

THE TEXTS

1. The Story

The New *Billy Budd* and the Novelistic Fallacy: The Chicago Text, *William T. Stafford* 3

Billy Budd, Sailor, *Herman Melville* 12

"Preface" from Freeman Text, *Herman Melville* 76

2. The Play

Billy Budd, *Louis O. Coxe and Robert Chapman* 77

Notes on the Play, *Louis O. Coxe and Robert Chapman* 126

THE CRITICS

1. Five Early Views

Sinners and Saints Alike, *Raymond M. Weaver* (1921) 131

The Inevitable Disaster of Good, *John Middleton Murry* (1924) 131

Innocence Vindicated, *John Freeman* (1926) 132

Revelation or Illusion? *Raymond M. Weaver* (1928) 133

Melville's Final Affirmation, *Lewis Mumford* (1929) 134

2. *Billy Budd* as Testament

Melville's Testament of Acceptance, *E. L. Grant Watson* 136

Billy Budd: Testament of Resistance, *Phil Withim* 140

3. Major Readings

Billy Budd AS SPIRITUAL AUTOBIOGRAPHY

Melville's *Billy Budd* as "An Inside Narrative," *William Braswell* 153

Billy Budd AS SOCIAL COMMENTARY

Expediency and Absolute Morality in *Billy Budd*, *Wendell Glick* 165

Billy Budd AS MYTH

The Rite of Sacrament, *Richard Chase* 173

Billy Budd AS ART

The Unity of *Billy Budd*, *Ray B. West, Jr.* 180

The Form of *Billy Budd*, *William York Tindall* 186

4. Christian Sources and Classical Parallels

Melville's Use of the Bible, *Nathalia Wright*   193
Melville's *Nunc Dimittis, Newton Arvin*   197
The Uses of Milton, *Lawrance Thompson*   201
Milton and Melville, *Henry F. Pommer*   202
A Caution about Sources, *Norman Holmes Pearson*   203
Billy Budd, Antigone, and *The Winter's Tale, Richard Chase*   203
Melville's Version of Tragedy, *Richard Harter Fogle*   206
Billy and Oedipus, *Herbert Weisinger and Adrian J. Jaffe*   210

5. Special Problems

THE CHARACTERS

The Case for Captain Vere, *Milton R. Stern*   211
The Case against Captain Vere, *Leonard Casper*   212
Billy Budd, *W. H. Auden*   215
Claggart—I, *W. H. Auden*   217
Claggart—II, *Geoffrey Stone*   218
The Dansker: Archetype of the Wise Man, *James Baird*   219

THE DIGRESSIONS

The Digressions in *Billy Budd, Mary Foley*   220
Billy in the Darbies, *M. L. Rosenthal and A. J. M. Smith*   223

THE AUTHOR

Herman Melville, *W. H. Auden*   225

6. Recent Criticism

Billy Budd and the Articles of War, *C. B. Ives*   227
Melville's *Billy Budd,* Chapter 1, *Leonard Nathanson*   234
Billy Budd and the Limits of Perception, *John W. Rathbun*   236

APPENDICES

Chronology   253
Study Questions   255
Theme Topics   257
Topics for Longer Essays and Term Papers   259
Bibliography: An Annotated Checklist of Studies of *Billy Budd*   263

THE TEXTS

1. THE STORY

The New *Billy Budd* and the
Novelistic Fallacy:
The Chicago Text

WILLIAM T. STAFFORD

SEVERAL YEARS AGO BRUCE HARKNESS PUBLISHED AN ELOQUENT PLEA
for more attention to the establishment of reliable texts of novels.[1]
The "novelistic fallacy," he said, is the view that because novels are
longer than poems and their wholes more important than their parts,
little attention need be paid to textual details: what matters a misprint or a misplaced comma in a work that contains thousands of
words? After giving a convincing number of instances in which
critics have made serious blunders by accepting inaccurate texts
(Melville's "soiled fish of the sea," for example[2]), Harkness concluded his essay by asking that critics pay more attention to textual
bibliography: "Can not we somehow insist that editing actually be
done—instead of the practice of putting a fancy introduction on a
poor text? Can not we have sound texts reproduced and publisher's
history stated by the editor? Can not we know *what it is* we have in
our hands?" In recent years an increasing amount of scholarly attention has been given to that most important task—by Harkness
himself on Conrad, by Matthew J. Bruccoli on Fitzgerald and James,
and by James B. Meriwether on Faulkner and Cozzens, to name but
three. Now new pertinence is given those questions and the general
problem of the text of novels by Hayford and Sealts's recently published edition of Melville's famous last tale.[3]

[1] "Bibliography and the Novelistic Fallacy," *Studies in Bibliography*, XII
(1959), 59–73.
[2] Harkness, p. 62. John W. Nichol was the first to point out that F. O. Matthiessen's praise of Melville's vivid image in *White-Jacket* was made without knowledge that "soiled" was a misprint for "coiled"—"Melville's 'Soiled' Fish of the
Sea," *American Literature*, XXI (Nov. 1949), 338–339.
[3] Harrison Hayford and Merton M. Sealts, Jr., eds., *Billy Budd, Sailor* (*An
Inside Narrative*): *Reading Text and Genetic Text, Edited from the Manuscript
with Introduction and Notes* (Chicago: Univ. of Chicago Press, 1962).

From "The New *Billy Budd* and the Novelistic Fallacy: An Essay-Review,"
Modern Fiction Studies, VIII (Autumn 1962), 306–311. Reprinted by permission
of the Purdue Research Foundation and of the author.

Billy Budd is a work that, though not published until 1924, is widely anthologized, often reprinted in student editions, and quite probably the one work by Melville more frequently taught in the classroom than *Moby-Dick*. In fact, at the time of this writing, at least seven paperback editions of the tale are in print, and it is a rare anthology of American literature that does not include it. In addition, critical comment on the story has been so extensive and varied, as the checklist in this issue of *Modern Fiction Studies* reveals, that even comment on James's "Turn of the Screw" is somewhat sketchy and limited by comparison. Yet until now we have not [306/307] had an accurate text of *Billy Budd*. Not wholly, of course, but partly for these reasons, the Hayford and Sealts edition is truly a significant event, possibly the most notable in Melville scholarship since, say, the discovery of *Billy Budd* and its initial publication by Raymond Weaver back in 1924.

To be sure, the sometimes stormy, unhappy history of the text since that time is well known to most Melville scholars: that Weaver's edition, even as revised in 1928, was no attempt to render all parts of the manuscript and therefore not totally reliable; that F. Barron Freeman's Harvard University Press edition of 1948, the first effort to establish a "definitive" text, was so filled with errors that the press (in June of 1951) temporarily withdrew the book from sale; that Miss Elizabeth Treeman, an editor for the Harvard Press, prepared a *Corrigenda* supposedly "correcting" Freeman's errors; that the Harvard Press (in June of 1953) again offered the book for sale when accompanied by Miss Treeman's *Corrigenda;* that Miss Treeman's corrections were worked into the edition first published in the college anthology edited by Bradley, Beatty, and Long (*The American Tradition in Literature,* 1956); and that this edition has been the one most widely used by scholars, editors, and anthologists since that date. This account does not mention three other editions (Jay Leyda's for *The Portable Melville* [Viking, 1952]; the unnamed editor of the edition in *Selected Writings of Herman Melville* [Modern Library, 1952]; and Milton R. Stern's edition in *Typee and Billy Budd* [Dutton-Everyman, 1958]). Although the editors of these three editions all individually collated the Freeman-Treeman text with the manuscript, they all, according to Hayford and Sealts, made only minor changes and perpetuated the major errors of the original Harvard edition, which was allowed to go out of print, incidentally, in March of 1958. Nor does this account mention the various reprintings of Weaver's edition, such as that of William Plomer, who edited the *Billy Budd* published by Lehmann in London (1946) and who made "a few small emendations" of his own. A reliable text was clearly needed.

Professors Hayford and Sealts date their formal, collaborative preparation of this edition as having begun in 1955, although they were concerned with the problem earlier. They have obviously worked with care, and their widespread knowledge of Melville's other writings, especially his later work, has served them well. The results are sometimes startling and, often enough, profoundly significant.

The editors organize their major comment in the "Introduction" around three subjects: "Growth of the Manuscript," "History of the Text," and "Perspectives for Criticism." Important findings are in each.

In the first place the editors accept the fact that the manuscript was in an incompleted form at the time of Melville's death. "More than once," they say, Melville "undertook to put his manuscript into fair-copy form, but each time he was led into further revision and elaboration." What Melville might have done had he continued to work on the manuscript they rightly cannot and do not say, pointing out that "the degree to which *Billy Budd* remained an 'unfinished' work is a matter for critical evaluation. . . ." Of [307/308] more significance to this reviewer is their story of *how* the story grew. I find their case convincing. It began, the editors contend, not with the *Somers* affair, but with a brief prose note to the ballad "Billy in the Darbies." They then see the tale developing through three successive stages following that beginning: the circumstances surrounding Billy in chains, how Billy got there, the "matter" of stage one; the creation of Claggart and its ramifications, stage two; and not until last, the creation and development of Vere. To be sure, they point to shifting "thematic emphases" and "modifications" as the novel expanded. And they also clearly see that "just where the emphasis finally lay" is "the issue that has engaged and divided the critics of *Billy Budd*." My account of course oversimplifies considerably the detail the editors provide in terms of what was left in, what out, what was added or subtracted, changed, reduced, or expanded at various stages. For example, the so-called digression on Nelson was at one stage not written, at another in, at still another out, and then back in. The name of the ship on which most of the action takes place was changed to *Bellipotent* from *Indomitable*—not vice versa, as previous editors have maintained, for it was a late change. The garbled news account and the ballad were reversed in order except during an initial stage and one of the last. Perhaps most importantly, it was a very late change that discarded what in effect had been the narrator's "underwriting" of Vere's view of the case to the one we all now know which brings "Vere's behavior very much into question."

What the editors call "three major errors" of Freeman's text all resulted (they say) from his mistaking (as did Weaver) the handwriting of Mrs. Melville for that of Melville himself. Two of them regard passages that Hayford and Sealts maintain were later superseded. The first is the passage subsequently printed as the "Preface" to *Billy Budd*. The second is a long paragraph of the chapter formerly titled "Lawyers, Experts, Clergy." The third is the title itself. The editors suggest that many of the other errors of the Freeman text resulted from his collating the manuscript with Weaver's 1928 version. And they state more than once that theirs "is based on a new and independent transcription of the manuscript, not on a corrected version of an earlier text."

But the real heart of the matter is the consequences for criticism of *Billy Budd* resulting from this new edition. And those consequences, it seems to me, are both greater and less—at any rate, somewhat different—from those the editors point to.

I cannot, for example, see anything of great critical import resulting from the title, *Billy Budd, Foretopman* or *Billy Budd, Sailor,* as long as the phrase "An Inside Narrative," the only crucial phrase in the title, is retained. And many widely used editions include that phrase. Nor can I see that there is any great critical consequence resulting from whether the ship is called *Bellipotent* or *Indomitable,* for the ironic contrast with the *Rights-of-Man* is apparent enough in either case, although *why* Melville preferred the former to the latter admittedly provides matter for interesting speculation. The Preface on the French Revolution is another case, for some ambitious [308/309] critical studies rest squarely on it. But even to that condition one might conceivably retort (although I do not think I would) that, given the somewhat ambiguous nature of the attitude displayed by the Preface, (1) it importantly supports the unmistakably ambiguous attitude toward Captain Vere; (2) it is a better tale that includes it, whether at the beginning or at Chapter 19, from which it was discarded; (3) in subsequent revisions Melville would probably have restored it, as he did the Nelson digression; and (4) if he did not, he should have.

Much more fruitful, it seems to me, are the editors' proposals along other lines. The much discussed *Somers* affair, for example, they convincingly relegate to the role of "cogent analogue," affecting perhaps Melville's conception of Vere late in the writing of the story, but not a primary source. Along with explorations they themselves make, they suggest the need for more examinations of literary parallels, American naval history, Melville's own experiences on the frigate *United States,* and closer study of Melville's late works.[4]

Ultimately, I suspect, their Genetic Text will have more significance than their Reading Text. It may well constitute the most important aspect of their work, for the opportunity it provides for studying Melville's writing method is, so far as I know, without parallel. And the editors see well what those opportunities are:

Wherein lay the difference between *Billy Budd* and the other late pieces? Did its quality of greatness emerge with one transforming major stroke some-

---

[4] One important anticipation of their plea is C. B. Ives's recent "*Billy Budd* and the Articles of War," *American Literature,* XXXIV (March 1962), 30–39, which demonstrates that Vere did not follow established court-martial procedure of the time.

where in the gradual process of growth by accretion? Were all the instances of his minute verbal revision necessary to its greatness, or were many of them merely nervous or fussy gestures? To what extent do the revisions show a sure intuition of what was vital in the work as it stood at the end in semi-final manuscript? To what extent are many of the revisions purely random strokes that overlie and obscure the emerging conception? Into what categories do the stylistic revisions fall? . . . Many problems relevant to interpretation and evaluation will likewise suggest themselves—inter-related problems about form, theme, and language, to which study of the Genetic Text may suggest answers.

To some of these problems they themselves of course provide tentative answers. In fact, they end their introduction by provocatively demonstrating how some of the revisions move key passages from exposition toward more and more objective dramatization. The highly charged and moving ambiguity that results surely accounts, at least in part, for the wide appeal the tale has had.

What then follows is their beautifully printed and readable Reading Text, 69 pages of finely printed Notes and Commentary, a Bibliography, and Textual Notes. And there are photographic plates of some of the crucial manuscript leaves. The Genetic Text is preceded by an "Analysis [309/310] of the Manuscript" and a "Table and Discussion of Foliations." The Genetic Text alone covers almost 150 printed pages.

The special virtue of their Genetic Text is that it ingeniously provides a literal transcription of the *Billy Budd* manuscript in a form that incorporates the editors' analysis of it. It is designed, they maintain, "to show the growth of the text, insofar as that can be seen from the surviving leaves." The running text is the earliest surviving version, with subsequent revisions elaborately and variously bracketed and with successive revisions clearly indicated. The reader can therefore follow a particular passage from the earliest surviving version through successive revisions to the latest surviving version. Each passage, moreover, by a somewhat elaborate system of leaf numbering, can easily be collated with comparable passages in the Reading Text. And by use of stage labels and successive foliations, one can indeed "learn much about the growth of the narrative as a whole." Their system is a difficult one to describe, one, in fact, that has to be seen to be clearly understood. I am nonetheless convinced that what their Genetic Text will eventually contribute to an understanding of Melville's creative processes is immeasurably large.

The Notes and Commentary might be almost too much of a good thing. Although delightfully prefaced and thus edged by Melville's marginal notation on an editor's footnote to Shakespeare—"Peace, peace, thou ass of a commentator"—the notes might at times give us more information than we really want to have. The editors have meticulously chased down every allusion. They report a handsome proportion of the voluminous commentary that has been written about the tale. And they provide a surprisingly large number of echoing and sometimes clarifying phrases from Melville's other works. A fair example is their "comment" on the phrase *a cat's-paw* for leaf 168:

Beside this passage in the manuscript Melville wrote in pencil the circled query "flaw?"—taken by Freeman (1948), pp. 15, 52, to apply to the entire paragraph. (Because "the Dansker's enigmatic reply to Billy's question about the afterguardsman" is insufficiently explained in the paragraph, Freeman holds, "Melville's suspicion of a flaw in his tale of Billy Budd is justified.") What Melville presumably had in mind, however, was the possible substitution of a more technical term for the phrase "light puff of air." "Flaw" in very much this same sense occurs both in *Clarel* (I.1.156–58, I.xiv.128–31, II.xxxvi.48–50) and in the poem "Pebbles" (*Poems*, p. 205), though elsewhere the word refers to a wind blowing suddenly and with more violence, as in *Redburn*, Ch. 16, and *Israel Potter*, Ch. 14, where "a sudden flaw of wind . . . came nigh capsizing them." In his set of Shakespeare (Sealts No. 460, HCL), VII, 374, Melville checked and queried a gloss-note to the phrase "winter's flaw" in *Hamlet*, V. 1, that defines "flaw" as "a violent gust of wind." Here, his indecision between "light puff of air" and "flaw" may reflect his uncertainty as to the exact shade of meaning that would be suggested by "flaw." Such concern for the phrasing shows Melville's meticulous regard not only for words themselves but for natural fact—a regard too often overlooked, as evidenced by those critics who see *Billy Budd* only as a treatment of abstract good and evil. [310/311]

Were I inclined seriously to quibble regarding apparatus, I would do so over the absence of an index, a very useful tool even in a work so conveniently cross-referenced as this one otherwise is.

The ultimate consequences of the edition are of course unpredictable. I nonetheless think they are likely to be immense, especially as scholars begin to explore the various ramifications of the Genetic Text. The Reading Text is far less revolutionary than I would have suspected, the controversial Preface notwithstanding, and will change very little, I predict, the critical disagreements regarding tone, intention, and theme. The position of the editors, it seems to me, silently supports this contention, for they appear to have felt that evaluation and interpretation of the whole not properly their task here, however varied and numerous their valuable insights to parts. Vere's agonizing dilemma, Claggart's noble ignobility, Billy's benediction, and the curiously appropriate honorific prose of the tale are all very much still with us—as they were even with Weaver's text, no less than with Freeman's.

Be that as it may, we do now appear to have a reliable text, even if we do have an unfinished work of art. Surely we "know *what it is*," to quote Harkness again, that "we have in our hands." But *Billy Budd, Sailor* is now as finished as it will ever be. And the widespread praise it has provoked—whatever the disagreements about meaning—testify adequately enough to the secure position it holds as one of Melville's most important novels. Professors Hayford and Sealts—and, yes, the University of Chicago Press—have done a much-needed job that deserves the highest praise. They have done it with care and dedication, with distinction—and with wit and good humor, too. [311]

Billy Budd, Sailor
(an inside narrative)

DEDICATED
TO
JACK CHASE
ENGLISHMAN
Wherever that great heart may now be
Here on Earth or harbored in Paradise

Captain of the Maintop
in the year 1843
in the U.S. Frigate
United States

1

In the time before steamships, or then more frequently than now, a stroller along the docks of any considerable seaport would occasionally have his attention arrested by a group of bronzed mariners, man-of-war's men or merchant sailors in holiday attire, ashore on liberty. In certain instances they would flank, or like a bodyguard quite surround, some superior figure of their own class, moving along with them like Aldebaran among the lesser lights of his constellation. That signal object was the "Handsome Sailor" of the less prosaic time alike of the military and merchant navies. With no perceptible trace of the vainglorious about him, rather with the offhand unaffectedness of natural regality, he seemed to accept the spontaneous homage of his shipmates.

A somewhat remarkable instance recurs to me. In Liverpool, now half a century ago, I saw under the shadow of the great dingy street-wall of Prince's Dock (an obstruction long since removed) a common sailor so intensely black that he must needs have been a native African of the unadulterate blood of Ham—a symmetric figure much above the average height. The two ends of a gay silk handkerchief thrown loose about the neck danced upon the displayed ebony of his chest, in his ears were big hoops of gold, and a Highland bonnet with a tartan band set off his shapely head. It was a hot noon in July; and his face, lustrous with perspiration, beamed with barbaric good humor. In jovial sallies right and left, his white teeth flashing into view, he rollicked along, the center of a company of his shipmates. These were made up of such an assortment of tribes and complexions as would have well fitted them to be marched up by Anacharsis Cloots before the bar of the first French Assembly as Representatives of the Human Race. At each spontaneous tribute rendered by the wayfarers to this black pagod of a fellow—the tribute of a pause and stare, and less frequently an [43/44] exclamation—the motley retinue showed that they took that sort of pride in the evoker of it which the Assyrian priests doubtless showed for their grand sculptured Bull when the faithful prostrated themselves.

To return. If in some cases a bit of a nautical Murat in setting forth his person ashore, the Handsome Sailor of the period in question

Reprinted from Herman Melville, *Billy Budd, Sailor (An Inside Narrative)*, ed. Harrison Hayford and Merton M. Sealts, Jr. (Chicago: University of Chicago Press, 1962), pp. 41–132, by permission of the University of Chicago Press, © 1962 by The University of Chicago.

evinced nothing of the dandified Billy-be-Dam, an amusing character all but extinct now, but occasionally to be encountered, and in a form yet more amusing than the original, at the tiller of the boats on the tempestuous Erie Canal or, more likely, vaporing in the groggeries along the towpath. Invariably a proficient in his perilous calling, he was also more or less of a mighty boxer or wrestler. It was strength and beauty. Tales of his prowess were recited. Ashore he was the champion; afloat the spokesman; on every suitable occasion always foremost. Close-reefing topsails in a gale, there he was, astride the weather yardarm-end, foot in the Flemish horse as stirrup, both hands tugging at the earing as at a bridle, in very much the attitude of young Alexander curbing the fiery Bucephalus. A superb figure, tossed up as by the horns of Taurus against the thunderous sky, cheerily hallooing to the strenuous file along the spar.

The moral nature was seldom out of keeping with the physical make. Indeed, except as toned by the former, the comeliness and power, always attractive in masculine conjunction, hardly could have drawn the sort of honest homage the Handsome Sailor in some examples received from his less gifted associates.

Such a cynosure, at least in aspect, and something such too in nature, though with important variations made apparent as the story proceeds, was welkin-eyed Billy Budd—or Baby Budd, as more familiarly, under circumstances hereafter to be given, he at last came to be called—aged twenty-one, a foretopman of the British fleet toward the close of the last decade of the eighteenth century. It was not very long prior to the time of the narration that follows that he had entered the King's service, having been impressed on the Narrow Seas from a homeward-bound [44/45] English merchantman into a seventy-four outward bound, H.M.S. *Bellipotent;* which ship, as was not unusual in those hurried days, having been obliged to put to sea short of her proper complement of men. Plump upon Billy at first sight in the gangway the boarding officer, Lieutenant Ratcliffe, pounced, even before the merchantman's crew was formally mustered on the quarter-deck for his deliberate inspection. And him only he elected. For whether it was because the other men when ranged before him showed to ill advantage after Billy, or whether he had some scruples in view of the merchantman's being rather short-handed, however it might be, the officer contented himself with his first spontaneous choice. To the surprise of the ship's company, though much to the lieutenant's satisfaction, Billy made no demur. But, indeed, any demur would have been as idle as the protest of a goldfinch popped into a cage.

Noting this uncomplaining acquiescence, all but cheerful, one might say, the shipmaster turned a surprised glance of silent reproach at the sailor. The shipmaster was one of those worthy mortals found in every vocation, even the humbler ones—the sort of person whom

everybody agrees in calling "a respectable man." And—nor so strange
to report as it may appear to be—though a ploughman of the troubled
waters, lifelong contending with the intractable elements, there was
nothing this honest soul at heart loved better than simple peace and
quiet. For the rest, he was fifty or thereabouts, a little inclined to
corpulence, a prepossessing face, unwhiskered, and of an agreeable
color—a rather full face, humanely intelligent in expression. On a fair
day with a fair wind and all going well, a certain musical chime in his
voice seemed to be the veritable unobstructed outcome of the inner-
most man. He had much prudence, much conscientiousness, and there
were occasions when these virtues were the cause of overmuch disquietude in him. On a passage, so long as his craft was in any proximity
to land, no sleep for Captain [45/46] Graveling. He took to heart
those serious responsibilities not so heavily borne by some shipmasters.

Now while Billy Budd was down in the forecastle getting his kit
together, the *Bellipotent's* lieutenant, burly and bluff, nowise disconcerted by Captain Graveling's omitting to proffer the customary
hospitalities on an occasion so unwelcome to him, an omission simply
caused by preoccupation of thought, unceremoniously invited himself
into the cabin, and also to a flask from the spirit locker, a receptacle
which his experienced eye instantly discovered. In fact he was one of
those sea dogs in whom all the hardship and peril of naval life in the
great prolonged wars of his time never impaired the natural instinct
for sensuous enjoyment. His duty he always faithfully did; but duty is
sometimes a dry obligation, and he was for irrigating its aridity,
whensoever possible, with a fertilizing decoction of strong waters. For
the cabin's proprietor there was nothing left but to play the part of the
enforced host with whatever grace and alacrity were practicable. As
necessary adjuncts to the flask, he silently placed tumbler and water
jug before the irrepressible guest. But excusing himself from partaking
just then, he dismally watched the unembarrassed officer deliberately
diluting his grog a little, then tossing it off in three swallows, pushing
the empty tumbler away, yet not so far as to be beyond easy reach, at
the same time settling himself in his seat and smacking his lips with
high satisfaction, looking straight at the host.

These proceedings over, the master broke the silence; and there
lurked a rueful reproach in the tone of his voice: "Lieutenant, you are
going to take my best man from me, the jewel of 'em."

"Yes, I know," rejoined the other, immediately drawing back the
tumbler preliminary to a replenishing. "Yes, I know. Sorry."

"Beg pardon, but you don't understand, Lieutenant. See here,
now. Before I shipped that young fellow, my forecastle was a rat-pit of
quarrels. It was black times, I tell you, aboard the [46/47] *Rights*
here. I was worried to that degree my pipe had no comfort for me. But
Billy came; and it was like a Catholic priest striking peace in an Irish
shindy. Not that he preached to them or said or did anything in

particular; but a virtue went out of him, sugaring the sour ones. They
took to him like hornets to treacle; all but the buffer of the gang, the
big shaggy chap with the fire-red whiskers. He indeed, out of envy,
perhaps, of the newcomer, and thinking such a "sweet and pleasant
fellow," as he mockingly designated him to the others, could hardly
have the spirit of a gamecock, must needs bestir himself in trying to
get up an ugly row with him. Billy forebore with him and reasoned
with him in a pleasant way—he is something like myself, Lieutenant,
to whom aught like a quarrel is hateful—but nothing served. So, in the
second dogwatch one day, the Red Whiskers in presence of the others,
under pretense of showing Billy just whence a sirloin steak was cut—
for the fellow had once been a butcher—insultingly gave him a dig
under the ribs. Quick as lightning Billy let fly his arm. I dare say he
never meant to do quite as much as he did, but anyhow he gave the
burly fool a terrible drubbing. It took about half a minute, I should
think. And, lord bless you, the lubber was astonished at the celerity.
And will you believe it, Lieutenant, the Red Whiskers now really loves
Billy—loves him, or is the biggest hypocrite that ever I heard of. But
they all love him. Some of 'em do his washing, darn his old trousers for
him; the carpenter is at odd times making a pretty little chest of
drawers for him. Anybody will do anything for Billy Budd; and it's the
happy family here. But now, Lieutenant, if that young fellow goes—I
know how it will be aboard the *Rights*. Not again very soon shall I,
coming up from dinner, lean over the capstan smoking a quiet pipe—
no, not very soon again, I think. Ay, Lieutenant, you are going to take
away the jewel of 'em; you are going to take away my peacemaker!"
And with that the good soul had really some ado in checking a rising
sob.

"Well," said the Lieutenant, who had listened with amused [47/
48] interest to all this and now was waxing merry with his tipple;
"well, blessed are the peacemakers, especially the fighting peacemakers. And such are the seventy-four beauties some of which you see
poking their noses out of the portholes of yonder warship lying to for
me," pointing through the cabin window at the *Bellipotent*. "But
courage! Don't look so downhearted, man. Why, I pledge you in
advance the royal approbation. Rest assured that His Majesty will be
delighted to know that in a time when his hardtack is not sought for
by sailors with such avidity as should be, a time also when some
shipmasters privily resent the borrowing from them a tar or two for the
service; His Majesty, I say, will be delighted to learn that *one* shipmaster at least cheerfully surrenders to the King the flower of his flock,
a sailor who with equal loyalty makes no dissent.—But where's my
beauty? Ah," looking through the cabin's open door, "here he comes;
and, by Jove, lugging along his chest—Apollo with his portmanteau!—
My man," stepping out to him, "you can't take that big box aboard a
warship. The boxes there are mostly shot boxes. Put your duds in a

bag, lad. Boot and saddle for the cavalryman, bag and hammock for the man-of-war's man."

The transfer from chest to bag was made. And, after seeing his man into the cutter and then following him down, the lieutenant pushed off from the *Rights-of-Man*. That was the merchant ship's name, though by her master and crew abbreviated in sailor fashion into the *Rights*. The hardheaded Dundee owner was a staunch admirer of Thomas Paine, whose book in rejoinder to Burke's arraignment of the French Revolution had then been published for some time and had gone everywhere. In christening his vessel after the title of Paine's volume the man of Dundee was something like his contemporary ship-owner, Stephen Girard of Philadelphia, whose sympathies, alike with his native land and its liberal philosophers, he evinced by naming his ships after Voltaire, Diderot, and so forth.

But now, when the boat swept under the merchantman's stern, and officer and oarsmen were noting—some bitterly and [48/49] others with a grin—the name emblazoned there; just then it was that the new recruit jumped up from the bow where the coxswain had directed him to sit, and waving hat to his silent shipmates sorrowfully looking over at him from the taffrail, bade the lads a genial good-bye. Then, making a salutation as to the ship herself, "And good-bye to you too, old *Rights-of-Man*."

"Down, sir!" roared the lieutenant, instantly assuming all the rigor of his rank, though with difficulty repressing a smile.

To be sure, Billy's action was a terrible breach of naval decorum. But in that decorum he had never been instructed; in consideration of which the lieutenant would hardly have been so energetic in reproof but for the concluding farewell to the ship. This he rather took as meant to convey a covert sally on the new recruit's part, a sly slur at impressment in general, and that of himself in especial. And yet, more likely, if satire it was in effect, it was hardly so by intention, for Billy, though happily endowed with the gaiety of high health, youth, and a free heart, was yet by no means of a satirical turn. The will to it and the sinister dexterity were alike wanting. To deal in double meanings and insinuations of any sort was quite foreign to his nature.

As to his enforced enlistment, that he seemed to take pretty much as he was wont to take any vicissitude of weather. Like the animals, though no philosopher, he was, without knowing it, practically a fatalist. And it may be that he rather liked this adventurous turn in his affairs, which promised an opening into novel scenes and martial excitements.

Aboard the *Bellipotent* our merchant sailor was forthwith rated as an able seaman and assigned to the starboard watch of the foretop. He was soon at home in the service, not at all disliked for his unpretentious good looks and a sort of genial happy-go-lucky air. No merrier man in his mess: in marked contrast to certain other individuals included like himself among the impressed portion of the ship's company; for these when not actively employed were sometimes, and more particularly in the [49/50] last dogwatch when the drawing near of twilight induced revery, apt to fall into a saddish mood which in some partook of sullenness. But they were not so young as our foretopman, and no few of them must have known a hearth of some sort, others may have had wives and children left, too probably, in uncertain circumstances, and hardly any but must have had acknowledged kith and kin, while for Billy, as will shortly be seen, his entire family was practically invested in himself.

2

Though our new-made foretopman was well received in the top and on the gun decks, hardly here was he that cynosure he had previously been among those minor ship's companies of the merchant marine, with which companies only had he hitherto consorted.

He was young; and despite his all but fully developed frame, in aspect looked even younger than he really was, owing to a lingering adolescent expression in the as yet smooth face all but feminine in purity of natural complexion but where, thanks to his seagoing, the lily was quite suppressed and the rose had some ado visibly to flush through the tan.

To one essentially such a novice in the complexities of factitious life, the abrupt transition from his former and simpler sphere to the ampler and more knowing world of a great warship; this might well have abashed him had there been any conceit or vanity in his composition. Among her miscellaneous multitude, the *Bellipotent* mustered several individuals who however inferior in grade were of no common natural stamp, sailors more signally susceptive of that air which continuous martial discipline and repeated presence in battle can in some degree impart even to the average man. As the Handsome Sailor, Billy Budd's position aboard the seventy-four was something [50/51] analogous to that of a rustic beauty transplanted from the provinces and brought into competition with the highborn dames of the court. But this change of circumstances he scarce noted. As little did he observe that something about him provoked an ambiguous smile in one or two harder faces among the bluejackets. Nor less unaware was he of the peculiar favorable effect his person and demeanor had upon the more intelligent gentlemen of the quarter-deck. Nor could this well have been otherwise. Cast in a mold peculiar to the finest physical examples of those Englishmen in whom the Saxon strain would seem not at all to partake of any Norman or other admixture, he showed in face that humane look of reposeful good nature which the Greek sculptor in some instances gave to his heroic strong man, Hercules. But this again was subtly modified by another and pervasive quality. The ear, small and shapely, the arch of the foot, the curve in mouth and nostril, even the indurated hand dyed to the orange-tawny of the toucan's bill, a hand telling alike of the halyards and tar bucket; but, above all, something in the mobile expression, and every chance attitude and movement, something suggestive of a mother eminently favored by Love and the Graces; all this strangely indicated a lineage in direct contradiction to his lot. The mysteriousness here became less mysterious through a matter of fact elicited when Billy at the capstan was being formally mustered into the service. Asked by the officer, a small, brisk little gentleman as it chanced, among other questions, his place of birth, he replied, "Please, sir, I don't know."

"Don't know where you were born? Who was your father?"

"God knows, sir."

Struck by the straightforward simplicity of these replies, the officer next asked, "Do you know anything about your beginning?"

"No, sir. But I have heard that I was found in a pretty silk-lined basket hanging one morning from the knocker of a good man's door in Bristol." [51/52]

"*Found,* say you? Well," throwing back his head and looking up and down the new recruit; "well, it turns out to have been a pretty good find. Hope they'll find some more like you, my man; the fleet sadly needs them."

Yes, Billy Budd was a foundling, a presumable by-blow, and, evidently, no ignoble one. Noble descent was as evident in him as in a blood horse.

For the rest, with little or no sharpness of faculty or any trace of the wisdom of the serpent, nor yet quite a dove, he possessed that kind and degree of intelligence going along with the unconventional rectitude of a sound human creature, one to whom not yet has been proffered the questionable apple of knowledge. He was illiterate; he could not read, but he could sing, and like the illiterate nightingale was sometimes the composer of his own song.

Of self-consciousness he seemed to have little or none, or about as much as we may reasonably impute to a dog of Saint Bernard's breed.

Habitually living with the elements and knowing little more of the land than as a beach, or, rather, that portion of the terraqueous globe providentially set apart for dance-houses, doxies, and tapsters, in short what sailors call a "fiddler's green," his simple nature remained unsophisticated by those moral obliquities which are not in every case incompatible with that manufacturable thing known as respectability. But are sailors, frequenters of fiddlers' greens, without vices? No; but less often than with landsmen do their vices, so called, partake of crookedness of heart, seeming less to proceed from viciousness than exuberance of vitality after long constraint: frank manifestations in accordance with natural law. By his original constitution aided by the co-operating influences of his lot, Billy in many respects was little more

than a sort of upright barbarian, much such perhaps as Adam presumably might have been ere the urbane Serpent wriggled himself into
his company.

And here be it submitted that apparently going to corroborate the
doctrine of man's Fall, a doctrine now popularly ignored, it [52/53] is
observable that where certain virtues pristine and unadulterate peculiarly characterize anybody in the external uniform of civilization, they
will upon scrutiny seem not to be derived from custom or convention,
but rather to be out of keeping with these, as if indeed exceptionally
transmitted from a period prior to Cain's city and citified man. The
character marked by such qualities has to an unvitiated taste an
untampered-with flavor like that of berries, while the man thoroughly
civilized, even in a fair specimen of the breed, has to the same moral
palate a questionable smack as of a compounded wine. To any stray
inheritor of these primitive qualities found, like Caspar Hauser, wandering dazed in any Christian capital of our time, the good-natured
poet's famous invocation, near two thousand years ago, of the good
rustic out of his latitude in the Rome of the Caesars, still appropriately
holds:

> Honest and poor, faithful in word and thought,
> What hath thee, Fabian, to the city brought?

Though our Handsome Sailor had as much of masculine beauty as
one can expect anywhere to see; nevertheless, like the beautiful woman
in one of Hawthorne's minor tales, there was just one thing amiss in
him. No visible blemish indeed, as with the lady; no, but an occasional
liability to a vocal defect. Though in the hour of elemental uproar or
peril he was everything that a sailor should be, yet under sudden
provocation of strong heart-feeling his voice, otherwise singularly
musical, as if expressive of the harmony within, was apt to develop an
organic hesitancy, in fact more or less of a stutter or even worse. In
this particular Billy was a striking instance that the arch interferer, the
envious marplot of Eden, still has more or less to do with every human
consignment to this planet of Earth. In every case, one way or another
he is sure to slip in his little card, as much as to remind us—I too have
a hand here.

The avowal of such an imperfection in the Handsome Sailor
should be evidence not alone that he is not presented as a conventional
hero, but also that the story in which he is the main figure is no
romance. [53/54]

3

At the time of Billy Budd's arbitrary enlistment into the *Bellipotent* that ship was on her way to join the Mediterranean fleet. No

long time elapsed before the junction was effected. As one of that fleet the seventy-four participated in its movements, though at times on account of her superior sailing qualities, in the absence of frigates, dispatched on separate duty as a scout and at times on less temporary service. But with all this the story has little concernment, restricted as it is to the inner life of one particular ship and the career of an individual sailor.

It was the summer of 1797. In the April of that year had occurred the commotion at Spithead followed in May by a second and yet more serious outbreak in the fleet at the Nore. The latter is known, and without exaggeration in the epithet, as "the Great Mutiny." It was indeed a demonstration more menacing to England than the contemporary manifestoes and conquering and proselyting armies of the French Directory. To the British Empire the Nore Mutiny was what a strike in the fire brigade would be to London threatened by general arson. In a crisis when the kingdom might well have anticipated the famous signal that some years later published along the naval line of battle what it was that upon occasion England expected of Englishmen; *that* was the time when at the mastheads of the three-deckers and seventy-fours moored in her own roadstead—a fleet the right arm of a Power then all but the sole free conservative one of the Old World—the bluejackets, to be numbered by thousands, ran up with huzzas the British colors with the union and cross wiped out; by that cancellation transmuting the flag of founded law and freedom defined, into the enemy's red meteor of unbridled and unbounded revolt. Reasonable discontent growing out of practical grievances in the fleet had been ignited into irrational combustion as by live cinders blown across the Channel from France in flames. [54/55]

The event converted into irony for a time those spirited strains of Dibdin—as a song-writer no mean auxiliary to the English government at that European conjuncture—strains celebrating, among other things, the patriotic devotion of the British tar: "And as for my life, 'tis the King's!"

Such an episode in the Island's grand naval story her naval historians naturally abridge, one of them (William James) candidly acknowledging that fain would he pass it over did not "impartiality forbid fastidiousness." And yet his mention is less a narration than a reference, having to do hardly at all with details. Nor are these readily to be found in the libraries. Like some other events in every age befalling states everywhere, including America, the Great Mutiny was of such character that national pride along with views of policy would fain shade it off into the historical background. Such events cannot be ignored, but there is a considerate way of historically treating them. If a well-constituted individual refrains from blazoning aught amiss or calamitous in his family, a nation in the like circumstance may without reproach be equally discreet.

Though after parleyings between government and the ringleaders, and concessions by the former as to some glaring abuses, the
first uprising—that at Spithead—with difficulty was put down, or
matters for the time pacified; yet at the Nore the unforeseen renewal
of insurrection on a yet larger scale, and emphasized in the confer-
ences that ensued by demands deemed by the authorities not only
inadmissible but aggressively insolent, indicated—if the Red Flag did
not sufficiently do so—what was the spirit animating the men. Final
suppression, however, there was; but only made possible perhaps by
the unswerving loyalty of the marine corps and a voluntary resumption
of loyalty among influential sections of the crews.

To some extent the Nore Mutiny may be regarded as analogous to
the distempering irruption of contagious fever in a frame constitu-
tionally sound, and which anon throws it off.

At all events, of these thousands of mutineers were some of [55/
56] the tars who not so very long afterwards—whether wholly prompted
thereto by patriotism, or pugnacious instinct, or by both—helped to
win a coronet for Nelson at the Nile, and the naval crown of crowns
for him at Trafalgar. To the mutineers, those battles and especially
Trafalgar were a plenary absolution and a grand one. For all that goes
to make up scenic naval display and heroic magnificence in arms, those
battles, especially Trafalgar, stand unmatched in human annals.

4

In this matter of writing, resolve as one may to keep to the main
road, some bypaths have an enticement not readily to be withstood. I
am going to err into such a bypath. If the reader will keep me
company I shall be glad. At the least, we can promise ourselves that
pleasure which is wickedly said to be in sinning, for a literary sin the
divergence will be.

Very likely it is no new remark that the inventions of our time
have at last brought about a change in sea warfare in degree corre-
sponding to the revolution in all warfare effected by the original introduction from China into Europe of gunpowder. The first European
firearm, a clumsy contrivance, was, as is well known, scouted by no
few of the knights as a base implement, good enough peradventure
for weavers too craven to stand up crossing steel with steel in frank
fight. But as ashore knightly valor, though shorn of its blazonry, did
not cease with the knights, neither on the seas—though nowadays in
encounters there a certain kind of displayed gallantry be fallen out of
date as hardly applicable under changed circumstances—did the
nobler qualities of such naval magnates as Don John of Austria, Doria,
Van Tromp, Jean Bart, the long line of British admirals, and the American Decaturs of 1812 become obsolete with their wooden walls. [56/
57]

Nevertheless, to anybody who can hold the Present at its worth

without being inappreciative of the Past, it may be forgiven, if to such
an one the solitary old hulk at Portsmouth, Nelson's *Victory,* seems to
float there, not alone as the decaying monument of a fame incorruptible, but also as a poetic reproach, softened by its picturesqueness,
to the *Monitors* and yet mightier hulls of the European ironclads. And
this not altogether because such craft are unsightly, unavoidably
lacking the symmetry and grand lines of the old battleships, but
equally for other reasons.

There are some, perhaps, who while not altogether inaccessible to
that poetic reproach just alluded to, may yet on behalf of the new
order be disposed to parry it; and this to the extent of iconoclasm, if
need be. For example, prompted by the sight of the star inserted in the
Victory's quarter-deck designating the spot where the Great Sailor fell,
these martial utilitarians may suggest considerations implying that
Nelson's ornate publication of his person in battle was not only
unnecessary, but not military, nay, savored of foolhardiness and
vanity. They may add, too, that at Trafalgar it was in effect nothing
less than a challenge to death; and death came; and that but for his
bravado the victorious admiral might possibly have survived the
battle, and so, instead of having his sagacious dying injunctions
overruled by his immediate successor in command, he himself when
the contest was decided might have brought his shattered fleet to
anchor, a proceeding which might have averted the deplorable loss of
life by shipwreck in the elemental tempest that followed the martial
one.

Well, should we set aside the more than disputable point whether
for various reasons it was possible to anchor the fleet, then plausibly
enough the Benthamites of war may urge the above. But the *might-
have-been* is but boggy ground to build on. And, certainly, in foresight
as to the larger issue of an encounter, and anxious preparations for
it—buoying the deadly way and mapping it out, as at Copenhagen—
few commanders have [57/58] been so painstakingly circumspect as
this same reckless declarer of his person in fight.

Personal prudence, even when dictated by quite other than selfish
considerations, surely is no special virtue in a military man; while an
excessive love of glory, impassioning a less burning impulse, the honest
sense of duty, is the first. If the name *Wellington* is not so much of a
trumpet to the blood as the simpler name *Nelson*, the reason for this
may perhaps be inferred from the above. Alfred in his funeral ode on
the victor of Waterloo ventures not to call him the greatest soldier of
all time, though in the same ode he invokes Nelson as "the greatest
sailor since our world began."

At Trafalgar Nelson on the brink of opening the fight sat down
and wrote his last brief will and testament. If under the presentiment
of the most magnificent of all victories to be crowned by his own
glorious death, a sort of priestly motive led him to dress his person in
the jewelled vouchers of his own shining deeds; if thus to have

adorned himself for the altar and the sacrifice were indeed vainglory, then affectation and fustian is each more heroic line in the great epics and dramas, since in such lines the poet but embodies in verse those exaltations of sentiment that a nature like Nelson, the opportunity being given, vitalizes into acts.

5

Yes, the outbreak at the Nore was put down. But not every grievance was redressed. If the contractors, for example, were no longer permitted to ply some practices peculiar to their tribe everywhere, such as providing shoddy cloth, rations not sound, or false in the measure; not the less impressment, for one thing, went on. By custom sanctioned for centuries, and judicially maintained by a Lord Chancellor as late as Mansfield, that mode of manning the fleet, a mode now fallen into a sort of [58/59] abeyance but never formally renounced, it was not practicable to give up in those years. Its abrogation would have crippled the indispensable fleet, one wholly under canvas, no steam power, its innumerable sails and thousands of cannon, everything in short, worked by muscle alone; a fleet the more insatiate in demand for men, because then multiplying its ships of all grades against contingencies present and to come of the convulsed Continent.

Discontent foreran the Two Mutinies, and more or less it lurkingly survived them. Hence it was not unreasonable to apprehend some return of trouble sporadic or general. One instance of such apprehensions: In the same year with this story, Nelson, then Rear Admiral Sir Horatio, being with the fleet off the Spanish coast, was directed by the admiral in command to shift his pennant from the *Captain* to the *Theseus;* and for this reason: that the latter ship having newly arrived on the station from home, where it had taken part in the Great Mutiny, danger was apprehended from the temper of the men; and it was thought that an officer like Nelson was the one, not indeed to terrorize the crew into base subjection, but to win them, by force of his mere presence and heroic personality, back to an allegiance if not as enthusiastic as his own yet as true.

So it was that for a time, on more than one quarter-deck, anxiety did exist. At sea, precautionary vigilance was strained against relapse. At short notice an engagement might come on. When it did, the lieutenants assigned to batteries felt it incumbent on them, in some instances, to stand with drawn swords behind the men working the guns.

6

But on board the seventy-four in which Billy now swung his hammock, very little in the manner of the men and nothing obvious in the demeanor of the officers would have suggested [59/60] to an ordinary observer that the Great Mutiny was a recent event. In their general bearing and conduct the commissioned officers of a warship naturally take their tone from the commander, that is if he have that ascendancy of character that ought to be his.

Captain the Honorable Edward Fairfax Vere, to give his full title, was a bachelor of forty or thereabouts, a sailor of distinction even in a time prolific of renowned seamen. Though allied to the higher nobility, his advancement had not been altogether owing to influences connected with that circumstance. He had seen much service, been in various engagements, always acquitting himself as an officer mindful of the welfare of his men, but never tolerating an infraction of discipline; thoroughly versed in the science of his profession, and intrepid to the verge of temerity, though never injudiciously so. For his gallantry in the West Indian waters as flag lieutenant under Rodney in that admiral's crowning victory over De Grasse, he was made a post captain.

Ashore, in the garb of a civilian, scarce anyone would have taken him for a sailor, more especially that he never garnished unprofessional talk with nautical terms, and grave in his bearing, evinced little appreciation of mere humor. It was not out of keeping with these traits that on a passage when nothing demanded his paramount action, he was the most undemonstrative of men. Any landsman observing this gentleman not conspicuous by his stature and wearing no pronounced insignia, emerging from his cabin to the open deck, and noting the silent deference of the officers retiring to leeward, might have taken him for the King's guest, a civilian aboard the King's ship, some highly honorable discreet envoy on his way to an important post. But in fact this unobtrusiveness of demeanor may have proceeded from a certain unaffected modesty of manhood sometimes accompanying a resolute nature, a modesty evinced at all times not calling for pronounced action, which shown in any rank of life suggests a virtue aristocratic in kind. As with [60/61] some others engaged in various departments of the world's more heroic activities, Captain Vere though practical enough upon occasion would at times betray a certain dreaminess of mood. Standing alone on the weather side of the quarter-deck, one hand holding by the rigging, he would absently gaze off at the blank sea. At the presentation to him then of some minor matter interrupting the current of his thoughts, he would show more or less irascibility; but instantly he would control it.

In the navy he was popularly known by the appellation "Starry Vere." How such a designation happened to fall upon one who whatever his sterling qualities was without any brilliant ones, was in this wise: A favorite kinsman, Lord Denton, a freehearted fellow, had been the first to meet and congratulate him upon his return to England from his West Indian cruise; and but the day previous turning over a copy of Andrew Marvell's poems had lighted, not for the first time, however, upon the lines entitled "Appleton House," the name of one of the seats of their common ancestor, a hero in the German wars of the seventeenth century, in which poem occur the lines:

> This 'tis to have been from the first
> In a domestic heaven nursed,
> Under the discipline severe
> Of Fairfax and the starry Vere.

And so, upon embracing his cousin fresh from Rodney's great victory wherein he had played so gallant a part, brimming over with just family pride in the sailor of their house, he exuberantly exclaimed, "Give ye joy, Ed: give ye joy, my starry Vere!" This got currency, and the novel prefix serving in familiar parlance readily to distinguish the *Bellipotent*'s captain from another Vere his senior, a distant relative, an officer of like rank in the navy, it remained permanently attached to the surname. [61/62]

7

In view of the part that the commander of the *Bellipotent* plays in scenes shortly to follow, it may be well to fill out that sketch of him outlined in the previous chapter.

Aside from his qualities as a sea officer Captain Vere was an exceptional character. Unlike no few of England's renowed sailors, long and arduous service with signal devotion to it had not resulted in absorbing and *salting* the entire man. He had a marked leaning toward everything intellectual. He loved books, never going to sea without a newly replenished library, compact but of the best. The isolated leisure, in some cases so wearisome, falling at intervals to commanders even during a war cruise, never was tedious to Captain Vere. With nothing of that literary taste which less heeds the thing conveyed than the vehicle, his bias was toward those books to which every serious mind of superior order occupying any active post of authority in the world naturally inclines: books treating of actual men and events no matter of what era—history, biography, and unconventional writers like Montaigne, who, free from cant and convention, honestly and in the spirit of common sense philosophize upon realities. In this line of reading he found confirmation of his own more reserved thoughts— confirmation which he had vainly sought in social converse, so that as touching most fundamental topics, there had got to be established in him some positive convictions which he forefelt would abide in him essentially unmodified so long as his intelligent part remained un- impaired. In view of the troubled period in which his lot was cast, this was well for him. His settled convictions were as a dike against those invading waters of novel opinion social, political, and otherwise, which carried away as in a torrent no few minds in those days, minds by nature not inferior to his own. While other members of that aristocracy to which by birth he belonged were incensed at the innovators mainly because their theories were inimical to the privileged classes, Captain [62/63] Vere disinterestedly opposed them not alone because they seemed to him insusceptible of embodiment in lasting institutions, but at war with the peace of the world and the true welfare of mankind.

With minds less stored than his and less earnest, some officers of his rank, with whom at times he would necessarily consort, found him lacking in the companionable quality, a dry and bookish gentleman, as they deemed. Upon any chance withdrawal from their company one would be apt to say to another something like this: "Vere is a noble fellow, Starry Vere. 'Spite the gazettes, Sir Horatio" (meaning him who became Lord Nelson) "is at bottom scarce a better seaman or fighter. But between you and me now, don't you think there is a queer streak of the pedantic running through him? Yes, like the King's yarn in a coil of navy rope?"

Some apparent ground there was for this sort of confidential criticism; since not only did the captain's discourse never fall into the jocosely familiar, but in illustrating of any point touching the stirring personages and events of the time he would be as apt to cite some historic character or incident of antiquity as he would be to cite from the moderns. He seemed unmindful of the circumstance that to his bluff company such remote allusions, however pertinent they might really be, were altogether alien to men whose reading was mainly confined to the journals. But considerateness in such matters is not easy to natures constituted like Captain Vere's. Their honesty prescribes to them directness, sometimes far-reaching like that of a migratory fowl that in its flight never heeds when it crosses a frontier.

8

The lieutenants and other commissioned gentlemen forming Captain Vere's staff it is not necessary here to particularize, nor needs it to make any mention of any of the warrant officers. [63/64] But among the petty officers was one who, having much to do with the story, may as well be forthwith introduced. His portrait I essay, but shall never hit it. This was John Claggart, the master-at-arms. But that sea title may to landsmen seem somewhat equivocal. Originally, doubtless, that petty officer's function was the instruction of the men in the use of arms, sword or cutlass. But very long ago, owing to the advance in gunnery making hand-to-hand encounters less frequent and giving to niter and sulphur the pre-eminence over steel, that function ceased; the master-at-arms of a great warship becoming a sort of chief of police charged among other matters with the duty of preserving order on the populous lower gun decks.

Claggart was a man about five-and-thirty, somewhat spare and tall, yet of no ill figure upon the whole. His hand was too small and shapely to have been accustomed to hard toil. The face was a notable one, the features all except the chin cleanly cut as those on a Greek medallion; yet the chin, beardless as Tecumseh's, had something of strange protuberant broadness in its make that recalled the prints of the Reverend Dr. Titus Oates, the historic deponent with the clerical drawl in the time of Charles II and the fraud of the alleged Popish Plot. It served Claggart in his office that his eye could cast a tutoring glance. His brow was of the sort phrenologically associated with more than average intellect; silken jet curls partly clustering over it, making a foil to the pallor below, a pallor tinged with a faint shade of amber akin to the hue of time-tinted marbles of old. This complexion, singularly contrasting with the red or deeply bronzed visages of the sailors, and in part the result of his official seclusion from the sunlight, though it was not exactly displeasing, nevertheless seemed to hint of something defective or abnormal in the constitution and blood. But his general aspect and manner were so suggestive of an education and career incongruous with his naval function that when not actively engaged in it he looked like a man of high quality, social and moral, who for reasons of his own was keeping incog. Nothing [64/65] was known of his former life. It might be that he was an Englishman; and yet there lurked a bit of accent in his speech suggesting that possibly he was not such by birth, but through naturalization in early childhood. Among certain grizzled sea gossips of the gun decks and forecastle went a rumor perdue that the master-at-arms was a *chevalier* who had volunteered into the King's navy by way of compounding for some mysterious swindle whereof he had been arraigned at the King's Bench. The fact that nobody could substantiate this report was, of course, nothing against its secret currency. Such a rumor once started on the gun decks in reference to almost anyone below the rank of a commissioned officer would, during the period assigned to this narrative, have seemed not altogether wanting in credibility to the tarry old wiseacres of a man-of-war crew. And indeed a man of Claggart's accomplishments, without prior nautical experience entering the navy at mature life, as he did, and necessarily allotted at the start to the lowest grade in it; a man too who never made allusion to his previous life ashore; these were circumstances which in the dearth of exact knowledge as to his true antecedents opened to the invidious a vague field for unfavorable surmise.

But the sailors' dogwatch gossip concerning him derived a vague plausibility from the fact that now for some period the British navy could so little afford to be squeamish in the matter of keeping up the muster rolls, that not only were press gangs notoriously abroad both afloat and ashore, but there was little or no secret about another matter, namely, that the London police were at liberty to capture any

able-bodied suspect, any questionable fellow at large, and summarily
ship him to the dockyard or fleet. Furthermore, even among voluntary
enlistments there were instances where the motive thereto partook
neither of patriotic impulse nor yet of a random desire to experience a
bit of sea life and martial adventure. Insolvent debtors of minor grade,
together with the promiscuous lame ducks of morality, found in the
navy a convenient and secure refuge, [65/66] secure because, once
enlisted aboard a King's ship, they were as much in sanctuary as the
transgressor of the Middle Ages harboring himself under the shadow
of the altar. Such sanctioned irregularities, which for obvious reasons
the government would hardly think to parade at the time and which
consequently, and as affecting the least influential class of mankind,
have all but dropped into oblivion, lend color to something for the
truth whereof I do not vouch, and hence have some scruple in stating;
something I remember having seen in print though the book I cannot
recall; but the same thing was personally communicated to me now
more than forty years ago by an old pensioner in a cocked hat with
whom I had a most interesting talk on the terrace at Greenwich, a
Baltimore Negro, a Trafalgar man. It was to this effect: In the case of
a warship short of hands whose speedy sailing was imperative, the
deficient quota, in lack of any other way of making it good, would be
eked out by drafts culled direct from the jails. For reasons previously
suggested it would not perhaps be easy at the present day directly to
prove or disprove the allegation. But allowed as a verity, how significant would it be of England's straits at the time confronted by those
wars which like a flight of harpies rose shrieking from the din and dust
of the fallen Bastille. That era appears measurably clear to us who look
back at it, and but read of it. But to the grandfathers of us graybeards,
the more thoughtful of them, the genius of it presented an aspect like
that of Camoëns' Spirit of the Cape, an eclipsing menace mysterious
and prodigious. Not America was exempt from apprehension. At the
height of Napoleon's unexampled conquests, there were Americans
who had fought at Bunker Hill who look forward to the possibility
that the Atlantic might prove no barrier against the ultimate schemes
of this French portentous upstart from the revolutionary chaos who
seemed in act of fulfilling judgment prefigured in the Apocalypse.

But the less credence was to be given to the gun-deck talk touching Claggart, seeing that no man holding his office in a [66/67] man-
of-war can ever hope to be popular with the crew. Besides, in
derogatory comments upon anyone against whom they have a grudge,
or for any reason or no reason mislike, sailors are much like landsmen:
they are apt to exaggerate or romance it.

About as much was really known to the *Bellipotent's* tars of the
master-at-arms' career before entering the service as an astronomer
knows about a comet's travels prior to its first observable appearance
in the sky. The verdict of the sea quidnuncs has been cited only by

way of showing what sort of moral impression the man made upon rude uncultivated natures whose conceptions of human wickedness were necessarily of the narrowest, limited to ideas of vulgar rascality— a thief among the swinging hammocks during a night watch, or the man-brokers and land-sharks of the seaports.

It was no gossip, however, but fact that though, as before hinted, Claggart upon his entrance into the navy was, as a novice, assigned to the least honorable section of a man-of-war's crew, embracing the drudgery, he did not long remain there. The superior capacity he immediately evinced, his constitutional sobriety, an ingratiating defer- ence to superiors, together with a peculiar ferreting genius manifested on a singular occasion; all this, capped by a certain austere patriotism, abruptly advanced him to the position of master-at-arms.

Of this maritime chief of police the ship's corporals, so called, were the immediate subordinates, and compliant ones; and this, as is to be noted in some business departments ashore, almost to a degree inconsistent with entire moral volition. His place put various converg- ing wires of underground influence under the chief's control, capable when astutely worked through his understrappers of operating to the mysterious discomfort, if nothing worse, of any of the sea commonalty. [67/68]

9

Life in the foretop well agreed with Billy Budd. There, when not actually engaged on the yards yet higher aloft, the topmen, who as such had been picked out for youth and activity, constituted an aerial club lounging at ease against the smaller stun'sails rolled up into cushions, spinning yarns like the lazy gods, and frequently amused with what was going on in the busy world of the decks below. No wonder then that a young fellow of Billy's disposition was well content in such society. Giving no cause of offense to anybody, he was always alert at a call. So in the merchant service it had been with him. But now such a punctiliousness in duty was shown that his topmates would sometimes good-naturedly laugh at him for it. This heightened alacrity had its cause, namely, the impression made upon him by the first formal gangway-punishment he had ever witnessed, which befell the day following his impressment. It had been incurred by a little fellow, young, a novice afterguardsman absent from his assigned post when the ship was being put about; a dereliction resulting in a rather serious hitch to that maneuver, one demanding instantaneous promptitude in letting go and making fast. When Billy saw the culprit's naked back under the scourge, gridironed with red welts and worse, when he marked the dire expression in the liberated man's face as with his woolen shirt flung over him by the executioner he rushed forward from the spot to bury himself in the crowd, Billy was horrified. He resolved that never through remissness would he make himself liable to such a visitation or do or omit aught that might merit even verbal reproof. What then was his surprise and concern when ultimately he found himself getting into petty trouble occasionally about such matters as the stowage of his bag or something amiss in his hammock, matters under the police oversight of the ship's corporals of the lower [68/69] decks, and which brought down on him a vague threat from one of them.

So heedful in all things as he was, how could this be? He could not understand it, and it more than vexed him. When he spoke to his young topmates about it they were either lightly incredulous or found something comical in his unconcealed anxiety. "Is it your bag, Billy?" said one. "Well, sew yourself up in it, bully boy, and then you'll be sure to know if anybody meddles with it."

Now there was a veteran aboard who because his years began to disqualify him for more active work had been recently assigned duty as mainmastman in his watch, looking to the gear belayed at the rail roundabout that great spar near the deck. At off-times the foretopman had picked up some acquaintance with him, and now in his trouble it occurred to him that he might be the sort of person to go to for wise counsel. He was an old Dansker long anglicized in the service, of few words, many wrinkles, and some honorable scars. His wizened face, time-tinted and weather-stained to the complexion of an antique parchment, was here and there peppered blue by the chance explosion of a gun cartridge in action.

He was an *Agamemnon* man, some two years prior to the time of this story having served under Nelson when still captain in that ship immortal in naval memory, which dismantled and in part broken up to her bare ribs is seen a grand skeleton in Haden's etching. As one of a boarding party from the *Agamemnon* he had received a cut slantwise along one temple and cheek leaving a long pale scar like a streak of dawn's light falling athwart the dark visage. It was on account of that scar and the affair in which it was known that he had received it, as well as from his blue-peppered complexion, that the Dansker went among the *Bellipotent*'s crew by the name of "Board-Her-in-the-Smoke."

Now the first time that his small weasel eyes happened to [69/70] light on Billy Budd, a certain grim internal merriment set all his ancient wrinkles into antic play. Was it that his eccentric unsentimental old sapience, primitive in its kind, saw or thought it saw something which in contrast with the warship's environment looked oddly incongruous in the Handsome Sailor? But after slyly studying him at intervals, the old Merlin's equivocal merriment was modified; for now when the twain would meet, it would start in his face a quizzing sort of look, but it would be but momentary and sometimes replaced by an expression of speculative query as to what might eventually befall a nature like that, dropped into a world not without some mantraps and against whose subtleties simple courage lacking experience and address, and without any touch of defensive ugliness, is of little avail; and where such innocence as man is capable of does yet in a moral emergency not always sharpen the faculties or enlighten the will.

However it was, the Dansker in his ascetic way rather took to Billy. Nor was this only because of a certain philosophic interest in such a character. There was another cause. While the old man's eccentricities, sometimes bordering on the ursine, repelled the juniors, Billy, undeterred thereby, revering him as a salt hero, would make advances, never passing the old *Agamemnon* man without a salutation marked by that respect which is seldom lost on the aged, however crabbed at times or whatever their station in life.

There was a vein of dry humor, or what not, in the mastman; and, whether in freak of patriarchal irony touching Billy's youth and athletic frame, or for some other and more recondite reason, from the first in addressing him he always substituted *Baby* for Billy, the Dansker in fact being the originator of the name by which the foretopman eventually became known aboard ship.

Well then, in his mysterious little difficulty going in quest of the wrinkled one, Billy found him off duty in a dogwatch ruminating [70/71] by himself, seated on a shot box of the upper gun deck, now and then surveying with a somewhat cynical regard certain of the more swaggering promenaders there. Billy recounted his trouble, again wondering how it all happened. The salt seer attentively listened, accompanying the foretopman's recital with queer twitchings of his wrinkles and problematical little sparkles of his small ferret eyes. Making an end of his story, the foretopman asked, "And now, Dansker, do tell me what you think of it."

The old man, shoving up the front of his tarpaulin and deliberately rubbing the long slant scar at the point where it entered the thin hair, laconically said, "Baby Budd, *Jemmy Legs*" (meaning the master-at-arms) "is down on you."

"*Jemmy Legs!*" ejaculated Billy, his welkin eyes expanding. "What for? Why, he calls me 'the sweet and pleasant young fellow,' they tell me."

"Does he so?" grinned the grizzled one; then said, "Ay, Baby lad, a sweet voice has Jemmy Legs."

"No, not always. But to me he has. I seldom pass him but there comes a pleasant word."

"And that's because he's down upon you, Baby Budd."

Such reiteration, along with the manner of it, incomprehensible to a novice, disturbed Billy almost as much as the mystery for which he had sought explanation. Something less unpleasingly oracular he tried to extract; but the old sea Chiron, thinking perhaps that for the nonce he had sufficiently instructed his young Achilles, pursed his lips, gathered all his wrinkles together, and would commit himself to nothing further.

Years, and those experiences which befall certain shrewder men subordinated lifelong to the will of superiors, all this had developed in the Dansker the pithy guarded cynicism that was his leading characteristic. [71/72]

<h2 style="text-align:center">10</h2>

The next day an incident served to confirm Billy Budd in his incredulity as to the Dansker's strange summing up of the case submitted. The ship at noon, going large before the wind, was rolling on her course, and he below at dinner and engaged in some sportful talk with the members of his mess, chanced in a sudden lurch to spill the entire contents of his soup pan upon the new-scrubbed deck. Claggart, the master-at-arms, official rattan in hand, happened to be passing along the battery in a bay of which the mess was lodged, and the greasy liquid streamed just across his path. Stepping over it, he was proceeding on his way without comment, since the matter was nothing to take notice of under the circumstances, when he happened to observe who it was that had done the spilling. His countenance changed. Pausing, he was about to ejaculate something hasty at the sailor, but checked himself, and pointing down to the streaming soup, playfully tapped him from behind with his rattan, saying in a low musical voice peculiar to him at times, "Handsomely done, my lad! And handsome is as handsome did it, too!" And with that passed on. Not noted by Billy as not coming within his view was the involuntary smile, or rather grimace, that accompanied Claggart's equivocal words. Aridly it drew down the thin corners of his shapely mouth. But everybody taking his remark as meant for humorous, and at which therefore as coming from a superior they were bound to laugh "with counterfeited glee," acted accordingly; and Billy, tickled, it may be, by the allusion to his being the Handsome Sailor, merrily joined in; then addressing his messmates exclaimed, "There now, who says that Jemmy Leggs is down on me!"

"And who said he was, Beauty?" demanded one Donald with some surprise. Whereat the foretopman looked a little foolish, recalling that it was only one person, Board-Her-in-the-Smoke, [72/73] who had suggested what to him was the smoky idea that this master-at-arms was in any peculiar way hostile to him. Meantime that functionary, resuming his path, must have momentarily worn some expression less guarded than that of the bitter smile, usurping the face from the heart—some distorting expression perhaps, for a drummer-boy heedlessly frolicking along from the opposite direction and chancing to come into light collision with his person was strangely disconcerted by his aspect. Nor was the impression lessened when the official, impetuously giving him a sharp cut with the rattan, vehemently exclaimed, "Look where you go!"

11

What was the matter with the master-at-arms? And, be the matter what it might, how could it have direct relation to Billy Budd, with whom prior to the affair of the spilled soup he had never come into any special contact official or otherwise? What indeed could the trouble have to do with one so little inclined to give offense as the merchant-ship's "peacemaker," even him who in Claggart's own phrase was "the sweet and pleasant young fellow"? Yes, why should Jemmy Legs, to borrow the Dansker's expression, be "down" on the Handsome Sailor? But, at heart and not for nothing, as the late chance encounter may indicate to the discerning, down on him, secretly down on him, he assuredly was.

Now to invent something touching the more private career of Claggart, something involving Billy Budd, of which something the latter should be wholly ignorant, some romantic incident implying that Claggart's knowledge of the young bluejacket began at some period anterior to catching sight of him on board the seventy-four—all this, not so difficult to do, might avail in a way more or less interesting to account for [73/74] whatever of enigma may appear to lurk in the case. But in fact there was nothing of the sort. And yet the cause necessarily to be assumed as the sole one assignable is in its very realism as much charged with that prime element of Radcliffian romance, the mysterious, as any that the ingenuity of the author of *The Mysteries of Udolpho* could devise. For what can more partake of the mysterious than an antipathy spontaneous and profound such as is evoked in certain exceptional mortals by the mere aspect of some other mortal, however harmless he may be, if not called forth by this very harmlessness itself?

Now there can exist no irritating juxtaposition of dissimilar personalities comparable to that which is possible aboard a great warship fully manned and at sea. There, every day among all ranks, almost every man comes into more or less of contact with almost every other man. Wholly there to avoid even the sight of an aggravating object one must needs give it Jonah's toss or jump overboard himself. Imagine how all this might eventually operate on some peculiar human creature the direct reverse of a saint!

But for the adequate comprehending of Claggart by a normal nature these hints are insufficient. To pass from a normal nature to him one must cross "the deadly space between." And this is best done by indirection.

Long ago an honest scholar, my senior, said to me in reference to one who like himself is now no more, a man so unimpeachably respectable that against him nothing was ever openly said though among the few something was whispered, "Yes, X—— is a nut not to be cracked by the tap of a lady's fan. You are aware that I am the adherent of no organized religion, much less of any philosophy built into a system. Well, for all that, I think that to try and get into X——, enter his labyrinth and get out again, without a clue derived from some source other [than] what is known as 'knowledge of the world'— that were hardly possible, at least for me."

"Why," said I, "X——, however singular a study to some, [74/75] is yet human, and knowledge of the world assuredly implies the knowledge of human nature, and in most of its varieties."

"Yes, but a superficial knowledge of it, serving ordinary purposes. But for anything deeper, I am not certain whether to know the world and to know human nature be not two distinct branches of knowledge, which while they may coexist in the same heart, yet either may exist with little or nothing of the other. Nay, in an average man of the world, his constant rubbing with it blunts that finer spiritual insight indispensable to the understanding of the essential in certain exceptional characters, whether evil ones or good. In a matter of some importance I have seen a girl wind an old lawyer about her little finger. Nor was it the dotage of senile love. Nothing of the sort. But he knew law better than he knew the girl's heart. Coke and Blackstone hardly shed so much light into obscure spiritual places as the Hebrew prophets. And who were they? Mostly recluses."

At the time, my inexperience was such that I did not quite see the drift of all this. It may be that I see it now. And, indeed, if that lexicon which is based on Holy Writ were any longer popular, one might with less difficulty define and denominate certain phenomenal men. As it is, one must turn to some authority not liable to the charge of being tinctured with the biblical element.

In a list of definitions included in the authentic translation of Plato, a list attributed to him, occurs this: "Natural Depravity: a depravity according to nature," a definition which, though savoring of Calvinism, by no means involves Calvin's dogma as to total mankind. Evidently its intent makes it applicable but to individuals. Not many are the examples of this depravity which the gallows and jail supply. At any rate, for notable instances, since these have no vulgar alloy of the brute in them, but invariably are dominated by intellectuality, one must go elsewhere. Civilization, especially if of the austerer sort, is auspicious to it. It folds itself in the mantle of respectability. [75/76] It has its certain negative virtues serving as silent auxiliaries. It never allows wine to get within its guard. It is not going too far to say that it is without vices or small sins. There is a phenomenal pride in it that excludes them. It is never mercenary or avaricious. In short, the depravity here meant partakes nothing of the sordid or sensual. It is serious, but free from acerbity. Though no flatterer of mankind it never speaks ill of it.

But the thing which in eminent instances signalizes so exceptional a nature is this: Though the man's even temper and discreet bearing would seem to intimate a mind peculiarly subject to the law of reason, not the less in heart he would seem to riot in complete exemption from that law, having apparently little to do with reason further than to employ it as an ambidexter implement for effecting the irrational. That is to say: Toward the accomplishment of an aim which in wantonness of atrocity would seem to partake of the insane, he will direct a cool judgment sagacious and sound. These men are madmen, and of the most dangerous sort, for their lunacy is not continuous, but occasional, evoked by some special object; it is protectively secretive, which is as much as to say it is self-contained, so that when, moreover, most active it is to the average mind not distinguishable from sanity, and for the reason above suggested: that whatever its aims may be—and the aim is never declared—the method and the outward proceeding are always perfectly rational.

Now something such an one was Claggart, in whom was the mania of an evil nature, not engendered by vicious training or corrupting books or licentious living, but born with him and innate, in short "a depravity according to nature."

Dark sayings are these, some will say. But why? Is it because they somewhat savor of Holy Writ in its phrase "mystery of iniquity"? If they do, such savor was far enough from being intended, for little will it commend these pages to many a reader of today.

The point of the present story turning on the hidden nature [76/ 77] of the master-at-arms has necessitated this chapter. With an added hint or two in connection with the incident at the mess, the resumed narrative must be left to vindicate, as it may, its own credibility.

12

That Claggart's figure was not amiss, and his face, save the chin, well molded, has already been said. Of these favorable points he seemed not insensible, for he was not only neat but careful in his dress. But the form of Billy Budd was heroic; and if his face was without the intellectual look of the pallid Claggart's, not the less was it lit, like his, from within, though from a different source. The bonfire in his heart made luminous the rose-tan in his cheek.

In view of the marked contrast between the persons of the twain, it is more than probable that when the master-at-arms in the scene last given applied to the sailor the proverb "Handsome is as handsome does," he there let escape an ironic inkling, not caught by the young sailors who heard it, as to what it was that had first moved him against Billy, namely, his significant personal beauty.

Now envy and antipathy, passions irreconcilable in reason, nevertheless in fact may spring conjoined like Chang and Eng in one birth.
Is Envy then such a monster? Well, though many an arraigned mortal
has in hopes of mitigated penalty pleaded guilty to horrible actions,
did ever anybody seriously confess to envy? Something there is in it
universally felt to be more shameful than even felonious crime. And
not only does everybody disown it, but the better sort are inclined to
incredulity when it is in earnest imputed to an intelligent man. But
since its lodgment is in the heart not the brain, no degree of intellect
supplies a guarantee against it. But Claggart's was no vulgar form of
the passion. Nor, as directed toward Billy Budd, did it [77/78]
partake of that streak of apprehensive jealousy that marred Saul's
visage perturbedly brooding on the comely young David. Claggart's
envy struck deeper. If askance he eyed the good looks, cheery health,
and frank enjoyment of young life in Billy Budd, it was because these
went along with a nature that, as Claggart magnetically felt, had in its
simplicity never willed malice or experienced the reactionary bite of
that serpent. To him, the spirit lodged within Billy, and looking out
from his welkin eyes as from windows, that ineffability it was which
made the dimple in his dyed cheek, suppled his joints, and dancing in
his yellow curls made him pre-eminently the Handsome Sailor. One
person excepted, the master-at-arms was perhaps the only man in the
ship intellectually capable of adequately appreciating the moral phenomenon presented in Billy Budd. And the insight but intensified his
passion, which assuming various secret forms within him, at times
assumed that of cynic disdain, disdain of innocence—to be nothing
more than innocent! Yet in an aesthetic way he saw the charm of it, the
courageous free-and-easy temper of it, and fain would have shared it,
but he despaired of it.

With no power to annul the elemental evil in him, though readily
enough he could hide it; apprehending the good, but powerless to be
it; a nature like Claggart's, surcharged with energy as such natures
almost invariably are, what recourse is left to it but to recoil upon itself
and, like the scorpion for which the Creator alone is responsible, act
out to the end the part allotted it.

13

Passion, and passion in its profoundest, is not a thing demanding
a palatial stage whereon to play its part. Down among the groundlings, among the beggars and rakers of the garbage, profound passion
is enacted. And the circumstances that provoke [78/79] it, however
trivial or mean, are no measure of its power. In the present instance
the stage is a scrubbed gun deck, and one of the external provocations
a man-of-war's man's spilled soup.

Now when the master-at-arms noticed whence came that greasy

fluid streaming before his feet, he must have taken it—to some extent wilfully, perhaps—not for the mere accident it assuredly was, but for the sly escape of a spontaneous feeling on Billy's part more or less answering to the antipathy on his own. In effect a foolish demonstration, he must have thought, and very harmless, like the futile kick of a heifer, which yet were the heifer a shod stallion would not be so harmless. Even so was it that into the gall of Claggart's envy he infused the vitriol of his contempt. But the incident confirmed to him certain telltale reports purveyed to his ear by "Squeak," one of his more cunning corporals, a grizzled little man, so nicknamed by the sailors on account of his squeaky voice and sharp visage ferreting about the dark corners of the lower decks after interlopers, satirically suggesting to them the idea of a rat in a cellar.

From his chief's employing him as an implicit tool in laying little traps for the worriment of the foretopman—for it was from the master-at-arms that the petty persecutions heretofore adverted to had proceeded—the corporal, having naturally enough concluded that his master could have no love for the sailor, made it his business, faithful understrapper that he was, to foment the ill blood by perverting to his chief certain innocent frolics of the good-natured foretopman, besides inventing for his mouth sundry contumelious epithets he claimed to have overheard him let fall. The master-at-arms never suspected the veracity of these reports, more especially as to the epithets, for he well knew how secretly unpopular may become a master-at-arms, at least a master-at-arms of those days, zealous in his function, and how the bluejackets shoot at him in private their raillery and wit; the nickname by which he goes among them (Jemmy Legs) implying under the form of merriment their cherished disrespect and dislike. But in view of the greediness [79/80] of hate for pabulum it hardly needed a purveyor to feed Claggart's passion.

An uncommon prudence is habitual with the subtler depravity, for it has everything to hide. And in case of an injury but suspected, its secretiveness voluntarily cuts it off from enlightenment or disillusion; and, not unreluctantly, action is taken upon surmise as upon certainty. And the retaliation is apt to be in monstrous disproportion to the supposed offense; for when in anybody was revenge in its exactions aught else but an inordinate usurer? But how with Claggart's conscience? For though consciences are unlike as foreheads, every intelligence, not excluding the scriptural devils who "believe and tremble," has one. But Claggart's conscience being but the lawyer to his will, made ogres of trifles, probably arguing that the motive imputed to Billy in spilling the soup just when he did, together with the epithets alleged, these, if nothing more, made a strong case against him; nay, justified animosity into a sort of retributive righteousness. The Pharisee is the Guy Fawkes prowling in the hid chambers underlying some natures like Claggart's. And they can really form no conception of an unreciprocated malice. Probably the master-at-arms' clandestine persecution of Billy was started to try the temper of the man; but it had not developed any quality in him that enmity could make official use of or even pervert into plausible self-justification; so that the occurrence at the mess, petty if it were, was a welcome one to that peculiar conscience assigned to be the private mentor of Claggart; and, for the rest, not improbably it put him upon new experiments.

14

Not many days after the last incident narrated, something befell Billy Budd that more graveled him than aught that had previously occurred. [80/81]

It was a warm night for the latitude; and the foretopman, whose watch at the time was properly below, was dozing on the uppermost deck whither he had ascended from his hot hammock, one of hundreds suspended so closely wedged together over a lower gun deck that there was little or no swing to them. He lay as in the shadow of a hillside, stretched under the lee of the booms, a piled ridge of spare spars amidships between foremast and mainmast among which the ship's largest boat, the launch, was stowed. Alongside of three other slumberers from below, he lay near that end of the booms which approaches the foremast; his station aloft on duty as a foretopman being just over the deck-station of the forecastlemen, entitling him according to usage to make himself more or less at home in that neighborhood.

Presently he was stirred into semiconsciousness by somebody, who must have previously sounded the sleep of the others, touching his shoulder, and then, as the foretopman raised his head, breathing into his ear in a quick whisper, "Slip into the lee forechains, Billy; there is something in the wind. Don't speak. Quick, I will meet you there," and disappearing.

Now Billy, like sundry other essentially good-natured ones, had some of the weaknesses inseparable from essential good nature; and among these was a reluctance, almost an incapacity of plumply saying *no* to an abrupt proposition not obviously absurd on the face of it, nor obviously unfriendly, nor iniquitous. And being of warm blood, he had not the phlegm tacitly to negative any proposition by unresponsive inaction. Like his sense of fear, his apprehension as to aught outside of the honest and natural was seldom very quick. Besides, upon the present occasion, the drowse from his sleep still hung upon him.

However it was, he mechanically rose and, sleepily wondering what could be in the wind, betook himself to the designated place, a narrow platform, one of six, outside of the high bulwarks and screened by the great deadeyes and multiple columned lanyards of the shrouds and backstays; and, in a great [81/82] warship of that time, of dimensions commensurate to the hull's magnitude; a tarry balcony in short, overhanging the sea, and so secluded that one mariner of the *Bellipotent*, a Nonconformist old tar of a serious turn, made it even in daytime his private oratory.

In this retired nook the stranger soon joined Billy Budd. There was no moon as yet; a haze obscured the starlight. He could not distinctly see the stranger's face. Yet from something in the outline and carriage, Billy took him, and correctly, for one of the afterguard.

"Hist! Billy," said the man, in the same quick cautionary whisper as before. "You were impressed, weren't you? Well, so was I"; and he paused, as to mark the effect. But Billy, not knowing exactly what to make of this, said nothing. Then the other: "We are not the only impressed ones, Billy. There's a gang of us.—Couldn't you—help—at a pinch?"

"What do you mean?" demanded Billy, here thoroughly shaking off his drowse.

"Hist, hist!" the hurried whisper now growing husky. "See here," and the man held up two small objects faintly twinkling in the night-light; "see, they are yours, Billy, if you'll only ——"

But Billy broke in, and in his resentful eagerness to deliver himself his vocal infirmity somewhat intruded. "D—d—damme, I don't know what you are d—d—driving at, or what you mean, but you had better g—g—go where you belong!" For the moment the fellow, as confounded, did not stir; and Billy, springing to his feet, said, "If you d—don't start, I'll t—t—toss you back over the r—rail!" There was no mistaking this, and the mysterious emissary decamped, disappearing in the direction of the mainmast in the shadow of the booms.

"Hallo, what's the matter?" here came growling from a fore-castleman awakened from his deck-doze by Billy's raised voice. And as the foretopman reappeared and was recognized by him: [82/83] "Ah, Beauty, is it you? Well, something must have been the matter, for you st—st—stuttered."

"Oh," rejoined Billy, now mastering the impediment, "I found an afterguardsman in our part of the ship here, and I bid him be off where he belongs."

"And is that all you did about it, Foretopman?" gruffly demanded another, an irascible old fellow of brick-colored visage and hair who was known to his associate forecastlemen as "Red Pepper." "Such sneaks I should like to marry to the gunner's daughter!"—by that expression meaning that he would like to subject them to disciplinary castigation over a gun.

However, Billy's rendering of the matter satisfactorily accounted to these inquirers for the brief commotion, since of all the sections of a ship's company the forecastlemen, veterans for the most part and bigoted in their sea prejudices, are the most jealous in resenting territorial encroachments, especially on the part of any of the afterguard, of whom they have but a sorry opinion—chiefly landsmen, never going aloft except to reef or furl the mainsail, and in no wise competent to handle a marlinspike or turn in a deadeye, say.

15

This incident sorely puzzled Billy Budd. It was an entirely new experience, the first time in his life that he had ever been personally approached in underhand intriguing fashion. Prior to this encounter he had known nothing of the afterguardsman, the two men being stationed wide apart, one forward and aloft during his watch, the other on deck and aft.

What could it mean? And could they really be guineas, those two glittering objects the interloper had held up to his (Billy's) eyes? Where could the fellow get guineas? Why, even spare buttons are not so plentiful at sea. The more he turned the matter [83/84] over, the more he was nonplussed, and made uneasy and discomfited. In his disgustful recoil from an overture which, though he but ill comprehended, he instinctively knew must involve evil of some sort, Billy Budd was like a young horse fresh from the pasture suddenly inhaling a vile whiff from some chemical factory, and by repeated snortings trying to get it out of his nostrils and lungs. This frame of mind barred all desire of holding further parley with the fellow, even were it but for the purpose of gaining some enlightenment as to his design in approaching him. And yet he was not without natural curiosity to see how such a visitor in the dark would look in broad day.

He espied him the following afternoon in his first dogwatch below, one of the smokers on that forward part of the upper gun deck allotted to the pipe. He recognized him by his general cut and build more than by his round freckled face and glassy eyes of pale blue, veiled with lashes all but white. And yet Billy was a bit uncertain whether indeed it were he—yonder chap about his own age chatting and laughing in freehearted way, leaning against a gun; a genial young fellow enough to look at, and something of a rattlebrain, to all appearance. Rather chubby too for a sailor, even an afterguardsman. In short, the last man in the world, one would think, to be overburdened with thoughts, especially those perilous thoughts that must needs belong to a conspirator in any serious project, or even to the underling of such a conspirator.

Although Billy was not aware of it, the fellow, with a sidelong watchful glance, had perceived Billy first, and then noting that Billy was looking at him, thereupon nodded a familiar sort of friendly recognition as to an old acquaintance, without interrupting the talk he was engaged in with the group of smokers. A day or two afterwards, chancing in the evening promenade on a gun deck to pass Billy, he offered a flying word of good-fellowship, as it were, which by its unexpectedness, and equivocalness under the circumstances, so embarrassed Billy that he knew not how to respond to it, and let it go unnoticed. [84/85]

Billy was now left more at a loss than before. The ineffectual speculations into which he was led were so disturbingly alien to him that he did his best to smother them. It never entered his mind that here was a matter which, from its extreme questionableness, it was his duty as a loyal bluejacket to report in the proper quarter. And, probably, had such a step been suggested to him, he would have been deterred from taking it by the thought, one of novice magnanimity, that it would savor overmuch of the dirty work of a telltale. He kept the thing to himself. Yet upon one occasion he could not forbear a little disburdening himself to the old Dansker, tempted thereto perhaps by the influence of a balmy night when the ship lay becalmed; the twain, silent for the most part, sitting together on deck, their heads propped against the bulwarks. But it was only a partial and anonymous account that Billy gave, the unfounded scruples above referred to preventing full disclosure to anybody. Upon hearing Billy's version, the sage Dansker seemed to divine more than he was told; and after a little meditation, during which his wrinkles were pursed as into a point, quite effacing for the time that quizzing expression his face sometimes wore: "Didn't I say so, Baby Budd?"

"Say what?" demanded Billy.

"Why, *Jemmy Legs* is *down* on you."

"And what," rejoined Billy in amazement, "has *Jemmy Legs* to do with that cracked afterguardsman?"

"Ho, it was an afterguardsman, then. A cat's-paw, a cat's-paw!" And with that exclamation, whether it had reference to a light puff of air just then coming over the calm sea, or a subtler relation to the afterguardsman, there is no telling, the old Merlin gave a twisting wrench with his black teeth at his plug of tobacco, vouchsafing no reply to Billy's impetuous question, though now repeated, for it was his wont to relapse into grim silence when interrogated in skeptical sort as to any of his sententious oracles, not always very clear ones, rather partaking [85/86] of that obscurity which invests most Delphic deliverances from any quarter.

Long experience had very likely brought this old man to that bitter prudence which never interferes in aught and never gives advice.

<h1 style="text-align:center">16</h1>

Yes, despite the Dansker's pithy insistence as to the master-at-arms being at the bottom of these strange experiences of Billy on board the *Bellipotent*, the young sailor was ready to ascribe them to almost anybody but the man who, to use Billy's own expression, "always had a pleasant word for him." This is to be wondered at. Yet not so much to be wondered at. In certain matters, some sailors even in mature life remain unsophisticated enough. But a young seafarer of the disposition of our athletic foretopman is much of a child-man. And yet a child's utter innocence is but its blank ignorance, and the innocence more or less wanes as intelligence waxes. But in Billy Budd intelligence, such as it was, had advanced while yet his simple-mindedness remained for the most part unaffected. Experience is a teacher indeed; yet did Billy's years make his experience small. Besides, he had none of that intuitive knowledge of the bad which in natures not good or incompletely so foreruns experience, and therefore may pertain, as in some instances it too clearly does pertain, even to youth.

And what could Billy know of man except of man as a mere sailor? And the old-fashioned sailor, the veritable man before the mast, the sailor from boyhood up, he, though indeed of the same species as a landsman, is in some respects singularly distinct from him. The sailor is frankness, the landsman is finesse. Life is not a game with the sailor, demanding the long head—no intricate game of chess where few moves are made in straightforwardness [86/87] and ends are attained by indirection, an oblique, tedious, barren game hardly worth that poor candle burnt out in playing it.

Yes, as a class, sailors are in character a juvenile race. Even their deviations are marked by juvenility, this more especially holding true with the sailors of Billy's time. Then too, certain things which apply to all sailors do more pointedly operate here and there upon the junior one. Every sailor, too, is accustomed to obey orders without debating them; his life afloat is externally ruled for him; he is not brought into that promiscuous commerce with mankind where unobstructed free agency on equal terms—equal superficially, at least—soon teaches one that unless upon occasion he exercise a distrust keen in proportion to the fairness of the appearance, some foul turn may be served him. A ruled undemonstrative distrustfulness is so habitual, not with businessmen so much as with men who know their kind in less shallow relations than business, namely, certain men of the world, that they come at last to employ it all but unconsciously; and some of them would very likely feel real surprise at being charged with it as one of their general characteristics.

17

But after the little matter at the mess Billy Budd no more found himself in strange trouble at times about his hammock or his clothes bag or what not. As to that smile that occasionally sunned him, and the pleasant passing word, these were, if not more frequent, yet if anything more pronounced than before.

But for all that, there were certain other demonstrations now. When Claggart's unobserved glance happened to light on belted Billy rolling along the upper gun deck in the leisure of the second dogwatch, exchanging passing broadsides of fun with other young promenaders in the crowd, that glance would follow the [87/88] cheerful sea Hyperion with a settled meditative and melancholy expression, his eyes strangely suffused with incipient feverish tears. Then would Claggart look like the man of sorrows. Yes, and sometimes the melancholy expression would have in it a touch of soft yearning, as if Claggart could even have loved Billy but for fate and ban. But this was an evanescence, and quickly repented of, as it were, by an immitigable look, pinching and shriveling the visage into the momentary semblance of a wrinkled walnut. But sometimes catching sight in advance of the foretopman coming in his direction, he would, upon their nearing, step aside a little to let him pass, dwelling upon Billy for the moment with the glittering dental satire of a Guise. But upon any abrupt unforeseen encounter a red light would flash forth from his eye like a spark from an anvil in a dusk smithy. That quick, fierce light was a strange one, darted from orbs which in repose were of a color nearest approaching a deeper violet, the softest of shades.

Though some of these caprices of the pit could not but be observed by their object, yet were they beyond the construing of such a nature. And the thews of Billy were hardly compatible with that sort of sensitive spiritual organization which in some cases instinctively conveys to ignorant innocence an admonition of the proximity of the malign. He thought the master-at-arms acted in a manner rather queer at times. That was all. But the occasional frank air and pleasant word went for what they purported to be, the young sailor never having heard as yet of the "too fair-spoken man."

Had the foretopman been conscious of having done or said anything to provoke the ill will of the official, it would have been different with him, and his sight might have been purged if not sharpened. As it was, innocence was his blinder.

So was it with him in yet another matter. Two minor officers, the armorer and captain of the hold, with whom he had never exchanged a word, his position in the ship not bringing him into contact with them, these men now for the first began to cast [88/89] upon Billy, when they chanced to encounter him, that peculiar glance which evidences that the man from whom it comes has been some way tampered with, and to the prejudice of him upon whom the glance lights. Never did it occur to Billy as a thing to be noted or a thing suspicious, though he well knew the fact, that the armorer and captain of the hold, with the ship's yeoman, apothecary, and others of that grade, were by naval usage messmates of the master-at-arms, men with ears convenient to his confidential tongue.

But the general popularity that came from our Handsome Sailor's manly forwardness upon occasion and irresistible good nature, indicating no mental superiority tending to excite an invidious feeling, this good will on the part of most of his shipmates made him the less to concern himself about such mute aspects toward him as those whereto allusion has just been made, aspects he could not so fathom as to infer their whole import.

As to the afterguardsman, though Billy for reasons already given necessarily saw little of him, yet when the two did happen to meet, invariably came the fellow's offhand cheerful recognition, sometimes accompanied by a passing pleasant word or two. Whatever that equivocal young person's original design may really have been, or the design of which he might have been the deputy, certain it was from his manner upon these occasions that he had wholly dropped it.

It was as if his precocity of crookedness (and every vulgar villain is precocious) had for once deceived him, and the man he had sought to entrap as a simpleton had through his very simplicity ignominiously baffled him.

But shrewd ones may opine that it was hardly possible for Billy to refrain from going up to the afterguardsman and bluntly demanding to know his purpose in the initial interview so abruptly closed in the forechains. Shrewd ones may also think it but natural in Billy to set about sounding some of the other impressed men of the ship in order to discover what basis, if [89/90] any, there was for the emissary's obscure suggestions as to plotting disaffection aboard. Yes, shrewd ones may so think. But something more, or rather something else than mere shrewdness is perhaps needful for the due understanding of such a character as Billy Budd's.

As to Claggart, the monomania in the man—if that indeed it were—as involuntarily disclosed by starts in the manifestations detailed, yet in general covered over by his self-contained and rational demeanor; this, like a subterranean fire, was eating its way deeper and deeper in him. Something decisive must come of it.

18

After the mysterious interview in the forechains, the one so abruptly ended there by Billy, nothing especially germane to the story occurred until the event now about to be narrated.

Elsewhere it has been said that in the lack of frigates (of course better sailers than line-of-battle ships) in the English squadron up the Straits at that period, the *Bellipotent* 74 was occasionally employed not only as an available substitute for a scout, but at times on detached service of more important kind. This was not alone because of her sailing qualities, not common in a ship of her rate, but quite as much, probably, that the character of her commander, it was thought, specially adapted him for any duty where under unforeseen difficulties a prompt initiative might have to be taken in some matter demanding knowledge and ability in addition to those qualities implied in good seamanship. It was on an expedition of the latter sort, a somewhat distant one, and when the *Bellipotent* was almost at her furthest remove from the fleet, that in the latter part of an afternoon watch she unexpectedly came in sight of a ship of the enemy. It proved to be a frigate. The latter, perceiving through the glass that the weight of men and metal would be heavily [90/91] against her, invoking her light heels crowded sail to get away. After a chase urged almost against hope and lasting until about the middle of the first dogwatch, she signally succeeded in effecting her escape.

Not long after the pursuit had been given up, and ere the excitement incident thereto had altogether waned away, the master-at-arms, ascending from his cavernous sphere, made his appearance cap in hand by the mainmast respectfully waiting the notice of Captain Vere, then solitary walking the weather side of the quarter-deck, doubtless somewhat chafed at the failure of the pursuit. The spot where Claggart stood was the place allotted to men of lesser grades seeking some more particular interview either with the officer of the deck or the captain himself. But from the latter it was not often that a sailor or petty officer of those days would seek a hearing; only some exceptional cause would, according to established custom, have warranted that.

Presently, just as the commander, absorbed in his reflections, was on the point of turning aft in his promenade, he became sensible of Claggart's presence, and saw the doffed cap held in deferential expectancy. Here be it said that Captain Vere's personal knowledge of this petty officer had only begun at the time of the ship's last sailing from home, Claggart then for the first, in transfer from a ship detained for repairs, supplying on board the *Bellipotent* the place of a previous master-at-arms disabled and ashore.

No sooner did the commander observe who it was that now deferentially stood awaiting his notice than a peculiar expression came over him. It was not unlike that which uncontrollably will flit across the countenance of one at unawares encountering a person who, though known to him indeed, has hardly been long enough known for thorough knowledge, but something in whose aspect nevertheless now for the first provokes a vaguely repellent distaste. But coming to a stand and resuming much of his wonted official manner, save that a sort of impatience [91/92] lurked in the intonation of the opening word, he said "Well? What is it, Master-at-arms?"

With the air of a subordinate grieved at the necessity of being a messenger of ill tidings, and while conscientiously determined to be frank yet equally resolved upon shunning overstatement, Claggart at this invitation, or rather summons to disburden, spoke up. What he said, conveyed in the language of no uneducated man, was to the effect following, if not altogether in these words, namely, that during the chase and preparations for the possible encounter he had seen enough to convince him that at least one sailor aboard was a dangerous character in a ship mustering some who not only had taken a guilty part in the late serious troubles, but others also who, like the man in question, had entered His Majesty's service under another form than enlistment.

At this point Captain Vere with some impatience interrupted him: "Be direct, man; say *impressed men*."

Claggart made a gesture of subservience, and proceeded. Quite lately he (Claggart) had begun to suspect that on the gun decks some sort of movement prompted by the sailor in question was covertly going on, but he had not thought himself warranted in reporting the suspicion so long as it remained indistinct. But from what he had that afternoon observed in the man referred to, the suspicion of something clandestine going on had advanced to a point less removed from certainty. He deeply felt, he added, the serious responsibility assumed in making a report involving such possible consequences to the individual mainly concerned, besides tending to augment those natural anxieties which every naval commander must feel in view of extraordinary outbreaks so recent as those which, he sorrowfully said it, it needed not to name.

Now at the first broaching of the matter Captain Vere, taken by surprise, could not wholly dissemble his disquietude. But as Claggart went on, the former's aspect changed into restiveness under something in the testifier's manner in giving his testimony. [92/93] However, he refrained from interrupting him. And Claggart, continuing, concluded with this: "God forbid, your honor, that the *Bellipotent*'s should be the experience of the ——"

"Never mind that!" here peremptorily broke in the superior, his face altering with anger, instinctively divining the ship that the other was about to name, one in which the Nore Mutiny had assumed a singularly tragical character that for a time jeopardized the life of its commander. Under the circumstances he was indignant at the purposed allusion. When the commissioned officers themselves were on all occasions very heedful how they referred to the recent events in the fleet, for a petty officer unnecessarily to allude to them in the presence of his captain, this struck him as a most immodest presumption. Besides, to his quick sense of self-respect it even looked under the circumstances something like an attempt to alarm him. Nor at first was he without some surprise that one who so far as he had hitherto come under his notice had shown considerable tact in his function should in this particular evince such lack of it.

But these thoughts and kindred dubious ones flitting across his mind were suddenly replaced by an intuitional surmise which, though as yet obscure in form, served practically to affect his reception of the ill tidings. Certain it is that, long versed in everything pertaining to the

complicated gun-deck life, which like every other form of life has its
secret mines and dubious side, the side popularly disclaimed, Captain
Vere did not permit himself to be unduly disturbed by the general
tenor of his subordinate's report.

Furthermore, if in view of recent events prompt action should be
taken at the first palpable sign of recurring insubordination, for all
that, not judicious would it be, he thought, to keep the idea of
lingering disaffection alive by undue forwardness in crediting an
informer, even if his own subordinate and charged among other things
with police surveillance of the crew. This feeling would not perhaps
have so prevailed with him were it [93/94] not that upon a prior
occasion the patriotic zeal officially evinced by Claggart had somewhat
irritated him as appearing rather supersensible and strained. Furthermore, something even in the official's self-possessed and somewhat
ostentatious manner in making his specifications strangely reminded
him of a bandsman, a perjurous witness in a capital case before a court-
martial ashore of which when a lieutenant he (Captain Vere) had
been a member.

Now the peremptory check given to Claggart in the matter of the
arrested allusion was quickly followed up by this: "You say that there
is at least one dangerous man aboard. Name him."

"William Budd, a foretopman, your honor."

"William Budd!" repeated Captain Vere with unfeigned astonish-
ment. "And mean you the man that Lieutenant Ratcliffe took from the
merchantman not very long ago, the young fellow who seems to be so
popular with the men—Billy, the Handsome Sailor, as they call him?"

"The same, your honor; but for all his youth and good looks, a
deep one. Not for nothing does he insinuate himself into the good will
of his shipmates, since at the least they will at a pinch say—all hands
will—a good word for him, and at all hazards. Did Lieutenant
Ratcliffe happen to tell your honor of that adroit fling of Budd's,
jumping up in the cutter's bow under the merchantman's stern when
he was being taken off? It is even masked by that sort of good-
humored air that at heart he resents his impressment. You have but
noted his fair cheek. A mantrap may be under the ruddy-tipped
daisies."

Now the Handsome Sailor as a signal figure among the crew had
naturally enough attracted the captain's attention from the first.
Though in general not very demonstrative to his officers, he had
congratulated Lieutenant Ratcliffe upon his good fortune in lighting
on such a fine specimen of the *genus homo,* who in the nude might
have posed for a statue of young Adam before the Fall. As to Billy's
adieu to the ship *Rights-of-Man,* [94/95] which the boarding lieutenant had indeed reported to him, but, in a deferential way, more as a
good story than aught else, Captain Vere, though mistakenly understanding it as a satiric sally, had but thought so much the better of the

impressed man for it; as a military sailor, admiring the spirit that could take an arbitrary enlistment so merrily and sensibly. The foretopman's conduct, too, so far as it had fallen under the captain's notice, had confirmed the first happy augury, while the new recruit's qualities as a "sailor-man" seemed to be such that he had thought of recommending him to the executive officer for promotion to a place that would more frequently bring him under his own observation, namely, the captaincy of the mizzentop, replacing there in the starboard watch a man not so young whom partly for that reason he deemed less fitted for the post. Be it parenthesized here that since the mizzentopmen have not to handle such breadths of heavy canvas as the lower sails on the main-mast and foremast, a young man if of the right stuff not only seems best adapted to duty there, but in fact is generally selected for the captaincy of that top, and the company under him are light hands and often but striplings. In sum, Captain Vere had from the beginning deemed Billy Budd to be what in the naval parlance of the time was called a "King's bargain": that is to say, for His Britannic Majesty's navy a capital investment at small outlay or none at all.

After a brief pause, during which the reminiscences above men-tioned passed vividly through his mind and he weighed the import of Claggart's last suggestion conveyed in the phrase "mantrap under the daisies," and the more he weighed it the less reliance he felt in the informer's good faith, suddenly he turned upon him and in a low voice demanded: "Do you come to me, Master-at-arms, with so foggy a tale? As to Budd, cite me an act or spoken word of his confirmatory of what you in general charge against him. Stay," drawing nearer to him; "heed what you speak. Just now, and in a case like this, there is a yardarm-end for the false witness." [95/96]

"Ah, your honor!" sighed Claggart, mildly shaking his shapely head as in sad deprecation of such unmerited severity of tone. Then, bridling—erecting himself as in virtuous self-assertion—he circum-stantially alleged certain words and acts which collectively, if credited, led to presumptions mortally inculpating Budd. And for some of these averments, he added, substantiating proof was not far.

With gray eyes impatient and distrustful essaying to fathom to the bottom Claggart's calm violet ones, Captain Vere again heard him out; then for the moment stood ruminating. The mood he evinced, Claggart —himself for the time liberated from the other's scrutiny—steadily regarded with a look difficult to render: a look curious of the operation of his tactics, a look such as might have been that of the spokesman of the envious children of Jacob deceptively imposing upon the troubled patriarch the blood-dyed coat of young Joseph.

Though something exceptional in the moral quality of Captain Vere made him, in earnest encounter with a fellow man, a veritable touchstone of that man's essential nature, yet now as to Claggart and what was really going on in him his feeling partook less of intuitional conviction than of strong suspicion clogged by strange dubieties. The perplexity he evinced proceeded less from aught touching the man informed against—as Claggart doubtless opined—than from considerations how best to act in regard to the informer. At first, indeed, he was naturally for summoning that substantiation of his allegations which Claggart said was at hand. But such a proceeding would result in the matter at once getting abroad, which in the present stage of it, he thought, might undesirably affect the ship's company. If Claggart was a false witness—that closed the affair. And therefore, before trying the accusation, he would first practically test the accuser; and he thought this could be done in a quiet, undemonstrative way.

The measure he determined upon involved a shifting of the scene, a transfer to a place less exposed to observation than the [96/97] broad quarter-deck. For although the few gun-room officers there at the time had, in due observance of naval etiquette, withdrawn to leeward the moment Captain Vere had begun his promenade on the deck's weather side; and though during the colloquy with Claggart they of course ventured not to diminish the distance; and though throughout the interview Captain Vere's voice was far from high, and Claggart's silvery and low; and the wind in the cordage and the wash of the sea helped the more to put them beyond earshot; nevertheless, the interview's continuance already had attracted observation from some topmen aloft and other sailors in the waist or further forward.

Having determined upon his measures, Captain Vere forthwith took action. Abruptly turning to Claggart, he asked, "Master-at-arms, is it now Budd's watch aloft?"

"No, your honor."

Whereupon, "Mr. Wilkes!" summoning the nearest midshipman. "Tell Albert to come to me." Albert was the captain's hammock-boy, a sort of sea valet in whose discretion and fidelity his master had much confidence. The lad appeared.

"You know Budd, the foretopman?"

"I do, sir."

"Go find him. It is his watch off. Manage to tell him out of earshot that he is wanted aft. Contrive it that he speaks to nobody. Keep him in talk yourself. And not till you get well aft here, not till then let him know that the place where he is wanted is my cabin. You understand. Go.—Master-at-arms, show yourself on the decks below, and when you think it time for Albert to be coming with his man, stand by quietly to follow the sailor in."

19

Now when the foretopman found himself in the cabin, closeted there, as it were, with the captain and Claggart, he was surprised enough. But it was a surprise unaccompanied by apprehension [97/

98] or distrust. To an immature nature essentially honest and humane, forewarning intimations of subtler danger from one's kind come tardily if at all. The only thing that took shape in the young sailor's mind was this: Yes, the captain, I have always thought, looks kindly upon me. Wonder if he's going to make me his coxswain. I should like that. And may be now he is going to ask the master-at-arms about me.

"Shut the door there, sentry," said the commander; "stand without, and let nobody come in.—Now, Master-at-arms, tell this man to his face what you told of him to me," and stood prepared to scrutinize the mutually confronting visages.

With the measured step and calm collected air of an asylum physician approaching in the public hall some patient beginning to show indications of a coming paroxysm, Claggart deliberately advanced within short range of Billy and, mesmerically looking him in the eye, briefly recapitulated the accusation.

Not at first did Billy take it in. When he did, the rose-tan of his cheek looked struck as by white leprosy. He stood like one impaled and gagged. Meanwhile the accuser's eyes, removing not as yet from the blue dilated ones, underwent a phenomenal change, their wonted rich violet color blurring into a muddy purple. Those lights of human intelligence, losing human expression, were gelidly protruding like the alien eyes of certain uncatalogued creatures of the deep. The first mesmeristic glance was one of serpent fascination; the last was as the paralyzing lurch of the torpedo fish.

"Speak, man!" said Captain Vere to the transfixed one, struck by his aspect even more than by Claggart's. "Speak! Defend yourself!" Which appeal caused but a strange dumb gesturing and gurgling in Billy; amazement at such an accusation so suddenly sprung on inexperienced nonage; this, and, it may be, horror of the accuser's eyes, serving to bring out his lurking defect and in this instance for the time intensifying it into a convulsed tongue-tie; while the intent head and entire form straining forward in an agony of ineffectual eagerness to [98/99] obey the injunction to speak and defend himself, gave an expression to the face like that of a condemned vestal priestess in the moment of being buried alive, and in the first struggle against suffocation.

Though at the time Captain Vere was quite ignorant of Billy's liability to vocal impediment, he now immediately divined it, since vividly Billy's aspect recalled to him that of a bright young schoolmate of his whom he had once seen struck by much the same startling impotence in the act of eagerly rising in the class to be foremost in response to a testing question put to it by the master. Going close up to the young sailor, and laying a soothing hand on his shoulder, he said, "There is no hurry, my boy. Take your time, take your time." Contrary to the effect intended, these words so fatherly in tone, doubtless touching Billy's heart to the quick, prompted yet more violent efforts at utterance—efforts soon ending for the time in confirming the paralysis, and bringing to his face an expression which was as a crucifixion to behold. The next instant, quick as the flame from a discharged cannon at night, his right arm shot out, and Claggart dropped to the deck. Whether intentionally or but owing to the young athlete's superior height, the blow had taken effect full upon the forehead, so shapely and intellectual-looking a feature in the master-at-arms; so that the body fell over lengthwise, like a heavy plank tilted from erectness. A gasp or two, and he lay motionless.

"Fated boy," breathed Captain Vere in tone so low as to be almost a whisper, "what have you done! But here, help me."

The twain raised the felled one from the loins up into a sitting position. The spare form flexibly acquiesced, but inertly. It was like handling a dead snake. They lowered it back. Regaining erectness, Captain Vere with one hand covering his face stood to all appearance as impassive as the object at his feet. Was he absorbed in taking in all the bearings of the event and what was best not only now at once to be done, but also in the sequel? Slowly he uncovered his face; and the effect was as if the moon [99/100] emerging from eclipse should reappear with quite another aspect than that which had gone into hiding. The father in him, manifested towards Billy thus far in the scene, was replaced by the military disciplinarian. In his official tone he bade the foretopman retire to a stateroom aft (pointing it out), and there remain till thence summoned. This order Billy in silence mechanically obeyed. Then going to the cabin door where it opened on the quarter-deck, Captain Vere said to the sentry without, "Tell somebody to send Albert here." When the lad appeared, his master so contrived it that he should not catch sight of the prone one. "Albert," he said to him, "tell the surgeon I wish to see him. You need not come back till called."

When the surgeon entered—a self-poised character of that grave sense and experience that hardly anything could take him aback—Captain Vere advanced to meet him, thus unconsciously intercepting his view of Claggart, and, interrupting the other's wonted ceremonious salutation, said, "Nay. Tell me how it is with yonder man," directing his attention to the prostrate one.

The surgeon looked, and for all his self-command somewhat started at the abrupt revelation. On Claggart's always pallid complexion, thick black blood was now oozing from nostril and ear. To the gazer's professional eye it was unmistakably no living man that he saw.

"Is it so, then?" said Captain Vere, intently watching him. "I thought it. But verify it." Whereupon the customary tests confirmed the surgeon's first glance, who now, looking up in unfeigned concern, cast a look of intense inquisitiveness upon his superior. But Captain Vere, with one hand to his brow, was standing motionless. Suddenly, catching the surgeon's arm convulsively, he exclaimed, pointing down to the body, "It is the divine judgment on Ananias! Look!"

Disturbed by the excited manner he had never before observed in the *Bellipotent's* captain, and as yet wholly ignorant of the affair, the prudent surgeon nevertheless held his peace, [100/101] only again looking an earnest interrogatory as to what it was that had resulted in such a tragedy.

But Captain Vere was now again motionless, standing absorbed in thought. Again starting, he vehemently exclaimed, "Struck dead by an angel of God! Yet the angel must hang!"

At these passionate interjections, mere incoherences to the listener as yet unapprised of the antecedents, the surgeon was profoundly discomposed. But now, as recollecting himself. Captain Vere in less passionate tone briefly related the circumstances leading up to the event. "But come; we must dispatch," he added. "Help me to remove him" (meaning the body) "to yonder compartment," designating one opposite that where the foretopman remained immured. Anew disturbed by a request that, as implying a desire for secrecy, seemed unaccountably strange to him, there was nothing for the subordinate to do but comply.

"Go now," said Captain Vere with something of his wonted manner. "Go now. I presently shall call a drumhead court. Tell the lieutenants what has happened, and tell Mr. Mordant" (meaning the captain of marines), "and charge them to keep the matter to themselves."

20

Full of disquietude and misgiving, the surgeon left the cabin. Was Captain Vere suddenly affected in his mind, or was it but a transient excitement, brought about by so strange and extraordinary a tragedy? As to the drumhead court, it struck the surgeon as impolitic, if nothing more. The thing to do, he thought, was to place Billy Budd in confinement, and in a way dictated by usage, and postpone further action in so extraordinary a case to such time as they should rejoin the squadron, and then refer it to the admiral. He recalled the unwonted agitation [101/102] of Captain Vere and his excited exclamations, so at variance with his normal manner. Was he unhinged?

But assuming that he is, it is not so susceptible of proof. What then can the surgeon do? No more trying situation is conceivable than that of an officer subordinate under a captain whom he suspects to be not mad, indeed, but yet not quite unaffected in his intellects. To argue his order to him would be insolence. To resist him would be mutiny.

In obedience to Captain Vere, he communicated what had happened to the lieutenants and captain of marines, saying nothing as to the captain's state. They fully shared his own surprise and concern. Like him too, they seemed to think that such a matter should be referred to the admiral.

21

Who in the rainbow can draw the line where the violet tint ends and the orange tint begins? Distinctly we see the difference of the colors, but where exactly does the one first blendingly enter into the other? So with sanity and insanity. In pronounced cases there is no question about them. But in some supposed cases, in various degrees supposedly less pronounced, to draw the exact line of demarcation few will undertake, though for a fee becoming considerate some professional experts will. There is nothing namable but that some men will, or undertake to, do it for pay.

Whether Captain Vere, as the surgeon professionally and privately surmised, was really the sudden victim of any degree of aberration, every one must determine for himself by such light as this narrative may afford.

That the unhappy event which has been narrated could not have happened at a worse juncture was but too true. For it was close on the heel of the suppressed insurrections, an aftertime [102/103] very critical to naval authority, demanding from every English sea commander two qualities not readily interfusable—prudence and rigor. Moreover, there was something crucial in the case.

In the jugglery of circumstances preceding and attending the event on board the *Bellipotent,* and in the light of that martial code whereby it was formally to be judged, innocence and guilt personified in Claggart and Budd in effect changed places. In a legal view the apparent victim of the tragedy was he who had sought to victimize a man blameless; and the indisputable deed of the latter, navally regarded, constituted the most heinous of military crimes. Yet more. The essential right and wrong involved in the matter, the clearer that might be, so much the worse for the responsibility of a loyal sea commander, inasmuch as he was not authorized to determine the matter on that primitive basis.

Small wonder then that the *Bellipotent's* captain, though in general a man of rapid decision, felt that circumspectness not less than promptitude was necessary. Until he could decide upon his course, and in each detail; and not only so, but until the concluding measure was upon the point of being enacted, he deemed it advisable, in view of all the circumstances, to guard as much as possible against publicity. Here he may or may not have erred. Certain it is, however, that subsequently in the confidential talk of more than one or two gun rooms and cabins he was not a little criticized by some officers, a fact imputed by his friends and vehemently by his cousin Jack Denton to professional jealousy of Starry Vere. Some imaginative ground for invidious comment there was. The maintenance of secrecy in the matter, the confining all knowledge of it for a time to the place where the homicide occurred, the quarter-deck cabin; in these particulars lurked some resemblance to the policy adopted in those tragedies of the palace which have occurred more than once in the capital founded by Peter the Barbarian. [103/104]

The case indeed was such that fain would the *Bellipotent's* captain have deferred taking any action whatever respecting it further than to keep the foretopman a close prisoner till the ship rejoined the squadron and then submitting the matter to the judgment of his admiral.

But a true military officer is in one particular like a true monk. Not with more of self-abnegation will the latter keep his vows of monastic obedience than the former his vows of allegiance to martial duty.

Feeling that unless quick action was taken on it, the deed of the foretopman, so soon as it should be known on the gun decks, would tend to awaken any slumbering embers of the Nore among the crew, a sense of the urgency of the case overruled in Captain Vere every other consideration. But though a conscientious disciplinarian, he was no lover of authority for mere authority's sake. Very far was he from embracing opportunities for monopolizing to himself the perils of moral responsibility, none at least that could properly be referred to an official superior or shared with him by his official equals or even subordinates. So thinking, he was glad it would not be at variance with usage to turn the matter over to a summary court of his own officers, reserving to himself, as the one on whom the ultimate accountability would rest, the right of maintaining a supervision of it, or formally or informally interposing at need. Accordingly a drumhead court was summarily convened, he electing the individuals composing it: the first lieutenant, the captain of marines, and the sailing master.

In associating an officer of marines with the sea lieutenant and the sailing master in a case having to do with a sailor, the commander perhaps deviated from general custom. He was prompted thereto by the circumstance that he took that soldier to be a judicious person, thoughtful, and not altogether incapable of grappling with a difficult case unprecedented in his prior experience. Yet even as to him he was not without some latent misgiving, for withal he was an extremely good-natured [104/105] man, an enjoyer of his dinner, a sound sleeper, and inclined to obesity—a man who though he would always maintain his manhood in battle might not prove altogether reliable in a moral dilemma involving aught of the tragic. As to the first lieutenant and the sailing master, Captain Vere could not but be aware that though honest natures, of approved gallantry upon occasion, their intelligence was mostly confined to the matter of active seamanship and the fighting demands of their profession.

The court was held in the same cabin where the unfortunate affair had taken place. This cabin, the commander's, embraced the entire area under the poop deck. Aft, and on either side, was a small state-room, the one now temporarily a jail and the other a dead-house, and a yet smaller compartment, leaving a space between expanding forward into a goodly oblong of length coinciding with the ship's beam. A skylight of moderate dimension was overhead, and at each end of the oblong space were two sashed porthole windows easily convertible back into embrasures for short carronades.

All being quickly in readiness, Billy Budd was arraigned, Captain Vere necessarily appearing as the sole witness in the case, and as such temporarily sinking his rank, though singularly maintaining it in a matter apparently trivial, namely, that he testified from the ship's weather side, with that object having caused the court to sit on the lee side. Concisely he narrated all that had led up to the catastrophe, omitting nothing in Claggart's accusation and deposing as to the manner in which the prisoner had received it. At this testimony the three officers glanced with no little surprise at Billy Budd, the last man they would have suspected either of the mutinous design alleged by Claggart or the undeniable deed he himself had done. The first lieutenant, taking judicial primacy and turning toward the prisoner, said, "Captain Vere has spoken. Is it or is it not as Captain Vere says?"

In response came syllables not so much impeded in the utterance [105/106] as might have been anticipated. They were these: "Captain Vere tells the truth. It is just as Captain Vere says, but it is not as the master-at-arms said. I have eaten the King's bread and I am true to the King."

"I believe you, my man," said the witness, his voice indicating a suppressed emotion not otherwise betrayed.

"God will bless you for that, your honor!" not without stammering said Billy, and all but broke down. But immediately he was recalled to self-control by another question, to which with the same emotional difficulty of utterance he said, "No, there was no malice between us. I never bore malice against the master-at-arms. I am sorry that he is dead. I did not mean to kill him. Could I have used my tongue I would not have struck him. But he foully lied to my face and in presence of my captain, and I had to say something, and I could only say it with a blow, God help me!"

In the impulsive aboveboard manner of the frank one the court saw confirmed all that was implied in words that just previously had perplexed them, coming as they did from the testifier to the tragedy and promptly following Billy's impassioned disclaimer of mutinous intent—Captain Vere's words, "I believe you, my man."

Next it was asked of him whether he knew of or suspected aught savoring of incipient trouble (meaning mutiny, though the explicit term was avoided) going on in any section of the ship's company.

The reply lingered. This was naturally imputed by the court to the same vocal embarrassment which had retarded or obstructed previous answers. But in main it was otherwise here, the question immediately recalling to Billy's mind the interview with the afterguardsman in the forechains. But an innate repugnance to playing a part at all approaching that of an informer against one's own shipmates—the same erring sense of uninstructed honor which had stood in the way of his reporting the matter at the time, though as a loyal man-of-war's man it [106/107] was incumbent on him, and failure so to do, if charged against him and proven, would have subjected him to the heaviest of penalties; this, with the blind feeling now his that nothing really was being hatched, prevailed with him. When the answer came it was a negative.

"One question more," said the officer of marines, now first speaking and with a troubled earnestness. "You tell us that what the master-at-arms said against you was a lie. Now why should he have so lied, so maliciously lied, since you declare there was no malice between you?"

At that question, unintentionally touching on a spiritual sphere wholly obscure to Billy's thoughts, he was nonplussed, evincing a confusion indeed that some observers, such as can readily be imagined, would have construed into involuntary evidence of hidden guilt. Nevertheless, he strove some way to answer, but all at once relinquished the vain endeavor, at the same time turning an appealing glance towards Captain Vere as deeming him his best helper and friend. Captain Vere, who had been seated for a time, rose to his feet, addressing the interrogator. "The question you put to him comes naturally enough. But how can he rightly answer it?—or anybody else, unless indeed it be he who lies within there," designating the compartment where lay the corpse. "But the prone one there will not rise to our summons. In effect, though, as it seems to me, the point you make is hardly material. Quite aside from any conceivable motive actuating the master-at-arms, and irrespective of the provocation to the blow, a martial court must needs in the present case confine its attention to the blow's consequence, which consequence justly is to be deemed not otherwise than as the striker's deed."

This utterance, the full significance of which it was not at all likely that Billy took in, nevertheless caused him to turn a wistful interrogative look toward the speaker, a look in its dumb expressiveness not unlike that which a dog of generous breed might turn upon his master, seeking in his face some elucidation [107/108] of a previous gesture ambiguous to the canine intelligence. Nor was the same utterance without marked effect upon the three officers, more especially the soldier. Couched in it seemed to them a meaning unanticipated, involving a prejudgment on the speaker's part. It served to augment a mental disturbance previously evident enough.

The soldier once more spoke, in a tone of suggestive dubiety addressing at once his associates and Captain Vere: "Nobody is present—none of the ship's company, I mean—who might shed lateral light, if any is to be had, upon what remains mysterious in this matter."

"That is thoughtfully put," said Captain Vere; "I see your drift. Ay, there is a mystery; but, to use a scriptural phrase, it is a 'mystery of iniquity,' a matter for psychologic theologians to discuss. But what has a military court to do with it? Not to add that for us any possible investigation of it is cut off by the lasting tongue-tie of—him—in yonder," again designating the mortuary stateroom. "The prisoner's deed—with that alone we have to do."

To this, and particularly the closing reiteration, the marine soldier, knowing not how aptly to reply, sadly abstained from saying aught. The first lieutenant, who at the outset had not unnaturally assumed primacy in the court, now overrulingly instructed by a glance from Captain Vere, a glance more effective than words, resumed that primacy. Turning to the prisoner, "Budd," he said, and scarce in equable tones, "Budd, if you have aught further to say for yourself, say it now."

Upon this the young sailor turned another quick glance toward Captain Vere; then, as taking a hint from that aspect, a hint confirming his own instinct that silence was now best, replied to the lieutenant, "I have said all, sir."

The marine—the same who had been the sentinel without the cabin door at the time that the foretopman, followed by the master-at-arms, entered it—he, standing by the sailor throughout these judicial proceedings, was now directed to take him [108/109] back to the after compartment originally assigned to the prisoner and his custodian. As the twain disappeared from view, the three officers, as partially liberated from some inward constraint associated with Billy's mere presence, simultaneously stirred in their seats. They exchanged looks of troubled indecision, yet feeling that decide they must and without long delay. For Captain Vere, he for the time stood—unconsciously with his back toward them, apparently in one of his absent fits—gazing out from a sashed porthole to windward upon the monotonous blank of the twilight sea. But the court's silence continuing, broken only at moments by brief consultations, in low earnest tones, this served to arouse him and energize him. Turning, he to-and-fro paced the cabin athwart; in the returning ascent to windward climbing the slant deck in the ship's lee roll, without knowing it symbolizing thus in his action a mind resolute to surmount difficulties even if against primitive instincts strong as the wind and the sea. Presently he came to a stand before the three. After scanning their faces he stood less as mustering his thoughts for expression than as one inly deliberating how best to put them to well-meaning men not intellectually mature, men with whom it was necessary to demonstrate certain principles that were axioms to himself. Similar impatience as to talking is perhaps one reason that deters some minds from addressing any popular assemblies.

When speak he did, something, both in the substance of what he said and his manner of saying it, showed the influence of unshared studies modifying and tempering the practical training of an active career. This, along with his phraseology, now and then was suggestive of the grounds whereon rested that imputation of a certain pedantry socially alleged against him by certain naval men of wholly practical cast, captains who nevertheless would frankly concede that His Majesty's navy mustered no more efficient officer of their grade than Starry Vere.

What he said was to this effect: "Hitherto I have been but the witness, little more; and I should hardly think now to take another [109/110] tone, that of your coadjutor for the time, did I not perceive in you—at the crisis too—a troubled hesitancy, proceeding, I doubt not, from the clash of military duty with moral scruple—scruple vitalized by compassion. For the compassion, how can I otherwise than share it? But, mindful of paramount obligations, I strive against scruples that may tend to enervate decision. Not, gentlemen, that I hide from myself that the case is an exceptional one. Speculatively regarded, it well might be referred to a jury of casuists. But for us here, acting not as casuists or moralists, it is a case practical, and under martial law practically to be dealt with.

"But your scruples: do they move as in a dusk? Challenge them. Make them advance and declare themselves. Come now; do they import something like this: If, mindless of palliating circumstances, we are bound to regard the death of the master-at-arms as the prisoner's deed, then does that deed constitute a capital crime whereof the penalty is a mortal one. But in natural justice is nothing but the prisoner's overt act to be considered? How can we adjudge to summary and shameful death a fellow creature innocent before God, and whom we feel to be so?—Does that state it aright? You sign sad assent. Well, I too feel that, the full force of that. It is Nature. But do these buttons that we wear attest that our allegiance is to Nature? No, to the King. Though the ocean, which is inviolate Nature primeval, though this be the element where we move and have our being as sailors, yet as the King's officers lies our duty in a sphere correspondingly natural? So little is that true, that in receiving our commissions we in the most important regards ceased to be natural free agents. When war is declared are we the commissioned fighters previously consulted? We fight at command. If our judgments approve the war, that is but coincidence. So in other particulars. So now. For suppose condemnation to follow these present proceedings. Would it be so much we ourselves that would condemn as it would be martial law operating through us? For that law and the rigor of it, we are [110/111] not responsible. Our vowed responsibility is in this: That however pitilessly that law may operate in any instances, we nevertheless adhere to it and administer it.

"But the exceptional in the matter moves the hearts within you. Even so too is mine moved. But let not warm hearts betray heads that should be cool. Ashore in a criminal case, will an upright judge allow himself off the bench to be waylaid by some tender kinswoman of the accused seeking to touch him with her tearful plea? Well, the heart here, sometimes the feminine in man, is as that piteous woman, and hard though it be, she must here be ruled out."

He paused, earnestly studying them for a moment; then resumed.

"But something in your aspect seems to urge that it is not solely the heart that moves in you, but also the conscience, the private conscience. But tell me whether or not, occupying the position we do, private conscience should not yield to that imperial one formulated in the code under which alone we officially proceed?"

Here the three men moved in their seats, less convinced than agitated by the course of an argument troubling but the more the spontaneous conflict within.

Perceiving which, the speaker paused for a moment; then abruptly changing his tone, went on.

"To steady us a bit, let us recur to the facts.—In wartime at sea a man-of-war's man strikes his superior in grade, and the blow kills. Apart from its effect the blow itself is, according to the Articles of War, a capital crime. Furthermore ——"

"Ay, sir," emotionally broke in the officer of marines, "in one sense it was. But surely Budd purposed neither mutiny nor homicide."

"Surely not, my good man. And before a court less arbitrary and more merciful than a martial one, that plea would largely extenuate. At the Last Assizes it shall acquit. But how here? We proceed under the law of the Mutiny Act. In feature no [111/112] child can resemble his father more than that Act resembles in spirit the thing from which it derives—War. In His Majesty's service—in this ship, indeed—there are Englishmen forced to fight for the King against their will. Against their conscience, for aught we know. Though as their fellow creatures some of us may appreciate their position, yet as navy officers what reck we of it? Still less recks the enemy. Our impressed men he would fain cut down in the same swath with our volunteers. As regards the enemy's naval conscripts, some of whom may even share our own abhorrence of the regicidal French Directory, it is the same on our side. War looks but to the frontage, the appearance. And the Mutiny Act, War's child, takes after the father. Budd's intent or non-intent is nothing to the purpose.

"But while, put to it by those anxieties in you which I cannot but respect, I only repeat myself—while thus strangely we prolong proceedings that should be summary—the enemy may be sighted and an engagement result. We must do; and one of two things must we do— condemn or let go."

"Can we not convict and yet mitigate the penalty?" asked the sailing master, here speaking, and falteringly, for the first.

"Gentlemen, were that clearly lawful for us under the circumstances, consider the consequences of such clemency. The people"
(meaning the ship's company) "have native sense; most of them are
familiar with our naval usage and tradition; and how would they take
it? Even could you explain to them—which our official position forbids
—they, long molded by arbitrary dicipline, have not that kind of
intelligent responsiveness that might qualify them to comprehend and
discriminate. No, to the people the foretopman's deed, however it be
worded in the announcement, will be plain homicide committed in a
flagrant act of mutiny. What penalty for that should follow, they know.
But it does not follow. Why? they will ruminate. You know what
sailors are. Will they not revert to the recent outbreak at the Nore? Ay.
They know the well-founded alarm—[112/113] the panic it struck
throughout England. Your clement sentence they would account pusillanimous. They would think that we flinch, that we are afraid of
them—afraid of practicing a lawful rigor singularly demanded at this
juncture, lest it should provoke new troubles. What shame to us such a
conjecture on their part, and how deadly to discipline. You see then,
whither, prompted by duty and the law, I steadfastly drive. But I
beseech you, my friends, do not take me amiss. I feel as you do for this
unfortunate boy. But did he know our hearts, I take him to be of that
generous nature that he would feel even for us on whom in this
military necessity so heavy a compulsion is laid."

With that, crossing the deck he resumed his place by the sashed
porthole, tacitly leaving the three to come to a decision. On the cabin's
opposite side the troubled court sat silent. Loyal lieges, plain and
practical, though at bottom they dissented from some points Captain
Vere had put to them, they were without the faculty, hardly had the
inclination, to gainsay one whom they felt to be an earnest man, one
too not less their superior in mind than in naval rank. But it is not
improbable that even such of his words as were not without influence
over them, less came home to them than his closing appeal to their
instinct as sea officers: in the forethought he threw out as to the
practical consequences to discipline, considering the unconfirmed tone
of the fleet at the time, should a man-of-war's man's violent killing at
sea of a superior in grade be allowed to pass for aught else than a
capital crime demanding prompt infliction of the penalty.

Not unlikely they were brought to something more or less akin to
that harassed frame of mind which in the year 1842 actuated the
commander of the U.S. brig-of-war *Somers* to resolve, under the so-
called Articles of War, Articles modeled upon the English Mutiny Act,
to resolve upon the execution at sea of a midshipman and two sailors
as mutineers designing the seizure of the brig. Which resolution was
carried out though in [113/114] a time of peace and within not many
days' sail of home. An act vindicated by a naval court of inquiry
subsequently convened ashore. History, and here cited without comment. True, the circumstances on board the *Somers* were different

from those on board the *Bellipotent*. But the urgency felt, well-warranted or otherwise, was much the same.

Says a writer whom few know, "Forty years after a battle it is easy for a noncombatant to reason about how it ought to have been fought. It is another thing personally and under fire to have to direct the fighting while involved in the obscuring smoke of it. Much so with respect to other emergencies involving considerations both practical and moral, and when it is imperative promptly to act. The greater the fog the more it imperils the steamer, and speed is put on though at the hazard of running somebody down. Little ween the snug card players in the cabin of the responsibilities of the sleepless man on the bridge."

In brief, Billy Budd was formally convicted and sentenced to be hung at the yardarm in the early morning watch, it being now night. Otherwise, as is customary in such cases, the sentence would forthwith have been carried out. In wartime on the field or in the fleet, a mortal punishment decreed by a drumhead court—on the field sometimes decreed by but a nod from the general—follows without delay on the heel of conviction, without appeal.

22

It was Captain Vere himself who of his own motion communicated the finding of the court to the prisoner, for that purpose going to the compartment where he was in custody and bidding the marine there to withdraw for the time.

Beyond the communication of the sentence, what took place at this interview was never known. But in view of the character of the twain briefly closeted in that stateroom, each radically [114–115] sharing in the rarer qualities of our nature—so rare indeed as to be all but incredible to average minds however much cultivated—some conjectures may be ventured.

It would have been in consonance with the spirit of Captain Vere should he on this occasion have concealed nothing from the condemned one—should he indeed have frankly disclosed to him the part he himself had played in bringing about the decision, at the same time revealing his actuating motives. On Billy's side it is not improbable that such a confession would have been received in much the same spirit that prompted it. Not without a sort of joy, indeed, he might have appreciated the brave opinion of him implied in his captain's making such a confidant of him. Nor, as to the sentence itself, could he have been insensible that it was imparted to him as to one not afraid to die. Even more may have been. Captain Vere in end may have developed the passion sometimes latent under an exterior stoical or indifferent. He was old enough to have been Billy's father. The austere devotee of military duty, letting himself melt back into what remains primeval in our formalized humanity, may in end have caught Billy to his heart, even as Abraham may have caught young Isaac on the brink of resolutely offering him up in obedience to the exacting behest. But there is no telling the sacrament, seldom if any case revealed to the gadding world, wherever under circumstances at all akin to those here attempted to be set forth two of great Nature's nobler order embrace. There is privacy at the time, inviolable to the survivor; and holy oblivion, the sequel to each diviner magnanimity, providentially covers all at last.

The first to encounter Captain Vere in act of leaving the compartment was the senior lieutenant. The face he beheld, for the moment one expressive of the agony of the strong, was to that officer, though a man of fifty, a startling revelation. That the condemned one suffered less than he who mainly had effected the condemnation was apparently indicated by the former's exclamation in the scene soon perforce to be touched upon. [115/116]

23

Of a series of incidents within a brief term rapidly following each other, the adequate narration may take up a term less brief, especially if explanation or comment here and there seem requisite to the better understanding of such incidents. Between the entrance into the cabin of him who never left it alive, and him who when he did leave it left it as one condemned to die; between this and the closeted interview just given, less than an hour and a half had elapsed. It was an interval long enough, however, to awaken speculations among no few of the ship's company as to what it was that could be detaining in the cabin the master-at-arms and the sailor; for a rumor that both of them had been seen to enter it and neither of them had been seen to emerge, this rumor had got abroad upon the gun decks and in the tops, the people of a great warship being in one respect like villagers, taking microscopic note of every outward movement or non-movement going on. When therefore, in weather not at all tempestuous, all hands were called in the second dogwatch, a summons under such circumstances not usual in those hours, the crew were not wholly unprepared for some announcement extraordinary, one having connection too with the continued absence of the two men from their wonted haunts.

There was a moderate sea at the time; and the moon, newly risen and near to being at its full, silvered the white spar deck wherever not blotted by the clear-cut shadows horizontally thrown of fixtures and moving men. On either side the quarter-deck the marine guard under arms was drawn up; and Captain Vere, standing in his place surrounded by all the wardroom officers, addressed his men. In so doing, his manner showed neither more nor less than that properly pertaining to his supreme position aboard his own ship. In clear terms and concise he told them what had taken place in the cabin: that the master-at-arms was dead, that he who had killed him had been already [116/117] tried by a summary court and condemned to death, and that the execution would take place in the early morning watch. The word *mutiny* was not named in what he said. He refrained too from making the occasion an opportunity for any preachment as to the maintenance of discipline, thinking perhaps that under existing circumstances in the navy the consequence of violating discipline should be made to speak for itself.

Their captain's announcement was listened to by the throng of standing sailors in a dumbness like that of a seated congregation of believers in hell listening to the clergyman's announcement of his Calvinistic text.

At the close, however, a confused murmur went up. It began to wax. All but instantly, then, at a sign, it was pierced and suppressed by shrill whistles of the boatswain and his mates. The word was given to about ship.

To be prepared for burial Claggart's body was delivered to certain petty officers of his mess. And here, not to clog the sequel with lateral matters, it may be added that at a suitable hour, the master-at-arms was committed to the sea with every funeral honor properly belonging to his naval grade.

In this proceeding as in every public one growing out of the tragedy strict adherence to usage was observed. Nor in any point could it have been at all deviated from, either with respect to Claggart or Billy Budd, without begetting undesirable speculations in the ship's company, sailors, and more particularly men-of-war's men, being of all men the greatest sticklers for usage. For similar cause, all communication between Captain Vere and the condemned one ended with the closeted interview already given, the latter being now surrendered to the ordinary routine preliminary to the end. His transfer under guard from the captain's quarters was effected without unusual precautions —at least no visible ones. If possible, not to let the men so much as surmise that their officers anticipate aught amiss from them is the tacit rule in a military ship. And the more that some sort of trouble should really be apprehended, [117/118] the more do the officers keep that apprehension to themselves, though not the less unostentatious vigilance may be augmented. In the present instance, the sentry placed over the prisoner had strict orders to let no one have communication with him but the chaplain. And certain unobtrusive measures were taken absolutely to insure this point.

24

In a seventy-four of the old order the deck known as the upper gun deck was the one covered over by the spar deck, which last, though not without its armament, was for the most part exposed to the weather. In general it was at all hours free from hammocks; those of the crew swinging on the lower gun deck and berth deck, the latter being not only a dormitory but also the place for the stowing of the sailors' bags, and on both sides lined with the large chests or movable pantries of the many messes of the men.

On the starboard side of the *Bellipotent's* upper gun deck, behold Billy Budd under sentry lying prone in irons in one of the bays formed by the regular spacing of the guns comprising the batteries on either side. All these pieces were of the heavier caliber of that period. Mounted on lumbering wooden carriages, they were hampered with cumbersome harness of breeching and strong side-tackles for running them out. Guns and carriages, together with the long rammers and shorter linstocks lodged in loops overhead—all these, as customary, were painted black; and the heavy hempen breechings, tarred to the same tint, wore the like livery of the undertakers. In contrast with the funereal hue of these surroundings, the prone sailor's exterior apparel, white jumper and white duck trousers, each more or less soiled, dimly glimmered in the obscure light of the bay like a patch of discolored snow in early April lingering at some upland [118/119] cave's black mouth. In effect he is already in his shroud, or the garments that shall serve him in lieu of one. Over him but scarce illuminating him, two battle lanterns swing from two massive beams of the deck above. Fed with the oil supplied by the war contractors (whose gains, honest or otherwise, are in every land an anticipated portion of the harvest of death), with flickering splashes of dirty yellow light they pollute the pale moonshine all but ineffectually struggling in obstructed flecks through the open ports from which the tampioned cannon protrude. Other lanterns at intervals serve but to bring out somewhat the obscurer bays which, like small confessionals or side-chapels in a cathedral, branch from the long dim-vistaed broad aisle between the two batteries of that covered tier.

Such was the deck where now lay the Handsome Sailor. Through the rose-tan of his complexion no pallor could have shown. It would have taken days of sequestration from the winds and the sun to have brought about the effacement of that. But the skeleton in the cheek-bone at the point of its angle was just beginning delicately to be defined under the warm-tinted skin. In fervid hearts self-contained, some brief experiences devour our human tissue as secret fire in a ship's hold consumes cotton in the bale.

But now lying between the two guns, as nipped in the vice of fate, Billy's agony, mainly proceeding from a generous young heart's virgin experience of the diabolical incarnate and effective in some men—the tension of that agony was over now. It survived not the something healing in the closeted interview with Captain Vere. Without movement, he lay as in a trance, that adolescent expression previously noted as his taking on something akin to the look of a slumbering child in the

cradle when the warm hearth-glow of the still chamber at night plays
on the dimples that at whiles mysteriously form in the cheek, silently
coming and going there. For now and then in the gyved one's trance a
serene happy light born of some wandering reminiscence [119/120] or
dream would diffuse itself over his face, and then wane away only
anew to return.

The chaplain, coming to see him and finding him thus, and
perceiving no sign that he was conscious of his presence, attentively
regarded him for a space, then slipping aside, withdrew for the time,
peradventure feeling that even he, the minister of Christ though
receiving his stipend from Mars, had no consolation to proffer which
could result in a peace transcending that which he beheld. But in the
small hours he came again. And the prisoner, now awake to his
surroundings, noticed his approach, and civilly, all but cheerfully,
welcomed him. But it was to little purpose that in the interview following, the good man sought to bring Billy Budd to some godly understanding that he must die, and at dawn. True, Billy himself freely
referred to his death as a thing close at hand; but it was something in
the way that children will refer to death in general, who yet among
their other sports will play a funeral with hearse and mourners.

Not that like children Billy was incapable of conceiving what
death really is. No, but he was wholly without irrational fear of it, a
fear more prevalent in highly civilized communities than those so-
called barbarous ones which in all respects stand nearer to unadulterate Nature. And, as elsewhere said, a barbarian Billy radically
was—as much so, for all the costume, as his countrymen the British
captives, living trophies, made to march in the Roman triumph of
Germanicus. Quite as much so as those later barbarians, young men
probably, and picked specimens among the earlier British converts to
Christianity, at least nominally such, taken to Rome (as today converts
from lesser isles of the sea may be taken to London), of whom the
Pope of that time, admiring the strangeness of their personal beauty so
unlike the Italian stamp, their clear ruddy complexion and curled
flaxen locks, exclaimed, "Angles" (meaning *English*, the modern de-
rivative), "Angles, do you call them? And is it because they look so like
angels?" Had it been [120/121] later in time, one would think that the
Pope had in mind Fra Angelico's seraphs, some of whom, plucking
apples in gardens of the Hesperides, having the faint rosebud complexion of the more beautiful English girls.

If in vain the good chaplain sought to impress the young barbarian with ideas of death akin to those conveyed in the skull, dial,
and crossbones on old tombstones, equally futile to all appearance
were his efforts to bring home to him the thought of salvation and a
Savior. Billy listened, but less out of awe or reverence, perhaps, than
from a certain natural politeness, doubtless at bottom regarding all
that in much the same way that most mariners of his class take any

discourse abstract or out of the common tone of the workaday world. And this sailor way of taking clerical discourse is not wholly unlike the way in which the primer of Christianity, full of transcendent miracles, was received long ago on tropic isles by any superior *savage*, so called—a Tahitian, say, of Captain Cook's time or shortly after that time. Out of natural courtesy he received, but did not appropriate. It was like a gift placed in the palm of an outreached hand upon which the fingers do not close.

But the *Bellipotent's* chaplain was a discreet man possessing the good sense of a good heart. So he insisted not in his vocation here. At the instance of Captain Vere, a lieutenant had apprised him of pretty much everything as to Billy; and since he felt that innocence was even a better thing than religion wherewith to go to Judgment, he reluctantly withdrew; but in his emotion not without first performing an act strange enough in an Englishman, and under the circumstances yet more so in any regular priest. Stooping over, he kissed on the fair cheek his fellow man, a felon in martial law, one whom though on the confines of death he felt he could never convert to a dogma; nor for all that did he fear for his future.

Marvel not that having been made acquainted with the young sailor's essential innocence the worthy man lifted not a finger to avert the doom of such a martyr to martial discipline. So to do [121/122] would not only have been as idle as invoking the desert, but would also have been an audacious transgression of the bounds of his function, one as exactly prescribed to him by military law as that of the boatswain or any other naval officer. Bluntly put, a chaplain is the minister of the Prince of Peace serving in the host of the God of War—Mars. As such, he is as incongruous as a musket would be on the altar at Christmas. Why, then, is he there? Because he indirectly subserves the purpose attested by the cannon; because too he lends the sanction of the religion of the meek to that which practically is the abrogation of everything but brute Force.

25

The night so luminous on the spar deck, but otherwise on the cavernous ones below, levels so like the tiered galleries in a coal mine—the luminous night passed away. But like the prophet in the chariot disappearing in heaven and dropping his mantle to Elisha, the withdrawing night transferred its pale robe to the breaking day. A meek, shy light appeared in the East, where stretched a diaphanous fleece of white furrowed vapor. That light slowly waxed. Suddenly *eight bells* was struck aft, responded to by one louder metallic stroke from forward. It was four o'clock in the morning. Instantly the silver whistles were heard summoning all hands to witness punishment. Up through the great hatchways rimmed with racks of heavy shot the watch below came pouring, overspreading with the watch already on deck the space between the mainmast and foremast including that occupied by the capacious launch and the black booms tiered on either side of it, boat and booms making a summit of observation for the powder-boys and younger tars. A different group comprising one watch of topmen leaned over the rail of that sea balcony, no small one in a seventy-four, looking down [122/123] on the crowd below. Man or boy, none spake but in whisper, and few spake at all. Captain Vere— as before, the central figure among the assembled commissioned officers—stood nigh the break of the poop deck facing forward. Just below him on the quarter-deck the marines in full equipment were drawn up much as at the scene of the promulgated sentence.

At sea in the old time, the execution by halter of a military sailor was generally from the foreyard. In the present instance, for special reasons the mainyard was assigned. Under an arm of that yard the prisoner was presently brought up, the chaplain attending him. It was noted at the time, and remarked upon afterwards, that in this final scene the good man evinced little or nothing of the perfunctory. Brief speech indeed he had with the condemned one, but the genuine Gospel was less on his tongue than in his aspect and manner towards him. The final preparations personal to the latter being speedily brought to an end by two boatswain's mates, the consummation impended. Billy stood facing aft. At the penultimate moment, his words, his only ones, words wholly unobstructed in the utterance, were these: "God bless Captain Vere!" Syllables so unanticipated coming from one with the ignominious hemp about his neck—a conventional felon's benediction directed aft towards the quarters of honor; syllables too delivered in the clear melody of a singing bird on the point of launching from the twig—had a phenomenal effect, not unenhanced by the rare personal beauty of the young sailor, spiritualized now through late experiences so poignantly profound.

Without volition, as it were, as if indeed the ship's populace were but the vehicles of some vocal current electric, with one voice from alow and aloft came a resonant sympathetic echo: "God bless Captain Vere!" And yet at that instant Billy alone must have been in their hearts, even as in their eyes.

At the pronounced words and the spontaneous echo that voluminously rebounded them, Captain Vere, either through stoic self-control or a sort of momentary paralysis induced by [123/124] emotional shock, stood erectly rigid as a musket in the ship-armorer's rack.

The hull, deliberately recovering from the periodic roll to leeward, was just regaining an even keel when the last signal, a preconcerted dumb one, was given. At the same moment it chanced that the vapory fleece hanging low in the East was shot through with a soft glory as of the fleece of the Lamb of God seen in mystical vision, and simultaneously therewith, watched by the wedged mass of upturned faces, Billy ascended; and, ascending, took the full rose of the dawn.

In the pinioned figure arrived at the yard-end, to the wonder of all no motion was apparent, none save that created by the slow roll of the hull in moderate weather, so majestic in a great ship ponderously cannoned.

26

When some days afterwards, in reference to the singularity just mentioned, the purser, a rather ruddy, rotund person more accurate as an accountant than profound as a philosopher, said at mess to the surgeon, "What testimony to the force lodged in will power," the latter, saturnine, spare, and tall, one in whom a discreet causticity went along with a manner less genial than polite, replied, "Your pardon, Mr. Purser. In a hanging scientifically conducted—and under special orders I myself directed how Budd's was to be effected—any movement following the completed suspension and originating in the body suspended, such movement indicates mechanical spasm in the muscular system. Hence the absence of that is no more attributable to will power, as you call it, than to horsepower—begging your pardon."

"But this muscular spasm you speak of, is not that in a degree more or less invariable in these cases?"

"Assuredly so, Mr. Purser." [124/125]

"How then, my good sir, do you account for its absence in this instance?"

"Mr. Purser, it is clear that your sense of the singularity in this matter equals not mine. You account for it by what you call will power—a term not yet included in the lexicon of science. For me, I do not, with my present knowledge, pretend to account for it at all. Even should we assume the hypothesis that at the first touch of the halyards the action of Budd's heart, intensified by extraordinary emotion at its climax, abruptly stopped—much like a watch when in carelessly winding it up you strain at the finish, thus snapping the chain—even under that hypothesis how account for the phenomenon that followed?"

"You admit, then, that the absence of spasmodic movement was phenomenal."

"It was phenomenal, Mr. Purser, in the sense that it was an appearance the cause of which is not immediately to be assigned."

"But tell me, my dear sir," pertinaciously continued the other, "was the man's death effected by the halter, or was it a species of euthanasia?"

"*Euthanasia,* Mr. Purser, is something like your *will power:* I doubt its authenticity as a scientific term—begging your pardon again. It is at once imaginative and metaphysical—in short, Greek.—But," abruptly changing his tone, "there is a case in the sick bay that I do not care to leave to my assistants. Beg your pardon, but excuse me." And rising from the mess he formally withdrew.

27

The silence at the moment of execution and for a moment or two continuing thereafter, a silence but emphasized by the regular wash of the sea against the hull or the flutter of a sail caused by the helmsman's eyes being tempted astray, this emphasized [125/126] silence was gradually disturbed by a sound not easily to be verbally rendered. Whoever has heard the freshet-wave of a torrent suddenly swelled by pouring showers in tropical mountains, showers not shared by the plain; whoever has heard the first muffled murmur of its sloping advance through precipitous woods may form some conception of the sound now heard. The seeming remoteness of its source was because of its murmurous indistinctness, since it came from close by, even from the men massed on the ship's open deck. Being inarticulate, it was dubious in significance further than it seemed to indicate some capricious revulsion of thought or feeling such as mobs ashore are liable to, in the present instance possibly implying a sullen revocation on the men's part of their involuntary echoing of Billy's benediction. But ere the murmur had time to wax into clamor it was met by a strategic command, the more telling that it came with abrupt unexpectedness: "Pipe down the starboard watch, Boatswain, and see that they go."

Shrill as the shriek of the sea hawk, the silver whistles of the boatswain and his mates pierced that ominous low sound, dissipating it; and yielding to the mechanism of discipline the throng was thinned by one-half. For the remainder, most of them were set to temporary employments connected with trimming the yards and so forth, business readily to be got up to serve occasion by any officer of the deck.

Now each proceeding that follows a mortal sentence pronounced at sea by a drumhead court is characterized by promptitude not perceptibly merging into hurry, though bordering that. The hammock, the one which had been Billy's bed when alive, having already been ballasted with shot and otherwise prepared to serve for his canvas coffin, the last offices of the sea undertakers, the sailmaker's mates, were now speedily completed. When everything was in readiness a second call for all hands, made necessary by the strategic movement before mentioned, was sounded, now to witness burial.

The details of this closing formality it needs not to give. But [126/ 127] when the tilted plank let slide its freight into the sea, a second strange human murmur was heard, blended now with another inarticulate sound proceeding from certain larger seafowl who, their attention having been attracted by the peculiar commotion in the water resulting from the heavy sloped dive of the shotted hammock into the sea, flew screaming to the spot. So near the hull did they come, that the stridor or bony creak of their gaunt double-jointed

pinions was audible. As the ship under light airs passed on, leaving the
burial spot astern, they still kept circling it low down with the moving
shadow of their outstretched wings and the croaked requiem of their
cries.

Upon sailors as superstitious as those of the age preceding ours,
men-of-war's men too who had just beheld the prodigy of repose in the
form suspended in air, and now foundering in the deeps; to such
mariners the action of the seafowl, though dictated by mere animal
greed for prey, was big with no prosaic significance. An uncertain
movement began among them, in which some encroachment was
made. It was tolerated but for a moment. For suddenly the drum beat
to quarters, which familiar sound happening at least twice every day,
had upon the present occasion a signal peremptoriness in it. True
martial discipline long continued superinduces in average man a sort
of impulse whose operation at the official word of command much
resembles in its promptitude the effect of an instinct.

The drumbeat dissolved the multitude, distributing most of them
along the batteries of the two covered gun decks. There, as wonted,
the guns' crews stood by their respective cannon erect and silent. In
due course the first officer, sword under arm and standing in his place
on the quarter-deck, formally received the successive reports of the
sworded lieutenants commanding the sections of batteries below; the
last of which reports being made, the summed report he delivered
with the customary salute to the commander. All this occupied time,
which in the present case was the object in beating to quarters at an
hour prior to the customary one. That such variance from usage was
[127/128] authorized by an officer like Captain Vere, a martinet as
some deemed him, was evidence of the necessity for unusual action
implied in what he deemed to be temporarily the mood of his men.
"With mankind," he would say, "forms, measured forms, are everything; and that is the import couched in the story of Orpheus with his
lyre spellbinding the wild denizens of the wood." And this he once
applied to the disruption of forms going on across the Channel and the
consequences thereof.

At this unwonted muster at quarters, all proceeded as at the
regular hour. The band on the quarter-deck played a sacred air, after
which the chaplain went through the customary morning service. That
done, the drum beat the retreat; and toned by music and religious rites
subserving the discipline and purposes of war, the men in their wonted
orderly manner dispersed to the places allotted them when not at the
guns.

And now it was full day. The fleece of low-hanging vapor had
vanished, licked up by the sun that late had so glorified it. And the
circumambient air in the clearness of its serenity was like smooth white
marble in the polished block not yet removed from the marble-dealer's
yard.

28

The symmetry of form attainable in pure fiction cannot so readily be achieved in a narration essentially having less to do with fable than with fact. Truth uncompromisingly told will always have its ragged edges; hence the conclusion of such a narration is apt to be less finished than an architectural finial.

How it fared with the Handsome Sailor during the year of the Great Mutiny has been faithfully given. But though properly the story ends with his life, something in way of sequel will not be amiss. Three brief chapters will suffice.

In the general rechristening under the Directory of the craft [128 /129] originally forming the Navy of the French monarchy, the *St. Louis* line-of-battle ship was named the *Athée* (the *Atheist*). Such a name, like some other substituted ones in the Revolutionary fleet, while proclaiming the infidel audacity of the ruling power, was yet, though not so intended to be, the aptest name, if one consider it, ever given to a warship; far more so indeed than the *Devastation,* the *Erebus* (the *Hell*), and similar names bestowed upon fighting ships.

On the return passage to the English fleet from the detached cruise during which occurred the events already recorded, the *Bellipotent* fell in with the *Athée.* An engagement ensued, during which Captain Vere, in the act of putting his ship alongside the enemy with a view of throwing his boarders across her bulwarks, was hit by a musket ball from a porthole of the enemy's main cabin. More than disabled, he dropped to the deck and was carried below to the same cockpit where some of his men already lay. The senior lieutenant took command. Under him the enemy was finally captured, and though much crippled was by rare good fortune successfully taken into Gibraltar, an English port not very distant from the scene of the fight. There, Captain Vere with the rest of the wounded was put ashore. He lingered for some days, but the end came. Unhappily he was cut off too early for the Nile and Trafalgar. The spirit that 'spite its philosophic austerity may yet have indulged in the most secret of all passions, ambition, never attained to the fulness of fame.

Not long before death, while lying under the influence of that magical drug which, soothing the physical frame, mysteriously operates on the subtler element in man, he was heard to murmur words inexplicable to his attendant: "Billy Budd, Billy Budd." That these were not the accents of remorse would seem clear from what the attendant said to the *Bellipotent*'s senior officer of marines, who, as the most reluctant to condemn of the members of the drumhead court, too well knew, though here he kept the knowledge to himself, who Billy Budd was. [129/130]

29

Some few weeks after the execution, among other matters under the head of "News from the Mediterranean," there appeared in a naval chronicle of the time, an authorized weekly publication, an account of the affair. It was doubtless for the most part written in good faith, though the medium, partly rumor, through which the facts must have reached the writer served to deflect and in part falsify them. The account was as follows:

"On the tenth of the last month a deplorable occurrence took place on board H.M.S. *Bellipotent*. John Claggart, the ship's master-at-arms, discovering that some sort of plot was incipient among an inferior section of the ship's company, and that the ringleader was one William Budd; he, Claggart, in the act of arraigning the man before the captain, was vindictively stabbed to the heart by the suddenly drawn sheath knife of Budd.

"The deed and the implement employed sufficiently suggest that though mustered into the service under an English name the assassin was no Englishman, but one of those aliens adopting English cognomens whom the present extraordinary necessities of the service have caused to be admitted into it in considerable numbers.

"The enormity of the crime and the extreme depravity of the criminal appear the greater in view of the character of the victim, a middle-aged man respectable and discreet, belonging to that minor official grade, the petty officers, upon whom, as none know better than the commissioned gentlemen, the efficiency of His Majesty's navy so largely depends. His function was a responsible one, at once onerous and thankless; and his fidelity in it the greater because of his strong patriotic impulse. In this instance as in so many other instances in these days, the character of this unfortunate man signally refutes, if refutation were needed, that peevish saying attributed to the late Dr. Johnson, that patriotism is the last refuge of a scoundrel. [130/131]

"The criminal paid the penalty of his crime. The promptitude of the punishment has proved salutary. Nothing amiss is now apprehended aboard H.M.S. *Bellipotent*."

The above, appearing in a publication now long ago superannuated and forgotten, is all that hitherto has stood in human record to attest what manner of men respectively were John Claggart and Billy Budd.

30

Everything is for a term venerated in navies. Any tangible object associated with some striking incident of the service is converted into a monument. The spar from which the foretopman was suspended was for some few years kept trace of by the bluejackets. Their knowledge followed it from ship to dockyard and again from dockyard to ship, still pursuing it even when at last reduced to a mere dockyard boom. To them a chip of it was as a piece of the Cross. Ignorant though they were of the secret facts of the tragedy, and not thinking but that the penalty was somehow unavoidably inflicted from the naval point of view, for all that, they instinctively felt that Billy was a sort of man as incapable of mutiny as of wilful murder. They recalled the fresh young image of the Handsome Sailor, that face never deformed by a sneer or subtler vile freak of the heart within. This impression of him was doubtless deepened by the fact that he was gone, and in a measure mysteriously gone. On the gun decks of the *Bellipotent* the general estimate of his nature and its unconscious simplicity eventually found rude utterance from another foretopman, one of his own watch, gifted, as some sailors are, with an artless *poetic* temperament. The tarry hand made some lines which, after circulating among the shipboard crews for a while, finally got rudely printed at Portsmouth as a ballad. The title given to it was the sailor's. [131/132]

BILLY IN THE DARBIES

Good of the chaplain to enter Lone Bay
And down on his marrowbones here and pray
For the likes just o' me, Billy Budd.—But, look:
Through the port comes the moonshine astray!
It tips the guard's cutlass and silvers this nook;
But 'twill die in the dawning of Billy's last day.
A jewel-block they'll make of me tomorrow,
Pendant pearl from the yardarm-end
Like the eardrop I gave to Bristol Molly—
O, 'tis me, not the sentence they'll suspend.
Ay, ay, all is up; and I must up too,
Early in the morning, aloft from alow.
On an empty stomach now never it would do.
They'll give me a nibble—bit o' biscuit ere I go.
Sure, a messmate will reach me the last parting cup;
But, turning heads away from the hoist and the belay,
Heaven knows who will have the running of me up!
No pipe to those halyards.—But aren't it all sham?
A blur's in my eyes; it is dreaming that I am.
A hatchet to my hawser? All adrift to go?
The drum roll to grog, and Billy never know?
But Donald he has promised to stand by the plank;
So I'll shake a friendly hand ere I sink.
But—no! It is dead then I'll be, come to think.
I remember Taff the Welshman when he sank.

And his cheek it was like the budding pink.
But me they'll lash in hammock, drop me deep.
Fathoms down, fathoms down, how I'll dream fast asleep.
I feel it stealing now. Sentry, are you there?
Just ease these darbies at the wrist,
And roll me over fair!
I am sleepy, and the oozy weeds about me twist. [132]

"Preface" from Freeman Text

HERMAN MELVILLE

The year 1797, the year of this narrative, belongs to a period which [,] as every thinker now feels, involved a crisis for Christendom not exceeded in its undetermined momentousness at the time by any other era whereof there is record. The opening proposition made by the Spirit of that Age involved rectification of the Old World's hereditary wrongs. In France, to some extent, this was bloodily effected. But what then? Straightway the Revolution itself became a wrong-doer, one more oppressive than the kings. Under Napoleon it enthroned upstart kings, and initiated that prolonged agony of continual war whose final throe was Waterloo. During those years not the wisest could have foreseen that the outcome of all would be what to some thinkers apparently it has since turned out to be—a political advance along nearly the whole line for Europeans.

Now, as elsewhere hinted, it was something caught from the Revolutionary Spirit that at Spithead emboldened the man-of-war's men to rise against real abuses, long-standing ones, and afterwards at the Nore to make inordinate and aggressive demands—successful resistance to which was confirmed only when the ringleaders were hung for an admonitory spectacle to the anchored fleet. Yet in a way analogous to the operation of the Revolution at large—the Great Mutiny, though by Englishmen naturally deemed monstrous at the time, doubtless gave the first latent prompting to most important reforms in the British navy.

Reprinted by permission of the publishers from *Melville's Billy Budd*, edited by Frederick Barron Freeman and corrected by Elizabeth Treeman (Cambridge, Mass.: Harvard University Press, 1948, 1956). Copyright, 1948, 1956 by the President and Fellows of Harvard College.

2. THE PLAY

Billy Budd

LOUIS O. COXE AND ROBERT CHAPMAN

CHARACTERS

EDWARD FAIRFAX VERE, *Captain, Royal Navy*
PHILIP MICHAEL SEYMOUR, *First Officer*
JOHN RATCLIFFE, *First Lieutenant*
BORDMAN WYATT, *Sailing Master*
GARDINER, *a Midshipman*
REA, *a Midshipman*
SURGEON
JOHN CLAGGART, *Master-at-Arms*
SQUEAK, *Master-at-Arms' man*
THE DANSKER, *Mainmast man*
JENKINS, *Captain of the Maintop*
PAYNE, *Maintopman*
KINCAID, *Maintopman*
O'DANIEL, *Maintopman*
BUTLER, *Maintopman*
TALBOT, *Mizzentopman*
JACKSON, *Maintopman*
BILLY BUDD, *Foretopman*
HALLAM, *a Marine*
MESSBOY
STOLL, *Helmsman*
DUNCAN, *Mate of the Main Deck*
BYREN, *Relief Helmsman*
DRUMMER
OTHER SAILORS, *crew of the* INDOMITABLE

The entire action takes place aboard *H.M.S. Indomitable* at sea, August, 1798, the year following the Naval mutinies at Spithead and the Nore.

From *Billy Budd* by Louis O. Coxe and Robert Chapman. Copyright 1947 by Louis O. Coxe and Robert Chapman, as an unpublished play under the title *Uniform of Flesh.* Copyright 1949 by Louis O. Coxe and Robert Chapman, a revised version under the title *Billy Budd,* as an unpublished play. Copyright © 1951 by Louis O. Coxe and Robert Chapman. Reprinted by permission of Hill and Wang, Inc. The text here used is that of the first Dramabook Edition (New York: Hill and Wang, Inc., 1962).

ACT ONE

Scene 1

Although outside it is a fine morning in early August, the between-decks compartment of the crew's quarters assigned to the maintopmen is dark and shadowy except for the light spilling down the companionway from above and, through the open gun-ports, the flicker of sunlight reflected on the water. The smoking-lamp burns feebly over a wooden mess table and two benches lowered for use.

JENKINS sits at the table mending a piece of clothing. In the shadow THE DANSKER sits motionless on a low sea chest, smoking a pipe. Neither man speaks for a long minute.

Then JACKSON appears on deck at the top of the companion-way and lurches down into the compartment. He is doubled up in pain.

CLAGGART [*off*]. You there! Jackson!

JACKSON. Oh Christ, he's followed me!

JENKINS. Who?

JACKSON. Master-at-Arms. He'll send me aloft again sure, and I can't hang on . . .

JENKINS. What the devil's wrong with you, jack? Here, sit down.

CLAGGART [*entering down the companionway*]. Why have you come down off the mainmast, Jackson? Your watch over?

JACKSON. Sick, Mister Claggart, I'm bloody sick, so I'm shaking up there on the yard till I near fell off.

JENKINS. Grab an arm, mate, I'll take you along to sick-bay. [9/10]

CLAGGART. Stand away from him, Jenkins. [*To* JACKSON] Just where does this sickness strike you, in the guts, or limbs? Or in the head? Does it exist at all?

JENKINS. You can see he's sick as a puking cat, plain as your stick.

CLAGGART. The role of Good Samaritan hardly fits you, Jenkins. [*To* JACKSON] Now up, man. Turn topside.

JACKSON. I can't, I can't, I'm deathly sick, God help me, sir!

CLAGGART. That's hard. But this ship needs all hands. We're undermanned. The aches and pains of landsmen have their cures, but ours have none. You'll have to get aloft. Now move!

JACKSON. I ain't bluffing, sir, I swear I'm not! Please, Mister Claggart . . . I got Cooper's leave, he says all right, I can come down.

CLAGGART. You have not got my leave. Cooper is captain of the maintop and ought to know better. Four men to every spar, and no replacements. Now up. Back where you belong.

JACKSON [*starts up the ladder*]. God, sir, I can't, I can't stand it! It'll be my death, sure!

CLAGGART. No more talk, man! Up you get! Start! [JACKSON *goes painfully up the ladder and out of sight on deck.* CLAGGART *starts out after him.*]

JENKINS [*mutters*]. God damn your bloody heart!

CLAGGART. Did you say something, Jenkins? [JENKINS *does not answer.* CLAGGART *goes out, calling after* JACKSON.] Now Jackson, get along. Up! Up!

JENKINS. I'll stick him one day before long! I will, if I hang for it. [10/11]

Laughter and talk in the next compartment followed by entrance of BUTLER, TALBOT *and* KINCAID.

BUTLER. Messboy!

TALBOT. Haul in the slops!

KINCAID. Suppose we'll get the new man? The jack they 'pressed this morning off that merchantman? I see 'em come alongside just now.

TALBOT. I pity that poor bastard, so I do. I hear they get good pay on merchant ships. Eat good, too, and then treated like the God-damn Prince of Wales. [MESSBOY *enters with an iron pot of food and spits on the deck.*] Spit in it, damn you. Can't taste no worse.

MESSBOY. Ain't nobody making you eat it, mate. You can wash your feet in it if you like. [O'DANIEL *and* PAYNE *enter.*]

TALBOT. What's eating you, Jenkins? Ain't you going to join the banquet?

JENKINS. By God, I seen a thing just now I won't stand for! I'm sitting here off watch, and I seen it all. That blacksnake Claggart kicked Jackson back aloft, and him sick as a pinkass baby in a cradle, as any fool could see.

PAYNE. He's the Master-at-Arms, ain't he?

JENKINS. Cooper sent him down. Who's captain of the starboard watch, him or Claggart? Cooper could have found him a relief. Plain murder, by God!

TALBOT. You think Claggart can get way with what he does without Captain Starry Vere knows what's going on? Him and that red snapper Seymour, and them other bloody officers!

JENKINS. Jackson'll fall. By God, no man can hang to a spar sick like that. He'll fall sure. [11/12]

O'DANIEL. Tush, man, nobody falls in His Majesty's Navy. We lose our footing. 'Tis flying we do, to be sure.

TALBOT. I tell you it's Vere that's the cause of it! Our glorious fine Captain Vere, with a league of braid around his arm and a ramrod up his bum.

O'DANIEL. Vere, is it. As captains go, mate, let me tell you, he's an angel with a harp alongside of the skipper on the *Royal George*. Every day that one flogged a dozen men. Picked 'em by lottery, by God. Never took the gratings down till they was rusty with blood. Ho! This Vere's a saint in heaven after him.

JENKINS. Ram the *Royal George* and everybody in her! Claggart's the man we want, and the sooner the better, say I!

O'DANIEL. Ah, we'd had him puking his blood at Spithead, the devil rot his wick.

BUTLER. You was there, O'Daniel? At Spithead?

O'DANIEL. Aye. I was. Wherever you do find Englishmen doing a smart thing, you'll find an Irishman is at the bottom of it. Oho, fine it was, every day of it, with the officers quaking in their cabins, spitting green, and the whole English government wetting their breeches from the fear of us! Ah, lovely it was, lovely!

TALBOT. Belay your Irish noise, you fat-mouthed mackerel-snatcher. I'll tell you this, we need men on here is not afraid to use their knives if it come to that. And you can be bloody sure it will come to that, mind my word, Mickey Cork.

JENKINS. What did you ever use your knife for, Talbot, but to scratch your lice? Ah, you're a dancing daredevil, you are for sure.

TALBOT. I'll be happy to show you, if you like. [12/13]

JENKINS. Trouble will be hunting you out, mate, if you're not careful.

TALBOT. Trouble! You whoreson cockney cullion! There's not a man aboard don't know you for a coward, you whining bitch-boy!

JENKINS. Get out.

TALBOT. Damn your seed, I'm not afraid of you, or your sniveling hangbys, either!

JENKINS. Move! Get out of it, or by God I'll run my knife to the hilts in you!

TALBOT. You son of a whore! Pigsticker!

They attack one another with drawn knives, JENKINS *reaching suddenly across the table to seize* TALBOT. *Silently they thrash around the compartment upsetting benches and food while the others look on unmoved.*

O'DANIEL. Ah, I do love to see two Englishmen fighting each other. It's fonder they are of killing themselves than fighting their proper foes. [*Laughs hoarsely.*]

PAYNE. Tomorrow's rum on Jenkins. Any bets?

KINCAID. He never lost one yet.

JENKINS *throws* TALBOT *on the deck and holds the knife at his throat for a moment before letting him up, first taking his knife. He holds out his hand.*

JENKINS. I'm leading seaman in this compartment, mind that. [TALBOT *hits* JENKINS' *hand and goes off angrily.*]

KINCAID. You're captain, that's all right by me.

O'DANIEL. Eyes in the boat, lads. Here comes *pfft*-face. [13/14]

SQUEAK, BILLY *and* GARDINER *appear on deck and start down the companionway.*

GARDINER. Hang it, step lively, boy! Your ship is . . . Doff your hat to officers when they speak to you! By God, I'll teach you to touch your hat to a midshipman's coat, if it's only stuck on a broomstick to dry!

BILLY. Aye, sir. [*The men react to* GARDINER *with yawns and gestures behind his back.*]

GARDINER. Very well. Your ship is *H.M.S. Indomitable* now, and we sail her tautly, and we tolerate no nonsense. Is that clear?

BILLY. Aye, sir.

GARDINER [*to* SQUEAK]. See this new man is assigned to a watch, and get him squared away. [*To* BILLY] You're green, of course, I can see that. But I expect we'll ripen you. [*He trips going up the ladder and* SQUEAK *tries to help him.*] Carry on. [GARDINER *exits.*]

SQUEAK. My name's Squeak. I'm the Master-at-Arms' man. Have you met the Master-at-Arms yet, Mister Claggart? [BILLY *shakes his head.*] Oh you'll like him. He's a nice fellow. [O'DANIEL *chokes on his pipe smoke and the other men react similarly.*] Stow your gear along in there. This here's the larboard section of the maintop. Captain of the watch is Jenkins. Him, there. Report to him. [*He pats* BILLY *on the chest and grins before starting up the ladder.*]

JENKINS. What's a green hand dumped in here for?

SQUEAK. Complaining, Jenkins?

JENKINS. I'm asking. What's wrong with that?

SQUEAK. Mister Claggart wants him here, that's why. Maybe [14/15] he wants for Billy Boy to set you pigs an example. Refer any more complaints to the Master-at-Arms! [*Exits.* BILLY *grins at the men, who return his look.*]

BILLY. My name is Budd. Billy, if you like.

KINCAID. I'm Kincaid. This is where you swing your hammock. That's O'Daniel, this here's Payne, and Butler. This is Jenkins, captain of the watch, and that old jack's called the Dansker. Don't know why, unless maybe he's Danish. You never had a real name, Dansker?

THE DANSKER. Not for many years.

BUTLER. You'd be the new impressed man?

BILLY. Aye, so I am. I just came off the *Rights of Man* this morning.

THE DANSKER. Forget about the *Rights of Man* now, lad.

JENKINS. How long you been going to sea, baby?

BILLY. About ten years, but in the merchant service.

O'DANIEL. Merchant service! Whissht! [*Laughs hoarsely.*]

BILLY. I know I'm new at Navy work, and probably there'll be some things I'll need help with.

JENKINS. No doubt, little boy.

BILLY. I'll learn fast, never fear. But she's a big old girl, this ship. I never was in a ship-of-the-line before. I'd have got lost trying to find the mess by myself. Maybe fallen in the magazine!

O'DANIEL. Ah, you get used to it. She's big, is this tub, but she's not so big you can get lost in her.

PAYNE. Sometimes I wish to God you could. Maybe we could lose O'Daniel. [BILLY *laughs and the others join.*] [15/16]

BILLY. You're Irish, aren't you? I like the Irish. There was an Irishman on the *Rights of Man,* with big red whiskers . . . when I came away, he gave me a silver knife. This is it.

O'DANIEL. It's a beauty. Mind you keep an eye on it.

BUTLER. What's the matter, boy?

BILLY. I was just thinking, maybe I won't ever see my friends again.

O'DANIEL. If they was Irish, don't you worry at all. The Irish is liable to turn up almost anywheres, excepting England and the fires of hell, which is much the same.

PAYNE. Danny, if it wasn't for the harps, the devil wouldn't have nothing to do. What was potato-eaters doing on a merchant ship?

BILLY. Just sailors, like me. Most of us had no other home, even the skipper. He was a kind old bloke. Looked fierce, but he always had a kind word. Used to keep a bird in a cage in his cabin. The skipper let me feed the bird sometimes. Worms right out of the ship's biscuit. That was mostly all the meat we got.

O'DANIEL. The bargemen is in Navy biscuit would eat the bird.

KINCAID. Sit down here, Bill. Maggots or not, this is what we get. You hungry?

BILLY. I'm always hungry.

KINCAID. Try your first sample of His Majesty's bounty. We don't know what it is, but we been eating it for a long time.

BUTLER. Here, eat mine. Tastes like it's been eat before, anyhow.

JENKINS. Give him more lobscouse, Butler. We got to keep the roses in his cheeks, ain't we, boy? [16/17]

BILLY [laughing]. I could eat anything right now. Even this.

O'DANIEL. Help you to forget about home and mother, lad.

JENKINS. Tell us about home and mother, Baby Budd.

BILLY. There's not much to tell. I've got no home, and never had a family to remember.

JENKINS. Ain't that too bad.

BILLY. Oh, I'd feel a lot worse if I'd been 'pressed with a wife and children.

KINCAID. That's the truth.

O'DANIEL. We're all patriotic volunteers.

KINCAID. Guano! Wait till my hitch is up, you won't see no more of me.

BUTLER. Three weeks drunk in Portsmouth, then back in the ruddy fleet.

THE DANSKER. Men like us got no other home.

O'DANIEL. No other home, is it? Ah 'tis so thick the sweet thoughts is in here, I can scarce breathe.

PAYNE. Then you can strangle or get out.

JENKINS. Aye, get along, you lousy harp, give us some fresh air.

O'DANIEL. If you begged me to stay itself, I'd be off to where there's smarter lads. Boy, let you pay no heed to these white mice, mind what I say. And be hanged, the lot of yous! [He starts up the ladder.]

KINCAID. You'll catch it, Danny, if Captain holds an inspection.

O'DANIEL [returning]. Ah whissht, I was forgetting that. And [17/18] I do think that me figure shows up better here below than it does in the broad daylight.

BILLY. Inspection today?

PAYNE. Ah the Old Man crawls over the ship from arsehole to appetite any time he ain't got nothing else to do. You never know when till you see him.

KINCAID. What the devil he wants to inspect this hooker for, I can't figure. He's seen it before.

BUTLER. He ain't seen Billy.

BILLY. What's the Captain like? On the *Rights of Man,* the captain . . .

JENKINS. You going to jaw some more about that rocking horse? I suppose *you* was at Spithead, too?

BILLY. Spithead? Where is that?

JENKINS. A little party the Navy had a year ago. A mutiny, Baby, a mutiny. Know what that is?

BILLY. Why did they mutiny?

O'DANIEL. Arra, it's easy to see you're new to the Navy.

JENKINS. Jimmy-Legs is ten good goddam reasons for it, himself.

BILLY. Who's Jimmy-Legs?

KINCAID. Master-at-Arms. We call him Jimmy-Legs.

BUTLER. Watch out for that one, Billy.

PAYNE. He's the devil himself between decks.

O'DANIEL. What d'you expect, the saints of heaven? Not in an English tub. [18/19]

BILLY. Why don't you like the Master-at-Arms?

JENKINS. You'll find out soon enough, Baby.

BUTLER. Watch him, boy. Jenkins can tell you. He's had a time or two with Claggart.

JENKINS. Aye, and I'll have another, one day before too long.

BUTLER. Sure, Jenkins. You look after Bill.

JENKINS. How old are you, kid? Sixteen?

BILLY. I don't know, maybe . . . twenty.

JENKINS. He don't even know how old he is! My guess is, too young to know what his parts are for.

O'DANIEL. Is it anybody is that young?

KINCAID. Stow it, Jenkins. Come on, don't pay no attention to him. He's feeling ugly today.

JENKINS. Well now, ain't you getting holier than a bloody bishop. Let him talk up for himself, if he don't like it.

KINCAID. Stow it, I say. You got no reason to crawl over Bill. Let him be.

BILLY. That's all right, Tom. I don't mind a joke. Black's the white of me eye, mates! [*All laugh except* JENKINS.]

JENKINS. Mama taught you pretty manners, huh? Oh! Ain't got no mama, you say? Well now, think what that makes you! [*Laughs.*]

BILLY. Tell me what you mean, Mister Jenkins.

PAYNE. What's gnawing your arse, Jenkins? Can't you see the boy's trying to be friendly?

JENKINS. You forgetting who's leading seaman here? Come on, Baby, talk back, why don't you? Scared? [19/20]

BILLY. N-no. Why do you think I'd be scared, M-M-Mister Jenkins?

JENKINS. He stammers! What do you know! The little bastard's so scared he's stammering.

BILLY. Don't call me that again.

JENKINS. Sounds good, ha? Sounds fine. I like the way it rolls out of your mouth. Bastard Baby Budd . . .

> BILLY *strikes him.* JENKINS *staggers and falls, pulls a knife and gets up, lunging at* BILLY. PAYNE, BUTLER *and* KINCAID *get up and stand close to* BILLY, *silently protecting him.*

JENKINS. Get away, God damn you! He's got to find out who gives orders here.

KINCAID. Not this time, Jenkins. Lay off.

O'DANIEL. Belay it. You're wearing me out, the pair of yous.

BUTLER. Put away the knife. [JENKINS *sees their determination and relaxes a little, uncertain what to do.*]

BILLY. Will you shake hands? Or would you rather fight?

JENKINS. You little bas . . . [*Lunges forward.* BILLY *catches his arm and bends it, holding* JENKINS *cursing and powerless.*]

BILLY. That's enough, mate. Pipe down and let us be.

O'DANIEL. Good lad! Save the great strength is in you, Jenkins, for fighting the devil is after your soul.

JENKINS. All right, all right. You can let me go now.

O'DANIEL. Leave him go, lad. I won't hurt him at all.

BILLY. You're like Red Whiskers on the *Rights*, he liked to fight too. [*Freeing him.*] Will you shake hands, mate? [20/21]

JENKINS [*momentarily uncertain what to do*]. Shake hands, is it? . . . Well, you beat me fair. You got guts, which is more than I give you credit for. [*They shake hands.*]

KINCAID. You're a hell of a peacemaker, Bill.

PAYNE. That's the only time I ever hear Jenkins eating his own words.

O'DANIEL. Ah, that's a terrible diet, would make any man puke.

JENKINS. Don't you be getting any wrong ideas. I'm still a match for you!

KINCAID. Better belay your mess gear, Bill.

JENKINS. Where you come from, Baby?

PAYNE. Stow it! Jimmy-Legs! [BILLY *goes on talking as* CLAGGART *enters.*]

BILLY. I don't know, I guess from Portsmouth. I never lived ashore, that I can remember. Where do you come from? [*Drops a pot on deck.* CLAGGART *stands over him.*]

CLAGGART. Handsomely done, young fellow, handsomely done. And handsome is as handsome did it, too. You can wipe that up, Jenkins. [*To* BILLY] What is your name?

BILLY. Budd, sir. William Budd, ship *Rights of Man.*

CLAGGART. Your ship is *H.M.S. Indomitable* now.

BILLY. Aye, sir.

CLAGGART. You look sturdy. What was your station aboard the merchantman?

BILLY. M-m-mizzentopman, sir.

CLAGGART. You like that station? [21/22]

BILLY. Aye, sir, well enough.

CLAGGART. How long have you been at sea?

BILLY. Ten years, sir, near as I can tell.

CLAGGART. Education?

BILLY. None, sir.

CLAGGART. So. You come aboard with nothing but your face to recommend you. Well, while beauty is always welcome, that alone may not avail us much against the French. There are other requirements in the service.

BILLY. I'll learn quickly, sir.

CLAGGART. The sea's a taskmaster, young fellow. It salts the sweetness out of boyish faces. You cannot tell what motion lies asleep in that flat water. Down where the manta drifts, and the shark and ray, storms wait for a wind while all the surface dazzles.

BILLY. I am a seaman, sir. I love the sea. I've hardly lived ashore.

CLAGGART. Then let the wind and sea have license to plunder at their will. As of today, a new maintopman swings between sky and water. [*He turns toward the ladder and notices the mess on deck.*] I thought I asked you to wipe that up, Jenkins.

JENKINS. That's the messboy's job.

CLAGGART. Clean up, Jenkins. [JENKINS *hesitates.*] That is an order. Turn to.

BILLY. I'll give you a hand, Jenkins. Come on.

CLAGGART. Ah, there. See how helpful Billy is. Why can't you take a leaf from this innocent young David's book, Jenkins? [*Turns away.* JENKINS *accidentally brushes against him and receives* [22/23] *a savage cut from* CLAGGART's *rattan across his face.*] Watch what you're doing, man!

JENKINS. I swear . . . !

CLAGGART. Yes, what is it that you swear? Well, speak. Nothing at all to say? Then hear me: I have my methods with unruly tempers.

On deck there is a loud crescendo scream and a crash. Running footsteps, shouts, voice calling for the SURGEON. *The men surge toward the ladder.*

CLAGGART. Stand fast! [SQUEAK *enters down the hatchway, whispers to* CLAGGART.] All right, I know. [SQUEAK *comes down into the compartment and runs off.*]

JENKINS. It's Jackson! I knew it, by God, I told you so!

Men turn to stare at CLAGGART *as several sailors enter down the companionway, bearing the body of* JACKSON, *inert and shattered. They carry him through the compartment and off to sick-bay.*

SURGEON [*as he moves through the compartment*]. Clear the way, you men. Take him into the sick-bay, through here. Carry him gently. Easy, now. Easy. [*Exit.*]

JENKINS [*pointing to* CLAGGART]. He sent him back aloft. Killed him, he did!

O'DANIEL. Might as well have knifed him.

CLAGGART. Stand fast. Stop where you are. Your man Jackson is looked after.

O'DANIEL [*in a low voice*]. Then he's a dead man surely.

CLAGGART. Who spoke? [23/24]

JENKINS. We'll have a showdown now! After him, mates! Cut into him!

The men move toward CLAGGART *in a rush, drawing knives and cursing him, as* CAPTAIN VERE *appears in the companion hatchway.*

VERE. Stand fast! Hold where you are. Master-at-Arms, what is the matter here? [*The men stop in their tracks and stare at* VERE, *who comes part way down the ladder.*]

CLAGGART. These dogs are out of temper, sir.

VERE [*to men*]. You will come to attention when I address you! Let me remind you that this ship is at war. This is a wartime cruise, and this vessel sails under the Articles of War. Volunteer or 'pressed man, veteran seaman or recruit, you are no longer citizens, but sailors: a crew that I shall work into a weapon. One lawless act, one spurt of rebel temper from any man in this ship, high or low, I will pay out in coin you know of. You have but two duties: to fight and to obey, and I will bend each contumacious spirit, each stiff-necked prideful soul of you, or crush the spirit in you if I must. Abide by the Articles of War and my commands, or they will cut you down. Now: choose. [*The men are silent.*] Very well. Master-at-Arms, this accident on deck, the sailor fallen from the yardarm. Do you know how it occurred?

CLAGGART. I do not, sir.

VERE. You are his messmates. Does any man of you know how this occurred? [*To* BUTLER] You?

BUTLER. No, sir.

VERE. Jenkins, do you?

JENKINS [*hesitates a moment;* CLAGGART *moves slightly, tapping his hand with the rattan*]. No, Sir. [24/25]

VERE [*notices the cut on* JENKINS' *face*]. What's this, what's this? Speak up, man. I want no random bloodshed aboard this ship.

JENKINS. I . . . fell, Captain. Fell and . . . and cut my cheek.

VERE. I see. You fell. Master-at-Arms, you will excuse this man from duty till the Surgeon tends him.

CLAGGART. Aye, aye, sir.

VERE. We must not wound ourselves, draining the blood from enterprise that takes a whole man. [*He turns to go up the ladder and sees* BILLY.] Well. This is a new face. Who are you, boy?

CLAGGART. Maintopman 'pressed from the *Rights of Man* this morning, sir. William Budd.

VERE. Let him speak for himself. [BILLY *tries to speak but can only stammer incoherently.*] That's all right boy, take your time. No need to be nervous.

BILLY. I saw a man go aloft, sir, as I came on board just a while ago. He looked sick, sir, he did. This officer was there, too, he can tell you. [*To* CLAGGART] Don't you remember, sir?

VERE. Did you send a sick man aloft, Master-at-Arms?

CLAGGART. I did not, sir.

VERE. Very well. [*To* BILLY] Well, Budd, I hope you take to Navy life and duty without too much regret. We go to fight the French and shall need wits and hearts about us equal to the task.

BILLY. I'll do my best, sir.

VERE. I'm sure you will. We are all here to do our several duties, and though they may seem petty from one aspect, still [25/26] they must all be done. The Admiral himself looks small and idle to the man like you who can see him from the maintop, threading his pattern on the quarterdeck. The Navy's only life. [SURGEON *enters.*]

SURGEON. Captain—Jackson, the man who fell just now—he's dead, sir.

VERE [*after a pause*]. Carry on, Master-at-Arms. [*He goes out up the companionway.* SURGEON *exits.*]

CLAGGART. You've made a good impression on the Captain, Billy Budd. You have a pleasant way with you. If you wish to make a good impression on me, you will need to curb your tongue. Jenkins, I thought you were ordered to sick-bay. Jump to it. And I suggest you change that shirt. See how fouled it is with a peculiar stain. Why can't you keep clean like Billy here? [*He strikes* JENKINS *viciously on the arm with his rattan, smiles at him, and exits up the ladder.*]

JENKINS. God damn his flaming soul! I can't stand it no more!

BILLY. I don't see what you can do, mate. He didn't mean it when he hurt you then.

JENKINS. Listen boy, I know Jimmy-Legs. He lives on hurting people. Stay away from him, and keep your mouth shut, if you don't want trouble.

O'DANIEL. Did you hear the lad speak up to the skipper?

PAYNE. Aye, you watch your tongue, Bill. Claggart will be after you for talking up like that.

KINCAID. He's a cool one, Billy is. None of us got the nerve.

BUTLER. It's nerve gets a man in trouble in this tub.

THE DANSKER. Jimmy-Legs is down on you already, Billy. [26/27]

BILLY. Down on me? Why he's friendly to me.

JENKINS. Claggart don't make no friends.

O'DANIEL. You seen Jackson when they brought him below. That's how friendly he gets. [*Bosun's pipe off.*]

DUNCAN [*off*]. Relieve the watch!

KINCAID. First watch on the *Indomitable*, Bill. Better lay up to the mainmast and report. [*Exit.*]

BUTLER. Don't slip off the yardarm.

PAYNE. Watch your step.

BILLY. Not me. You watch for me. Got to find the mainmast, and I'm in a hurry.

O'DANIEL. You'll never find your way in this old tub. I'll come along and show you. If anybody comes calling for O'Daniel while I'm out, take the message.

PAYNE. O'Daniel couldn't find his breeches if they wasn't buttoned on. You come with me. [BILLY and PAYNE go off.]

JENKINS. Poor bastard. I pity him, I do.

BUTLER. He's dead, ain't he? Better off than us.

JENKINS. Not Jackson. I mean the baby here. Billy.

BUTLER. We could have fared worse for a messmate.

JENKINS. Aye. He can take care of himself. Heave up the table. [27/28]

Scene 2

In the early evening of the same day, the off-duty sections of the crew are mustered aft on the maindeck for JACKSON'S *funeral. Above them* CAPTAIN VERE *stands uncovered at the forward break of the quarterdeck, reading the Committal Prayer. The westward sky is bright yellow and red, but fades into darkness as the scene progresses.*

The men are uncovered and stand at attention.

VERE. Unto Almighty God we commend the soul of our brother departed and we commit his body to the deep, in sure and certain hope of the resurrection unto Eternal Life, through our Lord Jesus Christ, at whose coming in glorious majesty to judge the world, the sea shall give up her dead, and the corruptible bodies of those who sleep in Him shall be changed and made like unto His glorious body according to the mighty working whereby He is able to subdue all things unto Himself. Amen.

MEN. Amen.

Short drum-roll followed by a muffled splash as JACKSON'S *body slips over the side. Then the bosun's pipe. Officers cover and march off.*

CLAGGART. Ship's company: Cover! Petty officers, dismiss your divisions.

VOICE [*off*]. Carpenters and gunners: Dismiss!

VOICE [*off*]. Afterguardsmen: Dismiss!

VOICE [*off*]. Fore, main, and mizzentopmen: Dismiss! [*The men break formation and go off, excepting* BUTLER, JENKINS, PAYNE, KINCAID *and* BILLY, *who gather near the ratlines, at the rail.*] [28/29]

BUTLER. I suppose in this clear water you could see him go down for quite a way.

BILLY. We're moving slow in this calm.

JENKINS. There'll be wind enough before dawn.

BUTLER. And that's the end of Enoch Jackson. Over the side he goes, and his mates forget him.

JENKINS. Whatever's happened to Jackson, he ain't worried none. He's got a hundred fathoms over him to keep him warm and cosy.

BILLY. I'd rather be buried at sea than on the beach, when I come to die. Will you stand by the plank, Tom, so I'll shake a friendly hand before I sink? Oh! But it's dead I'll be then, come to think! [*All laugh.*]

PAYNE. Don't you worry none. By that time, you won't give a sail-maker's damn.

KINCAID. It's only living makes sense to me, anyhow.

BILLY. Aye, I like to live. Even when it seems bad, there's a lot that's good in it.

JENKINS. Maybe for you, Bill. You wouldn't know trouble if it come up and spit in your eye.

BILLY. Don't you try now, mate! You might miss, and I got a clean jumper on!

PAYNE. That's the way to be, if you ask me. There's always trouble, if you know where to look for it.

BUTLER. You don't have to see nothing if you close your eyes.

KINCAID. When I close my eyes I sleep sound as a drunk marine. [29/ 30]

BILLY. Aye, after I roll in my hammock, it's one, two, three, and I'm deep down under.

JENKINS. Well it's down under for me right now. Let's lay below.

KINCAID. Aye, we'll be on watch before long. Coming, Bill?

BILLY. I think I'll stay and watch the water for a while. I like to watch the sea at night.

JENKINS. Aye. It's deep and silent, and it can drown a man before he knows it.

BILLY. Sleep sound, mates. [*All but* JENKINS *go down the companion hatchway.*]

JENKINS. Billy: stay clear of Jimmy-Legs.

JENKINS *exits down the hatchway.* BILLY *is left alone staring over the side until* CLAGGART *enters. He does not see* BILLY, *but stops near the quarterdeck ladder and gazes fixedly seaward.*

BILLY. Good evening, sir.

CLAGGART [*startled, then subtly sarcastic*]. Good evening.

BILLY. Will it be all right if I stay topside a bit to watch the water?

CLAGGART. I suppose the Handsome Sailor may do many things forbidden to his messmates.

BILLY. Yes, sir. The sea's calm tonight, isn't it? Calm and peaceful.

CLAGGART. The sea's deceitful, boy: calm above, and underneath, a world of gliding monsters preying on their fellows. Murderers, all of them. Only the sharpest teeth survive.

BILLY. I'd like to know about such things, as you do, sir. [30/31]

CLAGGART. You're an ingenuous sailor, Billy Budd. Is there, behind that youthful face, the wisdom pretty virtue has need of? Even the gods must know their rivals, boy; and Christ had first to recognize the ills before he cured 'em.

BILLY. What, sir?

CLAGGART. Never mind. But tell me this: how have you stomach to stand here and talk to me? Are you so innocent and ignorant of what I am? You know my reputation. Jenkins and the rest are witnesses, and certainly you've heard them talking to me. Half of them would knife me in the back some night and do it gladly; Jenkins is thinking of it. Doubtless he'll try one day. How do you dare, then? Have you not intelligence enough to be afraid of me? To hate me as all the others do?

BILLY. Why should I be afraid of you, sir? You speak to me friendly when we meet. I know some of the men . . . are fearful of you, sir, but I can't believe they're right about it.

CLAGGART. You're a fool, fellow. In time, you'll learn to fear me like the rest. Young you are, and scarcely used to the fit of your man's flesh.

BILLY. I know they're wrong, sir. You aren't like they say. Nobody could be so.

CLAGGART. So . . . ? So what, boy? Vicious, did you mean to say, or brutal? But they aren't wrong, and you would see it, but for those blue eyes that light so kindly on your fellow men.

BILLY. Oh, I've got no education, I know that. There must be a lot of things a man misses when he's ignorant. But learning's hard. Must be sort of lonely, too.

CLAGGART. What are you prating of, half-man, half-child? Your messmates crowd around, admire your yellow hair and [31/32] your blue eyes, do tricks and favors for you out of love, and you talk about loneliness!

BILLY. I just noticed the way you were looking off to leeward as I came up, sir. Kind of sad, you were looking.

CLAGGART. Not sadness, boy. Another feeling, more like . . . pleasure. That's it. I can feel it now, looking at you. A certain . . . pleasure.

BILLY [*flattered*]. Thank you, sir.

CLAGGART [*annoyed at* BILLY's *incomprehension*]. Pah.

BILLY. Just talking with you, sir, I can tell they're wrong about you. They're ignorant, like me.

CLAGGART. Compliment for compliment, eh, boy? Have you no heart for terror, fellow? You've seen this stick in use. Have you not got sense and spleen and liver to be scared, even to be cowardly?

BILLY. No, sir, I guess not. I like talking to you, sir. But please, sir, tell me something.

CLAGGART. I wonder if I can. Well, ask it.

BILLY. Why do you want us to believe you're cruel, and not really like everybody else?

CLAGGART. I think you are the only child alive who wouldn't understand if I explained; or else you'd not believe it.

BILLY. Oh, I'd believe you, sir. There's much I could learn from you: I never knew a man like you before.

CLAGGART [*slowly*]. Do you—like me, Billy Budd?

BILLY. You've always been most pleasant with me, sir.

CLAGGART. Have I? [32/33]

BILLY. Yes, sir. In the mess, the day I came aboard. And almost every day you have a pleasant word.

CLAGGART. And what I have said tonight, are these pleasant words?

BILLY. Yes, sir. I was wondering . . . could I talk to you between watches, when you've nothing else to do?

CLAGGART. You're a plausible boy, Billy. Aye, the nights are long, and talking serves to pass them.

BILLY. Thank you, sir. That would mean a lot to me.

CLAGGART. Perhaps to me as well. [*Drops his rattan.* BILLY *picks it up and hands it back to him.* CLAGGART *stares at it a moment, then at* BILLY.] No. No! Charm me, too, would you! Get away!

BILLY [*surprised and puzzled*]. Aye, sir. [*He exits down the hatchway. After a pause in which* CLAGGART *recovers his self-control* SQUEAK *appears.*]

CLAGGART [*without turning*]. Come here. I thought I told you to put that new seaman Budd on report. Why was it not done?

SQUEAK. I tried, Mister Claggart, sir. I couldn't find nothing out of place. Gear all stowed perfect.

CLAGGART. Then disarrange it. You know the practice. I want him on report.

SQUEAK. Two of his messmates is ones nearly caught me at it before.

CLAGGART. Then be more careful. Now get along and see you make out something. [SQUEAK *scurries off belowdecks as* VERE *comes into sight on the quarterdeck.*]

VERE. Master-at-Arms. What is that man doing above decks? [33/34]

CLAGGART. Ship's corporal, sir. A routine report.

VERE. There is nothing in this ship of so routine a nature that I do not concern myself in it. Remember that.

CLAGGART. Aye, aye, sir. With your permission, sir. [*Exit.* VERE *walks along the deck and scans the sails as* SEYMOUR *enters.*]

SEYMOUR. Fine evening, sir.

VERE. Yes, a fine evening, Seymour. How is the glass?

SEYMOUR. Falling, I believe, sir. I think we'll toss a little before morning. Well, I suppose I should be in my cabin inspecting the deck logs.

VERE. Stay for a moment, Seymour. In the days and nights to come, you and I will not often have an opportunity to stand easy and talk.

SEYMOUR. Aye, sir. I expect the French will put us to our stations any hour now.

VERE. Are you impressed by omens, Seymour? This seaman we've just buried: I think of him as an omen of some sort, a melancholy prologue to this voyage.

SEYMOUR. Aye, sir. Hard on the sailor, certainly, but that's the service. But we've been lucky in other ways. An accident, now, that's unavoidable.

VERE. It was more than an accident, Seymour.

SEYMOUR. This maintop sailor? How do you mean, sir?

VERE. The man was sent aloft sick, by the Master-at-Arms, contrary to my standing order. Budd, the new seaman, implied as much, and the maintop watch confirmed it. The Master-at-Arms lied to me. [34/35]

SEYMOUR. What are you going to do, sir? What action can you take? He's a valuable man, one we can hardly do without as things are now.

VERE. I shall do nothing at present, only wait and observe him. No court-martial could do more than strip him of his rank for such misconduct. I will let him have his head until some act puts him squarely counter to the law, then let the law consume him.

SEYMOUR. Why trouble the natural order to no purpose? Shouldn't we let it be?

VERE. Must a man always shrug, let things alone and drift? Would to God I could take this power of mine and break him now, smash all the laws to powder and be a man again.

SEYMOUR. We must serve the law, sir, or give up the right and privilege of service. It's how we live.

VERE. Live? Oh, you're right. Below this deck are men who at a call skip on the hurling spars against the wind, at Beat-to-quarters run as if they willed it. Yet each of us steps alone within this pattern, this formal movement centered on itself. Men live and die, taken by pattern, born to it, knowing nothing. No man can defy the code we live by and not be broken by it.

SEYMOUR. You are the Captain, sir. You maintain that code.

VERE. Keep an order we cannot understand. That's true. The world demands it: demands that at the back of every peace-maker there be the gun, the gallows and the gaol. I talk of justice, and would turn the law gentle for those who serve here; but a Claggart stands in my shadow, for I need him. So the world goes, wanting not justice, but order . . . to be let alone to hug its own iniquities. Let a man work to windward [35/36] of that law and he'll be hove down. No hope for him, none. [*Enter* WYATT.]

WYATT. Eight o'clock report, sir. Ship inspected and all in order.

SEYMOUR. Very well, carry on. [WYATT *goes off.*] By your leave, sir. Good night. [*Exit.* VERE *remains, crosses to the hatch and looks down, then slowly upward at the set of the sails.*] [36/37]

Scene 3

The maindeck several nights later.

Four bells is struck offstage. A sailor climbs wearily down the ratlines, drops to the deck and goes below. CLAGGART *stands by the larboard rail.*

As BILLY *enters from below decks, he sees the Master-at-Arms.*

BILLY. Hello, sir. [CLAGGART *looks at him without answering, then turns and goes off forward.* THE DANSKER *follows* BILLY *up onto the deck.*] Well, that's all there is to tell, Dansker. I always lash my hammock just so, and stow my gear same as all the others. They don't get in trouble.

THE DANSKER. Mister Claggart is down upon you, Billy.

BILLY. Jimmy-Legs? Why he calls me the sweet and pleasant fellow, they tell me.

THE DANSKER. Does he so, Baby lad? Aye, a sweet voice has Mister Claggart.

BILLY. For me he has. I seldom pass him but there comes a pleasant word.

THE DANSKER. And that's because he's down upon you.

BILLY. But he's my friend. I know he talks a little strange, but he's my friend.

THE DANSKER. Nobody's friend is Jimmy-Legs. Yours the least of all, maybe. Lay aloft, Baby. You'll be late to relieve your watch.

BILLY. Aye, Dansker. [*He climbs up the ratlines out of sight.* THE DANSKER *watches him go.* CLAGGART *appears, but* THE DANSKER *ignores him and goes off aft. As* JENKINS *comes into view climbing down the ratlines,* CLAGGART *gestures off and* [37/38] *fades into a shadowy corner of the deck near the quarterdeck ladder.* SQUEAK *enters as* JENKINS *drops to the deck, and intercepts him as he starts down the companionway.*]

SQUEAK. It's all right, mate, slack off and stay a bit.

JENKINS. What do you want? I pick my own company.

SQUEAK. So does I, mate, so does I. And if I may make so bold to say it, you'll be smarter to pick your company more careful.

JENKINS. If you got something to say to me, talk up, else I'll get below.

SQUEAK. Don't be hasty, now, mate, don't be in a sweat. It's haste gets good men into trouble. What d'you think of our new hand here, Billy Boy? Mister Claggart's taken with him, too. Fine young fellow, ha?

JENKINS. Talk plain. What d'you mean?

SQUEAK. I overheard him talking just this day. Would maybe surprise you some, what he had to say about yourself and a few other lads.

JENKINS. What?

SQUEAK. Aoh, bit of talk about his messmates. He don't fancy us! Not like his feather boys aboard the merchantman.

JENKINS. You lying cut-throat, try something else! Billy's in my mess; since he come on board he's rare been out of my sight. You're lying, you bloody nark! I know you too well. You'll need to try some other way to get Bill into trouble. Get away, and don't come lying to me no more.

SQUEAK. Aoh, so it's that friendly you are! Well, now, ain't that sweet! You're not smart, Jenkins. Remember, man: I tried to help you out. When you're feeling the cat between your shoulders . . . [38/39]

JENKINS [*seizing him*]. Damn your lies! Get back to Jimmy-Legs and kiss his butt. And stay out of my way! [*Throws* SQUEAK *down and exits.* SQUEAK *watches him go.* CLAGGART *steps out of the shadows.*]

CLAGGART. I heard your little talk. You lack subtlety; but I'm the greater fool to use you in these matters. You're inept.

SQUEAK. Aoh! Why don't you do it yourself, if you don't need me!

CLAGGART. I need nobody, least of all a rum-soaked footpad from the Old Bailey. If you wish to have free rein with your distasteful habits, mind your cockney manners! I stand between you and the flogging whip. Improve your style, or you stand tomorrow forenoon at the gratings!

SQUEAK. I only meant as you could do it better, Mister Claggart, I wouldn't say nothing to . . .

CLAGGART [cuts him on the arm with his rattan]. Don't touch me!— Keep Budd in petty troubles, that you can do. Unlash his hammock. Keep him on report. In time I'll let you know what plans I have for him. Get aft! [SQUEAK, eager to get away, scuttles aft as THE DANSKER enters.] Well, old man. Moon's in and out tonight. There's weather somewhere. [THE DANSKER turns down the night lamp over the cabin door and starts off.] Stay and have a pipe.

THE DANSKER. I have the watch.

CLAGGART. You take your duties as seriously as ever.

THE DANSKER. Aye. They are all of life for an old seaman like me. [Turns to go.]

CLAGGART. You move away from me as though I were some kind of stalking beast. You avoid me, too. [39/40]

THE DANSKER. Your word, John, "too."

CLAGGART. You know what I mean. The hands detest me. You are a hand, older than most, and older in your hatred, I have no doubt. But why, man? You at least should see me as I am, a man who knows how the world's made: made as I am.

THE DANSKER. How can I know what goes on in your head?

CLAGGART. The enigmatic Dansker. Come, it's dark, we can drop disguises when night serves to hold the disclosing soul apart.

THE DANSKER. You know who you remind me of . . . maintopman: Billy Budd.

CLAGGART. More enigmas! That sunny, smiling infant with no spleen nor knowledge in his head?

THE DANSKER. I'll leave you now.

CLAGGART. No, stay a while. This is a night for secrets and disclosures.

THE DANSKER. You have half the truth and Billy Budd the other. He can't see there's evil in the world, and you won't see the good.

CLAGGART. So. And I take it you come in between.

THE DANSKER. I keep outside. I am too old to stand between sky and water.

CLAGGART. And yet you hate me, too.

THE DANSKER. I hate an incomplete man.

CLAGGART. Damn all this talk. Hate me and have done. Let it alone, I say. Whatever else it is, this thing is Man, still!

THE DANSKER. I'll be off. [40/41]

CLAGGART. Don't go. The moon's gone under. Let us talk this out. You are a wise man in your senile way.

THE DANSKER. Then take this for all my wisdom. You recognize the hatred of your shipmates as an honor paid to a soul they cannot understand. Your fine contempt for human love is nothing but regret.

CLAGGART. Stop there. I know the rest by heart. Nothing you say to me but clatters in my belly, watch on watch. Aye: when this arm moves out in gesture of love, it mocks me with a blow. Who lifts this arm? What officer commands this hireling flesh? Somewhere below the farthest marks and deeps, God anchors hearts, and his sea rusts mine hollow. The flukes break in the bottom, and I slack and stand, go in and out forever at God's humor. Look at this sea: for all her easy swell, who knows what bones, ribs and decay are fathomed at her base and move in her motion, so that on the flattest water, the very stricture of the dead can kill that beauty with a dance of death?—Here is a man. He holds, past fathom curves, drowned fleets of human agonies that gesture when the long tide pulls.

THE DANSKER. Aye, John. But you must know that other men are moved so. Look up some evening at the quarterdeck for another poor thoughtful devil like you, like me, pacing all night between his doubts.

CLAGGART. What, Vere? That fine-drawn manner doesn't deceive me. There's a whited sepulchre, like all soft-spoken charmers of this world.

THE DANSKER. You don't believe in anything besides yourself, eh John?

CLAGGART. I've said what I have said. I know myself, and look to that. You should try it. Go to your post, old man, and your [41/42] everlasting duties. [CLAGGART *turns away.* BILLY *scrambles into view down the ratlines and calls out excitedly.*]

BILLY. Quarterdeck ho!

RATCLIFFE [*coming forward to the forward break of the quarterdeck*]. Sound off!

BILLY. Strange sail one mile off the larboard beam!

CLAGGART [*to* THE DANSKER]. A Frenchman! Get to your station.

RATCLIFFE [*on the quarterdeck ladder*]. Mister Duncan! Sound Beat-to-quarters! Clear for action!

DUNCAN [*offstage*]. Aye aye, sir!

RATCLIFFE. Gardiner! [*Enter* GARDINER.]

GARDINER. Sir?

RATCLIFFE. Report to the Captain, strange sail on the larboard beam. Then send Payne to the wheel. [*Exit* GARDINER.] Master-at-Arms, send a man to the mast to relay lookout's reports. Inspect battle stations and report to me when they are fully manned.

CLAGGART. Aye aye, sir.[*Exit.*]

VOICE [*off*]. She's a French frigate! Steering east by south! [*Enter* VERE *and* SEYMOUR.]

VERE. Prepare to make chase. Have your quartermaster steer small.

RATCLIFFE. Aye aye, sir.

Enter the DRUMMER *and sound Beat-to-quarters. Men run on, to gun stations, rigging, crossing stage and off.* [42/43]

SEYMOUR. She's too fast for us, sir. We'll never come up with her.

VERE. We are bound to try, though we were sure to fail. And we may smell powder before this chase is over.

CLAGGART [*re-entering*]. Battle stations fully manned, sir!

SEYMOUR. May we try a shot at her now?

VERE. She's drawing south. Yes, commence firing, Mr. Seymour.

SEYMOUR. Larboard battery, fire one!

DUNCAN. Fire! [*Fire one gun.*]

VERE. Fire at will!

SEYMOUR. Fire at will!

Guns fire dissnchronously. [43/44]

ACT TWO

Scene 1

The quarterdeck and part of the maindeck a few minutes before 0800. A high wind. On the quarterdeck are LIEUTENANT WYATT, MIDSHIPMAN REA *and the helmsman,* STOLL.

REA. I'm glad this watch is over. I'm tired.

WYATT. Make your entry in the log before your relief comes up. Bring it out here and I'll sign it.

REA. Aye, sir. What was our last position, do you remember?

WYATT. Thirteen ten west, forty-three forty north.

REA. And an easterly breeze.

WYATT. Aye, make it so. That'll make Ratcliffe happy. Last time he had an east wind, she blew his hat over the side. And put down "Running ground swell."

REA. Aye aye, sir. [*Exits.*]

WYATT. Helmsman, keep her close-hauled.

STOLL. I can't, sir. Too much cloth in the wind.

WYATT. Well hold her close as you can, and let the next watch reef sail if they like.

STOLL. Aye aye, sir. [*Enter* RATCLIFFE.]

WYATT. Morning, Johnny! You're on time!

RATCLIFFE. What's the course?

WYATT. Steady south. Wind's easterly. Glass is dropping. [44/45]

RATCLIFFE. East wind? Damn it. [*Enter* BYREN, *the relief helmsman.*] By the way, you forgot to sign the order book.

WYATT. All right. Thanks.

STOLL. I've been relieved, sir. Byren has the helm.

WYATT. Very well. [*Exit* STOLL.] Who's mate of your watch?

RATCLIFFE. The Admiralty midshipman. That lobcock Gardiner, hang him. [*Eight bells.*]

WYATT. Where the devil is he? It's eight. [*Enter* REA *and* GARDINER *separately, meeting.*]

RATCLIFFE. There he comes. He looks happy. That means trouble for some poor devil. [GARDINER *snatches the log out of* REA's *hands and bounds up to the quarterdeck.*]

REA. I've been relieved, sir. Horatio, Lord Gardiner has the watch.

WYATT. Ah, Midshipman Gardiner. The backbone of the British Navy.

RATCLIFFE. The backside, if you ask me.

WYATT. All right, Rea. You can turn in. [REA *exits.*]

RATCLIFFE. Pity we lost that Frenchman last night. A little action would season the monotony of these interminable watches.

WYATT. Did you ever hear of a ship-of-the-line running down a frigate, even with the wind? Ah! it's a magnificent morning! Thickening overcast, heavy ground swell, a fresh levanter breeze, and you, Johnny, are the Pride of the Morning!

RATCLIFFE. Mmm. Has the skipper been on deck yet? [45/46]

WYATT. Not since sunrise. He came up then and paced the deck and stared off east like a sleepwalker. Then went below again without a word.

RATCLIFFE. He thinks too much.

WYATT. Well if you ever make captain, your crew won't have that to complain of, anyway. Am I relieved?

RATCLIFFE. Yes, I relieve you. [*Tosses his cap to* WYATT.] Here. Take this below, will you?

WYATT. What? You'll be out of uniform, man. Mister Gardiner wouldn't approve of your standing watch without a hat, would you, Midshipman Gardiner?

GARDINER. Sir, the Articles state that officers on watch . . .

RATCLIFFE. Well hang it, I lost twelve shillings the last time my hat went over the rail, and this is the only other one I've got. To hell with the Articles.

WYATT. Mind your language! It's downright mutinous. Well, don't expect me to stand your watches if you catch your death of cold. Good morning. [*Exit.*]

GARDINER. Midshipman Rea, sir, I don't like to say it, but his log entries are impossible.

RATCLIFFE. Then enter yourself, Mister Gardiner. So are you.

GARDINER. Yes sir. But I do think he ought to be told . . .

RATCLIFFE. Go find the Captain and report to him the wind's abeam. Respectfully suggest we ought to take in topsails.

GARDINER. Aye aye, sir. [*Goes down stairs.*]

RATCLIFFE. And don't forget to tell him I haven't got a hat.

GARDINER. What's that, sir? [46/47]

RATCLIFFE. Nothing, sir! You got my order. Dump your ballast and shove off!

GARDINER. I thought you spoke to me, sir.

RATCLIFFE. I avoid that whenever possible. Move!

GARDINER. Yes, sir.

RATCLIFFE. Ye gods, what a brat. Nothing off, helmsman. She's well enough thus.

BYREN. Nothing off, sir.

GARDINER [*nearly bumping into* VERE *as he emerges from cabin, followed by* SEYMOUR *and* HALLAM]. Atten-tion!

RATCLIFFE. Good morning, sir.

VERE. Morning, Mister Ratcliffe.

GARDINER [*starting after* VERE, *bumps into* HALLAM]. Damn it, man, watch what you're doing!

VERE. Midshipman Gardiner.

GARDINER. Sir?

VERE. How long, pray, have you been in this ship, or any ship?

GARDINER. This is my first cruise, sir.

VERE. Your first cruise. A wartime cruise as well. And you are a midshipman. A midshipman, Mister Gardiner, let me tell you, is neither fish, flesh, nor fowl, and certainly no seaman. You're a salt-water hermaphrodite, Mister Gardiner. And unless you have a mind to be generally known as Spit-kit Gardiner, I recommend more tolerance toward the men. Now, is that clear?

GARDINER. Aye aye, sir! [47/48]

VERE. Very well, you may carry on.

RATCLIFFE. We've a weather helm, sir, and bow seas.

VERE. Take in topsails, if you please, Mister Ratcliffe.

RATCLIFFE. Aye aye, sir. Mister Duncan!

DUNCAN [enters]. Aye, sir?

RATCLIFFE. Douse your topsails and topgallants. Haul in the weather braces.

DUNCAN. Aye aye, sir. [Exit.] Away aloft! Hands by topgallant sheets and halyards!

GARDINER. Aloft there! Keep fast the weather sheets till the yards are down, da . . . if you please!

RATCLIFFE. Get aloft yourself, Mister Gardiner, see they do it right, since you're not satisfied.

GARDINER. Sir, the Articles state that . . .

RATCLIFFE. Did you hear me?

GARDINER. Aye aye, sir. [Exits up ratlines.]

DUNCAN [off]. Haul taut!

VERE. You disapprove of Gardiner, Mister Ratcliffe?

RATCLIFFE. He seems to think he's the only midshipman aboard capable of doing anything properly. He's always looking at you as if your hat weren't squared.

VERE. That is an unfortunate simile under the present circumstances.

RATCLIFFE [caught]. Oh, I—er—Keep her close to the wind, helmsman. Don't fall away! [48/49]

DUNCAN [off]. Let go topgallant bowlines!

VERE. I think Gardiner has had enough correction for one day. Call him down to our level, Mister Ratcliffe.

RATCLIFFE. Aye, sir. Mister Gardiner! You may come off your perch now! [BILLY descends rigging and starts offstage.] What do you think of our new man Budd, Captain?

SEYMOUR. That boy did a smart piece of work for us last night, sir. He's the nimblest man on the tops I've ever watched. Wyatt wants him for captain of the foretop.

VERE. Very well, let Budd take the post. He certainly deserves it for his actions last night during the chase. I'll speak to him myself.

SEYMOUR. He'll like hearing it from you, sir.

VERE. Hallam, go call Budd, the lad moving forward there. [*Exit* HALLAM. GARDINER *appears, looking sick.*] Well done, Gardiner. You may lay below and draw an extra tot of rum. You looks . . . chilly.

GARDINER. Thank you, sir. [*Exit.*]

SEYMOUR. By the way, sir, Budd has been on the Master-at-Arms' report once or twice for some petty misdemeanor. Nothing serious. [*Steps aside with* RATCLIFFE. BILLY *enters, followed by* HALLAM.]

BILLY. You sent for me, sir?

VERE. Yes, Budd. Your division officer recommends you for a post of more responsibility. He thinks you can perform duties of a higher station, and so do I, after last night. So I've agreed that you shall have Williams' place on the foretop.

BILLY. But—Williams is captain of the foretop, sir. [49/50]

VERE. The station calls for a younger man. Lieutenant Wyatt asked for you, and the spirit you showed last night warrants it. That is a real honor for a man so new on board.

BILLY. The Navy's new to me, Captain, but I hardly know anything else but the sea and ships.

VERE. And how do you like us, now that the awesomeness has worn away a bit?

BILLY. The Navy's a bustling world, sir. Bigger than the *Rights of Man,* and I get lost sometimes. But my mates lend me a hand. Why even Jimmy-Legs—beg pardon, sir, the Master-at-Arms, I mean—he's good to me, too.

VERE. The sea and the Navy exact a discipline, but it need not be a harsh one. In some ways I envy the man who dances across the tops and seems to rule the ship and sea below. Up there is a pleach of ropes for you to make a world of. Though winds have their way with tackle of your world, you live at ease against your strength and the round bole of the mast in your back. You are a king up there, while the water curds and frolics at the forefoot. I envy you that stance.

BILLY. You can trust me, Captain.

VERE. I do, boy. Very well, that's all.

BILLY. Aye aye, sir. Thank you, sir, thank you! [*Runs off.*]

VERE. Hallam, find the Master-at-Arms and bid him report to me.

HALLAM. Aye aye, sir. [*Exit.* SEYMOUR *joins* VERE.]

VERE. If I had a son, I'd hope for one like Budd.

SEYMOUR. Aye, sir. Fine boy. He's a force for order in this ship, certainly. I hope his charm's contagious. [50/51]

VERE. One such is enough. Men cannot stand very much perfection. It's a disease that we stamp out at its first rash showing. [*Enter* CLAGGART. SEYMOUR *withdraws.*] Master-at-Arms, I want to make a change on the Watch, Quarter and Station Bill. I needn't have troubled you about it until later, but I am especially interested in this change.

CLAGGART. The time of day is indifferent to me, sir.

VERE. Williams, present captain of the foretop, is assigned to the afterguard. I am replacing him with Budd.

CLAGGART. William Budd, sir? You do not mean the so-called Handsome Sailor?

VERE. Aye, William Budd, the new seaman from the *Rights of Man.*

CLAGGART. I know him, sir.

VERE. Do you find anything unusual in this replacement?

CLAGGART. You must be aware, sir, that he is . . .

VERE. Well? That he is what? I know he's an able seaman.

CLAGGART. Nothing, sir. But I wondered if he were entirely trustworthy. He has been aboard such a brief time.

VERE. Long enough to prove himself to me, and to his shipmates.

CLAGGART. Very good, sir.

VERE. He is captain of the foretop. That is all.

CLAGGART. With your permission, sir. Will there not be some dissatisfaction among the foretopmen who have been aboard much longer than Budd? [51/52]

VERE. Master-at-Arms: I concern myself with these matters. They are none of your function. Until such time as the senior topmen formally object to Budd for incapacity, he is captain of the foretop. Make it so on the Bill. [*Exit.*]

RATCLIFFE. What are you waiting for, man? Light to dawn? Promotion? You got the order.

CLAGGART. With your permission, sir.

As CLAGGART *goes off,* RATCLIFFE *spits over the rail.* [52/53]

Scene 2

Forward part of the deck. Night. Eight bells. A man descends the rigging and goes off. CLAGGART *enters, stands by the hatch for a moment, then exits forward.* BILLY *comes down off watch, drops to the deck and remains in shadow, leaning over the rail, looking seaward.* JENKINS *stealthily and silently comes up from below deck.*

BILLY. Jenkins! What you doing topside . . . [JENKINS *puts his hand over Billy's mouth.*]

JENKINS [*in a whisper*]. Stow the noise! [*Releases* BILLY.]

BILLY. You're after Mister Claggart, like you said you would!

JENKINS. Well? What about it? You try and stop me?

BILLY. He knows, Jenkins! I tell you, he knows! He's ready for you!

JENKINS. Then by God, I'll oblige him! I been waiting up here every night, waiting for him to come by when it's dark. Now get away and let me do it!

BILLY. No! I won't let you hang yourself!

JENKINS. I don't give a fiddler's damn what happens to me! Move out of my way, mate!

BILLY. No! Give me the knife.

JENKINS. The knife's for Claggart. You're a nice boy, Bill, but I ain't playing with you. You get away below, quick. This game ain't for boys.

BILLY. Damme, no, Jenkins! You'll hang yourself!

JENKINS. Take your hands off! The moon's under, I can do it now! Oh, sweet mother of God, leave me go! [53/54]

BILLY. No!

JENKINS. Yes, by God!

JENKINS *strikes* BILLY; *struggle, in which* BILLY *wrests knife from* JENKINS, *and it falls on deck.* BILLY *knocks* JENKINS *down.*

CLAGGART [*offstage*]. What's that noise? Stand where you are! [*Entering.*] You again! Well? Explain this pageant.

BILLY. He . . . I had to hit him, sir. He struck at me.

CLAGGART. Mm. And drew that knife on you, too, no doubt.

BILLY. Yes, sir.

CLAGGART. I have been waiting, forward there, for Jenkins. You intercepted him, I take it.

BILLY. I didn't know you were looking for him, sir.

CLAGGART. You shouldn't meddle, my fine young friend, in matters that don't concern you! I was expecting him. [*Enter* THE DANSKER.] There, help the body up. I do not thank you, boy, for cheating me of the pleasure of his punishment.

WYATT [*offstage*]. What's the disturbance there? You, forward on the spar-deck!

CLAGGART. Master-at-Arms reports all in order, sir!

WYATT [*offstage*]. Stand where you are.

CLAGGART. The sweet and pleasant fellow saved you, Jenkins. But I reserve you still for my own justice in due time. Say nothing to this officer. [*Enter* WYATT.]

WYATT. What's the matter, Master-at-Arms? It's an odd hour for stargazing.

CLAGGART. A slight matter, sir. I found these two men together here on deck, contrary to the Captain's orders. I was sending them below when you called out. [54/55]

WYATT. Oh, is that all. Carry on, then.

CLAGGART. Aye aye, sir. Now then, get below, both of you. [*Enter* VERE *followed by* HALLAM. THE DANSKER *goes off*.] Attention!

VERE. Wyatt, what's this mean?

WYATT. Two men on deck without permission, sir.

VERE. Is there no more to this? The story's lame, man. What occurred? [*Silence*.] Very well, then. Go along, both of you.

BILLY. Aye aye, sir. Come along, mate. [*Exits with* JENKINS.]

VERE. Your knife, Master-at-Arms?

CLAGGART. William Budd's, sir, I believe.

VERE. Return it to him. [*Exits with* HALLAM *and* WYATT.]

CLAGGART *raps rail with rattan.* SQUEAK *approaches warily.*

CLAGGART. Listen carefully; you may make up for your late mistakes if you do this smartly. Give Budd just time enough to get to sleep. At four bells wake him. Bring him to the lee forechains. You understand?

SQUEAK. Mister Claggart, sir . . . we done enough to him. He's a good lad, Mister Claggart. Couldn't it be somebody else? Jenkins, maybe?

CLAGGART. So. He's softened your heart too, eh? Do as you're ordered, man, or I'll see your back laid raw with a flogging whip! Remember: I will be watching you. Bring him to the lee forechains. And when you're there . . .

SQUEAK. Dansker. [*Moving forward*.]

CLAGGART. Step back, you fool. Wait for me.

Exit SQUEAK. THE DANSKER *enters.* [55/56]

THE DANSKER. Baby saved you, eh? And you are angry.

CLAGGART. Saved me, you say? From what? I've tried to tempt Jenkins to this blow, so as to break his toplofty spirit with his neck; and I am "saved" by that guileless idiot! He'd turn the other cheek to me, in Christian kindness! Well: there's a second pleasure in striking that same face twice. I can destroy him, too, if I choose to do it!

THE DANSKER. Crazy, crazy!

CLAGGART. All right, old man, call it madness then. Whatever its name, it will plunder the sweetness from that face, or it will kill us both.

THE DANSKER. You are afraid of him.

CLAGGART. Afraid? Of Budd? What nonsense is that?

THE DANSKER. He usurps the crew; they turn from hating you to loving him, and leave you impotent.

CLAGGART. That bastard innocent frighten me! That witless kindness that spills from him has neither force nor aim. Stand out from between us, or you founder together, sink in five hundred fathoms with him, if I want it so!

THE DANSKER. Aye, then, if you take that tack, let it be both of us. You expect me to sit by and watch your deliberate arm seize him and force him under?

CLAGGART. Why not? You have always done that. I thought your practice was to stay outside. What breeds the saintly knight errant in you?

THE DANSKER. I am old, but I have some manhood left.

CLAGGART. What can you do? You've drifted with the tide too long, old one. You are as involved as I am now. [56/57]

THE DANSKER. So you may say. In this ship a man lives as he can, and finds a way to make life tolerable for himself. I did so. That was a fault. But no longer.

CLAGGART. Stand clear. You haven't courage to cross me.

THE DANSKER. Eh, I'm not afraid of you; I see your scheme.

CLAGGART. Damn your feeble, ineffectual eyes! [*Striking him;* THE DANSKER *falls.*] You can see only what I let you see!

THE DANSKER. Say what you like. I see your scheme; so will Captain if need be.

CLAGGART [*pulling him to his feet*]. Take a warning for yourself, old man. And keep away! You are on watch, eh? Well, go back to sleep again, or I'll report you. [THE DANSKER *exits.* CLAGGART *watches him go, then violently breaks his rattan and throws the pieces over the side.*] [57/58]

Scene 3

Forward part of the main deck. Four bells. CLAGGART *stands with one hand on the rail, waiting. After a short pause, hearing a sound, he fades into shadow.* SQUEAK *enters, bending over and running.*

SQUEAK. Hsssssssssst! [BILLY, *sleepy and rubbing his eyes, enters.*]

BILLY. You brought me all the way up here, out of my hammock. Now what do you want?

SQUEAK. I heard you're captain of the foretop, Bill. That right?

BILLY. Aye. What's that to do with you?

SQUEAK. Ah, now you can be more use to your shipmates than ever you was before.

BILLY. What?

SQUEAK. You was impressed, now, weren't you? Well, so was I. We're not the only impressed ones, Billy. There's a gang of us. Could you help . . . at a pinch?

BILLY. What do you mean?

SQUEAK. See here . . . [*Holds up two coins.*] Here's two gold guineas for you, Bill. Put in with us. Most of the men aboard are only waiting for a word, and they'll follow you. There's more for you where these come from. What d'you say? If you join us, Bill, there's not a man aboard won't come along! Are you with us? The ship'll be ours when we're ready to take it!

BILLY. Damme, I don't know what you're driving at, but you had better go where you belong! [SQUEAK, *surprised, does not move.* BILLY *springs up.*] If you don't start, I'll toss you back over the rail! [SQUEAK *decamps.* BILLY *watches him and starts off himself.* THE DANSKER, *offstage, calls out.*] [58/59]

THE DANSKER. Hallo, what's the matter? [*Enters.*] Ah, Beauty, is it you again? Something must have been the matter, for you stammered. [CLAGGART *appears and comes forward.*]

CLAGGART. You seem to favor the maindeck, Billy Budd. What brings you topside at this hour, man, against my orders and the Captain's?

BILLY. I . . . found an afterguardsman in our part of the ship here, and I bid him be off where he belongs.

THE DANSKER. And is that all you did about it, boy?

BILLY. Aye, Dansker, nothing more.

CLAGGART. A strange sort of hour to police the deck. Name the afterguardsman.

BILLY. I . . . can't say, Mister Claggart. I couldn't see him clear enough.

THE DANSKER. Don't be a fool, speak up, accuse him.

CLAGGART. Well?

BILLY. I can't say, sir.

CLAGGART. You refuse? Then get below, and stay where you belong.

BILLY. Aye aye, sir. Good night, sir. Good night, Dansker. [*Exits.*]

CLAGGART. I'm glad you saw this mutinous behavior.

THE DANSKER. Your crazy brain squeezes out false conclusions. He has done nothing except find you out, though he's too innocent to know it.

CLAGGART. I am not hoodwinked by his weak excuse. What else would he be doing at this hour, but fanning rebel tempers like his own? [59/60]

THE DANSKER. I stood in the shadows forward when your pander Squeak slipped by me, running from this place. You set him on, on purpose to trap Billy.

CLAGGART. And I will do that, old man. But you will say nothing about it; see you don't. [*Enter* VERE *followed by* HALLAM.]

VERE. Well, Master-at-Arms. You stand long watches.

CLAGGART. Sir. May I take the liberty of reserving my explanation for your private ear. I believe your interest in this matter would incline you to prefer some privacy.

VERE [*to* THE DANSKER *and* HALLAM]. Leave us. Hallam, stand within hail. [THE DANSKER *and* HALLAM *go off.*] Well? What is it you wish to say, Master-at-Arms?

CLAGGART. During my rounds this night, I have seen enough to convince me that one man aboard, at least, is dangerous; especially in a ship which musters some who took a guilty part in the late serious uprisings . . .

VERE. You may spare a reference to that.

CLAGGART. Your pardon, sir. Quite lately I have begun to notice signs of some sort of movement secretly afoot, and prompted by the man in question. I thought myself not warranted, so long as this suspicion was only indistinct, in reporting it. But recently . . .

VERE. Come to the point, man.

CLAGGART. Sir, I deeply feel the cruel responsibility of making a report involving such serious consequences to the sailor mainly concerned. But God forbid, sir, that this ship should suffer the experience of the Nore.

VERE. Never mind that! You say there is one dangerous man. Name him. [60/61]

CLAGGART. William Budd, the . . . captain of the foretop.

VERE. William Budd?

CLAGGART. The same, sir. But for all his youth and appealing manners, a secret, vicious lad.

VERE. How, vicious?

CLAGGART. He insinuates himself into the good will of his mates so that they will at least say a word for him, perhaps even take action with him, should it come to that. With your pardon, sir; you note but his fair face; under that there lies a man-trap.

VERE [*after a pause*]. Master-at-Arms, I intend to test your accusation here and now. Hallam! [*Enter* HALLAM.]

HALLAM. Aye, sir.

VERE. Find Budd, the foretopman. Manage to tell him out of earshot that he is wanted here. Keep him in talk yourself. Go along.

HALLAM. Aye aye, sir. [*Exits.*]

VERE [*angry and perturbed*]. Do you come to me with such a foggy tale, Master-at-Arms? As to William Budd, cite me an act, or spoken word of his, confirming what you here in general charge against him. Wait; weigh what you speak. Just now, and in this case, there is the yardarm end for false witness.

CLAGGART. I understand, sir. Tonight, when on my rounds, discovering Budd's hammock was unused, I combed the ship, and found him in conclave with several growlers; men, who, like himself, spread unrest and rebellion in the crew. They were collected here, near the lee forechains, and when I ordered them below, young Budd and others threatened me, and swore they'd drop me, and some officers they hate, overboard, some misty night. Should you, sir, desire substantial proof, it is not far. [61/62]

Enter HALLAM, *followed by* BILLY.

VERE. Hallam, stand apart and see that we are not disturbed. [HALLAM *exits.*] And now, Master-at-Arms, tell this man to his face what you told me of him.

CLAGGART [*moving near to* BILLY, *and looking directly at him*]. Certainly, sir. I said this man, this William Budd, acting so out of angry resentment against impressment and his officers, against this ship, this Service, and the King, breeds in the crew a spirit of rebellion against the officers, the mates, and me, urging some outrage like the late revolt. I myself have seen and heard him speak with manifest malingerers and men who growl of mistreatment, harshness, unfair pay and similar complaints. I say this man threatened his officers with murder, and was bent tonight on urging other men to act concertedly in mutiny. I have nothing further to say, sir.

BILLY *tries to speak, but can make only incoherent sounds. He seems to be in pain from the contortions of his face and the gurgling which is all he can effect for speech.*

VERE. Speak, man, speak! Defend yourself! [*Remembering* BILLY's *impediment, goes to him and puts a hand on his shoulder reassuringly.*] There is no hurry, boy. Take your time, take your time.

After agonized dumb gesturing and stammering, increased by VERE's *kindness,* BILLY's *arm hits out at* CLAGGART. CLAGGART *staggers, falls, lies still.*

VERE. Stand back, man! It was a lie, then! [BILLY, *shaking, only stares at the body.* VERE *raises the body to a sitting position. Since* CLAGGART *remains inert,* VERE *lowers him again slowly, then rises.* BILLY *tries again to speak, without success; he is crying and badly frightened.*] No need to speak now, Billy. Hallam! [*Enter* HALLAM.] Tell the Surgeon I wish to see [62/63] him here at once. And bid Mister Seymour report to my cabin without delay. [*To* BILLY] Retire to the stateroom aft. Remain there till I summon you. [BILLY *exits.* VERE *waits, turning once to stare at* CLAGGART's *body. Enter the* SURGEON.] Surgeon, tell me how it is with him. [SURGEON *bends over* CLAGGART *briefly, then looks up in surprise.*] Come, we must dispatch. Go now. I shall presently call a drumhead court to try the man who out of God's own instinct dropped him there. Tell the lieutenants that a foretopman has, in an accidental fury, killed this man. Inform the Captain of Marines as well, and charge them to keep the matter to themselves. [SURGEON *exits.*] The divine judgment of Ananias! Struck dead by the Angel of God . . . and I must judge the Angel. Can I save him? Have I that choice? [63/64]

ACT THREE

Scene 1

Captain Vere's cabin, a quarter of an hour later. VERE *and* SEYMOUR.

SEYMOUR. Budd beat a man to death! What had he done?

VERE. Lied again: lied to Budd's face, hoping to kill him by it. Oh, the boy was tempted to it past endurance.

SEYMOUR. False witness has its penalty, sir. Budd has set our justice right.

VERE. Aye, too right. This natural, right act, done in an instinct's fever of recognition, was late and fatal.

SEYMOUR. What are you going to do, Captain? Isn't this last lie of the Master-at-Arms the very act you were waiting for, so as to let the law destroy him, as you said? He should have suffered at the yardarm if Billy hadn't killed him.

VERE. Yes. He should. But by fair process of authority. Budd has prevented that, and turned the law against himself.

SEYMOUR. You can't condemn the boy for answering with his arm for lack of words! The motive was clearly justified.

VERE. Aye, but was the act? For God's sake try, try to convince me I am wrong!

SEYMOUR. This Master-at-Arms, you knew him for a liar, a vicious dog.

VERE. A dog's obeyed in office. Claggart was authority.

SEYMOUR. Then authority's an evil! [64/65]

VERE. It often is. But it commands, and no man is its equal, not Billy, nor I. It will strike us down, and rightly, if we resist it.

SEYMOUR. Rightly! What power gives evil its authority? We should thank God the man's dead, and the world well rid of that particular devil.

VERE. Our life has ways to hedge its evil in. No one must go above them; even innocents. Laws of one kind or other shape our course from birth to death. These are the laws pronouncing Billy's guilt; Admiralty codes are merely shadows of them.

SEYMOUR. That's tyranny, not law, forcing conformity to wrongs, giving the victory to the devil himself!

VERE. I thought so once. But without this lawful tyranny, what should we have but worse tyranny of anarchy and chaos? So aboard this man-of-war. Oh, if I were a man alone, manhood would declare for Billy.

SEYMOUR. Then do it. Put your strength and your authority behind Budd, and let him go.

VERE. When I think I could have watched him grow in comely wholeness of manhood . . . all lost now. What could have been, quenched in evil, swept out by that undertow.

SEYMOUR. It's more than anyone can have to answer for, Captain; to his peers, or to his God. Let him go free and try on mortal flesh! Will you urge a noose for him, marked like a common felon, and that devil still to have his wish, killing the boy at last?

VERE. Can I do otherwise? I'd give my life to save his, if I could.

SEYMOUR. It's in your hands, Captain. Only you can help him now. [65/66]

VERE. Billy, Billy. What have we done to you? [Knock.] Yes, come in. [Enter HALLAM.]

HALLAM. Lieutenants Ratcliffe and Wyatt, sir.

VERE. Let them come in. [Enter RATCLIFFE and WYATT.]

SEYMOUR. You both know why you've been summoned hither?

WYATT. Yes, sir.

RATCLIFFE. Aye, sir, in a general sort of way.

SEYMOUR. Then take your chairs. Ratcliffe. You here, Wyatt. You are appointed members of a court-martial convened under extraordinary circumstances by Captain Vere. I am Senior Member, and I declare this court open. [WYATT, RATCLIFFE, *and* SEYMOUR *sit.* VERE *remains standing, apart.*] Sentry, bring the prisoner in. [HALLAM *salutes and exits.*] As you know, the Master-at-Arms has been killed by the foretopman, Budd. Whether by accident or by design, and whether the act shall carry the penalty of death or no, you are to decide. There is only one witness, Captain Vere. I shall call upon him to give his deposition as soon as the sentry brings in the prisoner. [*An uneasy silence.*]

WYATT. Budd wouldn't kill a minnow without good reason.

RATCLIFFE. What did the . . .

SEYMOUR. I had rather you did not express an opinion until after you have heard the evidence. [*Another awkward silence.* HALLAM *finally enters with* BILLY.] Sentry, stand outside. [*Exit* HALLAM.] You may sit down.

BILLY. Th-th-thank you, sir.

SEYMOUR. Captain: will you be good enough to give us your account? [66/67]

VERE [*turning towards them*]. I speak not as your Captain, but as witness before this court. The Master-at-Arms early this morning detailed to me an account of mutinous sentiments expressed by Budd, and in particular, spoke of overhearing a specific conversation last night on the mid-watch. He alleged that Budd offered him violence and threatened further violence against the officers.

WYATT. Budd a mutineer! That's absurd, he's the best-liked man . . .

SEYMOUR. Lieutenant Wyatt. Please do not interrupt the witness.

RATCLIFFE. Did the Master-at-Arms specify who the other malcontents were, sir?

VERE. He did not. He said merely that he was in possession of substantial proof of his accusation.

SEYMOUR. With your permission, sir . . . Budd, did you speak with anyone in the Master-at-Arms' hearing last night?

BILLY. I . . . spoke a little . . . with the Dansker, sir.

WYATT. Who is the Dansker?

BILLY. He's just called the Dansker, sir. He's always called so.

RATCLIFFE. I know him. A mainmast sailor.

SEYMOUR. Sentry. [*Enter* HALLAM.]

HALLAM. Sir.

SEYMOUR. Do you know a mainmast sailor referred to as "the Dansker"?

HALLAM. Aye, sir.

SEYMOUR. Go on deck and find him. Let him know apart that he is wanted here, and arrange it so that none of the other [67/68] people notice his withdrawing. See you do it tactfully. I want no curiosity aroused among the men.

HALLAM. Aye aye, sir. [*Exits.*]

SEYMOUR. Please go on.

VERE. I sent at once for Budd. I ordered the Master-at-Arms to be present at this interview, to make his accusation to Budd's face.

RATCLIFFE. May I ask what was the prisoner's reaction on being confronted by the Master-at-Arms?

VERE. I perceived no sign of uneasiness in his demeanor. I believe he smiled.

RATCLIFFE. And for the Master-at-Arms?

VERE. When I directed him to repeat his accusation, he faced Budd and did so.

WYATT. Did Budd reply?

VERE. He tried to speak, but could not frame his words.

SEYMOUR. And then, sir?

VERE. He answered with blows, and his accuser fell. . . . It was apparent at once that the attack was fatal, but I summoned the Surgeon to verify the fact. That is all. [*Turns away.*]

SEYMOUR [*to* BILLY]. You have heard Captain Vere's account. Is it, or is it not, as he says?

BILLY. Captain Vere tells the truth. It is just as Captain Vere says, but it is not as the Master-at-Arms said. I have eaten the King's bread, and I am true to the King.

VERE. I believe you, boy.

BILLY. God knows . . . I . . . thank you, sir. [68/69]

SEYMOUR. Was there any malice between you and the Master-at-Arms?

BILLY. I bore no malice against the Master-at-Arms. I'm sorry he is dead. I did not mean to kill him. If I'd found my tongue, I would not have struck him. But he lied foully to my face, and I . . . had to say . . . something . . . and I could only say it . . . with a blow. God help me.

SEYMOUR. One question more—you tell us that what the Master-at-Arms said against you was a lie. Now, why should he have lied with such obvious malice, when you have declared that there was no malice between you? [BILLY *looks appealingly at* VERE.] Did you hear my question?

BILLY. I . . . I . . .

VERE. The question you put to him comes naturally enough. But can he rightly answer it? Or anyone else, unless, indeed, it be he who lies within there. [*Knock and enter immediately* HALLAM.]

HALLAM. The mainmast man, sir.

SEYMOUR. Send him in. [HALLAM *nods off and* THE DANSKER *enters.* HALLAM *withdraws, closing door.*] State your name and station.

THE DANSKER. I have no name. I'm called the Dansker, that's all I know. Mainmast man.

SEYMOUR. You have been summoned in secrecy to appear as a witness before this court, of which I am Senior Member. I may not at this time disclose to you the nature of the offense being tried. However, the offender is William Budd, foretopman. [*Pause.*] Do you consent to give this court your testimony, though ignorant of the case at trial, and further, to keep in strictest confidence all that passes here? [69/70]

THE DANSKER. Aye.

SEYMOUR [*pushes forward a Bible*]. Do you so swear?

THE DANSKER [*touching the Bible*]. I do.

SEYMOUR. Then this is my question. In your opinion, is there malice between Budd and the Master-at-Arms?

THE DANSKER. Aye.

VERE [*wheeling around*]. How!

SEYMOUR. Explain your statement.

THE DANSKER. How should he not have hated him?

SEYMOUR. Be plain, man. We do not deal in riddles here.

THE DANSKER. Master-at-Arms bore malice towards a grace he could not have. There was no reason for it.

RATCLIFFE. In other words, this malice was one-sided?

THE DANSKER. Aye.

RATCLIFFE. And you cannot explain how it arose?

THE DANSKER. Master-at-Arms hated Billy . . .

SEYMOUR. One moment. I notice that you have been using the past tense in your testimony. Why?

THE DANSKER. I look around and sense finality here.

WYATT. You cannot explain further the cause of Claggart's hate for Budd?

THE DANSKER. Master-at-Arms made his world in his own image. Pride was his demon, and he kept it strong by others' fear of him. Billy could not imagine such a nature, saw nothing but a lonely man, strange, but a man still, nothing to be feared. So Claggart, lest his world be proven false, planned Billy's death. The final reason is beyond my thinking. [70/71]

VERE. Aye, that is thoughtfully put. There is a mystery in iniquity. But it seems to me, Seymour, that the point we seek here is hardly material.

SEYMOUR. Aye, sir. Very well, you may go.

THE DANSKER. One thing more. Since this Master-at-Arms first came on board from God knows where, I have seen his shadow lengthen along the deck, and being under it, I was afraid. Whatever happened here, I am in part to blame—more than this lad. [*To* BILLY] I am an old man, Billy. You—try to—forgive me. [*Exits.*]

SEYMOUR. Have you any further questions to put to the accused?

RATCLIFFE. No.

WYATT. None.

SEYMOUR. William Budd, if you have anything further to say for yourself, say it now.

BILLY [*after glance at* VERE]. I have said all, sir.

SEYMOUR. Sentry. [*Enter* HALLAM.] Remove the prisoner to the after compartment. [HALLAM *and* BILLY *exit. A long pause.*] Have you anything to say, Ratcliffe?

RATCLIFFE. Yes, sir. Claggart was killed because Budd couldn't speak. In that sense, that he stammers, he's a cripple. You don't hang a man for that, for speaking the only way he could.

WYATT. If you condemn him, it's the same thing as condoning the apparent lie the Master-at-Arms clearly told. I'd have struck him, too. The boy is clearly innocent, struck him in self-defense.

RATCLIFFE. Aye. I'm ready to acquit him now.

SEYMOUR. Good. Then we can reach a verdict at once. [71/72]

VERE. Hitherto I have been a witness at this trial, no more. And I hesitate to interfere, except that at this clear crisis you ignore one fact we cannot close our eyes to.

SEYMOUR. With your pardon, sir, as Senior Member of this court, I must ask if you speak now as our commanding officer or as a private man.

VERE. As convening authority, Seymour. I summoned this court, and I must review its findings and approve them before passing them on to the Admiralty.

SEYMOUR. Aye, sir, that is your right.

VERE. No right. Which of us here has rights? It is my duty, and I must perform it. Budd has killed a man—his superior officer.

SEYMOUR. We have found a verdict, sir.

VERE. I know that, Seymour. Your verdict sets him free, and so would I wish to do. But are we free to choose as we would do if we were private citizens? The Admiralty has its code. Do you suppose it cares who Budd is? Who you and I are?

SEYMOUR. We don't forget that, sir. But surely Claggart's tales were simply lies. We've established that.

VERE. Aye. But the Nore and Spithead were brute facts, and must not come again. The men were starved out before, but if they should think we are afraid . . .

RATCLIFFE. Captain, how could they? They certainly know Budd is no mutineer.

WYATT. Of course not. Since he came on board, he's done more to keep the crew in hand than any of us.

SEYMOUR. That's true. The men took naturally to him. [72/73]

VERE. As officers we are concerned to keep this ship effective as a weapon. And the law says what we must do in such a case as this. Come now, you know the facts, and the Mutiny Act's provisions. At sea, in time of war, an impressed man strikes his superior officer, and the blow is fatal. The mere blow alone would hang him, at least according to the Act. Well then, the men on board know that as well as you and I. And we acquit him. They have sense, they know the proper penalty to follow, and yet it does not follow.

SEYMOUR. But they know Budd, sir, and Claggart too, I daresay. Would they not applaud the decision that frees Budd? They would thank us.

WYATT. String him to a yard, and they'll turn round and rescue him, and string us up instead!

RATCLIFFE. Aye, that's a point. It's twice as dangerous to hang the boy as it would be to let him go. If there's a mutinous temper in the crew, condemning Budd would surely set it off.

VERE. That is possible. Whatever step we take, the risk is great; but it is ours. That is what makes us officers. Yet if in fear of what our office demands we shirk our duty, we only play at war, at being men. If by our lawful rigor mutiny comes, there is no blame for us. But if in fear, miscalled a kind of mercy, we pardon Budd against specific order, and then the crew revolts, how culpable and weak our verdict would appear! The men on board know what our case is, how we are haunted by the Spithead risings. Have they forgotten how the panic spread through England? No. Your clemency would be accounted fear, and they would say we flinch from practising a lawful rigor lest new outbreaks be provoked. What shame to us! And what a deadly blow to discipline!

RATCLIFFE. I concede that, sir. But this case is exceptional, and pity, if we are men, is bound to move us, Captain. [73/74]

VERE. So am I moved. Yet we cannot have warm hearts betraying heads that should be cool. In such a case ashore, an upright judge does not allow the pleading tears of women to touch his nature. Here at sea, the heart, the female in a man, weeps like a woman. She must be ruled out, hard though it be. [*Pause.*] Still silent? Very well, I see that something in all your downcast faces seems to urge that not alone the heart moves hesitancy. Conscience, perhaps. The private conscience moves you.

WYATT. Aye, that's it, sir. How can we condemn this man and live at peace again within ourselves? We have our standards; ethics, if you like.

VERE. Challenge your scruples! They move as in a dusk. Come, do they import something like this: if we are bound to judge, regardless of palliating circumstances, the death of Claggart as the prisoner's deed, then does that deed appear a capital crime whereof the penalty is mortal? But can we adjudge to summary and shameful death a fellow creature innocent before God, and whom we feel to be so? Does that state the case rightly?

SEYMOUR. That is my feeling, sir.

VERE. You all feel, I am sure, that the boy in effect is innocent; that what he did was from an unhappy stricture of speech that made him speak with blows. And I believe that, too; believe as you do, that he struck his man down, tempted beyond endurance. Acquit him, then, you say, as innocent?

RATCLIFFE. Exactly! Oh I know the Articles prescribe death for what Budd has done, but that . . .

WYATT. Oh, stow the Articles! They don't account for such a case as this. You yourself say Budd is innocent.

VERE. In intent, Wyatt, in intent. [74/75]

WYATT. Does that count for nothing? His whole attitude, his motive, count for nothing? If his intent . . .

VERE. The intent or non-intent of Budd is nothing to the purpose. In a court more merciful than martial it would extenuate, and shall, at the last Assizes, set him free. But here we have these alternatives only: condemn or let go.

SEYMOUR. But it seems to me we've got to consider the problem as a moral one, sir, despite the fact that we're not moralists. When Claggart told you his lie, the case immediately went beyond the scope of military justice.

VERE. I, too, feel that. But do these gold stripes across our arms attest that our allegiance is to Nature?

RATCLIFFE. To our country, sir.

VERE. Aye, Ratcliffe; to the King. And though the sea, which is inviolate Nature primeval, though it be the element whereon we move and have our being as sailors, is our official duty hence to Nature? No. So little is that true that we resign our freedom when we put this on. And when war is declared, are we, the fighters commissioned to destroy, consulted first?

WYATT. Does that deny us the right to act like men? We're not trying a murderer, a dockside cut-throat!

VERE. The gold we wear shows that we serve the King, the Law. What does it matter that our acts are fatal to our manhood, if we serve as we are forced to serve? What bitter salt leagues move between our code and God's own judgments! We are conscripts, every one, upright in this uniform of flesh. There is no truce to war born in the womb. We fight at command.

WYATT. All I know is that I can't sit by and see Budd hanged!

VERE. I say we fight by order, by command of our superiors. And if our judgments approve the war, it is only coincidence. [75/76] And so it is with all our acts. So now, would it be so much we ourselves who speak as judges here, as it would be martial law operating through us? For that law, and for its rigor, we are not responsible. Our duty lies in this: that we are servants only.

RATCLIFFE. The Admiralty doesn't want service like that. What good would it do? Who'd profit by Budd's death?

WYATT. You want to make us murderers!

SEYMOUR. Wyatt! Control yourself!

VERE. What is this vessel that you serve in, Wyatt, an ark of peace? Go count her guns; then tell your conscience to lie quiet, if you can.

RATCLIFFE. But that is war. This would be downright killing!

SEYMOUR. It's all war, Ratcliffe; war to the death, for all of us.

VERE. You see that, Seymour? That this war began before our time?

SEYMOUR. And will end long after it.

VERE. Here we have the Mutiny Act for justice. No child can own a closer tie to parent than can that Act to what it stems from: War. This is a wartime cruise and in this ship are Englishmen who fight against their wills, perhaps against their conscience, 'pressed by war into the service of the King. Though we as fellow creatures understand their lot, what does it matter to the officer, or to the enemy? The French will cut down conscripts in the same swath with volunteers, and we will do as much for them. War has no business with anything but surfaces. War's child, the Mutiny Act, is featured like the father.

RATCLIFFE. Couldn't we mitigate the penalty if we convict him?

VERE. No, Ratcliffe. The penalty is prescribed. [76/77]

RATCLIFFE. I'd like to think it over, Captain. I'm not sure.

VERE. I repeat, then, that while we ponder and you hesitate over anxieties I confess to sharing, the enemy comes nearer. We must act, and quickly. The French close in on us; the crew will find out shortly what has happened. Our consciences are private matters, Ratcliffe. But we are public men, controlling life and death within this world at sea. Tell me whether or not in our positions we dare let our consciences take precedence of the code that makes us officers and calls this case to trial.

RATCLIFFE. [after a pause; quietly]. No, sir.

WYATT. Can you stand Budd's murder on your conscience?

SEYMOUR. Wyatt! Hold your tongue!

WYATT [jumping up]. I say let him go!

SEYMOUR. Sit down, sir!

VERE. Let him speak.

WYATT. I won't bear a hand to hang a man I know is innocent! My blood's not cold enough. I can't give the kind of judgment you want to force on us! I ask to be excused from sitting upon this court.

SEYMOUR. Do you know what you're saying? Sit down and hold your tongue, man!

VERE. The kind of judgment I ask of you is only this, Wyatt: that you recognize your function in this ship. I believe you know it quite as well as we, yet you rebel. Can't you see that you must first strip off the uniform you wear, and after that your flesh, before you can escape the case at issue here? Decide you must, Wyatt. Oh you may be excused and wash your hands of it, but someone must decide. We are the law; law orders us to act, and shows us how. Do you imagine Seymour, or Ratcliffe [77/78] here, or I, would not save this boy if we could see a way consistent with our duties? Acquit Budd if you can. God knows I wish I could. If in your mind as well as in your heart, you can say freely that his life is not forfeit to the law we serve, reason with us! Show us how to save him without putting aside our function. Or if you can't do that, teach us to put by our responsibility and not betray ourselves. Can you do this? Speak, man, speak! Show us how! Save him, Wyatt, and you save us all. [WYATT slowly sits down.] You recognize the logic of the choice I force upon you. But do not think me pitiless in thus demanding sentence of a luckless boy. I feel as you do for him. But even more, I think there is a grace of soul within him that shall forgive the law we bind him with, and pity us, stretched on the cross of choice. [Turns away.]

SEYMOUR. Well, gentlemen. Will you decide. [Officers write their verdicts on paper before them, and hand them to SEYMOUR, who rises, *draws his dirk and places it on the table, pointing forward.*] He is condemned, sir. Shall we appoint the dawn? [78/79]

Scene 2

CAPTAIN VERE'S *cabin, 0400. Ship's bell strikes offstage.* VERE *sitting alone at his desk. Knock at the door.*

VERE. Come in. [*Enter* SEYMOUR.] Oh, it's you, Seymour.

SEYMOUR. It's eight bells, Captain.

VERE. What's the hour of sunrise?

SEYMOUR. Four fifty-two, sir.

VERE. Eight bells. And one bell at four-thirty. Odd and even numbers caught between two hands. Budd shall not live to hear the odd made even or wrong made right.—Call all hands to quarters at four-thirty.

SEYMOUR. Aye aye, Captain. [*Turns irresolutely.*]

VERE. The wind has slackened, I think. How is the glass?

SEYMOUR. It's risen slightly. Sea has flattened out.

VERE. Fair weather after foul . . . it's all nature, nature and law. How exigent are these Mediterranean climates of the heart, and temperate zones of mind!

SEYMOUR. Have you been here all night, sir?

VERE. All night, Seymour . . . all my life moving between dark and dark. It has been a long night, but day will be quick and deadly on the mainyard. D'you think, Seymour, a man can forgive a wrong done of the heart's own election?

SEYMOUR. Most people are decent enough. You can forgive them trespasses.

VERE. No, by God. There's wickedness alive. It's dead now in one man, but it's alive to feel and smell at night. . . . Seymour, go below. Get Budd and bring him here. [79/80]

SEYMOUR. But Captain . . .

VERE. Do as you're told. Get Budd and bring him here. [SEYMOUR *exits.* VERE *sits motionless for a few moments, then rises and goes to the cabin door.*] Sentry.

HALLAM. Yes, sir?

VERE. Who has the deck this watch?

HALLAM. Mister Ratcliffe, Captain.

VERE. Very well. [*Pause.*] Sentry!

HALLAM. Sir?

VERE. When Mister Seymour has returned, admit him right away.

HALLAM. Aye aye, Captain.

VERE. The wind's still sharp. You must be cold there, Hallam. Go to the leeward side. I'll be responsible.

HALLAM. Thank you, sir. This is the coldest hour now, just before sunrise.

VERE [*closes door, returns slowly to his desk*]. The lamp holds steady when the vessel heels. Does the law hang straight in crooked lives? It burns, and shapes nothing but shadows here, plumb in the twisting cabin of the mind. [*Footsteps, voices,* VERE *turns to door. Enter* SEYMOUR, BILLY, *and* HALLAM.] Take off the manacles. [HALLAM *frees* BILLY.]

SEYMOUR [*to* HALLAM]. Outside, man. Bear a hand. [*Exits with* HALLAM.]

VERE. Sit down. No, it's better that I stand.

BILLY. I was thinking, locked up below there . . . the Captain knows the rights of all this. He'll save me if it's right. Then you sent for me. Is there hope for me, Captain? [*80/81*]

VERE. Billy, what hope is there?

BILLY. Tell me why. I only want to understand.

VERE. How young you still are, Billy! Oh, I can tell you this: nothing is lost of anything that happens. I have given you the judgment of the world . . . deadly constraint . . . a length of hemp and a yard-arm. I have done this to you, no one else.

BILLY. I can't get the rights of all that's happened.

VERE. There's not much right, Billy. Only necessity. You and Claggart broke man's compromise with good and evil, and both of you must pay the penalty.

BILLY. Penalty? What for? Would anyone make laws just to be broken by fellows like me?

VERE. Aye, boy. You have learned this late. Most of us find out early and trim to a middle course.

BILLY. Do you mean . . . it's better to be like that?

VERE. Better as this world goes. When a man is born, he takes a guilt upon him, I can't say how or why. And life takes its revenge on those who hurt its pride with innocence.

BILLY. Do you think Claggart knew it would come to this?

VERE. He knew he would kill you, and he died to gain that end. But if you trust me, he'll not win entirely.

BILLY. How could he hate me like that?

VERE. The world we breathe is love and hatred both, but hatred must not win the victory.

BILLY. Claggart is dead. Now I'm to hang. Doesn't that show the law is wrong, when it can't choose between him and me?

VERE. Yes, it's all wrong, all wrong. [81/82]

BILLY. I don't know, Captain. I never was a hand to wonder about things, but now I think that maybe there's a kind of cruelty in people that's just as much a part of them as kindness, say, or honesty, or m-m-m . . . I can't find words, I guess, Captain.

VERE. There are no words. We are all prisoners of deadly forms that are made to break us to their measure. Nothing has power to overcome them, except forgiveness. . . . Can you forgive what I have done?

BILLY. I *can* trust you, can't I? *Can* you show me it's all right, my being . . .

VERE [*turns away; a long pause*]. It's nearly dawn, lad. In the Spanish villages they're lighting fires.

BILLY. I'm not afraid, sir. [*Steps toward* VERE.] It's getting light.

VERE. There's no time for either of us left. Go, take the morning. God knows you have the right to it. And when you are on the mainyard, think of me, and pray for those who must make choices. Hallam. [*Enter* HALLAM *in doorway.*] Take Budd into your charge. [BILLY *and* HALLAM *go out.*] Time has run out. [82/83]

Scene 3

Main deck aft. Drum-to-formation. Crew forming up. WYATT, MIDSHIPMEN GARDINER *and* REA.

WYATT. Bear a hand. Form the men up in ranks.

GARDINER. Aye, sir. All right, you! Close ranks! Move up, Stoll. That's better. Talbot, square your hat. Form up straight there, damn it! [*Drum.* MEN *come to attention.*]

WYATT. Division commanders report!

VOICE [*off*]. Carpenters and gunners, present or accounted for, sir!

VOICE [*off*]. Marine Detachment, present or accounted for, sir!

VOICE [*off*]. Afterguard, present or accounted for, sir!

GARDINER. Fore, main and mizzentopmen . . . one absentee!

WYATT. All hands will stand by to witness punishment! Stand easy.

VOICES [*off*]. Stand easy! [WYATT *walks away from men. Murmur in ranks.*]

KINCAID. Where the devil is Billy? He wasn't in his hammock when they piped us up.

O'DANIEL. He'll be getting himself in trouble if he don't fall in.

KINCAID. Who the hell they punishing, and what for?

JENKINS. It's got to be flogging, or they wouldn't have us all up here.

KINCAID. Vere never flogs anybody. And there ain't no gratings up. [83/84]

THE DANSKER. They flog men at noon. The early morning's for hanging.

KINCAID. Hanging! [*The word travels back.*] Who? What for?

O'DANIEL. The skipper, he don't confide in me no more.

KINCAID. I thought they waited till they got ashore before they hanged a man.

THE DANSKER. Not in wartime.

JENKINS. He goes up them ratlines, out on the yard, they slips a noose around his neck, and then he jumps and hangs himself.

O'DANIEL. They'd have the devil's work getting O'Daniel to jump.

KINCAID. It's jump, or get pushed.

JENKINS. Where's Claggart? God, you don't suppose it's Claggart! Oh, Judas, let it be that fishblooded nark!

KINCAID. Not him. He's too smart, he is.

JENKINS. Where is he, then? He ain't here.

THE DANSKER. He is here.

KINCAID. Where? I don't see him.

THE DANSKER. He is here.

KINCAID. Ah . . . you're balmy, old man.

Enter VERE, SEYMOUR, RATCLIFFE *and the* SURGEON. *Drum sounds Attention.*

WYATT [*to* SEYMOUR]. Ship's company present to witness execution, sir.

SEYMOUR. Very well. [*To* VERE.] Ship's company present to witness execution, sir. [VERE *nods.*] [84/85]

SEYMOUR [*to* WYATT]. Lieutenant Wyatt, have the prisoner brought forward.

WYATT. Aye aye, sir. [*Marches to wing.*] Sentries, bring forward the prisoner. [*Marches back to his post.*]

Enter BILLY *with two sentries. Astonished murmur through the crew, who momentarily break ranks.*

WYATT. No talking in ranks! [*Continued restless movement and murmurings.*] Form up!

GARDINER. You men are at attention!

WYATT [*over subdued muttering*]. You hear me? Silence in ranks!

Silence. SENTRIES *lead* BILLY *to the foot of the ropes.* SEYMOUR *looks at* VERE, *who nods.* SEYMOUR *steps forward and reads.*

SEYMOUR. Proceedings of the court-martial held aboard *H.M.S. Indomitable* on the eighth August, 1798. Convened under the authority of Edward Fairfax Vere, Senior Captain, Royal Navy, and composed of the First Officer, the Sailing Master, and the First Lieutenant of said vessel. In the case of William Budd, foretopman, Royal Navy. While attached and so serving in the aforesaid vessel, he did, on the 8th day of August, 1798, strike and kill his superior officer, one John Claggart, Master-at-Arms, Royal Navy.

Crew breaks out uneasily, astonished, talking excitedly.

JENKINS. Billy! Did you, boy?
VOICE. Good lad!
VOICE. Serves him proper!   *All together.*
KINCAID. Hi, Billy! Hurrah!

WYATT. Quiet! Silence, you men! Form up!

GARDINER. Stand at attention, hang you! Silence in the ranks! [85/86]

WYATT. Do you hear? [*Excited muttering, low voices.*]

SEYMOUR. You will be silent and remain at strict attention until dismissed. [*Silence.*] . . . Master-at-Arms, Royal Navy. Therefore, the court sentences the aforementioned William Budd, foretopman, Royal Navy, to die by hanging on the first watch of the day following these proceedings. By authority of his Gracious Majesty George Rex and Alan Napier, Viscount Kelsey, First Sea Lord. Signed, Philip Seymour, Senior Member.

During the last phrases of the reading, the crew, upon hearing the sentence, breaks out again, some stepping foward, shouting; they are in an ugly temper.

VOICES. No he don't!
Not if I know it!
Hang the jemmies instead, I say!
Not Billy, you bloody swineheads!   *All together.*
Not him, by Christ!
You ain't hanging Billy, damn your eyes!
Let them dance on a rope's end!

WYATT. Stand back! Sentries, guard your prisoner, if you have to fire!

GARDINER. Stand back, you damned clods! Keep back!

SEYMOUR [*steps forward*]. Silence there! You will resume discipline instantly! Be warned. [*Waits a silent moment. Men stop in disordered formation.*] Stand back into ranks.

GARDINER. Form up again, quick about it now! [*There is a surly movement into irregular lines.*]

SEYMOUR [*warily resuming procedure*]. Prisoner, have you anything to say? [BILLY *shakes his head.*] If you have nothing to say, when the drum roll is sounded, you will proceed to carry out the sentence of this court. [*Signals to* WYATT.] [86/87]

WYATT. Sound off!

Drum roll. BILLY *turns and starts up the ropes.*

VOICES. Get him! Now!
Bill! Stay where you are, boy, don't do it!
Wait, Billy! Wait!   } *All together.*
Rush the deck, mates! Don't let them do it!
We're here, Bill, don't you worry!

BILLY [*stops, turns forward, looks at* VERE, *and shouts out loud and clear, without trace of stammer*]. God bless Captain Vere!

A second's pause; VERE *is profoundly shaken;* BILLY *goes quickly up the ropes and out of sight. The crew moves back a step, is silent; officers and men in deep breathless quiet watch him out of sight and are staring overhead as the curtain falls.* [87]

Notes on the Play

LOUIS O. COXE AND ROBERT CHAPMAN

IT IS DIFFICULT NOW, IN RETROSPECT, TO DETERMINE HOW AND WHY WE arrived at a decision to make Melville's novel into a play. We had of course been familiar with the story for some time, and when in 1947 we actually began discussing the dramatic problems entailed in writing a play on the theme Melville gives us, we had only recently been very close to the novel. Perhaps the "Melville Revival" influenced us; it may have been the desire to find a theme and action that was inherently poetic and non-realistic. Above all, one idea or purpose seems clear: that we saw in *Billy Budd* a morality play.

From *Billy Budd* (New York: Hill and Wang, Inc., 1962), pp. 88–90. Reprinted by permission of Hill and Wang, Inc.

History and the literature of the past serve many functions for the present. Men like to think that they look at the past and its works objectively, with an evaluating eye, yet most of us know that any age seeks from the past justifications and flatteries; looks for ideas in a literature of another time and selects from them those that seem peculiarly pertinent to the seeker, whether the ideas found be actually *there* or not. Writers and critics have a way of reviving the dead with the purpose of forcing them to say certain things we wish they had said, or to reaffirm what they perhaps did say, though too often in accents and in a tone to which we do violence in our translation. But this is no evil, and surely it is a mark of greatness in a writer if his accents and tone are various enough to command the languages of various times and places. For us, as inchoate playwrights, in January of 1947, Melville's story of good, evil, and the way the world takes such absolutes was material enough for two veterans of a war, a depression, and the moving cold front.

Today morality is not popular; perhaps it has never really been so. In our day it is popularly lamented and celebrated in absentia, much modern criticism being devoted to the discovery of morality in the least likely places. Yet to find the stuff of dramatic morality pure is no easy task, since, however hard [88/89] one may try, Freud will turn up and all one's efforts will post off to the clinic and the analyst's couch to work out there a modern salvation. Thus a critic can say of our play that such a phenomenon as Claggart could never appear in our world with all we know of the psyche and the ego. We doubt that. We are certain that neither a Billy nor a Claggart ever was or could be, and, to undercut a little ground, we add that the same is true of an Oedipus. But all these personae are true as symbol, figuring as they do certain permanent attitudes, qualities, moral images. It is just this figuring forth that Melville's novel so preeminently effects for our time, and if we do indeed lament a lack of standards for this age we can at least see in *Billy Budd* the potentiality of a new vision, a vision that allows a man to think generally about absolutes without feeling he is violating "truth" because he has not polled a sample of his generation to get the "facts." The trouble is, Melville has stated a fact, but it is not the kind of fact men either like or know what to do with.

Perhaps all this has less to do than we think with how our play got written or even started. Once that start was made, however, we found ourselves bound by the novel, and it was only after some experimentation that we realized how little Melville had given us that was theatrical or, perhaps, finished. There was certainly little reason why he should; the drama is surely in the novel, but it is an inner, imagined drama. Our job was to put it on a stage and give flesh to the finely articulated skeleton—no small task in view of the deceptive nature of the novel. What seems to the casual reader mere padding in *Billy Budd* (the novel) is vital information—about the great mutinies, the

Napoleonic Wars, the British Navy, the moral and social climate. And Melville was assuming an audience of some culture (if at this stage he was able to assume an audience at all) which would know about the Rights of Man, the Terror, Rodney, and what manner of man Captain Vere is intended to represent. All this we had to show, to bring to life and to give to the audience [89/90] in such a way that the information might not arrive as information but as an ambience. We do not say that we have done this, only that it must be done if there is to be a real play. This is a morality play and we do not apologize for its being such.

The version presented here is that of the final Broadway production. The play in this form has passed through several stages. The original version, given by the Experimental Theatre in 1949, was in stricter poetic form and was more austere in tone and structure; much of it seemed to us too bald and expository. We have tried to thicken the texture of the play with much added dramatic incident, contrapuntal conflict, and realistic speech. There is, of course, some danger that we have fallen between two stools: what we have done may not entirely please either the average theatregoer or the Melville scholar. But for our part we have done! Our original faith in the novel remains and supports our faith in our own work. We will look far before we find another theme of equal interest or vitality. [90]

THE CRITICS

1. FIVE EARLY VIEWS

Sinners and Saints Alike

RAYMOND M. WEAVER (1921)

THE NOVEL, *Billy Budd,* IS BUILT AROUND THE CHARACTER OF JACK CHASE, the "Handsome Sailor." In the character of Billy Budd, Melville attempts to portray the native purity and nobility of the uncorrupted man. Melville spends elaborate pains in analysing "the mystery of iniquity," and in celebrating by contrast the god-like beauty of body and spirit of his hero. Billy Budd, by his heroic guilelessness is, like an angel of vengeance, precipitated into manslaughter; and for his very righteousness he is hanged. *Billy Budd,* finished within a few months before the end of Melville's life, would seem to teach that though the wages of sin is death, that sinners and saints alike toil for a common hire. In *Billy Budd* the orphic sententiousness is gone, it is true. But gone also is the brisk lucidity, the sparkle, the verve. Only the disillusion abided with him to the last. [381]

From R. M. Weaver, *Herman Melville, Mariner and Mystic,* Introduction by Mark Van Doren (New York: Pageant Books Inc., 1960), p. 381, by permission of the publisher. [Editor's title.]

The Inevitable Disaster of Good

JOHN MIDDLETON MURRY (1924)

WITH THE MERE FACT OF THE LONG SILENCE IN OUR MINDS WE COULD NOT help regarding "Billy Budd" as the last will and spiritual testament of a man of genius. We could not help expecting this, if we have any imaginative understanding. Of course, if we are content to dismiss in our minds, if not in our words, the man of genius as mad, there is no

From "Herman Melville's Silence," *Times Literary Supplement,* No. 1173 (July 10, 1924), p. 433, by permission of The Times Publishing Company Limited. All Rights Reserved. (C.) [Editor's title.]

need to trouble. Some one is sure to have told us that "Billy Budd," like "Pierre," is a tissue of naivety and extravagance: that will be enough. And, truly, "Billy Budd" is like "Pierre"—startlingly like. Once more Melville is telling the story of the inevitable and utter disaster of the good and trying to convey to us that this must be so and ought to be so—chronometrically and horologically. He is trying, as it were with his final breath, to reveal the knowledge that has been haunting him— that these things must be so and not otherwise.

Billy Budd is a foretopman, pressed out of the merchant service into the King's Navy in the year of the Nore mutiny. He is completely good, not with the sickly goodness of self-conscious morality, but as one born into earthly paradise—strong, young, manly, loyal, brave, unsuspecting, admired by his officers and adored by his shipmates. And he is hated by the master-at-arms, the policeman of the lower deck. Claggart hates him, simply because he is Billy Budd, with the instinctive hatred of the evil for the good. Melville is careful to explain that there is no reason whatever for his hatred; he puts it deliberately before us as naked and elemental—the clash of absolutes. Claggart is subtle and cool, he works quietly, and he is also a man of courage. He involves Billy Budd in the thin semblance of revolutionary mutiny. The master-at-arms deliberately risks his own life in order to destroy his enemy's. He risks it, and loses it, for in the privacy of his own cabin the captain confronts the accuser with his victim, and in a flash of anger Budd strikes the master-at-arms dead. The moment in the story is unearthly. But Billy is doomed: he has killed his officer in time of war. The captain who understands and loves him presides over the court-martial, and Budd is condemned to be hanged at dawn. . . . ["Billy Budd"] was Melville's final word, worthy of him, indisputably a passing beyond the nihilism of "Moby Dick" to what may seem to some simple and childish, but will be to others wonderful and divine. [433]

Innocence Vindicated

JOHN FREEMAN (1926)

LIKE *Moby-Dick* THIS LATE AND PURE SURVIVAL OF MELVILLE'S GENIUS has a double interest, the interest of story and the interest of psychology. *Billy Budd* is the narrative of one who, like Pierre, is unpracticed

From John Freeman, *Herman Melville* (New York: The Macmillan Co., 1926), pp. 131, 135–136, by permission of the publisher. [Editor's title.]

in the ways of life and the hates of other men; guilelessness is a kind of genius and the better part of innocence in this handsome young sailor. [131/135]

Exaltation of spirit redeems such a scene [as the hanging scene] from burdens which otherwise might appear too painful to be borne. And beyond this, it is innocence that is vindicated, more conspicuously in death than it could be in life. . . . The ultimate opposition is shown clearly . . . in this public vindication of the law, and the superior assertion at the very moment of death of the nobility of pure human spirit. *Moby-Dick* ends in darkness and desolation, for the challenge of Ahab's pride is rebuked by the physical power and the unhumanness of Nature; but *Billy Budd* ends in a brightness of escape, such as the apostle saw when he exclaimed, "Death, where is thy sting!"

Finished but a few months before the author's death and only lately published, *Billy Budd* shows the imaginative faculty still secure and powerful, after nearly forty years' supineness, and the not less striking security of Melville's inward peace. . . . In his last days he reenters an Eden-like sweetness and serenity . . . and sets his brief, appealing tragedy for witness that evil is defeat and natural goodness invincible in the [135/136] affections of man. In this, the simplest of stories, told with but little of the old digressive vexatiousness, and based upon recorded incidents, Herman Melville uttered his everlasting yea, and died before a soul had been allowed to hear him. [136]

Revelation or Illusion?

RAYMOND M. WEAVER (1928)

JUST AS SOME THEOLOGIANS HAVE PRESENTED THE FALL OF MAN AS EVIDENCE of the great glory of God, in similar manner Melville studies the evil in Claggart in vindication of the innocence of Billy Budd. For, primarily, Melville wrote *Billy Budd* in witness to his ultimate faith that evil is defeat and natural goodness invincible in the affections of man. *Billy Budd*, as *Pierre*, ends in disaster and death; in each case inexperience and innocent and seraphic impulse are wrecked against the malign forces of darkness that seem to preside [1/li] over external human destiny. In *Pierre*, Melville had hurled himself into a fury of vituperation against the world; with *Billy Budd* he would justify the ways of

From the Introduction to *Shorter Novels of Herman Melville* (New York: Liveright Publishing Corp., 1928), pp. l–li, by permission of Sidney A. Burrell. [Editor's title.]

God to man. Among the many parallels of contrast between these two books, each is a tragedy (as was Melville's life), but in opposed senses of the term. For tragedy may be viewed not as being essentially the representation of human misery, but rather as the representation of human goodness or nobility. All of the supremest art is tragic: but the tragedy is, in Aristotle's phrase, "the representation of Eudaimonia," or the highest kind of happiness. There is, of course, in this type of tragedy, with its essential quality of encouragement and triumph, no flinching of any horror of tragic life, no shirking of the truth by a feeble idealism, none of the compromises of the so-called "happy ending." The powers of evil and horror must be granted their fullest scope; it is only thus we can triumph over them. Even though in the end the tragic hero finds no friends among the living or dead, no help in God, only a deluge of calamity everywhere, yet in the very intensity of his affliction he may reveal the splendour undiscoverable in any gentler fate. Here he has reached, not the bottom, but the crowning peak of fortune—something which neither suffering nor misfortune can touch. Only when worldly disaster has worked its utmost can we realize that there remains something in man's soul which is for ever beyond the grasp of the accidents of existence, with power in its own right to make life beautiful. Only through tragedy of this type could Melville affirm his everlasting yea. The final great revelation—or great illusion—of his life, he uttered in *Billy Budd*. [li]

Melville's Final Affirmation

LEWIS MUMFORD (1929)

BILLY BUDD, HIS FINAL NOVEL, IS NOT A FULL-BODIED STORY: THERE IS statement, commentary, illustration, just statement, wise commentary, apt illustration: what is lacking is an independent and living creation. The epithets themselves lack body and colour: Billy Budd has nothing to compare with the description of boiling whale oil in Moby Dick—"a wild Hindoo odour, like the left wing of the Day of Judgement."

Billy Budd . . . lacks the fecundity and energy of White Jacket: the story itself takes place on the sea, but the sea itself is missing, and

From *Herman Melville* (New York: Harcourt, Brace & World, Inc., 1929), pp. 353–354, 356–357, by Lewis Mumford, copyright, 1929, by Harcourt, Brace & World, Inc.; renewed, 1957, by Lewis Mumford. Reprinted by permission of the publishers. [Editor's title.]

even the principal characters are not primarily men: they are actors and symbols. [353/354] The story gains something by this concentration, perhaps: it is stripped for action, and even Melville's deliberate digressions do not halt it. Each of the characters has a Platonic clarity of form. . . . [354/356]

Billy Budd is the story of three men in the British Navy; it is also the story of the world, the spirit, and the devil. Melville left a note, crossed out in the original manuscript, "Here ends a story not unwarranted by what happens in this incongruous world of ours—innocence and infirmity, spiritual depravity and fair respite." The meaning is so obvious that one shrinks from underlining it. Good and evil exist in the nature of things, each forever itself, each doomed to waı with the other. In the working out of human institutions, evil has a place as well as the good: Vere is contemptuous of Claggart, but cannot do without him: he loves Budd as a son and must condemn him to the noose: justice dictates an act abhorrent to his nature, and only his inner magnanimity keeps it from being revolting. These are the fundamental ambiguities of life: so long as evil exists, the agents that intercept it will also be evil, whilst we accept the world's conditions: the universal articles of war on which our civilizations rest. Rascality may be punished; but beauty and innocence will suffer in that process far more. There is no comfort, in the perpetual Calvary [356/357] of the spirit, to find a thief nailed on either side. Melville had been harried by these paradoxes in Pierre. At last he was reconciled. He accepted the situation as a tragic necessity; and to meet that tragedy bravely was to find peace, the ultimate peace of resignation, even in an incongruous world. As Melville's own end approached, he cried out with Billy Budd: God Bless Captain Vere! In this final affirmation Herman Melville died. . . . [357]

2. *BILLY BUDD* AS TESTAMENT

Melville's Testament of Acceptance

E. L. GRANT WATSON

THE STYLE OF THIS PRODUCT OF MELVILLE'S LAST YEARS IS STRIKINGLY DIF-
ferent from the exuberant and highly-colored prose of that great
period of more ardent creation (1850–1852) which produced *Mardi,
Moby-Dick,* and *Pierre.* Though it lacks that fine extravagance of the
earlier books, which laid on the color with prodigality, *Billy Budd* is as
rich, or even richer, in Melville's peculiar and elaborate symbolism;
and this symbolism becomes all the more effective for being presented
in a dry and objective manner. The fine flourishes, the purple patches,
which scintillate brilliantly in *Moby-Dick,* and the deep sombre melancholy of *Pierre* are not here. The grandiloquence of youth which
tempted Stevenson's very partial appreciation is here transformed into
the dignity of an achieved detachment. The story develops simply,
always unhurried, yet never lagging. Each character is described with
the patience which the complex intention of the theme demands—the
color of the eyes, the clothes, the complexion, the color of the skin, of
the blood under the skin, the past, the present—these are hints at a
deep and [319/320] solemn purpose, one no less ambitious than to
portray those ambiguities of good and evil as the mutually dependent
opposites, between which the world of realization finds its being.

The title *Billy Budd* is not without significance, and would strike
some readers in its crude simplicity as proof that Melville was lacking
in a sense of humor. How could any man, they would argue, write a
tragedy and call it *Billy Budd?* But a sense of humor, like almost
everything else, is relative. Melville certainly lacked it in the crude
form; but he was always conscious of those occasions when he might
seem, to a superficial view, to be wanting it. He is particularly
conscious of the obvious, but not in the obvious manner; and when he
uses such a name as Billy Budd to set as the hub round which his own
philosophy of life must revolve, he does so consciously, choosing the
obvious to carry the transcendental. "I have ever found the plain
things, the knottiest of all," he has written; and so he has made the
simple man, the every-day Billy, the handsome sailor, the hero of a

From *The New England Quarterly,* VI (June 1933), 319–327, by permission
of the publisher.

tragedy. Humor is appreciated most easily when larger things contract suddenly to smaller things—as when a man slips on a piece of orange-peel, thus converting his intention of going about his business to the abrupt act of falling on his back-side. Yet a more imaginative intelligence might, with a sense of humor just as true, see in the fall, the destiny of man, with full chorus of pities and ironic spirits. The easy contraction will seem to the sophisticated too facile to provoke a smile, a larger humor is found in the reverse process, namely in a filling in, in an exaggeration from the particular to the [320/321] general. With such an added pinch of imagination, the obvious thing becomes the centre of mystery. And so, with a sense of humor which perceived both the obvious and the peculiar quality of the name, Melville deliberately chose "Billy Budd." Moreover, he made the hero of this, his gospel story (as it might well be called), a foundling of uncertain parentage, whose "entire family was practically invested in himself."

It is a mistake for critics to try to tell stories which authors must have told better in their texts. The critic's function is rather to hint at what lies beneath—hidden, sometimes, under the surface. Melville called his story "an inside narrative," and though it deals with events stirring and exciting enough in themselves, it is yet more exciting because it deals with the relation of those principles which constitute life itself. A simple-mindedness unaffected by the shadow of a doubt, a divine innocence and courage, which might suggest a Christ not yet conscious of His divinity, and a malice which has lost itself in the unconscious depths of mania—the very mystery of iniquity—these opposites here meet, and find their destiny. But Melville's theme is even larger. All the grim setting of the world is in the battleship *Indomitable;* war and threatened mutiny are the conditions of her existence. Injustice and inhumanity are implicit, yet Captain Vere, her commander, is the man who obeys the law, and yet understands the truth of the spirit. It is significant of Melville's development since the writing of *Moby-Dick* and *Pierre,* that he should create this naval captain—wholly pledged to the unnaturalness of the law, but sufficiently touched, at the same time, by the divine difference from ordinary sanity [321/322] (he goes by the nick-name of "Starry Vere"), as to live the truth *within* the law, and yet, in the cruel process of that very obedience, to redeem an innocent man from the bitterness of death imposed by the same law. A very different ending this from the despairing acts of dissolution which mar the conclusions of the three earlier books: *Mardi, Moby-Dick,* and *Pierre.*

Melville is no longer a rebel. It should be noted that Billy Budd has not, even under the severest provocation, any element of rebellion in him; he is too free a soul to need a quality which is a virtue only in slaves. His nature spontaneously accepts whatever may befall. When impressed from the merchant-ship, the *Rights of Man,* he makes no demur to the visiting lieutenant's order to get ready his things for trans-shipment. The crew of the merchant-ship are surprised and reproachful at his uncomplaining acquiescence. Once aboard the battleship, the young sailor begins to look around for the advantages of chance and adventure. Such simple power to accept gives him the buoyancy to override troubles and irritations which would check inferior natures.

Yet his complete unconsciousness of the attraction, and consequent repulsion, that his youthful beauty and unsophisticated good-fellowship exercise on Claggart, makes it only easier for these qualities to turn envy into hatred. His very virtue makes him the target for the shaft of evil, and his quality of acceptance provokes to action its complementary opposite, the sense of frustration that can not bear the consciousness of itself, and so has to find escape in mania. Thus there develops the conflict between unconscious virtue (not even aware of [322/323] its loss of Eden and unsuspecting of the presence of evil) and the bitter perversion of love which finds its only solace in destruction.

And not only Billy Budd is marked by this supreme quality of acceptance. Captain Vere, also, possesses it, but with full consciousness, and weighted with the responsibility of understanding the natural naturalness of man's volition and the unnatural naturalness of the law. . . . In Captain Vere we find a figure which may interestingly be compared to Pontius Pilate. Like Pilate, he condemns the just man to a shameful death, knowing him to be innocent, but, unlike Pilate, he does not wash his hands, but manfully assumes the full responsibility, and in such a way as to take the half, if not more than the half, of the bitterness of the execution upon himself. We are given to suppose that there is an affinity, a [323/324] spiritual understanding between Captain Vere and Billy Budd, and it is even suggested that in their partial and separate existence they contribute two essential portions of that larger spirit which is man. . . . There are darker hints: those deep, far-away things in Vere, those occasional flashings-forth of intuition—short, quick probings to the very axis of reality. Though the book be read many times, the student may still remain baffled by Melville's significant arrangement of images. The story is so solidly filled out as to suggest dimensions in all directions. As soon as the mind fastens upon one subject, others flash into being.

Melville reported in *Pierre* how he fished his line into the deep sea of childhood, and there, as surely as any modern psychoanalyst, discovered all the major complexes that have since received baptism at the hands of Freudians. He peered as deep as any into the origins of sensuality, and in conscious understanding he was the equal of any modern psychologist; in poetic divination he has the advantage of most. No doubt the stresses of his own inner life demanded this exceptional awareness. In this book of his old age, the images which he chose for the presentation of his final wisdom, move between the antinomies of love and hate, of innocence and malice. From behind— from far behind the main pageant of the story—there seem to fall suggestive shadows of primal, sexual simplicities. In so conscious a symbolist as Melville, it would be surprising if there should be no meaning or half-meaning in the spilling of Billy's soup towards the homosexually-disposed [324/325] Claggart, in the impotence of Billy's speech in the presence of his accuser, in his swift and deadly answer, or the likening of Claggart's limp, dead body to that of a snake.

It is possible that such incidents might be taken as indications of some unresolved problem in the writer himself. This may be, but when we remember how far Melville had got in the process of self-analysis in *Pierre*, and when we have glanced at the further analysis that is obvious in the long narrative poem *Clarel*, it seems likely that this final book, written nearly forty years after *Pierre*, should contain a further, deeper wisdom. And as the philosophy in it has grown from that of rebellion to that of acceptance, as the symbolic figures of unconscious forces· have become always more concrete and objective, so we may assume that these hints are intentional, and that Melville was particularly conscious of what he was doing.

But let no one suppose that he would ever pin an image to his scale of value, as an entomologist would pin an insect to his board; there is always in his interpretation a wide spaciousness. He lifts some familiar object, holding it to his light, that it may glow and illumine some portion of what must always remain vast and unknown. For his suggestive use of words, and the special values he gives them, and the large implication he can in this way compress into a sentence, the passage which tells how Billy Budd was hanged from the main yardarm of the battle-ship *Indomitable* is a good example: [Last part of Chapter 26.] [325/326] Here is Melville at his very best, at his deepest, most poetic, and therefore at his most concentrated, most conscious. Every image has its significant implication: the very roll of the heavily-cannoned ship so majestic in moderate weather—the musket in the ship-armourer's rack; and Billy's last words are the triumphant seal of [326/327] his acceptance, and they are more than that, for in this supreme passage a communion between personality at its purest, most God-given form, and character, hard-hammered from the imperfect material of life on the battleship *Indomitable*, is here suggested, and one feels that the souls of Captain Vere and Billy are at that moment strangely one.

In this short history of the impressment and hanging of a handsome sailor-boy, are to be discovered problems almost as profound as those which puzzle us in the pages of the Gospels. *Billy Budd* is a book to be read many times, for at each reading it will light up, as do the greater experiences of life, a beyond leading always into the unknown. [327]

Billy Budd: Testament of Resistance

PHIL WITHIM

WHEN E. L. G. WATSON WROTE HIS FAMOUS ARTICLE, "MELVILLE'S TESTA-ment of Acceptance," he made no attempt to prove his view. All he attempted, all he achieved, was to suggest a way of looking at the story. "Melville," said Watson, "is no longer a rebel." He has come to accept the presence of evil, and he has ceased to blame God for its existence. Other critics began to write on *Billy Budd* in the same vein. Their positions varied somewhat, but the tenor, the direction of the viewpoint was always the same: Melville had mellowed, he was resigned, as Freeman says, to the recognition of necessity.[1] In F. O. Matthiessen's words, "He has come to respect necessity. . . . Melville could now face incongruity; he could accept the existence of both good and evil. . . ." Or as Willard Thorp remarks, "In the end Melville called the truce."

There was, however, some dissent; both Alfred Kazin and Richard Chase indicated dissatisfaction with the "testament of acceptance" theory. In 1950 Joseph Schiffman, in an article which reviewed all these interpretations as well as those of Mumford, Weir, and Sedgwick, put forth a suggestion, which he credited to Gay Wilson Allen, "that *Billy Budd* might best be understood as a work of irony." Since this article appeared, a number of other critics have also objected to the "testament of acceptance" theory or have supported an ironic interpre-tation; sometimes they have done both.

This paper is another step in this same direction. It accepts the point of view that *Billy Budd* was written in a basically ironic style: it will attempt to establish a thesis in harmony with all of the parts of [115/116] the story and to demonstrate that the "testament of accept-ance" theory is essentially self-contradictory.

The body of the story is concerned with the relationships of three men: Billy Budd, John Claggart, and Captain Vere. Whatever argu-ments may rage concerning other elements of the story, there is general agreement as to the character and significance of Billy Budd

[1] F. Barron Freeman, ed., *Melville's Billy Budd* (Cambridge, 1948), p. 115. All page references to *Billy Budd* are from this edition and will be inserted in parentheses directly following the quotations.

From *Modern Language Quarterly,* XX (June 1959), 115–127, by permission of publisher and author.

and John Claggart. Billy Budd is the Handsome Sailor uniting "strength and beauty," whose moral nature is not "out of keeping with the physical make" (p. 135). Claggart is Billy's reverse. He is pale and unhealthy looking; his visage seems to hint of something defective or abnormal in the constitution and blood. This contrasts with the conjunction in Billy of beauty and goodness. Claggart had an "evil nature, not engendered by vicious training or corrupting books or licentious living, but born with him and innate, in short 'a depravity according to nature'" (p. 187).

Melville is explicit about his desire to have Billy and Claggart taken as types of good and bad, and this, I think, is the chief argument against those who, like Matthiessen and Freeman, consider homosexualism an aspect of the problem. For if Melville had desired to hint at homosexualism, he would not have denied its possibility; when speaking of Claggart's peculiar nature, he says, "In short the depravity here meant partakes nothing of the sordid or sensual" (p. 186). And speaking of Billy, he says he was "preëminently the Handsome Sailor" (p. 192) who, as Melville has told us in the opening pages of the book, typifies strength united to beauty. In those descriptions of Billy emphasizing his delicate color and the fine detail of his features, the point is to impress us with his purity, his aristocratic heritage, not his femininity. Melville takes care to remind the reader that Billy had thrashed the bully, Red Whiskers (p. 139).

But it is around the third figure, Captain Vere, that the greatest disagreement has arisen. This suggests that a detailed examination of his character and function is essential to any understanding of the novel. He is described as apparently the best type of British naval man:

always acquitting himself as an officer mindful of the welfare of his men, but never tolerating an infraction of discipline; thoroughly versed in the science of his profession, and intrepid to the verge of temerity, though never injudiciously so. (p. 160)

He loves to read, particularly those books "treating of actual men and events no matter of what era—history, biography and unconventional writers, who, free from cant and convention, like Montaigne, honestly, and in the spirit of common sense philosophize upon realities" (pp. 163–64). In the reading he found

confirmation of his own more reserved thoughts—confirmation which he had vainly sought in social converse, so that as touching most fundamental topics, there had got to be established in him some positive convictions which he forefelt would abide in him essentially unmodified so long as his intelligent part remained unimpaired. (p. 164) [116/117]

This particular sentence creates a question as to Melville's meaning. Does he suggest here that the only result of Vere's reading is that his mind becomes more and more firmly fixed on his earliest opinions, that no author can ever modify them, either because he will not let their ideas penetrate or because he never reads books that do not agree with him; or does Melville imply that Vere's opinions are instinctively right and that all the books in Vere's library, "compact, but of the best" (p. 163) agree with him unfailingly? But it is as yet too early to decide. Melville continues to describe Vere as one whose "settled convictions were as a dyke against those invading waters of novel opinion social political and otherwise" (p. 164) and as one who opposed these novel opinions because they seemed to him not only "incapable of embodiment in lasting institutions, but at war with the peace of the world and the true welfare of mankind" (p. 164). This last phrase sounds suspiciously like cant, like sarcasm. Vere's reasons here are such terribly stock arguments that it is hard to accept them at face value.

The possibility arises that the reader is expected to understand that Vere's reasoning is presented without comment because it is simply and transparently a rationalization of an uninformed and bigoted man who reads only those authors who reinforce his views. But if this possibility is to be accepted as fact, the reader must find other implied criticism of Vere, and, indeed, it does not take much searching. Melville, for example, goes to the trouble of devoting several pages to Nelson, the greatest of English captains,[2] pointing out with approval that Nelson challenged death by his brilliant apparel.

Personal prudence even when dictated by quite other than selfish consideration is surely no special virtue in a military man; while an excessive love of glory, impassioning a less burning impulse the honest sense of duty, is the first. (p. 157)

Nelson, of course, dies a soldier's death, while Vere dies drugged and ashore before ever reaching fame. Nelson is a fighter in direct contact with the enemy; but Vere, in the encounter described in *Billy Budd*, does not have an opportunity to catch the opposing ship. Vere is

[2] Wendell Glick, in his article "Expediency and Absolute Morality in *Billy Budd*," *PMLA*, LXVIII (1953), 103–10, devotes much attention to the Nelson episode, equating Nelson not with Vere but with Billy, and discovers both to be heroic. This may be true, although the differences in station, occasion, and motivation seem to be unsurmountable obstacles to such an interpretation. On the other hand, it seems natural to compare Nelson with Vere: both are captains of ships in time of war, both are asked to deal with mutiny. An additional difficulty with Glick's article lies in the fact that his defense is built on the following unsupported statement: "[Melville] agreed with the Captain that justice to the individual is not the ultimate loyalty in a complex culture; the stability of the culture has the higher claim, and when the two conflict, justice to the individual must be abrogated to keep the order of society intact" (p. 104). Since this is exactly the point in question, so far as any interpretation of the meaning of *Billy Budd* is concerned, it seems facile to present it as axiomatic.

frequently used for diplomatic missions, the very opposite of a captain's usual job; Vere, says Melville, though a man of "sturdy qualities was without brilliant ones" (p. 162). Nelson is asked to take command [117/118] of a ship recently involved in the Great Mutiny, for "it was thought that an officer like Nelson was the one, *not indeed to terrorize the crew into base subjection,* but to win them, by force of his mere presence back to an allegiance if not as enthusiastic as his own, yet as true" (p. 159; italics mine). Vere, in a similar situation, hangs Billy, "thinking perhaps that under existing circumstances in the navy the consequence of violating discipline should be made to speak for itself" (p. 254).

It is clear that this comparison is not favorable to Captain Vere, and if we look back to earlier descriptions, we find that they apparently contain an implied criticism: "ever mindful of the welfare of his men, but never tolerating an infraction of discipline"; "intrepid to the verge of temerity, though never injudiciously so." The second half of each statement could merely qualify the virtue mentioned in the first half, or it could cancel the virtue completely.[3]

After Claggart accuses Billy of projected mutiny, Vere decides to confront the two men with each other in his cabin. There Billy, infuriated by the charge, confused and frustrated by his stammer, strikes Claggart dead. Apparently Vere's purpose in bringing them together is to find out the truth.[4] But how does he expect the interview

[3] Cf. James E. Miller, Jr., *"Billy Budd:* The Catastrophe of Innocence," *MLN,* LXXIII (1958), 168–76. Miller uses the quotations I have just cited to demonstrate the opposite of my point, namely, that Vere, as opposed to both Billy (all heart) and Claggart (all mind), "is the man of moderation with heart and intellect in ideal balance," who recognizes the "wide and necessary separation of heavenly wisdom and earthly wisdom and the 'impossibility' of the application of the one in the province of the other." In this interpretation Vere becomes a "Hero of Humanity" who shields society from the cataclysmic consequences of Billy's "nakedly spontaneous and raw innocence."

Apparently Miller does not take the quotations in question ironically, whereas I do. But how does one know when to read any line ironically? The answer, I suppose, must be: when such a reading is suggested by and found to be consistent with the total context. In this article, I have tried to submit my own reading to such a test, but I do not find that Miller has. Rather, pretty much abandoning *Billy Budd,* he retreats to *Pierre,* to the Plinlimmon pamphlet, to its famous distinction between heavenly and earthly truth and to its call for a "virtuous expediency." Unfortunately, this pamphlet is not the clearest of Melville's work, and in Willard Thorp's words, "the critics will argue its significance perpetually."

It would seem, therefore, an invalid critical procedure to attempt to explain the uncertain meanings of *Billy Budd* by an appeal to the uncertain meanings of *Pierre.* Even if Melville's intentions, ironic or otherwise, in *Pierre* were crystal clear, which they are not, there is no guarantee that *Billy Budd* embodies them, forty years later.

[4] This point is taken from Lawrance Thompson's *Melville's Quarrel with God* (Princeton, 1952), a book which has been widely and deservedly criticized as totaling somewhat less than the sum of its parts; yet many of those parts are valuable for their detailed analyses and suggestive insights.

to accomplish this? Claggart would have accused, and Billy would have denied. There seems to be no relevant reason for Vere's decision. Claggart had suggested that there was substantiating evidence not far away, but Vere had not sent for it, since he wished to keep the affair secret because he was afraid of the crew. In short, Vere's decision is based on the single element of prudence, and he ignores all other [118/119] elements inherent in the situation. Now Claggart is dead. As Vere looks on, he cries, " 'Struck dead by an angel of God. Yet the Angel must hang' " (p. 229). Vere must have acute perception, indeed, to see so quickly to the heart of so complex a situation. He realizes instantly that there is no alternative to Billy's death.

Vere calls a court-martial, reserving, however, "to himself as the one on whom the ultimate accountability would rest, the right of maintaining a supervision of it, or formally or informally interposing at need" (p. 236). During the trial the members of the court seem reluctant to hang Billy, and the Captain has to talk them into it. But it is hard to understand why Vere called the court at all. What purpose does it serve? Was it called to guide him to a right decision? But Vere had already made his decision. In any case the court did not guide him; he guided the court. Perhaps he thought the court would overrule him and free the boy. But Vere had reserved for himself the right of supervising and interfering at need. Apparently all Vere wants is to have on record a trial agreeing with his decision.

Vere begins his argument (pp. 224-48) by saying that he would not interfere with their deliberations, but that he sees them at a crisis proceeding " 'from the clashing of military duty with moral scruple.' " He advises them to " 'strive against scruples that may tend to enervate decision.' " When the men look startled, he explains thus:

"How can we adjudge to summary and shameful death a fellow-creature innocent before God, and whom we feel to be so?—Does that state it aright? You sign sad assent. Well, I too feel that, the full force of that. It is Nature. But do these buttons that we wear attest that our allegiance is to Nature? No, to the King."

This is the main basis of his argument: we do not serve nature but the king.

"We fight at command. If our judgments approve the war, that is but coincidence. So in other particulars. . . . Would it be so much we ourselves that would condemn as it would be martial law operating through us? For that law and the rigor of it, we are not responsible. Our vowed responsibility is in this: That however pitilessly that law may operate, we nevertheless adhere to it and administer it."

The officer of marines points out that Budd "proposed neither mutiny nor homicide." Vere agrees with him, saying that, after all, " 'At the Last Assizes it shall acquit,' " but **not** now. " 'War looks but to the frontage, the appearance. And the Mutiny Act, War's child, takes after the father. Budd's intent or non-intent is nothing to the purpose.'"

No one at any time questions his argument. No one suggests that the king's law should be in harmony with nature's law, or that if there is disagreement between them, the allegiance must be to the higher and the more universal law of nature. No one asks Vere to support his peculiar thesis; it is merely slipped in, so to speak, with the analogy of the buttons: because the men wear the king's buttons, they [119/120] are to violate natural laws. Even though Vere has admitted that the Mutiny Act looks only to frontage, to the appearance, no one suggests that the point of justice is to see through appearance to reality. But the reason that no one questions Vere's arguments is that no one understands them. "Loyal lieges, plain and practical . . . they were without the faculty, hardly had the inclination to gainsay one whom they felt to be an earnest man, one too not less their superior in mind than in naval rank" (pp. 248–49).

Vere, however, soon gives them an argument they can understand, for when the junior lieutenant asks why, if they must convict, they cannot mitigate the sentence, Vere replies that they cannot because the crew " 'will ruminate. You know what sailors are. Will they not revert to the recent outbreak at the Nore. . . . Your clement sentence they would account pusillanimous. They would think that we flinch, that we are afraid of them.' " And this is the only argument the court really understands, for, as Melville says, "it is not improbable that even such of his words as were not without influence over them, less came home to them than his closing appeal to their instincts as sea-officers. . . ." So for all the finely spun thought, the issue is decided by fear. When subtle arguments fail, Vere calls on, not a rational argument, but an emotional one: an appeal to fear.

Another clue to Vere's thinking comes after Billy has been hanged. The men are put to work at various tasks; they are swept into the routine as fast as possible. Melville writes of this:

"With mankind" he would say "forms, measured forms are everything; and that is the import couched in the story of Orpheus with his lyre spellbinding the wild denizens of the woods." And this [Vere] once applied to the disruption of forms going on across the Channel and the consequences thereof. (p. 272)

Stripped of verbiage, Vere is saying that men cannot think for themselves, that form and habit can control men as if they were no more than beasts. Vere, in an earlier passage, had thought to himself that Billy was a " '*King's bargain*,' that is to say, for His Britannic Majesty's navy a capital investment at small outlay or none at all" (p. 220). In this light, Vere, far from being a wise man, balanced in his judgments and fair in his attitudes, is discovered to be narrow, literal, prejudiced, completely circumscribed by the needs of the navy, less compassionate than his officers, and lastly, guilty of that worst of naval sins, over-prudence.

The core of Vere's argument is that we must bow to necessity; " 'For that law and the rigor of it, we are not responsible. Our vowed responsibility is in this: That however pitilessly that law may operate, we nevertheless adhere to it and administer it' " (pp. 245–46). A logical extension of this argument is that man should abdicate responsibility for unjust law and enforce it mechanically. Man should not try to change that which is wrong, but merely accept injustice and tyranny and lie supinely beneath them; man is to stand by and watch [120/121] the innocent as indiscriminately ground under the heel of unresisted law as are the evil.

Melville makes his opposition to this view clear by dedicating the book to Jack Chase, his companion years before on the frigate *United States*. It was this voyage that became the story of *White-Jacket*, the novel that cried out so eloquently against impressment, flogging, the captain's tyranny. Jack Chase is here mentioned by name and is referred to as "a stickler for the Rights of Man and the liberties of the world." It would be ironic indeed to dedicate *Billy Budd* to such a man if the novel was devoted to submission. However, the preface (pp. 131–32) helps to make clear the direction of the book. In it, Melville speaks of the French Revolution as an expression of "the Spirit of that Age [which] involved the rectification of the Old World's hereditary wrongs." He points out that, although the revolution had in its turn become an oppressor, the outcome was "a political advance along nearly the whole line for Europeans," and he concludes by saying,

in a way analogous to the operation of the Revolution at large the Great Mutiny, though by Englishmen naturally deemed monstrous at the time, doubtless gave the first latent prompting to most important reforms in the British Navy.

In short, tyranny can be successfully resisted.

We can now be sure of the direction of the theme of *Billy Budd*. In local context it suggests that it is wrong to submit to unjust law. Those in power, such as Vere, should do all they can to resist the evil inherent in any institution or government. All men are flawed, but not all men are depraved; and we must not let those institutions designed to control the evil destroy the good. In a larger context, man should not resign himself to the presence of evil but must always strive against it. It is possible to check the validity of this view by making sure that the various incidents, descriptions, and points reinforce it, and that they also contradict the "testament of acceptance" theory.

Observe that Vere dies drugged and on shore before he has "attained to the fullness of fame" (p. 275). In other words, Vere's end is suitable to one who did not deserve such renown as the daring and imprudent Nelson, a man capable, as Vere is not, of inspiring his men to loyalty, of substituting persuasion for coercion.

Observe that Claggart is characterized as civilized and intellectual:

the man's even temper and discreet bearing would seem to intimate a mind peculiarly subject to the law of reason, not the less in his heart he would seem to riot in complete exemption from that law having apparently little to do with reason further than to employ it as an ambidexter implement for effecting the irrational. (p. 186)

But such men, continues Melville,

are true madmen, and of the most dangerous sort, for their lunacy is not continuous [121/122] but occasional [,] evoked by some special object; it is probably secretive which is as much to say it is self contained, so that when moreover, most active it is to the average mind not distinguishable from sanity. . . . (p. 187)

This material comes into sharper focus when considered in relationship to Vere. He, like Claggart, is civilized; he, like Claggart, is intellectual; and he, like Claggart, uses reason to a bad end. Melville had suggested that Claggart was mad, and yet in Chapter 21, the surgeon, after seeing Claggart's body and hearing Vere say that the boy must hang, cannot banish this treasonable thought: "Was Captain Vere suddenly affected in his mind . . .? Was he unhinged?" (p. 231). The surgeon reports, as instructed by Vere, to the lieutenants and the captain of the marines. "They fully stared at him in surprise and concern. Like him they seemed to think that such a matter should be reported to the Admiral" (p. 232). Melville pushes further; in the next chapter he says,

Who in the rainbow can draw the line where the violet tint ends and the orange tint begins? . . . So with sanity and insanity. . . . Whether Captain Vere, as the Surgeon professionally and primarily surmised, was really the sudden victim of any degree of aberration, one must determine for himself by such light as this narrative can afford. (p. 233)

Observe that Billy was removed from a ship called the *Rights of Man* by a lieutenant named Ratcliffe.

Observe that, although Vere was "solicitous of his men's welfare," yet the day after Billy was impressed, the captain flogged "a little fellow, young, a novice an after-guardsman absent from his assigned post when the ship was being put about . . ." (p. 174). It is useful to remember here that, when Melville was a novice, he was almost flogged for the same reason, but was saved by the interference of Jack Chase.

Observe that white is not used to portray innocence, as Matthiessen suggests; on the contrary, it is used as Melville had used it in

Moby-Dick: to imply terror and possibly evil. For example, Claggart is described as pale in visage; Billy, when accused of treachery, appears "struck as by white leprosy" (p. 225); the young man who tries to persuade Billy to join a mutiny had "glassy eyes of pale blue, veiled with lashes all but white" (p. 202); Claggart's voice is silvery and low; the whistles used to pipe the men to witness the punishment of Billy are silver whistles; the moon that shines at midnight as Vere tells the men about Billy's sentence silvers the white spar-deck (p. 254) as, in the ballad also, it silvers the bay where Billy lies shackled, awaiting death. In this light the whiteness of Billy's clothes may not be a sign of his purity but of the evil which is successfully destroying him; and the "circumambient air in the clearness of its serenity . . . like smooth white marble" (p. 273), which surrounds him as he hangs from the yardarm, may be more concerned with all-conquering evil than with submissive purity. [122/123]

Observe that Vere appears at the court-martial as the sole witness, "and as such temporarily sinking his rank, though singularly maintaining it in a matter apparently trivial, namely, that he testified from the ship's weather-side with that object having caused the court to sit on the lee-side" (p. 238). Vere thus chooses the side which puts him literally and metaphorically above the court and gives him, in the slang meaning of the term, the advantage.

Vere, when preparing to address the court, that is, to persuade it to his opinion, paces the cabin,

in the returning ascent to windward, climbing the slant deck in the ship's lee roll; without knowing it symbolizing thus in his action a mind resolute to surmount difficulties even if against primitive instincts strong as the wind and the sea. (p. 243)

But Melville has suggested already that the instincts of the untutored barbarian are sounder than the civilized intellect.

Observe that this is corroborated in the very next paragraph. "When speak he did, something both in the substance of what he said and his manner of saying it, showed the influence of unshared studies modifying and tempering the practical training of an active career" (p. 243). But practicality is exactly what is called for. Vere never refers to these qualities, preferring instead to weave a complex skein of thought which none of his court, though thoroughly competent, can follow.

Even the governing circumstance of the entire story, namely, the recent mutinies and the consequent peril hovering over the fleet, does not go unchallenged by Melville. For at the conclusion of Vere's speech, just after his appeal to the fear of a new revolt, Melville describes the court's frame of mind as akin to that

which in the year 1842 actuated the commander of the U.S. brig-of-war *Somers* to resolve, under the so-called Articles of War, Articles modelled upon the English Mutiny Act, to resolve upon the execution at sea of a midshipman and two petty-officers as mutineers designing the seizure of the brig. Which resolution was carried out though in a time of peace and within not many days sail of home. An act vindicated by a naval court of inquiry subsequently convened ashore. History, and here cited without comment. True, the circumstances on board the *Somers* were different from those on board the *Indomitable*. But the urgency felt, well-warranted or otherwise, was much the same. (p. 249)

Thus, Melville introduces a case whose justice had been considered extremely dubious and which, after forty years, was still being debated in the papers. Melville does not stop here; the last two [123/124] sentences state that the circumstances are not the same, and that perhaps the need for swift action on the *Indomitable* is urgent and perhaps it is not. Thus even the circumstance responsible for Vere's basic motive is undermined.

It should be pointed out that the adherents of the "testament of acceptance" theory have to deal not only with the unsuitability of Captain Vere as a spokesman for Melville, but they also have to explain away the presence of a number of contradictions which arise in the story solely as a result of their position. For example, if the story concerns the acceptance of necessary evil, then why does Melville continue beyond the death of Billy, where, and only where, an emotional equilibrium favorable to such an acceptance is attained? Vere's untimely death would be a poor reward for so faithful a servant and in the "acceptance" context would be meaningless, for the point is made and the tale ended with Billy's death. Only an ironical reversing of the point would justify continuation of the story.

It is even possible to bring into question the tone of the hanging scene. Joseph Schiffman, B. R. McElderry, and Harry Campbell have each noted contradictions in this scene that arise only if the story is interpreted as an "acceptance." Schiffman points out that, even though the crew echoes Billy's cry, "God bless Captain Vere," they are not thinking of the captain, for, in Melville's words, "yet at that instant Billy alone must have been in their hearts, even as he was in their eyes" (p. 265).

B. R. McElderry demonstrates that Billy's cry is not unprecedented in the literature of the sea; he cites two plays and a novel by Marryat which have similar scenes. Thus Billy's cry is

what Melville said it was: "a conventional felon's benediction directed aft towards the quarters of honor . . ." It is the traditional ritual of the condemned man forgiving the official who is duty bound to order his death.

If this episode is taken ironically, then it fits the rest of the story as so far interpreted and acquires tremendous power. For Billy is willing to die as Isaac or as Christ was willing; he accepts all the captain's arguments, but it is Billy alone who is noble. The captain suffers and wishes he could avoid this duty, but he has no nobility and above all no trust in man. Yet Billy's very acceptance of his role is the evidence that proves man can be trusted, that man can rise above the need for forms.

Harry Campbell has ,analyzed the hanging scene and perceives therein an attempt on Melville's part to strike a balance between the sacrificial religious aspect and the aspect of the scene as sheer injustice, as an execution. For example, Melville says that "Billy ascended; [124/125] and ascending, took the full rose of the dawn." But he ascends only to the yardarm, where he remains a pinioned figure. Campbell also notes that the reading of the early *Baby Budd, Sailor* for "rosy dawn" was the powerful religious term "shekinah" (p. 339) and that the "silence accompanying the ascension" (p. 340) later becomes "The silence at the moment of execution" (p. 269). This last change, particularly, suggests that Melville wants us to realize that Billy's death, though noble, is still unjust. If Vere had had such nobility and strength, Billy need not have died. As Kark Zink has said, "The lesson is not that Billy learns to accept the necessary harshness of the forms, but that in their high impersonality there is a dangerous lack of discrimination—dangerous to the individual and to the social structure itself."

Another contradiction inherent in the "acceptance" theory lies in Melville's argument that barbarians with their instincts and warm hearts have sounder values than civilized men with their intricate intellects and their rabied hearts. Would it not be contradictory for Melville to suggest this not once, but twice, and then have Vere, Melville's foremost spokesman, weave a complex intellectual argument? Would it not be contradictory for Melville to have Billy die bravely, crying "God bless Captain Vere," and then have Vere say directly that mankind is a denizen of the forest and must be controlled by form and routine?

Would it not be contradictory, in the "testament of acceptance" framework, for Melville to use for the captain's name a word which at first glance suggests *veritas* "truth," but on second glance can as easily suggest *veritus* "fear," or on third glance, *vir* "man"?

Would it not be contradictory for him to use as symbols of evil flogging, impressment, arbitrary hanging, when these evils had been corrected by the time that he wrote this story, partly through his own writing?

Would it not be contradictory for Melville to use Vere as a symbol of the proper recognition of necessary evil: a man who had opposed the French Revolution and all its new social and political doctrines which since have changed the globe and reduced tyranny, injustice, poverty, and disease? Might it not be argued that, since Vere was wrong in his judgment of these attempts to change existing evils, he might also be wrong about the case in hand?

Would it not be contradictory for Melville to have a captain who is intelligent and widely read in both the ancients and the moderns, who does not apply this breadth of experience, who sees no larger context than the immediate needs of the navy?

Again, would it not be contradictory for Melville to represent Billy as inarticulate, nonthinking, naïve, emotionally adolescent, and morally undeveloped, and then expect the reader to accept his cry, "God [125/126] bless Captain Vere," as indicative of full understanding, instinctive or otherwise?

And finally, is not the "acceptance" theory contradictory to all that Melville stood for and fought for throughout his entire life? He had been a seaman and had witnessed at first hand the floggings and the tyrannies of the captains. He had never approved of such practices, and in *White-Jacket* he thundered against them from every angle.

No matter, then, what may be the consequences of its abolition; no matter if we have to dismantle our fleets, and our unprotected commerce should fall a prey to the spoiler, the awful admonitions of justice and humanity demand that abolition without procrastination; in a voice that is not to be mistaken, demand that abolition to-day. It is not a dollar-and-cent question of expediency; it is a matter of *right and wrong*. And if any man can lay his hand on his heart, and solemnly say that this scourging is right, let that man but once feel the lash on his own back, and in his agony you will hear the apostate call the seventh heavens to witness that it is *wrong*. And, in the name of immortal manhood, would to God that every man who upholds this thing were scourged at the gangway till he recanted.

Melville was a fighter, he was stubborn, he never accepted the easy way out. Would it not then be contradictory for him, after a lifetime of resisting practical evil in the world at large and metaphysical evil in his novels, at the very end to discover that he had been wrong all along and that his duty had always been to lie down and accept evil as unavoidable?

It is now possible to review the story swiftly. It begins with a cue from a narrator; a rebellion, like the French Revolution or the Spithead Mutiny, may result in good, although in the beginning it may not seem so. Thus, rebellion is justified in the first pages, the implication being that evil can and perhaps should be resisted. We have seen how the various characteristics of the three main actors are clues to the working out of this theme. Claggart is evil through and through; he possesses the perverted intelligence of a serpent, an intelligence used for irrational purposes. Billy Budd, on the contrary, is pure innocence, acting and judging on instinct alone. When Vere is introduced, his central characteristic is his intellection, by means of which he can justify or rationalize an over-prudence that leads to injustice. The chapter on Nelson reminds us that Vere's kind of caution and Vere's way of preventing possible mutiny are not admirable.

It may be argued that, while both Vere and Claggart possess intelligence, Vere uses his wisely and justly. But this argument collapses when it is perceived that Vere does not do what reason would suggest in so dubious a case, i.e., jail Billy until they reach land. The real point is, of course, that Vere does not act on reason and intelligence at all, but on fear; his intelligence, instead of being a guide, is a perverted instrument. Such scenes as the confusion of the officers and the doubt of the surgeon concerning Vere's sanity make sense only when regarded as putting into issue Vere's stature and ability.

It may also be argued that such episodes are intended to demonstrate [126/127] that Vere and only Vere has the intelligence and insight to perceive the deeper issues. But this explanation falls to the ground when it is realized that Vere's whole argument is irrational and that his final appeal is to brute force. The ballad at the end becomes particularly rich in this context. Billy is to be sacrificed, but unjustly and unnecessarily so. The ballad, written by one of his comrades who does not understand the issues but who feels obscurely the truth of the matter in spite of a calumnious official report, speaks of Billy as unafraid but sad. Billy, being innocence personified, does not fear death; but as an unjust sacrifice, he is pictured as alone and unhappy. He longs for companionship and affection and thinks wistfully of his friends; in the end he contemplates with a melancholy resignation his death:

> Fathoms down, fathoms down, how I'll dream fast asleep.
> I feel it stealing now. Sentry, are you there?
> Just ease these darbies at the wrist,
> And roll me over fair.
> I am asleep, and the oozy weeds about me twist.
>
> (p. 281)

Thus, Billy's cry, "God Bless Captain Vere," is the crowning irony and really the climax of the story, for he was hanged unjustly. Melville says here that a harsh truth of this harsh world is that good folk can be misled, that they can be abused by the evil simply because they are trusting. Thus Melville reminds us that we must keep up the good fight: evil must not remain uncontested. And he does so not by a call to arms but by demonstrating the consequences of unresisting acquiescence. [127]

3. MAJOR READINGS

BILLY BUDD AS SPIRITUAL AUTOBIOGRAPHY

Melville's *Billy Budd* as "An Inside Narrative"

WILLIAM BRASWELL

As with *Moby-Dick* and many other classics, it is possible to find different meanings in *Billy Budd*, complementary rather than conflicting, by reading it on different levels. One way of reading it which seems to me worthy of further exploration is as "an inside narrative," which Melville himself called it in a subtitle in parentheses. This phrase may obviously be interpreted in various ways. It may be taken merely to imply that the story is restricted to the inner life of a single ship. It may also be taken as a hint that the story is "inside" in a family sense, on account of the part played in the *Somers* affair by Melville's cousin Guert Gansevoort. But it seems to me that Melville intended the subtitle in still another sense. I believe that *Billy Budd* may justifiably and profitably be considered as an inside narrative about a tragic conflict in Melville's own spiritual life. The *Indomitable*, which may be regarded merely as a man-of-war, or, on another plane, as the world of Christendom, appears to me acceptable also as a microcosm, the world of an individual—specifically, the world of Herman Melville —and the story of what happened aboard the *Indomitable*, the symbolical projection of a personal crisis and the resolution of it. This is not to say that *Billy Budd* is an allegory, nor to argue that its symbols have fixed, rigidly restricted meanings throughout the narrative; in fact, the shifting similitudes and the rich allusiveness suggest new truths every time one reads the novel. Still, a general symbolical pattern may be discerned.

1

With the *Indomitable* a microcosm representing Melville, certain aspects of his being are dramatized in Captain Vere, Billy Budd, and Claggart. The devine, or semidivine, origin of Melville's being is suggested in the fact that Vere is of noble lineage and that Billy and

From *American Literature*, XXIX (May 1957), 133–146, by permission of publisher and author.

Claggart, although their origin is uncertain, are reputed to have noblemen's blood in their veins. The King is a symbol of the Deity: [133/134] he does not physically appear in the story, but he is the supreme authority under whose law the ship operates.

Billy Budd and Claggart are contrasting symbols. Billy, the handsome, strong, lovable sailor, represents the good tendencies, the tendencies often designated as "the heart," and the epithet "welkin-eyed"[1] suggests a celestial quality. During his service aboard the *Rights of Man* it is said that a virtue goes out of him, sugaring the sour members of the crew. He is innocent as Adam before the fall. After he has been impressed for duty aboard the *Indomitable*, he is so unsuspecting and so unfamiliar with the ways of evil that at first he thinks Claggart likes him. Later he is horrified by the false charges that Claggart brings against him. He strikes his accuser the fatal blow only because an impediment in speech prevents him from defending himself orally.

Billy's character arouses pity, but so does Claggart's. In defining Claggart's evil nature, Melville suggests analogies between him and Milton's Satan, especially Satan's being cast into hell for his plot against the Deity and his part in bringing about the fall.[2] Claggart's history is obscure, but it is rumored that he "was a *chevalier* who had volunteered into the King's navy by way of compounding for some mysterious swindle whereof he had been arraigned at the King's Bench."[3] His pallor is "in part the result of his official seclusion from the sunlight."[4] While his office keeps him below decks, "welkin-eyed" Billy is a man of the top. At an unforeseen encounter of the two "a red light" flashes forth from Claggart's violet eyes "like a spark from an anvil in a dusk smithy."[5] Yet, looking on Billy before he brings about his downfall, Claggart is filled with sadness, like Satan looking on Adam in the Garden of Eden. Claggart's lifeless body is compared to a dead snake. His depravity, like Billy's goodness, is according to nature. He is the only person aboard with the exception of Vere who is "intellectually" capable of realizing the moral phenomenon of Billy's character; yet, "apprehending the good, but powerless to be it," a nature such as Claggart's [134/135] has no recourse left but "to recoil upon itself and like the scorpion for which the Creator alone is responsible, act out to the end the part allotted it."[6] With freedom of will denied him, Claggart is doomed to the role he plays.

---

[1] *Melville's Billy Budd,* ed. F. Barron Freeman (Cambridge, Mass., 1948), pp. 136, 192. References throughout are to this edition, as corrected by the *Corrigenda* published by the same press.

[2] Norman Holmes Pearson, "Billy Budd: 'The King's Yarn,'" *American Quarterly,* III, 99–114 (Summer 1951), contains provocative discussion of Milton's influence on *Billy Budd.*

[3] *Billy Budd,* p. 169.

[4] *Ibid.,* p. 168.

[5] *Ibid.,* p. 208.

[6] *Ibid.,* p. 192.

He has further symbolical significance. As Billy symbolizes the heart, so Claggart roughly symbolizes "the head." His brow is "of the sort phrenologically associated with more than average intellect."[7] A significant comparison of the two men points out that if Billy's "face was without the intellectual look of the pallid Claggart's, not the less was it lit, like his, from within, though from a different source. The bonfire in his heart made luminous the rose-tan in his cheek."[8] The intellectual Claggart's bleached complexion suggests that he is sicklied o'er with the pale cast of thought. The contrasting symbolism of the two men is subtly indicated also in the fatal scene in Vere's quarters when Billy is confronted with Claggart's charges against him. Billy's impediment in speech here becomes a superb figure for the inarticulateness of the heart. Captain Vere's soothing words, instead of calming Billy, touch his "heart to the quick," so that, still unable to speak, he strikes Claggart a powerful blow upon "the forehead, so shapely and intellectual-looking a feature in the master-at-arms. . . ."[9] A line not used in the final version, as transcribed by Freeman, describes Billy's blow as "electrically energized by the inmost spasm of his heart."[10] The blow comes then, in effect, directly from the heart to the head.* And as a result of it, Captain Vere is confronted by a crisis.

But this terrific blow of Billy's, this lashing out of the heart at the evil represented by Claggart—is there anything comparable to it, symbolically, in Melville's own life? I believe that there is. It seems to me that the part of the narrative leading up to the dramatic scene in Vere's quarters may be said to represent the early part of Melville's spiritual life.

With ruddy-cheeked, welkin-eyed Billy sauntering on the deck in the sunshine, joking with friends, and with the pallid, scheming Claggart slyly promoting his own interests below deck, but still not openly asserting himself, Captain Vere has no problem out of the ordinary to contend with. The relationship between heart and head [135/136] in Melville's early life seems to have been, on the whole, well-balanced, with the heart somewhat predominant. There are signs of a

[7] *Ibid.*, p. 168.
[8] *Ibid.*, p. 190.
[9] *Ibid.*, p. 226.
[10] *Ibid.*, p. 228, n. 45.

---

* Author's additional note (1960): A student who read this article, and who accepted Billy and Claggart as symbols of heart and head respectively, asked me what Captain Vere symbolizes. I regretted then not having been so explicit as to say that Captain Vere symbolizes the will: he is the final authority on all matters aboard ship and he determines the ship's course of action; he has the ultimate responsibility of choosing between right and wrong. The psychology of the soul as Melville presents it in *Billy Budd* is relatively simplified; he was more elaborate and involved in dramatizing aspects of the soul in *Mardi* and *Pierre*, as I attempted to show in Chap. VI, *Melville's Religious Thought* (Durham, 1943).

dichotomy between heart and head at the end of *Mardi,* where all the travelers except Taji are converted to the religion of the heart practiced on the island of Serenia, but Taji sails out into the open sea in pursuit of the ultimate truth. Melville's next two books, *Redburn* and *White-Jacket,* show his compassionate heart in their fervent preaching of Christian charity, but there is ample evidence that during the period in which he wrote these novels he continued assiduously to cultivate the head.

Moby-Dick is predominantly an expression of the heart, but with a difference that sets it off from the earlier books. In addition to the compassion for mankind, there is now an impassioned hatred for the source of man's grief. In the early pages of the novel, when preparing for the entrance of Captain Ahab, Melville writes with admiration for the type of pageant character who has a "globular brain" and a "ponderous heart."[11] However one may feel about Ahab's brain, he is a man of greater heart than some critics apparently have realized. There has been a tendency of late in certain quarters to interpret *Moby-Dick* too much in the manner of a Sunday School pamphlet in which the sad fate of wicked, crazy old Ahab is intended to illustrate for Everyman-Ishmael what will happen to him if he is not a good boy. Obviously Ahab's intention is insane, as he himself admits, and from the beginning it is clear that he is doomed; but despite the tyranny with which his madness makes him drive his crew, he is a noble character with a capacity for great love. On an early appearance he is pictured, in a way to remind one of Christ, as standing before his men "with a crucifixion in his face";[12] and the Iron Crown of Lombardy which he wears was made partly of nails used in the crucifixion. He has one of those great hearts capable of feeling in one pang the sum total of pains diffused through feebler men's whole lives. He feels as though he "were Adam, staggering beneath the piled centuries since Paradise."[13] In a letter to Hawthorne, Melville said that "the reason the mass of men fear God, and *at bottom dislike* Him, is because they rather distrust His heart, and fancy Him all brain like a watch."[14] Ahab says that he himself [136/137] only feels, feels, feels; God alone has the right to think. His hostility toward God is based on his conception that God is without love for mankind. The plight of crazy Pip makes him exclaim, "There can be no hearts above the snow-line."[15] In the last days of the voyage the despairing Starbuck shows

[11] *Moby-Dick,* ed. Luther S. Mansfield and Howard P. Vincent (New York, 1952), p. 73.
[12] *Ibid.,* p. 122.
[13] *Ibid.,* p. 535.
[14] Julian Hawthorne, *Nathaniel Hawthorne and His Wife: A Biography* (Boston, 1885), I, 404.
[15] *Moby-Dick,* p. 514.

sound perception in addressing Ahab as "grand old heart," "noble heart."[16]

At first glance it may seem incredible that there should be a symbolical relationship between Captain Ahab and Billy Budd. Ahab, of course, is a much more complex character than Billy; and, in fact, it would be possible to point out similarities between him and both Vere and Claggart. But the parallels between him and Billy seem especially significant. Consider the conflicts in which the two men become embroiled. On the one hand, there are Ahab and Billy, symbols of man's naturally good heart outraged by evil, and, on the other hand, their adversaries, Moby Dick and Claggart, symbols of evil (to Ahab, Moby Dick symbolizes "all evil").[17] One may smile at the suggestion that in the whiteness of the whale and the pallor of Claggart there is a subtle tie between the adversaries of Ahab and Billy. More important, Moby Dick is an "agent"[18] of the Deity, to use Ahab's label, and Claggart, a petty officer in His Majesty's Navy, is likewise symbolically an agent of the Deity. Thus both Ahab and Billy rebel, in effect, against the highest authority: Ahab's "blasphemy" in harpooning Moby Dick is matched by Billy's "mutiny" in striking the master-at-arms during war. In both fables the symbol of the heart, when injured, strikes back in retaliation. It might be argued with some justice that Ahab brought his injury on himself, but as Billy incurred Claggart's enmity while going about routine duties aboard ship, so Ahab was on a routine whaling cruise when he first encountered Moby Dick. Melville uses the same figure, a firing cannon, to express the terrific feeling of the two men against their opponents. Billy's blow against Claggart's pallid brow is explosive, from "the heart": "quick as the flame from a discharged cannon at night, his right arm shot out, and Claggart dropped to the deck."[19]And Ahab's chest is compared to a mortar which bursts his "hot heart's shell"[20] upon the White Whale.

The hero of Melville's next book, Pierre, is quite as violent as Ahab and Billy in his ultimate reaction to evil. Highly idealistic [137/138] and full of love for mankind, Pierre vows in the beginning that he will be ruled by the heart. His preference for heart over head is shown in his exclamation that "the brains grow maggoty without a heart; but the heart's the preserving salt itself, and can keep sweet without the head."[21] Pierre's following the dictates of the heart, however, his attempt to live according to the ideals of Christ, leads to such maddening entanglements that his love turns to hate. He fires his

[16] *Ibid.*, pp. 535, 558.
[17] *Ibid.*, p. 181.
[18] *Ibid.*, p. 162.
[19] *Billy Budd*, p. 226.
[20] *Moby-Dick*, p. 181.
[21] *Pierre; or, The Ambiguities*, ed. Henry A. Murray (New York, 1949), p. 377.

pistols pointblank at his chief antagonist in the evil world closing in about him. In prison he reflects on the joy he might have known had he been "heartless," but realizing that now he must endure hell in both this world and the next, he cries out his defiance of the Deity: "Well, be it hell. I will mould a trumpet of the flames, and, with my breath of flame, breathe back my defiance!"[22]

There is no doubt that Pierre, Ahab, and Billy all had Melville's deepest sympathy. "I stand for the heart. To the dogs with the head!"[23] Melville wrote to Hawthorne. But he ultimately realized that a rebellious heart could bring him to disaster—in fact, threatened to do so.

It is generally recognized that Pierre, a book of overwrought emotion, of indignation, represents a climax of some sort in Melville's life. It is one of the most baffling and most terrifying books ever written. Not long after it was published Melville's nervousness and strange behavior alarmed some of his family to the point of their having him examined for insanity. He was pronounced sane, but it is well known that he suffered much anguish during this period.

His condition soon after writing Pierre is symbolized, I believe, by the tragic situation aboard the Indomitable just after Billy has struck Claggart. The fact that the crisis in Billy Budd comes during a time of war when there is grave danger of mutiny suggests symbolically how critical matters were with Melville himself. Aboard the Indomitable decisive action is necessary to prevent possible anarchy. I believe that the action of Captain Vere in regard to Billy indicates symbolically how Melville, with his faculties threatening mutiny, resolved his own greatest personal crisis.

2

Before going into more detail about the symbolism, however, it is necessary to analyze the role of Captain Vere, because on whatever [138/139] plane one reads the novel, he is the key figure. The good-hearted Billy Budd and the evil Claggart have inspired relatively little dissent among critics: one is inescapably good as the other is inescapably evil. The crux of the problem is what to make of their commanding officer, who alone sees and understands the situation, and yet, knowing Billy to be essentially innocent, summarily has him hanged for striking the blow that accidentally kills the master-at-arms. Most criticism of the novel treats Vere sympathetically, as a conscientious man who does his duty as he sees it. But some of the later criticism pictures him as a monstrous villain—a depraved martinet who enforces ironclad laws regardless of whether they violate individual rights. He is charged with overweening personal ambition,

---

[22] Ibid., p. 424.
[23] Julian Hawthorne, op. cit., I, 404.

hypocrisy, and the abuse of confidence. His part in the trial scene is denounced as odious.[24]

Melville himself makes no explicit judgment on Vere's part in having Billy hanged. In one very important sentence he puts it up to the reader himself to judge the reasonableness of Captain Vere's actions. Just after Vere has told the Surgeon that a drumhead court is to be convened immediately to determine Billy's fate, the Surgeon reflects: Why such haste? Should not Billy be confined and the case later be referred to the Admiral? Was Vere mentally unhinged? Melville says that the line of demarcation between sanity and insanity is as difficult to draw as the line between two merging colors in a rainbow, and then adds: "Whether Captain Vere, as the Surgeon professionally and primarily surmised, was really the sudden victim of any degree of aberration, one must determine for himself by such light as this narrative may afford."[25]

Though Melville is ostensibly noncommittal, the way in which he narrates the story reveals something of his attitude toward Vere. Lawrance Thompson is alone, so far as I know, in assuming that the narrative passages in the novel as distinguished from the dramatic passages, to use his phraseology, are related by a stupid narrator whose admiration for Vere should not be attributed to Melville.[26] Unless more convincing argument than Thompson's is advanced, there is no reason for doubting that Melville intended himself to be [139/ 140] thought of as the narrator. As such, he uses a shifting point of view, looking now into the mind of one character, now into the mind of another, making general comments from time to time, and presenting scenes of dramatic action, but also shutting himself off from a scene entirely when he chooses.

He portrays Vere as both an admirable man and an excellent officer. Though not brilliant, Vere has a superior mind and a marked liking for books by authors who "in the spirit of common sense philosophize upon realities."[27] He has won distinction as an intrepid fighter. He runs a taut ship, but he has always acquitted himself as "an officer mindful of the welfare of his men."[28] In view of his role in the trial, his concern for the welfare of his men should be especially noted.

Vere is a man of firm principles, and Melville says it is well that he is, since he lives in the tempestuous era of the French Revolution. "His

[24] For derogatory comments on Vere, see, for instance, Joseph Schiffman, "Melville's Final Stage, Irony: A Re-examination of *Billy Budd* Criticism," *American Literature*, XXII, 128–136 (May, 1950); "Letter from E. M. Forster," *The Griffin*, I, 4–6 (1951); and Lawrance Thompson, *Melville's Quarrel with God* (Princeton, 1952), chap. xi.

[25] *Billy Budd*, p. 233.

[26] Thompson, *op. cit.*, pp. 359–360.

[27] *Billy Budd*, p. 164.

[28] *Ibid.*, p. 160.

settled convictions were as a dyke against those invading waters of novel opinion[,] social[,] political[,] and otherwise, which carried away as in a torrent no few minds in those days, minds by nature not inferior to his own." He disinterestedly opposed the theories not only "because they seemed to him incapable of embodiment in lasting institutions, but at war with the peace of the world and the true welfare of mankind."[29]

It is impossible to appreciate Vere's actions without relating them to the world he lives in. Except in regard to the one particular allusion to it, the case of Captain MacKenzie and the three executions aboard the United States brig *Somers* during peacetime in 1842 should perhaps best be forgotten when one is attempting to analyze the character of Captain Vere, because in spite of what the historical incident may possibly have contributed to Melville's imaginative creation, what he tells about Vere is another story, about another man, at another time. There is particular significance in the choice of 1797 as the time for the action of the story. England is at war with France, now in the excesses of the Revolution; and England herself has lately been rocked by mutinies at Spithead and the Nore. The first of the mutinies was comparatively mild: the sailors complained about undesirable conditions and were granted concessions. But the Great Mutiny, which occurred the following month, was more "menacing to England than the contemporary manifestoes [140/141] and conquering and proselyting armies of the French Directory." To the British Empire it was "what a strike in the fire-brigade would be to London threatened by general arson." Melville's vivid figures leave no doubt as to the devastating effect upon Christendom which Vere and other loyal Englishmen feared was imminent unless rigid control were maintained:

that was the time when at the mast-heads of the three-deckers and seventy-fours moored in her own roadstead—a fleet, the right arm of a Power then all but the sole free conservative one of the Old World, the blue-jackets, to be numbered by thousands ran up with huzzas the British colors with the union and cross wiped out; by that cancellation transmuting the flag of founded law and freedom defined, into the enemy's red meteor of unbridled and unbounded revolt. Reasonable discontent growing out of practical grievances in the fleet had been ignited into irrational combustion as by live cinders blown across the Channel from France in flames.[30]

After the mutiny had been quelled, it was feared that there would be further uprisings. To illustrate the precautionary measures taken at sea against such hazards, Melville points out that, with the fleet off the Spanish coast, Nelson was transferred to a ship just arrived from the Nore, with the hope that his presence would win back the loyalty of

[29] *Ibid.*, p. 164.
[30] *Ibid.*, pp. 150–151.

the late mutineers. Engagements with the enemy might take place at any hour. When they did occur, officers assigned to batteries felt it necessary at times to stand with drawn swords behind the gunners.

It is clear that Billy's fatal blow could not have been struck at a worse time. Though Vere would rather confine Billy and submit his case later to the Admiral, he feels it incumbent on him, as an officer responsible for the efficiency of a fighting unit, to act on the case immediately. Ironically, with Claggart lying dead on the deck, the essentially innocent man and the bearer of false witness have in effect changed places, so that Claggart, legally viewed, appears the victim of "the most heinous of military crimes. Yet more. The essential right and wrong involved in the matter, the clearer that might lie, so much the worse for the responsibility of a loyal sea-commander inasmuch as he was not authorized to determine the matter on that primitive basis."[31]

Vere advises the court that Billy's intent is not to be considered, [141/142] that the court must confine itself to the consequence of the blow. He knows, of course, that this is a hard doctrine for the young officers to accept:

How can we adjudge to summary and shameful death a fellow-creature innocent before God, and whom we feel to be so?—Does that state it aright? You sign sad assent. Well, I too feel that, the full force of that. It is Nature. But do these buttons that we wear attest that our allegiance is to Nature? No, to the King. Though the ocean, which is inviolate Nature primeval, though this be the element where we move and have our being as sailors, yet as the King's officers lies our duty in a sphere correspondingly natural? So little is that true, that in receiving our commissions we in the most important regards ceased to be natural free-agents. When war is declared are we the commissioned fighters previously consulted? We fight at command. If our judgements approve the war, that is but coincidence. So in other particulars. So now. For suppose condemnation to follow these present proceedings. Would it be so much we ourselves that would condemn as it would be martial law operating through us? For that law and the rigour of it, we are not responsible. Our vowed responsibility is in this: That however pitilessly that law may operate, we nevertheless adhere to it and administer it.[32]

To convict and yet mitigate the penalty would have a disastrous effect on the ship's company. Long accustomed to arbitrary discipline, the crew would be bewildered, Vere reasons, by seeing clemency granted a seaman who had murdered the master-at-arms: such a disposition of the case would be virtually an invitation to further mutiny.

Vere's speech to the court is the hardest thing in the book for readers to accept. E. M. Forster's and Eric Crozier's "tidying up" Vere in the trial scene of the libretto they wrote for Benjamin Britten's

[31] *Ibid.*, pp. 234–235.
[32] *Ibid.*, pp. 244–246.

music resulted in Vere's not counseling the court.[33] But as Melville wrote the novel, there is no denying that Vere alone is ultimately responsible for the execution of Billy.

Billy Budd does not condemn Captain Vere. When Vere privately tells Billy of the verdict, what takes place between the two is not revealed, but with "each radically sharing in the rarer qualities of our nature—so rare indeed as to be all but incredible to average [142/143] minds however cultivated"[34]—Billy understands and approves what Vere has done. His final words, uttered just before his execution, are, "God bless Captain Vere!"[35] It has been suggested that this remark is ironical, but Billy, we are explicitly told, is incapable of conscious irony, and nobody has yet presented convincing argument that Melville meant the remark to be taken so.

Vere is portrayed as suffering more than Billy. The relationship between the two, suggestive as it is of the relationship between Abraham and Isaac, and between God the Father and the Son, apparently enables Billy to understand that Vere's role is necessitated by his adherence to forms which he holds dearer than life itself—forms for which Vere ultimately gives his own life. "With mankind," Vere believes, "forms, measured forms, are everything; and that is the story of Orpheus with his lyre spellbinding the wild denizens of the wood."[36] In an ideal world, Billy would not be punished; but in the tense man-of-war world of which the *Indomitable* is a part, forms dictate the execution of a murderer if anarchy is not to prevail. The "union and cross" on the British flag—symbols torn off by the mutineers—represent "founded law and freedom defined" as against "unbridled and unbounded revolt." Vere agonizingly perceives the injustice effected at times by adhering to forms, but he sets imperfect order above anarchic disorder. After each of the incidents which emotionally upset the ship's company—the announcement of the verdict, the execution, and the burial—Vere maintains discipline through enforcement of forms, issuing routine orders that he knows the men will obey.

The chief reason for immediate action on Billy's case is that an encounter with the enemy might take place at any time, and any weakening of discipline might result in defection that would mean defeat. Soon after the execution, and before the *Indomitable* rejoins the Mediterranean fleet, there is an engagement with the enemy. The well-disciplined British sailors fight valiantly and win the victory. Vere himself is fatally wounded fighting for his beloved forms.

The internal evidence as a whole shows, it seems to me, that

---

[33] See Forster on their feeling it necessary to "tidy up" Vere ("Letter from E. M. Forster," *op. cit.*, pp. 4–6). Their libretto was published by Boosey & Hawkes (London, 1951).

[34] *Billy Budd*, p. 251.

[35] *Ibid.*, p. 264.

[36] *Ibid.*, p. 272.

Melville looked upon Vere as a sympathetic character. There is also a bit of external evidence of Melville's attitude toward the tragically involved commander. On the back of the dedication page of the [143/ 144] novel, Melville wrote the following annotation: "Both directly and indirectly the era lent emphasis to the difficulties professional and moral falling on Captain Vere by reason of the tragic event just recounted; difficulties not adequately to be estimated by the sea-officers of our time; and still less by landsmen."[37] If readers of today, whether military or civilian, cannot adequately estimate the moral and professional difficulties that fell on Captain Vere, are they qualified to pass judgment on his resolution of the difficulties? The implication appears to be that Melville himself does not condemn Vere. The reader, of course, as Melville remarked, is free to judge Vere for himself.

3

As an inside narrative, *Billy Budd* reveals Melville telling his own story as objectively as he could, not with self-pity, but with self-respect. Instead of being called his "Testament of Acceptance," it might perhaps better be called his apologia. In the character of Billy Budd he presents, one may say, the dominant tendencies of his young manhood; in Captain Vere he presents in essence the later Melville. The name *Budd* suggests youth; in a manuscript line not used in the final version Billy, who is also called Baby Budd, is referred to as "a flower of masculine strength and beauty, a flower, scarce yet released from the bud."[38] The name *Vere* brings to mind the Latin word for man, *vir*. The crucial point in Melville's development came when he realized the necessity for curbing the wild, rebellious spirit manifested in *Moby-Dick* and *Pierre*. The fact that the rebelliousness was inspired, in part at least, by the highest idealism was no justification for its being tolerated, especially since it threatened to destroy his whole being.

Nearly forty years before Melville wrote *Billy Budd*, he developed the theme, most notably in Plinlimmon's tract in *Pierre*, that the heavenly wisdom of Christ is not in accord with the wisdom of this earth, and that anyone who attempts to live strictly by heavenly ideals is likely to become involved in "strange, *unique* follies and sins."[39] At the time of writing *Pierre* Melville was so wrapped up in his idealistic young hero that he presented the coldly rational Plinlimmon in a very satirical manner. It is worth remembering that although Pierre proceeds to his downfall, he does not throw [144/145] away Plinlimmon's pamphlet, but carries it about unknowingly in the lining of his

[37] *Ibid.*, p. 234, n. 12.
[38] *Ibid.*, p. 219, n. 88.
[39] *Pierre*, p. 250.

overcoat—tucked away in his subconscious, as it were. The passing years brought about a change in Melville's attitude toward the teachings of the pamphlet. In writing *Billy Budd* he was sympathetic toward not only the Christlike Billy but also the philosophical Vere.

When Vere tells the court that in administering the laws of His Majesty's Navy they are restricted to considering the act alone, not the intent or nonintent, when he says that they are not responsible for the severity of the laws they administer, one should recall that as the King symbolizes the Deity, the laws in effect in His Majesty's Navy are symbolically the universal laws to which man must adapt himself, no matter what his personal opinion of them may be. It is only natural that Vere and his officers should be moved with pity for the essentially innocent sailor, but as commissioned officers their allegiance, as Vere points out, is not to Nature, but to the King, or God. The *Indomitable* proves its loyalty to the King by observing his rigid laws and by defeating the enemy ship, significantly named the *Athéiste*. Though this loyalty symbolizes Melville's realization that man must accept his place in the universal scheme decreed by God, one should not overlook the fact that the loyalty is based more on a sense of duty—in fact, of necessity—than on love. On the *Indomitable* it is Billy Budd rather than the King who is loved: the men preserve bits of the spar from which Billy was hanged as though they were chips from the Cross, and Vere's final words, uttered not with remorse, but with poignancy, are, "Billy Budd, Billy Budd."

At Melville's death there was found among his manuscripts together with *Billy Budd* a sketch entitled "Daniel Orme." Though it is too slight to have much value as literature, it is important as a brief symbolical self-portrait, and particularly so, in my opinion, since its kindred imagery and symbolism confirm much of what has been said here about *Billy Budd*.[40] There are striking parallels in the experiences of Orme and Vere.

Both men spend most of their lives at sea aboard battleships, and though Orme, retired at the end, has not been in command of a ship, [145/146] he has been a "captain of the top." Both men are respected by their shipmates, but both remain somewhat apart. Vere is suspected by the Surgeon of suffering mental aberrations, and, similarly, Orme is suspected by some of his shipmates of piracy, which here, as in "I and My Chimney," symbolizes insanity. Orme, like Vere, is wounded fighting for "forms." Across the crucifix tattooed over his heart he bears a scar, which it is intimated he received repelling boarders; and Vere, under the flag of the "union and cross," is fatally wounded fighting the

[40] On "Daniel Orme" as a self-portrait see William Braswell, *Melville's Religious Thought* (Durham, 1943), pp. 124–126. Richard Chase, *Herman Melville: A Critical Study* (New York, 1949), p. 298, and Newton Arvin, *Herman Melville* (New York, 1950), p. 288, both consider the sketch a self-portrait.

Athéiste. In his last days Orme frequently contemplates his scarred image of the crucifixion, and Vere dies murmuring of the crucified Billy Budd. In view of Melville's sea-and-land symbolism, with the sea representing abstract truth and the land empirical truth, it is important that both men die in port: Orme is found dead near a battery of rusty guns on a cliff looking seaward; Vere dies not aboard the *Indomitable* but on the gun-studded Rock of Gibraltar. Both men die calmly, with no apparent remorse.

It is not surprising that in these two symbolical narratives the image of the crucifixion figures so prominently. For Melville it had long been an image of human life, more suggestive of man's suffering than of man's hope. Men are "Cross-bearers all," to quote a phrase from *Clarel.*[41] In *Billy Budd* he develops the theme in all its magnitude; and for those who read the "inside narrative" he tells how he bore his own cross. [146]

[41] *Clarel* (London, 1924), IV, xxxiv.

BILLY BUDD AS SOCIAL COMMENTARY

Expediency and Absolute Morality in *Billy Budd*

WENDELL GLICK

"RESOLVE AS ONE MAY TO KEEP TO THE MAIN ROAD," MELVILLE WROTE in *Billy Budd,* "some bypaths have an enticement not readily to be withstood. Beckoned by the genius of Nelson, knowingly, I am going to err in such a bypath."[1] With these words of caution to the reader who might object to the "literary sin" of digression, the author of *Moby Dick* launched into a spirited encomium upon the heroism of Lord Nelson, defending the Admiral against any "martial utilitarians" and "Benthamites of war" who might interpret his acts of "bravado" at Trafalgar which had resulted in his death to have been foolhardy and

[1] Herman Melville, *Billy Budd,* ed. F. Barron Freeman (Cambridge, Mass., 1948), p. 154 n. Citations to *Billy Budd* in the text of this article are to this, the best critical edition so far available.

From *PMLA,* LXVIII (March 1953), 103–110, by permission of the publisher and author.

vain. For what reason, the question arises, did Melville feel that the eulogy on Nelson could justifiably be included in *Billy Budd*? What is the meaning of the attack upon Benthamites and utilitarians? This was no pot-boiler which required padding; surely his inclusion of the highly emotional defense of Nelson is significant for other reasons than that the chapter makes "more understandable Melville's hearty interest in martial exploits, sayings, and songs."[2]

At the time Melville was writing and revising *Billy Budd* he was in no mood to trifle with peccadilloes. "My vigor sensibly declines," he had written to Archibald MacMechan on 5 December 1889: "What little of it is left I husband for certain matters yet incomplete, and which indeed, may never be completed."[3] He could hardly have been husbanding his strength to communicate his "hearty interest in martial exploits"; his digression away from his narrative in order to praise Nelson must have served in his mind the more serious purpose of clarifying one of the "truths" for which, as he pointed out, *Billy Budd* was but the vehicle. The purpose of this article is to call attention to an aspect of one of these truths, heretofore unnoticed. Although it is much more, *Billy Budd* is the cogent fruition of a lifetime of observation and study of the eternal conflict between absolute morality and social expediency; and the digression on Nelson, though it intrudes upon the plot, is central to an understanding of Melville's final resolution of this crucial problem.

In writing *Billy Budd*, Melville made clear at the outset of his novel, he was writing no "romance"; he would not be bound, consequently, in [103/104] his delineation of the "Handsome Sailor," by any of the conventions usually followed in depicting a romantic hero. Nor would he be bound to refrain from digressing if digression served his purposes. His interest was less in art than in "Truth uncompromisingly told" (pp. 149 and 274). He was quite willing, he asserted, to sacrifice "the symmetry of form attainable in pure fiction" and to risk "ragged edges" on his final work if by so doing he could tell a story "having less to do with fable than with fact" (p. 274). Thus relieved both from the conventional restrictions usually imposed by art and from the financial exigencies which had dictated the content of some of his early works, he would be free to deal forthrightly and honestly with issues far too serious to be treated cavalierly.

For his *raisonneur* Melville chose Captain "Starry" Vere, a clear-headed realist possessed of sufficient perspective as a result of broad human experience and extensive reading to enable him to weigh the most difficult alternatives and choose rationally between them. No person with lesser qualifications would serve. For the choice which

---

[2] For this reason, Freeman suggests, the digressions on Nelson are "important" (p. 42).

[3] Leon Howard, *Herman Melville* (Berkeley, 1951), p. 328.

Captain Vere had to make involved more than a simple distinction between blacks and whites; instead it was a choice between two standards of human behavior, to each of which man owed unquestioning loyalty. The Captain's decision, moreover, was to be Melville's as well; and Melville felt no disposition in the waning years of his life to trifle with reality and call the process truth-seeking.

Melville sympathized with Billy Budd as completely as did Captain Vere. He appreciated with the Captain the stark injustice of a situation which finds the individual condemned for adherence to a standard of behavior most men would consider noble and right. But he agreed with the Captain that justice to the individual is not the ultimate loyalty in a complex culture; the stability of the culture has the higher claim, and when the two conflict, justice to the individual must be abrogated to keep the order of society intact. Turning their backs upon one of the most cherished systems of ideas in the American tradition, a system typified by such individualists as Thoreau and Emerson, Melville and Captain Vere brought in the verdict that the claims of civilized society may upon occasion constitute a higher ethic than the claims of "natural law" and personal justice (p. 245). The ultimate allegiance of the individual, in other words, is not to an absolute moral code, interpreted by his conscience and enlivened by his human sympathies, but to the utilitarian principle of social expediency.

To isolate his problem, to strip it of all irrelevant issues preparatory to making a critical examination of it, Melville chose as his setting a British vessel at sea. The ship-of-the-line *Indomitable,* a smooth-functioning [104/105] microcosm of society as a whole, was threatened with mutiny. Though the threat was remote, whatever would contribute to the end of knitting together the diverse individuals who made up the crew into a homogeneous unit which would act efficiently in an emergency was fully justified; conversely, that which jeopardized even slightly the clock-like functioning of the crew it was necessary to stamp out ruthlessly. His highest obligation, as Captain Vere conceived of it, was the preservation of the tight little society into which the crew had been welded, and the prevention of anything resembling anarchy. The transcendent responsibility of the leaders of the English nation, moreover, was the same as his own, writ large. An intensive study of history had confirmed his "settled convictions" against "novel opinion, social, political, and otherwise, which carried away as in a torrent no few minds in those days"; and he was "incensed at the innovators," not because their theories were inimical to the private interests of the privileged classes of which he was a member, but because such theories "seemed to him incapable of embodiment in lasting institutions," and "at war with the peace of the world and the good of mankind" (pp. 163–164). The world as he viewed it was ruled by "forms"; "with mankind," Melville quotes him as saying, "forms, measured forms, are everything"; that was the import which he saw "in the story of Orpheus, with his lyre, spellbinding the wild denizens of the woods" (p. 272). To preserve the ordered functioning of his crew Captain Vere was willing to sacrifice even the ideal of justice when the absolute necessity arose. What he objected to in Claggart was not that Claggart was remiss in his "duty of preserving order" but that the Master at Arms abridged the ideal of justice unnecessarily, even when the autonomy and general good of the crew were not at stake. Still, the maintenance of order came first, and it was rigorously safeguarded on the *Indomitable* "almost to a degree inconsistent with entire moral volition" (pp. 172–173).

To the idea that order in society should be maintained at all cost Captain Vere adhered "disinterestedly," not because he desired such a regimented society, but because he believed it to be a practical necessity of this world. Like Plotinus Plinlimmon of *Pierre,* he preferred Christian ("Chronometrical") standards of absolute morality to the more mundane, utilitarian standard of expediency; but like Plinlimmon, he had concluded that Christian ideals were unworkable in everyday situations. He was fully aware that a regimented society abridged many private rights, but he realized also that in the absence of such a society a state of anarchy and chaos inevitably arose in which every human right was sacrificed. An ordered society at least guaranteed the preservation of *some* rights; and though this fell far short of the ideal of the preservation [105/106] of *all,* it was far better than the sort of "society" which, in the idealistic attempts to guarantee all rights, degenerated into chaos and so permitted their complete and total destruction. It was not a question of insuring all individual rights or a part of them; the choice was between insuring a part of them or none. The ideal society which abridged no prerogatives and guaranteed all private liberties was, in the considered opinion of Captain Vere, a figment of the imagination.

Recent events, Melville makes abundantly plain, had been responsible for the Captain's position. The Nore Mutiny, though it had been precipitated by the failure of the authorities to redress the legitimate grievances of the seamen, had threatened the military usefulness of the "indispensable fleet" upon which the stability of the entire English nation depended, and consequently had been ruthlessly suppressed (pp. 150–153). The cataclysmic French Revolution had taught its bitter lesson, both to Captain Vere and to his creator. To the Captain the principle involved in the two events was the same: the English sailors at Nore, in running up "the British colors with the union cross wiped out," had transmuted "the flag of founded law and freedom defined" into "the red meteor of unbridled and unbounded revolt" of the French. "Reasonable discontent," Melville pointed out, "growing out of practical grievances in the fleet had been ignited into irrational combustion as by live cinders blown across the Channel from

France in flames" (p. 151). No price was too great to pay to keep such unhinging forces of anarchy in check; in giving his life to destroy the *Athéiste*, Captain Vere sacrificed himself in defense of the *sine qua non* of civilized existence and in opposition to the false, unworkable doctrines of the French Revolution. The triumph of the *Indomitable* over the *Athéiste* was the triumph of order over chaos.

Yet how staggering was the cost of a stable society! Having decided upon the absolute necessity for maintaining unweakened the strength of the social fabric, Melville shuddered when he contemplated the price exacted in terms of human values; and *Billy Budd* became the balance-sheet upon which he reckoned the price men have to pay for the ordered society which they have to have. The most obvious price was the destruction of "Nature's Nobleman," the superlatively innocent person: every Billy Budd impressed by an *Indomitable* is forced to leave his *Rights-of-Man* behind. To the destruction of innocent persons, moreover, it was necessary to add the mental suffering of the individual forced to make moral judgments. But the total cost is not met even by the sacrifice of Billy Budds and the suffering of Captain Veres; social stability based upon expediency is paid for also with a general, blighting, human mediocrity. The standards of any civilized society are the standards of [106/107] the great mass of men who make up its bulk; and when maintenance of the stability of society becomes the supreme obligation of every person, the result is a levelling of the superior persons down to the level of the mass. The chief personal virtue becomes "prudence"; the end most worth seeking for becomes "that manufacturable thing known as respectability," so often allied with "moral obliquities" (p. 147), and occasionally, as in the case of Claggart, indistinguishable even from "natural depravity." "Civilization," Melville remarks categorically, "especially of the austerer sort, is auspicious" to natural depravity because natural depravity "folds itself in the mantle of respectability" by avoiding "vices or small sins" and by refraining from all excesses; in short, by exhibiting the prudence which is the only virtue society demands. The natural depravity of Claggart was so insidious because it lacked the trappings in which society expects to see evil garbed, and instead, prudently enfolded itself in "the mantle of respectability" (pp. 185–186). Prudence, while being the mark of the socially adjusted man who rigidly adheres to the utilitarian principle of expediency, may also be the last refuge of scoundrels.

But even when prudence did not take the extreme form of moral obliquity, even when it was not "habitual with the subtler depravity" (p. 195), as it proved to be in the case of Claggart, it left its mark upon the people in the world of Billy Budd. The most "prudent" characters discharged faithfully their "duty" to their king even when to do so clashed with moral scruple, but they fell far short of the personal heroism which inspires others and vitalizes them into acts. Captain

Graveling of the *Rights-of-Man* was "the sort of person whom every-body agrees in calling 'a respectable man'"; he was a lover of "peace and quiet" and the possessor of "much prudence" which caused "overmuch disquietude in him," but he was by and large a pedestrian individual who could hardly be depended upon to make any signal contribution to human progress (p. 137). The old ascetic Dansker had learned from experience a "bitter prudence" which had taught him never to interfere, never to give advice, in other words, to solve the problem of his social responsibility by escaping into a shell of cynicism, and by so doing had disqualified himself for service to society (p. 205). The *Indomitable's* "prudent surgeon" was singularly un-equipped to pass moral judgments and would have "solved" the problem of Billy's murder of Claggart by dropping the whole affair into the lap of the Admiral (pp. 229, 231). Even Captain Vere, who possessed in eminent measure the "two qualities not readily inter-fusable" demanded of every English sea-commander at the time, "prudence and rigor" (p. 234), did not earn Melville's highest accolade as a member of "great Nature's nobler order" until he let himself [107/108] "melt back into what remains primeval in our formalized human-ity"; in short, until he forgot temporarily his "military duty," his prudence, and acted in a manner difficult to reconcile with strict social expediency (p. 252).[4]

To what do these examples of prudence, the highest ethic of utilitarian philosophers, add up? Simply this: in making social ex-pediency an ethic superior to absolute morality, Melville found himself pushed perilously close to a *Weltanschauung* which would admit slight, if any, possibility of personal greatness. Could prudence ever be truly heroic? A society which elevated prudence above all other virtues seemed to be anathema to the sort of moral adventuresomeness which Melville loved, and which for him set the great man off from the mediocre one. Yet such a society seemed to be the only sort which could safeguard men from the perils of "irrational combustion" which followed hard upon an idealism permitted to run its free course unrestrained. Here lay a crucial dilemma: was the race doomed to accept mediocrity as the price of its self-preservation, or was it still possible in a complex society for great private virtues to generate and grow?

Emotionally unequipped to reconcile himself to the bleaker alter-native toward which both his experience and his reason had led him, Melville turned to history in the hope of discovering a figure of heroic dimensions whose life would free him from his impasse. Having played the role of champion of man's dignity and greatness for a lifetime, he did not feel that he could relinquish it now; and in the person of Nelson, "the greatest sailor since the world began," he found

---

[4] Melville conjectures that this is what transpired while the Captain spoke with Billy privately in the cabin.

his answer.[5] Though he recognized that many changes had take. place since Trafalgar, that the "symmetry and grand lines" of Nelson's *Victory* seemed obsolete in a world of "*Monitors* and yet mightier hulls of the European ironsides," he nonetheless insisted that "to anybody who can hold the Present at its worth without being inappreciative of the Past," the "solitary old hulk at Portsmouth" spoke eloquent truth. If he could no longer embrace the simple faith of his youth when he had believed in a law "coeval with mankind, dictated by God himself, superior in obligation to any other," when he had advocated the abolition of flogging on the grounds that "it is not a dollar-and-cent question of expediency; it is a matter of *right and wrong*";[6] if the corrosive years had eaten away for him such immutable standards, he could at least salvage somehow a foundation for personal greatness and heroism. Nelson was the man he needed. [108/109]

He admitted that strict "martial utilitarians," believers in the rigorous application of an inexorable social expediency to every particular situation, would be inclined to take issue with his estimate of Nelson's greatness, even perhaps "to the extent of iconoclasm." For Nelson's exposure of his own person in battle at Trafalgar appeared on the surface to have been militarily inexpedient, even vain and foolhardy; his value to the cause for which he fought was so great that he should have sacrificed his natural desire for personal heroism to the higher principle of preserving a life which was indispensable to the general good. Had his life been preserved and his command of the fleet therefore been retained, the mistakes made by his successor in command might have been avoided; and his sagacity might well have averted the shipwreck with its horrible loss of life which followed the battle. So the "Benthamites of war" argued, and, Melville admitted, with some plausibility; using only the immediate circumstances of the engagement as their criteria they could convict Nelson of behavior out of harmony with the general good, and on these grounds strip him of the glory with which Englishmen had invested him.

But to this sort of iconoclasm Melville would not accede for a moment. "Personal prudence," he countered, "even when dictated by quite other than selfish considerations, is surely no special virtue in a military man; while an excessive love of glory, exercising to the uttermost heartfelt sense of duty, is the first." The Benthamites were wrong; in applying their principle of social expediency to Nelson's deed "of foolhardiness and vanity" they failed to calculate the strength of purpose which such a "challenge to death" injects into the arteries of a nation. Nelson's deed was "expedient" to a degree they lacked the vision to perceive; his name had become a "trumpet to the blood" more stimulating even to the hearts of Englishmen than the name of

---

[5] The scattered references to *Billy Budd* which follow are to Ch. iv, pp. 154–157, passim.

[6] *White Jacket* (Boston, 1892), pp. 138, 139.

Wellington; the act which on the surface seemed sheer "bravado" still inspired posterity to deeds of greatness.

Unless, Melville argued, Nelson's "challenge to death" could be considered an act of supreme heroism, conformable to the highest ideals governing human behavior, no deed could be truly heroic; and this possibility he refused to entertain. The vitality of Nelson's example was immortal. In 1891, shortly after he had made his own will, Melville composed this enthusiastic tribute to another great man who had also glimpsed a premonition that death was near:

At Trafalgar, Nelson, on the brink of opening the fight, sat down and wrote his last brief will and testament. If under the presentiment of the most magnificent of all victories, to be crowned by his own glorious death, a sort of priestly motive led him to dress his person in the jewelled vouchers of his own shining deeds; if [109/110] thus to have adorned himself for the altar and the sacrifice were indeed vainglory, then affectation and fustian is each truly heroic line in the great epics and dramas, since in such lines the poet but embodies in verse those exaltations of sentiment that a nature like Nelson, the opportunity being given, vitalizes into acts. (p. 157)

The question naturally arises whether Melville intended the digression on Nelson to illuminate the final scene of the novel. Might the answer be that the hanging of Billy Budd is Melville's final commentary upon the theme of the impracticability of absolute standards in a world necessarily ruled by expediency? Billy's noble devotion to absolute justice and right throughout the novel made him a sort of personification of the moral law; his death must have meant for Melville, consequently, that the standard of behavior to which Billy gave his allegiance, though a noble one, is simply unworkable when applied to complex social relationships. There was something unearthly about the death of Billy Budd: he was "an angel of God" (p. 229), returning without fear to his Maker; his pinioned figure at the yard-end behaved like that of no mortal man; to the sailors aboard the *Indomitable* the spar from which Billy's body had hung was thought of for some years as a piece of the Cross. The luminous night of the morning when Billy was to be hanged passed away like the prophet Elijah disappearing into heaven in his chariot and dropping his mantle to Elisha. Billy was too good for this world; he properly belonged to another, not to this; and the moral principles from which he acted were appropriate enough for the world to which he belonged. But in a society composed of men, not angels—in a society in which even Claggarts are to be found—an inferior standard, that of expediency, is the only workable one.[7] [110]

    [7] This article is peripheral to a study of the concept of "expediency" in American thought, undertaken with the aid of a grant from the American Council of Learned Societies.

BILLY BUDD AS MYTH

The Rite of Sacrament

RICHARD CHASE

AT THE DEEP LEVELS OF *Billy Budd* THERE IS A MASSIVE AND TERRIBLE image, which, it seems to me, moved the aged Melville so overpoweringly that he was unable to give it direct expression. As Melville says at one point in *Billy Budd*, "every . . . form of life has its secret mines and dubious sides; the side popularly disclaimed." On the night before Billy Budd's execution, the ship, with its decks, is like the story itself. "The night was luminous on the spar-deck, but otherwise in the cavernous ones below—levels so very like the tiered galleries in a coalmine."

The real theme of *Billy Budd* is castration and cannibalism, the ritual murder and eating of the Host. During his trial Billy proclaims his faithfulness to the king and to Captain Vere by saying, "I have eaten the King's bread, and I am true to the King." When, "without remorse," the dying Captain Vere murmurs, "Billy Budd, Billy Budd," he expresses faithfulness, dependence, and longing. He had eaten of the Host, and he was true to the Host. After forty years Melville had returned to the theme of *Typee*. In that book the young hero had extricated himself from the valley by a sudden exchange of passivity for action. Billy Budd is fatally passive, his acts of violence being unconsciously calculated to ensure his final submission. All of Billy's conscious acts are toward passivity, the first one being his quick acquiescence in his impressment, an act which causes the hero-worshipping sailors to regard him with "surprise" and "silent reproach." In symbolic language, Billy Budd is seeking his own castration—seeking to yield up his vitality to an authoritative but kindly father, whom he finds in Captain Vere. When anyone else stirs the depths of Billy's longing, threatening to bring his unconscious thoughts to consciousness, he flies into a sudden rage. When Red-Whiskers, a sailor who had once been a butcher, maliciously digs Billy in the ribs

From Richard Chase, *Herman Melville: A Critical Study* (New York: Macmillan, 1949), pp. 269–277. Copyright 1949 by Richard Chase and used with permission of The Macmillan Company. [Editor's title.]

to show him "just whence a sirloin steak was cut," Billy gives him a "terrible drubbing." And when the minion of Claggart approaches Billy on the moonlit deck and, holding out two shining guineas, says, "See, they are yours, Bill," Billy Budd stammeringly threatens to toss him over the rail. The persistent feminine imagery Melville associates with Billy and his statement that "above all" there was "something in the mobile [269/270] expression, and every chance attitude and movement suggestive of a mother eminently favored by Love and the Graces," indicate that Billy has identified himself with the mother at a pre-Oedipean level and has adopted the attitude of harmlessness and placation toward the father in order to avoid the hard struggle of the Oedipus conflict. The Oedipus conflict entails, of course, the idea of one's incestuous guilt and one's desire to kill one's father. The psycho-analyst might say that Billy Budd has avoided the Oedipus struggle by forming an attachment to the mother at the prephallic level of "oral eroticism" and has allayed his fears of castration by symbolically castrating himself (by being consciously submissive) and by repressing his rage and hostility against the father in order to placate him. That all Billy's rage and hostility against the father are unconscious is symbolized by the fact that whenever it is aroused it cannot find expression in spoken language. Billy can only stutter and use his fists. This is a mechanism for keeping himself from admitting his own guilt and his own destructiveness. For indeed Billy destroys not only Claggart but himself—and even Captain Vere. For a cloud seems to pass over Vere in his last days, and he dies without achieving the rewards his character had seemed to predestine him to achieve; he dies longing for a "child-man" he had once known.

The food symbolism need not be labored. It recurs frequently, and it is the symbolism which takes us down most swiftly into the coherent lower strata of the story, where there is "a subterranean fire . . . eating its way deeper and deeper." Melville even symbolizes moral qualities by their taste, the innocent character having an "untampered-with flavor like that of berries" as against the guilty character, which has the "questionable smack of a compounded wine." Frequently Billy Budd is compared with animals—a heifer, a horse, a dog, a nightingale, a goldfinch. When he is hanged, he ascends to the yardarm like a "singing-bird," watched from below by a "wedged mass of upturned faces"—as if the sailors were birds expecting to be fed. It is said of Billy Budd (the Lamb of God) that the serpent has never bitten him, but after the accusation Claggart is described as a snake.

The idea of Billy as Host is established early in the story. When the lieutenant of the *Indomitable* goes aboard the *Rights-of-Man* in [270/271] search of new hands and immediately selects Billy Budd, he drinks some of the captain's grog almost as if conscious of performing a ritual. "Lieutenant," says the captain, "you are going to take my best man from me, the jewel of 'em.'" "'Yes, I know,' rejoined the other, immediately drawing back the tumbler preliminary to a replenishing; 'yes, I know. Sorry.'" The captain, referring to the pacifying effect Billy has had on his troublesome sailors, then says, "A virtue went out of him, sugaring the sour ones. They took to him like hornets to treacle." Metaphors such as these evoke the primitive rite of slaughtering the young hero in order to eat his flesh and thus obtain his "virtue," his strength, or his heroic quality.

Later in the story Billy Budd spills his soup at mess, and Claggart, happening to pass by at the moment, is inwardly enraged, though outwardly he is only suavely and ambiguously satirical. Melville seems to feel that the enormous eruption of hostile emotion in Claggart may strike the reader as excessive and hence unbelievable. He therefore prefaces one of his comments on the spilled soup with a paragraph which says in effect that the most ordinary event may be a symbolic act which can arouse momentous passions:

> Passion, and passion in its profoundest, is not a thing demanding a palatial stage whereupon to play its part. Down among the groundlings, among the beggars and rakers of the garbage, profound passion is enacted. And the circumstances that provoke it, however trivial or mean, are no measure of its power.

The palatial stage is surely the conscious mind or the realm of conscious art, and the abode of beggars and rakers of the garbage is the unconscious mind. There are "beggars" in the unconscious mind, calling the ego back among the rakers of garbage, as Billy Budd calls his own ego back. And is not this whole passage intended as a statement that *Billy Budd* does not present the reader with a "palatial stage" where profoundest passions are enacted but that, instead, these passions are being enacted "down among the groundlings"? This comes close to telling us not only what is wrong with the story—simply that its profound passions do not find adequate objective representation—but also what is wrong with Billy Budd as tragic hero—that there is no "palatial stage" in his [271/272] personality, no conscious structure, no mind whose disintegration we should watch with pity and terror rather than merely with bewilderment and an obscure sense of loss.

When Claggart spies the spilled soup, it seemed to him "the sly escape of a spontaneous feeling on Billy's part more or less answering to the antipathy on his own." He feels that Billy has insulted him. But what is the nature of the insult? Presumably that, in spilling the soup, Billy has symbolically exposed himself to Claggart as the Host, the vessel from which issues "virtue." ("Handsomely done, my lad!" cries Claggart. "And handsome is as handsome did it, too!") The spilled soup has also exposed Claggart's guilt as an eater of the Host and, furthermore, Claggart's fear of his own unconscious desire to be like

Billy; for the psychological content of Claggart's desire to share Billy's innocence is his desire to be the passive Host.

Melville tells us that Claggart's jaw is heavy out of proportion with his otherwise delicately shaped face—Claggart's unconscious motives center upon orality. This occurs to us when, for example, he smiles at Billy Budd with an ambiguously "glittering dental satire." One of Claggart's "cunning corporals" is called Squeak, "so nicknamed by the sailors on account of his squeaky voice and sharp visage ferreting about the dark corners of the lower decks after interlopers, satirically suggesting to them the idea of a rat in a cellar." Squeak spies on Billy Budd and in this capacity is described as the "purveyor" who "feeds Claggart's passions."

I am sure that much of the sacramental symbolism in *Billy Budd* is conscious and intended. But some of it may be less conscious. One cannot be sure how much Melville means by pointing out that two other partisans of Claggart in compromising Billy Budd (two of Claggart's "messmates," they are called) are the Armourer and the Captain of the Hold; but it is a haunting idea that the Armourer represents Teeth and the Captain of the Hold represents Belly. Nor can one say what Thyestean implications there may be in the use of parts of the body in referring to Claggart, whose nickname is Jimmy Legs and whose official title is Master-at-Arms.

As the story concludes, the grim symbolism occurs more frequently and with more intensity. In the captain's cabin Claggart's "mesmeric glance," which Melville compares with "the hungry [272/273] lurch of the torpedo fish," quickly determines Billy's fate. It is the overt threat of castration which always sets off the explosion of Billy's unconscious fears and resentments. There is a terrible upwelling of his passive emotions, as if in a last attempt to control their aggressive counterparts. Briefly Billy has the expression of "a condemned vestal priestess at the moment of her being buried alive, and in the first struggle against suffocation"—images which convey both the desire for, and the fear of, castration.[1] But such emotions as these Billy cannot express consciously. He stutters, and strikes Claggart.

Describing the scene in which Vere informs Billy Budd of the sentence, Melville says, "there is no telling the sacrament." There is no telling; but the sacrament can be symbolized. Lying manacled on the

---

[1] The psychoanalysts tell us that suffocation is sometimes identified in the unconscious with castration. In connection with the cabin scene, the following passage is significant: "Quite often a patient begins to stutter when he is particularly eager to prove a point. Behind his apparent zeal he has concealed a hostile or sadistic tendency to destroy his opponent by means of words, and the stuttering is both a blocking of and a punishment for this tendency. Still more often stuttering is exacerbated by the presence of prominent or authoritative persons, that is, of paternal figures against whom the unconscious hostility is most intense." O. Fenichel, *The Psychoanalytic Theory of Neuroses*, pp. 312–313.

deck during the night, Billy is like "a patch of discolored snow . . . lingering at some upland cave's black mouth." His terrible experiences are of the order that "devour our human tissues." The skeleton begins to show under Billy's cheek for the first time; he lies between two cannon as if "nipped in the vise of fate." After the hanging of this Lamb of God, after the chaplain has knelt down "on his marrow bones" to pray (as the ballad of "Billy in the Darbies" says), after the night has passed and it is full day, "the fleece of low-hanging vapor had vanished, licked up by the sun that late had so glorified it." The very patriarch of the universe feeds on Billy Budd.

The passage Melville calls "Digression" is difficult and obscure; but I venture the following account. The purser and the surgeon discuss the absence of spasm in Billy's body. (They are at mess during this discussion: we are continually reminded in *Billy Budd* of the verbal kinship of "mess" with the ritual word "mass.") The purser is "a rather ruddy, rotund person, more accurate as an accountant than profound as a philosopher." The surgeon is "spare [273/274] and tall" (the same words used to describe Claggart): he is caustic, austere, and something of an intellectual. The two men are opposite types. The purser is the unthinking human animal who kills, vicariously, in order to eat. He is the simple cannibal, as is indicated by his placid rotundity (his being like a purse) and by his crude belief that Billy controlled his spasm by "will power." The surgeon is, like Claggart, a lean, emotionally complex and ambivalent sadist: he is more interested in murder than in food, as may be symbolized by his hastily leaving the mess table to get back to a patient in the sick bay. Thus, this very horrifying passage is not really a digression: it is a brief scene which universalizes the theme of the story by presenting two opposite mythical types of man lingering, as it were, over the body.

As the body of Billy Budd, wrapped in canvas and weighted with cannon balls, slides over the rail, the sailors "who had just beheld the prodigy of repose in the form suspended in air" think of the same form "foundering in the deeps"—an image of the act of eating. Over the spot where Billy has sunk, gaunt sea birds wheel and scream; and though the birds are predictably moved by "mere animal greed for prey," the sight has a surprising effect on the sailors. "An uncertain movement began among them, in which some encroachment was made." It is a brief moment of potentially mutinous commotion, which we can understand by noticing that the captain and his officers are symbolically connected with the birds, a connection the sailors unconsciously make. Immediately after the hanging, there had been a similar murmurous impulse to mutiny among the sailors. But the ship's officers had acted quickly. Their authoritative voice was heard in the whistle of the boatswain and his mates, which was "shrill as the shriek of the sea-hawk," which "pierced the low ominous sound" and "dissipated" it, so that in a moment or two "the throng was thinned by one half."

In a man-of-war world, Melville is saying, law feeds on man, being only a translation into social forms of that "horrible vulturism of earth" of which he had spoken in *Moby-Dick*. And with a complex human vulturism Captain Vere feeds on Billy Budd. Notice the sexual-sacramental character of Vere's reaction to Billy's spontaneous "God bless Captain Vere." At these words, "Captain Vere, either through stoic self-control or a sort of momentary [274/275] paralysis induced by emotional shock, stood erectly rigid as a musket in the ship-armor's rack." The sexual spasm does not occur in Billy Budd because Billy's vitality or "virtue" has been symbolically transferred to Vere. And yet the transference is ambiguous; paralysis and rigidity suggest death just as surely as erection and the potentiality of the musket suggest life. New vitality has been given to Vere as captain and exponent of martial law (Vere as "musket"), but as man and father he has been stricken.

The intimation of Melville's passages about Lord Nelson is that had Nelson been aboard the *Indomitable* instead of Vere (the two are inferentially compared on several occasions), all this might not have happened, or—and perhaps this is the central point—if it had happened, no subsequent cloud would have passed over Nelson, as it does over Vere. Nelson is the invulnerable and fully mature father, a mythical hero standing behind Captain Vere, a less majestic figure. Nelson already has the qualities of Billy Budd, so that the ritual transference of vitality need not ruin him with its cruel ambiguities. Nelson has the heroic vitality of Billy Budd and the brilliance and audacity of the "jewel" among sailors; it is Nelson's fatherhood which allows him to make "ornate publication" of the very qualities, in sublimated form, which Billy Budd, in the form of infantile rage and hostility, represses. As Melville presents him, Nelson, the "Great Sailor," is the ultimate heroic possibility of the man-of-war world. But he is not of that order of hero represented by Jack Chase; Jack Chase symbolizes a culture beyond the boundaries of Nelson's world. Nelson would never leave his ship to take part in a republican revolution, as Jack Chase did. He is the mythical father whose very presence on board ship, as Melville says, is enough to forestall an incipient mutiny —the uprising, that is, of the sons against the father.

The imposing structure of personality Melville attributes to Nelson is beyond the reach of Captain Vere because Vere's moral stability is not proof against the uprising of the sons. In Claggart he sees his own hostility toward Billy Budd. (The relation of Vere to Claggart and Billy is the relation of a father to his sons, one of whom assumes the aggressive and hostile role of the father and the other of whom assumes the passive role of the mother.) In Billy Budd, Captain Vere sees his own imperfectly redeemed childhood. [275/276] Vere, imposing and even heroic as he is, must repeatedly return to his own childhood to feed on it and to murder it. For him there is no other way of supporting, of nourishing, the structure of consciousness, order, authority, and legality which constitutes the man-of-war world. The man-of-war world destroys itself by feeding on its own vitality, as the vulture feeds upon Prometheus.

This is in itself a moving idea; and so is the implied identification of Billy Budd with Christ. But is there not still another source of the massive emotion which rests uneasily beneath the imperfect surface of *Billy Budd?* Consider the connections Melville makes between the captains and literature. Nelson's ship is "poetic"; it has "symmetry" and "grand lines." Of Nelson at Trafalgar, Melville writes:

> If under the presentiment of the most magnificent of all victories, to be crowned by his own glorious death, a sort of priestly motive led him to dress his person in the jewelled vouchers of his own shining deeds; if thus to have adorned himself for the altar and the sacrifice were indeed vainglory, then affectation and fustian is each truly heroic line in the great epics and dramas, since in such lines the poet embodies in verse those exaltations of sentiment that a nature like Nelson, the opportunity being given, vitalizes into acts.

Homer is a kind of Nelson. They are the same mythical hero—great captains of the mind, the sea, and the man-of-war world. The author of *Moby-Dick* was such a captain.

Captain Vere "loved books." His name, "Vere," signifies (besides "man") "truth"; he is a speaker of the truth. Both his mien and his interests connect him with different kinds of literature than that associated with Nelson. He likes books "treating of actual men and events, no matter of what era." Such a man of truth is Herman Melville, who writes concerning *Billy Budd:* "The symmetry of form attainable in pure fiction cannot so readily be achieved in a narration essentially having less to do with fable than with fact. Truth uncompromisingly told will always have its ragged edges."

In *Typee,* Melville had already pictured himself as Billy Budd, the youth with the nameless malady who shrank with such inexplicable fear from the tattooing instrument, tipped with a shark's tooth, and who discovered that his elders—the fathers and the warriors of the tribe—were cannibals. [276/277]

Lord Nelson is not on "the main road"; he is on "a bypath." The central autobiographical figure in *Billy Budd* is Captain Vere. The dark and moving image of the book is Melville as the devourer of his own childhood. An old man with sons of his own, Melville is overwhelmingly moved with pity for the passive, hermaphrodite youth, an image of himself, who must continuously be killed in the rite of the sacrament if books are to be written or the man-of-war world sustained—or indeed if life is to go on at all.

Surely, then . . . I contradict myself. Billy Budd *is* a deep one and a man-trap (but if he is, he cannot be "innocent"!). His personality has extensive moral significance and psychological reality. He is highly effective, since he kills Claggart and even Captain Vere. And Captain Vere, not Billy Budd, is the tragic hero of the story.

It seems to me, however, that how one judges *Billy Budd* depends on what level of the story one is talking about. Potentially the story is one of the great tragedies of Western literature. But the upper level, the conscious structure, the "palatial stage" is far too uncreated, self-contradictory, and noncommittal to articulate the underlying images. At the explicit symbolic and dramatic levels of the story Melville draws back in awe from Billy Budd and can speak of him only by painful acts of will which in the very process of becoming articulate cut themselves off from the deepest sources of emotion and thus remain inexpressive. Billy Budd's stammering is Melville's own. When Billy Budd speaks articulately, he misrepresents his own deepest emotions. So does Melville. [277]

BILLY BUDD AS ART

The Unity of *Billy Budd*

RAY B. WEST, JR.

. . . THE SUBJECT OF [*Billy Budd*] IS ADEQUATELY SUGGESTED IN MEL-ville's brief preface, the opening sentence of which reads as follows:

> The year 1797, the year of this narrative, belongs to a period which as every thinker now feels, involved a crisis for Christendom not exceeded in its undetermined momentousness at the time by any other era whereof there is record.

This crisis, of course, represents the events surrounding the revolution in France, and it is significant that Melville apparently saw the events of the mutinies at Spithead and at the Nore as symbolic of the threat to world order posed by the revolution. Any reader of Melville knows that he was greatly concerned with the historic development of mankind and that he saw Christianity as the center of an order which seemed gradually but inevitably to be passing away. It was probably because of this view that he could think of himself only as a nominal,

From *Hudson Review*, V (Spring 1952), 120–127. Reprinted by permission of the author.

not an orthodox, Christian. Any reader of *Clarel* understands the approximate terms upon which this state of mind was based [121/ 122] during the later years of Melville's life. Both *Clarel* and *Billy Budd* might have been titled, less imaginatively, "The Crisis of Christendom", with Christendom standing not only for the formal aspects of religion, but for all of the philosophical, political, and moral concerns of Man.

In these terms Billy Budd is Man—Christian man as well as historic man. Though he is presented with obvious simplicity, he contains the ambiguities of all of Melville's heroes from Ahab to The Confidence Man. In Christian terms he is Christ, but with typical Christian ambiguity, he is both the Son of Man and the Son of God. Whence came he? In philosophical and political terms, he sailed first as a common sailor on the *Rights of Man,* but was later impressed aboard his Majesty's warship the *Indomitable.* It is remarkable how little attention critics have paid to the names of these two vessels, as well as to the ship which appears at the end of the story: the French warship *Athéiste,* formerly the *St. Louis.* The contrast between life aboard the *Rights of Man* and that aboard the *Indomitable* is the contrast between the Lockean and the Hobbesian points of view. The order of the first is that imposed by Billy's primitive innocence: the common-sense example of good backed up by physical force when necessary. The *Indomitable* is ruled by a concept of absolute order imposed by authority and depending upon fealty to the source of legislated power. Historically, however, it is the distinction between primitive society (which, of course, Melville knew well and at first hand) and the era of what he called "citified man". Theologically, it is the contrast of pagan and Christian order.

Freeman presents evidence to show that at one point Melville considered naming the *Indomitable,* the *Bellipotente.* Such a title must have seemed to him finally too inclusive, too pointedly aimed at the religious level of his tale. Nevertheless, the religious level is primary during the period of Billy's difficulties aboard the second ship, and the parallel of Billy's execution for technical mutiny and the crucifixion have been clearly and commonly seen. Christ's godlike innocence is mirrored in Billy's natural innocence; Christ's humanity in Billy's natural (physical) defect of speech; Christ's agony in submitting to the Will of Heaven in Billy's submission to the authority of Captain Vere. Captain Vere's exclamation following the death of Claggart (the naturally depraved) by the hand of Billy—"Struck dead by an angel of God. Yet the Angel must hang!"—reflects the paradox of atonement by which Christ suffered the agony of death in order to release mankind from the bondage of evil.

It is clear that Melville saw the idea of the Fall and the Atonement as an accurate image of man's predicament . . .; this level of

Billy Budd is the one [with] which critics have primarily concerned themselves. What is important is that Melville held it *as image*, not as orthodox religion. As such it was nearer an aesthetic than a theological concept. This is important, because it follows that the crucifixion [122/123] becomes tragedy, mirroring man's incompleteness; the victory over evil is transient and incomplete. . . .*

In *Billy Budd* Melville is merely consulting "historic memory", and what he discovers is that man and God are always the same. Billy is budding man, yet he is also the budding God. As primitive man Billy lives at comparative ease with his shipmates aboard the *Rights of Man*—a society similar to that pictured in *Typee*. Transferred, however, to the *Indomitable*—emerging into the era of citified man, he has left nature behind him, except as he himself represents it aboard the second vessel. As a representative of nature, he does the *natural* thing, strikes out at the evil with which he is confronted. It is Claggart's eloquence (the ability to make a fair case for an evil cause) which is the mark of his duplicity. The mark of primitive man is his completeness, his oneness with nature; but he lacks eloquence, he depends upon intuition and action. Citified man faces nature, as John Crowe Ransom has stated handsomely in a recent article, "in guilt and fear toward that Nature who no longer contained him but indifferently confronted him." Melville has Captain Vere say, after acknowledging that Billy's action was no more than "natural": "But do these buttons that we wear attest that our allegiance is to Nature? No, to the King."

The question I take it Melville is raising here is this: If the King's authority is gone, and Nature's, what then supports us? Billy dies for his impulsive act with a prayer for Captain Vere (*vir*—man) upon his lips. A little later the *Indomitable* meets up with the French warship *Athéiste* (formerly the King's ship, the *St. Louis*) and engages her. The *Indomitable* survives the engagement, sinking the *Athéiste*, but Captain Vere, who is also the old god, perhaps even the father of Billy, dies with Billy's name upon his lips, not, as Melville says, "in accents of remorse", but as though transferring his authority to his son: Billy the Son of God and the Son of Man; God become Man and Man become God.

It seems clear that this is Melville's view of the crucifixion—the old God superseded by the new; God as myth. The story of Billy Budd then represents the origin of myth, myth which mirrors man's tragic situation; but is not an attempt at tragedy itself. It is set in a period which represents, in Melville's words, "a crisis for Christendom", a period in which atheism is averted but [123/124] which has only

---

* Deleted passages are quotations from *Clarel* and other late poems of Melville that clarify the direction of his thinking at the time he composed *Billy Budd*. Pertinent quotations from these verses are utilized later in the essay, but quoted without reference to their source. [Ed.]

(possibly) in the story of Billy Budd brought forth a new myth to replace it. *Billy Budd* is to be seen, then, somewhat as prophecy, or as an expression of faith. . . .

[Melville's tale] is [thus] an example of how the new birth will come, winning for mankind a unity such as they knew under Christianity, under the gods of antiquity, or in their primitive innocence. . . .

If the subject of *Billy Budd* is, as we suggest, the renewal of myth, is it Melville's intention to imply that we are simply awaiting the arrival of a new Messiah? In one sense, yes. We must not assume, as did Tully, that since the old gods are gone no new ones will arise to perform the unification performed by the old. On the other hand, Melville is quite specific about a certain danger—the danger of following false gods; and he is equally specific about the method whereby he believes the new will be enabled to arise. It is this which the critics of *Billy Budd* have heretofore failed to see in those pages which they have labeled extraneous.

Let us begin first with the danger. I have said that the victim of Billy's natural wrath, Claggart, clothed his duplicity by a fairness of appearance which included his ability to speak falsehood under the appearance of truth. Undisguised truth (which is what Billy's innocence represents) is hateful because antipodal to evil. Billy is budding man—primitive man: John Locke's *tabula rasa*. Claggart is the Hobbesian man in whom cunning and intelligence have been substituted for brute force. Mythical man (or Captain Vere) stands squarely between these two opposing concepts. He is intelligent but dreamy—sometimes known as "Starry" Vere. He wears the authority of his office openly [124/125] and plainly, as did Lord Nelson, who insisted upon wearing the scarlet and gold-braid even in the midst of battle. The life of Vere (and Nelson) is open to scrutiny, and upon a certain level it is reflected in the beauty of their vessels, the ornaments of their office, the attractions of ceremony, and the eloquence of their commands. Upon another level, however, such ornaments only served to mask the ugly injustices afflicting the common sailors under their command. Here is Melville's dilemma, and the dilemma which supplies the dramatic framework for his tale. If we correct the injustices in the name of humanity, do we not almost commit ourselves to the giving up of all of those beauties which the old order had cherished? Yes, Melville finally concedes, we do. We exchange Nelson's ornate dress for drab, because in calling attention to himself, Nelson endangered the lives of those under him. We relinquish the ceremony of authority, because to delay weighing anchor as Nelson did was dangerous and impractical in a world where ceremony is no longer observed. We surrender the grand lines of Nelson's flagship *Victory* to the more functional and less beautiful design of the *Monitor*. Yet we do not accede to the demands of revolution—atheism. We have come full circle, but only in the sense that pagan civilization had come full circle at the time of Tully. . . .

We then are faced by the same danger which Captain Vere faced in his engagement with the *Athéiste:* civil barbarism. The *Athéiste* is, significantly, not a vessel in its own right, but one merely captured and renamed. The question of identity here is related to Melville's concept of truth and reality. Atheism, which was the product of popular science, was doomed simply because it did not express truth and reality. Captain Vere was doomed, but for an entirely different reason ("The gods are gone"); the *Indomitable* survived both the *St. Louis* and the *Athéiste,* but the implication is clear that the crisis is one merely of discovering a new captain. Melville's attitude toward popular science is further clarified in an ironic passage labeled "A Digression", which occurs in the narrative just after Billy's death. The Purser and the ship's Surgeon are discussing what everyone had considered the remarkable nature of Billy's dying. The Purser suggested that willpower might have been responsible for the absence of the usual physical manifestations, but the Surgeon ridicules such an idea, saying it is not more attributable to will-power than to horsepower. He admits that the event was phenomenal only "in the sense that it was an appearance the cause of which is not immediately to be assigned." The Purser then suggests euthanasia. "*Euthanasia*", the Surgeon replies, "is something like your *will-power;* I doubt its authenticity as a scientific term. . . . It is at once imaginative and metaphysical—in short, Greek."

It seems clear that if Melville was optimistic it was not with the arrogant optimism of Nineteenth Century science. This is further indicated in the report of Billy's death supplied by a writer of popular prose, the reporter of [125/126] *News from the Mediterranean;* here (as with the Surgeon) the truth is hidden beneath a false appearance of truth. If Claggart represents malicious evil (natural depravity), the Surgeon represents the evil of ignorance, while the popular reporter, pretending to serve constituted authority, tells the grossest falsehood of all. All are forms of dissimulation—the dangers confronting modern man in his search for truth. Where then does truth lie?

The answer, of course, is inherent in the novel itself. . . . Christianity and all it implies has fallen into decay. The spirit exhales, but only momentarily, awaiting the propitious moment again to belly philosophy's sails. Billy's act of innocent heroism supplies the opportunity—creates the situation. Authoritarianism and a changing concept of man's individual worth had conspired to bring about the destruction of the old gods. Billy's act (and by extension, Christ's) is seen more as tragic circumstance than as actual atonement. From Billy's act then springs the new myth, sung to the tune of a simple sailor's ballad. It is "verse, popular verse" which bellies the sails, which supplies the common man with a means of confronting the facts, not only of Billy's death, but of his own. It is not orthodox Christianity. It is not popular science. It is the simple creative act which pierces the mask of falsehood and error, which sees man's existence as an heroic submission to fate, but which is in constant rebellion against those forms which result in man's injustice to man.

If it seems odd that so apparent and so integrated a theme should have been missed by so many readers, the fact of its having been missed is only additional evidence of the difficulty which the modern reader has with the ironic style in which Billy is composed. The difficulty is multiplied in this case, because Melville did not employ (indeed, could not have employed) the lyric-ironic style of *Moby Dick*, to which we have, after a lapse of many years, become accustomed. Accompanying the positive theme of man's rejuvenation through myth, there is also, as we have indicated, the negative one of modern man's situation in an over-materialistic society: "atheized into a smatterer". In a satiric-ironic manner, Melville pretends to adopt the very style of the popular-prose writer against whom his book is at least partially directed. Despite the fact that his central theme betrays his principal intention—he had elsewhere [126/127] written, "It is not the purpose of literature to purvey news",—he pretended to have written a story which, as he says, "has less to do with fable than with fact". He speaks of digressions and ragged edges, as though the very essence of truth lay in its absence of form. He pretends, in other words, to have written the very book which claims arrest of the advance of truth, or fable, or of instituted creeds; but the theme itself, the form which he has created in *Billy Budd*, tinctures the very book which he pretends to have written—the book of factual information concerning a mutiny at sea.

Contrary to current critical opinion, then, *Billy Budd* as a unified work not only is not marred by digressions and irrelevancies, it is a triumph of architectonic structure. When Melville protests that as a writer of "facts" he is prevented from achieving "an architectural finial", he is merely calling attention (in a method not uncommon in literature) to his central theme, which is in fact presented as an architectural finial, since it lies imbedded in the popular ballad "Billy in the Darbies", which ends the book. . . . This is not great poetry, but it was not intended to be. Neither is it, as one critic calls it, doggerel. It is intended merely to represent the primitive, but universal, ability of man to temper the harsh facts of death, to come to terms with nature, through art. It represents Melville's final expression of faith in mankind—faith in the ability of the common man to see beyond the misrepresentations of evil, however disguised; faith that the essential beauty and heroism of man will always be recognized and celebrated in artistic form, however crude.

Billy Budd is not in itself a tragedy, although it is an expression of belief in the tragic predicament of man. If we need distinguish it by supplying a name, I would suggest that it be called satiric-allegory. It does not pretend to the organ voice of *Moby Dick*. It combines the biting irony of Swiftian satire with the lyric hopefulness of John Bunyan. That it has been so little understood need not finally surprise us when we consider the history of Melville's literary career from *Mardi* onward. Among other things, *Billy Budd* suggests the possibility that Melville believed the rich tongue of Shakespeare (the use of which he borrowed in *Moby Dick* and *Pierre*) to be as obsolete as the scarlet and gold of Lord Nelson's office. Perhaps this is why he chose to write otherwise in his final work. [127]

The Form of *Billy Budd*

WILLIAM YORK TINDALL

Billy Budd SEEMS TO MAKE SOMETHING ALMOST TOO TIDY OUT OF WHAT remains uncertain in *Moby Dick*. Melville's story of the captain, the villain, and the tar, apparently less a story than a commentary on one, may strike the hasty reader as a product of reason rather than imagination, as something reduced to discourse for ready apprehension by basic Englishmen. What had to be said has been said by Captain Vere or Melville himself. As critics, therefore, we may feel frustrated, as Romantics we may prefer a little teasing mystery around, and as esthetes, confronted with discourse, we are sure that talking about a thing is less admirable than embodying it in image or action. Of Kierkegaard's three categories, the esthetic, the moral, and the divine, Melville seems to have chosen the second—to the applause of some and the departure of others, for *Don Giovanni* maybe.

That the matter of *Billy Budd* gratifies what Melville calls "the moral palate" is plain from the plainest rehearsal. The scene is a British frigate during the Napoleonic wars. Two mutinies have justified fears of more. Against this ominous background, Billy, an innocent aboard, is accused for no good reason by Claggart, a petty officer, of plotting mutiny. The captain, a reasonable man, doubts Claggart's story and brings Billy in to confront his lying accuser. Overcome by a stutterer's indignation, the innocent foretopman, unable to speak a word, strikes

From "The Ceremony of Innocence," in R. M. McIver, ed., *Great Moral Dilemmas in Literature, Past and Present* (New York: Harper & Row, 1956), pp. 73–81, by permission of publisher and author. [Editor's title.]

Claggart dead with a fist like a ham. Captain Vere is faced with a dilemma. Though he believes in Billy's innocence, naval law and prudence alike demand punishment for the [73/74] impetuous seaman while pity and reason counsel mercy. Internal debate inclines the captain toward conviction, and Billy, condemned despite the "troubled conscience" of his judges, is hanged.

The subject is a quandary or what Melville calls "the intricacies involved in the question of moral responsibility." As the captain ponders "the moral phenomenon presented in Billy Budd" and the "elemental evil" of Claggart, he fathoms the "mystery of iniquity." The case of Billy seems, as the captain says, a matter for "psychologic theologians."

Although, as T. S. Eliot observes in *After Strange Gods,* "It is . . . during moments of moral and spiritual struggle . . . that men (in fiction) . . . come nearest being real," Billy and Claggart, who represent almost pure good and pure evil, are too simple and too extreme to satisfy the demands of realism; for character demands admixture. Their all but allegorical blackness and whiteness, however, are functional in the service of Vere's problem, and Vere, goodness knows, is real enough. Claggart is black because, as Philipp G. Frank once observed, a sinner is necessary for the realization of a moral code; and an innocent is almost equally instructive. These abstractions, a sacrifice of verisimilitude to tactical necessity, reveal the "moral quality" of the captain's mind, which becomes a theater for contending opposites and eventual choice. Such dramatic crises are not only the favorite stuff of novelists but of philosophers and poets as well: Kierkegaard wrote *Either/Or* and Yeats "The Choice."

Not only rational, Vere's choice involves his whole sensitive, adult being. Agony shows on his face as he emerges from his interview with Billy, and a final exclamation shows how deeply he is stirred. Involving more than black and white, the captain's choice is between two moral codes, military and natural. The first is evident; the second is either that of the noble savage, in whom Melville was interested, or what Western culture takes for granted. In other words, the captain's conflict is between the balanced claims of justice and equity, order and confusion, law and grace, reason and feeling, or, as Melville puts it, "military duty" and "moral scruple." Vere's eloquent and moving speech to the drumhead court, the climax of such drama as there is, leaves little to add about these issues and his dilemma. [74/75]

The conflict of military with natural may occupy the stage, but Melville recognizes other codes, that of custom or respectability, for example. Claggart's "natural depravity" appears in respectable guise. Melville also recognizes the cultural, psychological, and absolute bases for morality, and hints in a very modern way at their operation.

"Moral," Melville's favorite word—in this book at least—is one which, though commonly taken for granted, is slippery. I have read a

thing in which "moral" means something else on every page. What
Yvor Winters means by it escapes me. Vague and general like F. R.
Leavis's "awareness of life" or narrow and definite like the *quid agas* of
Scholastic philosophers, the word needs fixing before use. As I shall
use it and as I think Melville did, morality implies not only action but
motive, attitude, and being. It involves a sense of obligation to self,
community, and the absolute, which provide a frame by conscience,
law, tradition, or revelation. If we demand a single equivalent, Melville's "responsibility" will do.

Vere's action, however sudden and whether we approve of it or
not, is plainly responsible. Billy and Claggart act, to be sure: one bears
false witness and the other delivers a blow, but neither actor follows
reason and each is more important for what he is than what he does. If
being as well as action can be moral, however, they are moral figures,
too, existing like cherubs or fiends in a moral atmosphere. Good and
bad, they occupy the region of good and evil.

It is agreed by most that moral substance is necessary for the
novel. Not the pure form of Flaubert's desire, and falling far short of
the condition of music, the novel is an arrangement of references to
vital issues, without which it is empty. A value of Joyce's *Ulysses*, for
example, is the feeling and idea of charity. That moral substance fails
to insure greatness, however, is proved by the works of Horatio Alger;
and that it fails to guarantee moral effect is proved by those of Mickey
Spillane. The errors of censors and formalists show the folly of judging
by morality alone or arrangement alone. Not moral idea but its
embodiment in what Eliot called objective correlatives, suitably ar-
ranged, determines value. Far from inciting action as moralizing does,
embodied morality invites contemplation, and to become an object of
contemplation, substance must be distanced by form. The [75/76]
question is not how much morality is there but how much is under
control, how fully insight and moral intelligence have submitted to
esthetic discipline. Our problem, then, is not morality itself but moral
art or morally significant form.

Captain Vere's speech to the court adequately embodies the idea
of "moral responsibility" in dramatic form; but we must find if Billy's
history has found fitting embodiment. At first reading, that history
seems a curious and eccentric structure of essays on ethics, digressions
or "bypaths," character sketches, and chronicles of the navy, an
arrangement that after uncertain progress tails inconclusively off. Such
image and action as we find, failing to halt the lamentable decline,
seem occasions for analysis or digression, like biblical texts in a pulpit.
Since the crucial interview between Vere and Billy is disappointingly
offstage, Melville seems to have avoided the dramatic possibilities of
his theme. That the book calls for the dramatization he failed to give it,
is proved by attempts at play and opera, which, while affirming
excellence of theme, imply that action or image are better ways of

presenting it. But something that continues to fascinate us in its present form and calls forth responses beyond the capacity of discourse, suggests art of another kind. Maybe Melville avoided drama in the interests of a less obvious medium.

Moby Dick assures us that Melville was an artist, not a lecturer on ethics. He not only worked three years on *Billy Budd*, but he seems to have regarded the result with far from senile favor. The first version, recently detected in manuscript by F. Barron Freeman, reveals more action and less discourse; yet this version, which corresponds more happily to what we think fiction should be, is not so effective as the one before us with all its weight of digression and analysis.

That Melville was aware of form is clear from passages in *Billy Budd*. When Captain Vere says, "With mankind forms, measured forms, are everything," he probably means usage and custom; but Melville himself, applying Vere's remark to esthetics, says that the symmetry of form desirable in pure fiction cannot be achieved in factual narrative like this. The story is not factual in fact. But Melville, wanting it to seem so, excuses apparent formlessness as a form for [76/77] giving the illusion of a bare report; for truth, he continues, will always have its ragged edges and matters of fact must lack the finish of an "architectural finial." Aware of loose structure and inconclusive ending, he justifies them for what seem wrong reasons. Not reasons, however, but what he made must detain us while we scout further possibilities. The curious form he made may be functional and, for all our hasty impression and his explanation, effective. Is the book as shapeless as he implies? Or, if shapeless, is shapelessness a kind of shape? Is the book as pedestrian, discursive, and factual as he claims and as we had supposed on first looking into it?

What seems at first to be factual is presented, we find, in part by images and allusions that are incompatible with pretense of factuality. Though unapparent, those images are livelier than we thought. Consider the coloring of the scene between decks before the execution as Billy lies in white amid profound blackness. Catching up the abstract whiteness and blackness of Billy and Claggart, this image of black and white embodies them. At the execution the rosy dawn that seems "the fleece of the Lamb of God seen in mystical vision" promises a kind of renewal while implying much else. Circling birds after the burial at sea offer by the aid of tradition some spiritual import. And that spilt soup, perhaps more action than image, carries suggestions beyond the demands of plot, suggestions so indefinite, what is more, that they confound its rational progress. Even the names of ships, though serving a more comprehensible purpose, are as significant as those in *Moby Dick*. Billy is removed from the *Rights of Man*, for instance, and Vere is mortally wounded by a shot from the *Athéiste*.

The words of *Billy Budd* carry more than denotation. "Sinister dexterity," at once witty and desolating, sounds like something from

Finnegans Wake, where, indeed, it reappears. Vere's last words, "Billy Budd," are equivocal. Do they imply feeling, regret, self-realization, understanding? Are they a form for something incompletely realized? However "factual" the words of this pseudoreport, they function like the words of poetry.

Not only last words and indeterminate images but a number of hints about Billy's "all but feminine" nature plague our assumptions. [77/78] Roses and lilies dye his cheeks. He comports himself like a "rustic beauty" at times and like a vestal virgin at others. These qualities and appearances, astonishing in an able seaman, calling forth an "ambiguous smile" from one or another of his shipmates, suggest psychological depths and motives below the level of the plain report. By virtue of such intimations Billy seems at once more and less bottomless than we had supposed, and so do the motives of Claggart, if not those of the captain himself. Among such suggestions, avoidance of the obviously dramatic becomes implicit embodiment that escapes the limits of drama.

What pleases me most, however, is the accompaniment of biblical allusions which, however unobtrusive and irregular, recurs like Wagnerian *leitmotiv.* Time and again Billy is compared to Adam and Jesus. Billy's innocence is as much that of Adam before the Fall as that of the more secular noble savage. As a "peacemaker," a term implying beatitude, Billy seems destined for "crucifixion"; and his hanging, condensing events, becomes an ascension. Vere is compared to Abraham about to sacrifice Isaac, obeying God's will with fear and trembling. Becoming a shadow of God, Vere weighs the claims of Adam and Satan. Claggart, whose denunciation is reported in Mosaic terms as "false witness," is compared not only to the Serpent of Eden but to Ananias and to one struck dead by an angel of God, "yet," as the captain says, "the angel must hang!" Man's fall and redemption and all troubles between seem suggested by this large though not fully elaborated analogy, which, bringing to mind the mythical parallels in *Ulysses* and *The Waste Land,* removes Billy a little farther from the abstraction to which, for all his stutter and those rosy cheeks, he seems committed. However incapable of supporting this mythical burden, he becomes by its aid almost as portentous as choosing Vere. The sailors, whose testimony cannot be ignored, are more impressed by Billy than by Vere, reason and all. Not only being and secular victim, Billy becomes saint and martyr and his hanging an omen. Pieces of the spar to which he quietly ascends are venerated like pieces of the true cross, suitable for reliquaries or the holiest of duffle bags. By the aid of myth and military ritual the [78/79] story of Billy, transformed from an essay on good, evil, and choice, approaches what Yeats called "the ceremony of innocence."

We must conclude that Melville avoided the attractions of the obvious in the interests of indefinite suggestiveness and myth. His work, whatever its air of the factual and the discursive, is symbolist and richer for scarcity of drama and image. Such drama and images as are there function more intensely in their abstract context than profusion could. That the structure as a whole also serves esthetic purpose is likely. As we have seen, the book is a queer arrangement of discourse, action, image, and allusion, with discourse predominating. We have seen how image and action work in this mixture; but we must examine the function of discourse. In such context, discourse, increasing tension, makes allusion and image dramatic or enlarges them, and, working with allusion, image, and action may produce a third something by juxtaposition as in Eliot's *Four Quartets* or Wallace Stevens' *Notes Toward a Supreme Fiction.* Seeming now a structure of conflicts, not only of men and codes but of methods, which become a technical echo of the theme, the book emerges as a structural drama or a drama of structure. An ending that seemed weak afterthought (and was not there in the first version) now unifies all. Vere's exclamation, the saint's legend, and inconclusiveness, working together, comprise a form, which may tail off but tails suggestively off, leaving endless reverberations in our minds. There is more mystery around than we had thought, and we may agree with dying Gertrude Stein that answers are less important than questions. What at a superficial reading had the appearance of exhaustive discourse becomes inexhaustible. The shapeless thing becomes suggestive shape. Neither as loose nor as tight as it once seemed, the strange sequence of precise discourse and indefinite suggestiveness corresponds to our experience of life itself. That the form Melville made fascinates while it eludes and teases is shown no less by popular favor than by the abundance of critical comment.

However different it looks, *Billy Budd* is not altogether different in kind from *Moby Dick,* another structure of digression, discourse, action, and image. The proportions and impact may be different, the [79/80] images of *Moby Dick* may be more compelling, but both serve symbolic suggestion and both are forms for offering a vision of reality. Not the tidy discourse of our first impression, the work is almost as inexplicable as *Moby Dick.*

What exactly does this form present? It is impossible to answer this question for any symbolist work; for works of this kind escape discursive accounting. We may say that *Billy Budd* is a vision of man in society, a vision of man's moral quandary or his responsibility; but its meaning is more general than these, and that is why it haunts us. So haunted, I find the work not an essay or a moral issue but a form for embodying the feeling and idea of thinking about a moral issue, the experience of facing, of choosing, of being uneasy about one's choice, of trying to know. Not a conclusion like a sermon, *Billy Budd* is a vision of confronting what confronts us, of man thinking things out with all the attendant confusions and uncertainties. Disorder is a form for this and the apparently formless book a formal triumph. To do what it does it has to be a fusion of tight-loose, shapeless-shaped, irrelevant-precise, suggestive-discursive—a mixture of myth, fact, and allusion that has values beyond reference. The discursive parts represent our attempts at thinking, while the action, images, and allusions represent what we cannot think but must approximate. Arrangement of these discordant elements forms a picture of a process.

From my guess at meaning it follows that the center of this form is neither Vere nor Billy but rather the teller of the story or Melville himself. Though ghostlier, he is not unlike the Marlow of Conrad's *Lord Jim* and *Heart of Darkness* or the Quentin of Faulkner's *Absalom, Absalom!* Using Vere and Billy as materials, Melville's thought-process, like those of Marlow and Quentin, is the heart of this darkness and its shape the objective correlative, a form for something at once imperfectly understood and demanding understanding. Morality, the substance of this form, becomes an element that limits and directs the feelings and ideas created by the whole. Moral substance, what is more, may be what engages our minds while the form does its work. Value, not from morality alone, issues from the form that includes it and in which it serves. If the form [80/81] concerned less, I repeat, it would be trivial, but without its formal presentation the morality would remain in Sunday school.

United now, the beautiful and the good create a vision larger than either, a vision transcending the case of Billy Budd or the quandary of Captain Vere. The teller, now any man, presents man's feeling in the face of any great dilemma. Thought and feeling, outdistancing themselves, become objects of contemplation, remote yet immediate. The effect of this form is moral in the sense of enlarging our awareness of human conditions or relationships and of improving our sensitivity. In such a form Kierkegaard's esthetic, moral, and divine become a single thing. [81]

4. CHRISTIAN SOURCES AND CLASSICAL PARALLELS

Melville's Use of the Bible

NATHALIA WRIGHT

WHEN THE THEME OF THE CRUCIFIXION IS TAKEN UP FINALLY IN *Billy Budd*, the New Testament story is clearly visible. Fundamentally, of course, the two main characters in the novel are embodiments of two abstractions. In one sense Budd is simple nature, a barbarian, "Adam . . . ere the urbane Serpent wriggled himself into his company." Yet his innocence is more than that of a natural man, completely unarmed in the world. It is a divine innocence, incorruptible by society or the forces of darkness. It is a communicable quality, too, to such an extent that Billy's captain on [128/129] the *Rights of Man* says of him, as Jesus said of himself: " 'Not that he preached to them or said or did anything in particular; but a virtue went out of him, sugaring the sour ones.' "

The spiritual antithesis of Billy is Claggart, the master-at-arms, who represents "depravity according to nature." It is a quality not consisting of petty vices nor engendered by experience, but innately residing in his inmost being. He is not so much an evil man as an evil principle, described by such words as those in Proverbs 21:10, which Melville marked: "The soul of the wicked desireth evil. . . ." Admittedly Melville had some Biblical parallel in mind, for when he came to analyze Claggart he indulged in an illuminating digression. Recording a youthful conversation with a friend on the subject of penetrating character, he quoted the friend as saying:

"Coke and Blackstone hardly shed so much light into obscure spiritual places as the Hebrew prophets. And who were they? Mostly recluses."
At the time my inexperience was such that I did not quite see the drift of all this. It may be that I see it now. And, indeed, if that lexicon which is based on Holy Writ were any longer popular, one might with less difficulty define and denominate certain phenomenal men. As it is, one must turn to some authority not liable to the charge of being tinctured with the Biblical element. [129/130]

From *Melville's Use of the Bible* (Durham: Duke University Press, 1949), pp. 128–135, by permission of the publisher.

193

Yet while Billy and Claggart are essentially abstractions, arrayed against each other by their very natures, for the purposes of the plot they play the roles of Jesus and Judas. Though he is not a creature of the secondary or auxiliary nature of Judas, Claggart is as effective a betrayer of an innocent man to authority. His first attempt is by bribery: he has a seaman offer Billy two guineas to join a proposed mutiny group. When that temptation is withstood, Claggart falsely charges that Billy is disloyal to the king. Only in this way, by treachery, can evil reach good. So Jesus was betrayed by Judas after he had resisted the temptations of Satan in the wilderness, and above him on the cross was hung the same charge: treason.

Both these indictments, moreover, go unanswered. When Budd is brought into the cabin and hears Claggart's accusation he does not utter a word in self-defense, just as Jesus remained silent before the priests and elders. The experience has brought out his defect of speech and he is momentarily paralyzed, though making agonized efforts to speak and defend himself. Perceiving the situation, Vere offers him more time in which to reply, but he is not successful in soothing the sailor:

Contrary to the effect intended, these words, so fatherly in tone, doubtless touching Billy's heart to the quick, prompted yet more violent efforts at utterance—efforts soon ending for the time in confirming the paralysis, and bringing to the face an expression which was as a crucifixion to behold.

Then comes Budd's response to Claggart's accusation, not consciously but instinctively. There can be no compromise between the two forces which they represent, and Claggart falls fatally under Budd's blow. Nor can there be compromise between what remains: between Budd and the king's statute, under which he is now subject to trial. It does not matter that in nature he is free; it does not matter [130/131] that in breaking an immediate law he thereby kept one higher. Nor does his intent enter into the case; he is judged solely by his deed. The purity of his conscience is reserved for consideration until the Last Assizes, where, as Vere remarks, it will surely acquit him. Here he is the double victim of malignity and of custom.

Thus poignantly and dramatically did Melville distinguish between the false and the true charge against Budd. The distinction is the same in the trial of Jesus. The charge of treason which the members of the Sanhedrin proffered, though necessary for his official execution, was not only false, it was superficial in their own minds. Their true grievance against him was the fact that in obeying the spirit of the law, even more faithfully than they, Jesus violated its letter. Under a similar primitive code both he and the Handsome Sailor are condemned: the Mosaic law and the Mutiny Act. The similarity between the two codes is not insignificant. For the Mutiny Act, demanding a life for a life, is in effect the same penalizing legalism as the Old Testament ethic. . . .

Throughout these scenes Captain Vere stands in two relationships to Budd. Primarily he is the military superior and disciplinarian. He sacrifices everything to the end of having Billy convicted, calling a drumhead court together lest in the delay he be swayed by the essential right and wrong of the case from the execution of his duty as administrator of the drastic law. Like Pilate, he condemns to death a man whom he knows to be innocent, though unlike Pilate he accepts the full responsibility of his act. Melville may have known, too, that apocryphal story that Pilate was haunted by the memory of Jesus during his last years as praetor of Hispania Tarraconensis. Not far from this locality Vere murmurs Budd's name as he lies dying on Gibraltar. [131/132]

Yet Vere also appears in the role of Billy's father; as Abraham to Isaac, as God to Jesus—or rather, not as Abraham to Isaac. Among numerous figures of speech emphasizing the general father-son relationship of the two men this one, brief as it is, provides a revealing contrast with the particular relationship which Melville was also at pains to establish between them. In the private interview between the foretopman and his captain before the execution Melville imagines:

The austere devotee of military duty, letting himself melt back into what remains primeval in our formalised humanity, may in the end have caught Billy to his heart, even as Abraham may have caught young Isaac on the brink of resolutely offering him up in obedience to the exacting behest.

The figure is moving, but the parallel can be carried no further. For Isaac did not die. Even waiving the fact that his near sacrifice is a deliberate scheme of the Old Testament Jehovah, the obedience of Isaac and of Billy Budd are two different things. Isaac was not taken into Abraham's confidence any more than Abraham was taken into Jehovah's. All is blind obedience, dependent on a jealous and capricious deity.

Not so is the sympathy between Budd and Vere. The sailor and the officer meet as equals; neither conceals anything from the other. When confused at the trial Budd turns to Vere, his accuser, for counsel. His only concern is to have himself cleared in the mind of his captain, to be understood if not to understand; when that is accomplished he has no fear of the future. Their interview alone in Vere's cabin is not unlike the episode in Gethsemane. Afterward the foretopman possesses a peace marvelous and ineffable, which even the chaplain cannot fathom. As he goes to his death his last words are, " 'God bless Captain Vere!' " [132/133] . . .

But Melville read something . . . [else] into the Crucifixion story. There he found one more illustration for his notion that beyond the farthest known truth there is yet an untrodden realm, an undisclosed mystery. Unlike Jehovah in the Old Testament, God the Father seems to practice as well as to command obedience; [133/134] hence his enigmatical willingness for Jesus to die. And so in *Billy Budd* even he who administers the law is bound by it. It is the fact that Vere did not formulate the Mutiny Act which makes possible the community of spirit between him and Billy Budd. Both are subject to a power beyond themselves.

What this power is, what this realm is in which, as in Hebrew wisdom, God himself does not reign, Melville never concluded. But it is clearly not simply evil. It is beyond good or evil; it is beyond conflict. The realm in which Budd meets Vere is not the same as that in which he meets Claggart, and beyond them all is an utterly amoral, mysteriously influential *terra incognita*. The last of all Melville's symbols, the death of Captain Vere in the encounter with the *Athéiste*, is a fitting one. Religion, even in its noblest aspect, remained for him penultimate.

The mystery in *Billy Budd* is thus not altogether one of iniquity. It is the mystery of a boundless creation, an infinite number of superficially exclusive, deeply related spheres. Symbolic of their existence and of their interdependence is the fact that all nature is affected at Budd's death, as it was at the death of Jesus. . . . The moral conflict is not confined to its own world but reaches beyond it, even to the unyielding elements. When Budd's body is hoisted aloft the violent motion usually noticeable at hangings is absent; it is suspended quietly above the heads of his comrades. At the same moment the appearance of the sea and sky becomes phenomenal:

. . . the vapoury fleece hanging low in the east, was shot through with a soft glory as of the fleece of the Lamb of God seen in mystical vision, and simultaneously therewith, watched by the wedged mass of upturned faces, Billy ascended; and ascending, took the full rose of the dawn.[134/135]

It is not accidental that the description contains a suggestion of the Ascension and of the doctrine of the Atonement. For in the manuscript of *Billy Budd* the word "shekinah" is crossed out in favor of "rose," and at the beginning of the next chapter Melville first referred to Billy's "ascension" but changed it to his "execution."

Finally, when Billy's remains are lowered into the sea, throngs of birds fly screaming to the spot and circle it as the ship passes out of sight. And at last it is related that for several years the sailors of the *Indomitable* knew the whereabouts of the spar from which Billy was suspended, following it from ship to dockyard to ship again. "To them a chip of it was as a piece of the Cross." . . . [135]

Melville's *Nunc Dimittis*

NEWTON ARVIN

. . . THE REAL FEELING OF *Billy Budd* . . . IS VERY DEEP AND VERY AF-
fecting; it triumphs even over the stiff-jointed prose, the torpidity of
the movement, the excess of commentary, and Melville's failure to
quicken any of the scenes with a full dramatic life. In spite of these
blemishes of form and manner, the persons in *Billy Budd* and the
moral drama they enact have too much largeness, as well as too much
subtlety, in their poetic representativeness, not to leave a permanent
stamp on the imagination.

For the tale of the Handsome Sailor and his unhappy end has an
archetypal depth and scope that no reader can quite mistake; it is
Melville's version of a primordial fable, the fable of the Fall of Man,
the loss of Paradise. There are vibrations in it of the Book of Genesis,
of the *Works and Days*, of Milton; there are other vibrations that are
pure Melville. Billy himself, at any rate, is on one level Primal Man; he
is Adam; indeed, it is said of him that, in the nude, he "migh. have
posed for a statue of young Adam before the fall." His physical beauty,
certainly, is such as the First Man's would necessarily be; but so, too,
and of course more vitally, is the purity of his innocence, his incapacity
so much as to imagine evil, his utter freedom from all malice and envy,
and his helplessness in the presence of the wrong. His goodness,
moreover, is not mere blank innocence; it is an active and disarming
good nature also, and it draws upon him the spontaneous affection of
his mates. But there is a complete absence from it of any intellectual
element whatever; the illiterate and mindless Billy is "radically" a
barbarian. And perfect as Billy is in the innocence of his heart, he is
touched nevertheless by the primordial imperfection of humanity. His
stutter [294/295] is a symbol of this, and there is a mysterious justice
in the fact that this stutter is his undoing.

If Billy is the Adam of this naval Eden, Claggart is of course its
Satan. Malign as he is, Claggart, like the Great Enemy in *Paradise
Lost*, has a certain nobility of form and type. In physical presence,
with his tall figure, his shapely forehead, and his curling black hair, he
is quite without meanness, and it is only his strangely protuberant chin
and his unwholesome pallor of complexion that hint at the depravity of
his being. That depravity is inherent and terrible, but it does not

From *Herman Melville: A Critical Biography* (New York: William Sloane
Associates, Inc., 1950), pp. 294–299, copyright 1950 by William Sloane Associates,
Inc., by permission of William Sloane Associates, Inc. [Editor's title.]

express itself in what are called vices or small sins. As a naval officer, Claggart is a model of dutifulness and patriotism, and intellectually he is a man of marked superiority. He is dominated, indeed, by his intellectuality; dominated by it, at any rate, in his *means*, for his aims are mad; with all his "rationality," he is completely exempt, at heart, from the law of reason. Instinctively he hates the good; hates Billy precisely because he is innocent and guileless. In the deepest sense Claggart is a rebel and a traitor, like his great exemplar; a rebel against the law of reason and a traitor to the image of man. There is a Guy Fawkes, as Melville says, prowling in the hid chambers of his nature, and it is wholly suitable that the charge he brings against an innocent man should be the charge of mutiny. It is true that Billy has been guiltless of what he is accused of; guiltless of rebellion and disobedience; but was not that the sin to which Satan tempted the first of men? and is it not fitting that Claggart should now impute it to Billy? There is a strong suggestion of the old serpent in the master-at-arms, and when, after his death, Billy and Captain Vere attempt to raise his body to a sitting posture, "it was like handling a dead snake."

Now that he has struck dead an officer of the Navy, Billy is indeed objectively guilty, under the Mutiny Act, of a crime of exactly the same heinousness as that with which he was falsely charged. It may be that, as the officer of marines protests, Budd *intended* neither mutiny nor homicide; Adam did [295/296] not *intend* disobedience either, and, as Captain Vere observes, "Budd's intent or non-intent is nothing to the purpose." The Mutiny Act, like war, of which it is the offspring, "looks but to the frontage," and Captain Vere, as the embodiment of naval authority, the Jehovah of the drama, has no choice but to administer, dutifully and grimly, the harsh terms of that Act. In order to do so, he must suppress not only the heart within him but his private conscience: it is the "imperial" conscience, formulated in the Naval Code, under which he officially proceeds. This means adjudging to death a youth toward whom he is drawn emotionally as a father to a son. Imaginably, Billy might *be* his son, for Billy is a foundling and one in whom noble descent is as evident as in a blood horse; and the aristocratic Captain Vere, a bachelor, "was old enough to have been Billy's father." The sacrifice of Billy by Captain Vere is a re-enactment of the sacrifice of Isaac by Abraham, though it is a completed one; and Vere does not turn aside from his duty, anguishing though it is. Billy is hanged at the yard-arm, and Vere, a few months later, mortally wounded by a shot from the *Athéiste*, dies with Billy's name on his lips.

Such is this rewriting of the first three chapters of Genesis, this late-nineteenth-century *Paradise Lost*. Budd owes much of its subliminal effect on the imagination to the fact that it repeats, with variations, that primordial pattern. Yet quite as real as the repetition, and at least as vital, are the variations. There is no Eve in this Eden, for one thing, but far more importantly, the tale does not have, after all, the un-equivocal spiritual and moral simplicity of the Christian legend or of any of its theological formulations. It abounds in what Melville himself calls ambiguities; it suggests no unambiguous dogma. There is a strain of irony in it that has no parallel in Genesis or in Milton. . . . [296/ 297] Unlike the world of theology, Melville's world is insuperably incomprehensible, and he makes no claim to comprehending it.

The drama of the Fall of Man is a drama in which divine and absolute justice is countered by infernal evil in a contest for the immortal soul of God's creature, Man, and in which Man, yielding to the temptation of the evil spirit, turns rebel against God's will, disobeys it, and involves himself and all his posterity in the guilt of Original Sin. Billy, on the contrary, is no rebel against divine justice, and he is not guilty, even symbolically, of disobeying some tran-scendent will. He is an unwitting, impulsive offender against the Mutiny Act, the child of war, itself an evil and infecting with evil everything that relates to it. Captain Vere makes no mistake about that. To the protest of the officer of marines that Billy intended no mutiny, he replies: "Surely not, my good man. And before a court less arbitrary and more merciful than a martial one that plea would largely extenuate. At the Last Assizes it shall acquit." If there is a divine justice, Billy is innocent in its eyes; he goes to his death as a penalty for breaking a law that has no absolute sanction whatever. His impediment in speech is a symbol of his irreducible imperfection as a man; it is not a symbol of total depravity, and Vere's real feeling about Billy breaks out when, gazing at Claggart's dead body, he cries: "Struck dead by an angel of God."

There is a far more enigmatic intertangling of good and evil in this universe of Melville's final vision than in the universe of theology or of dogmatic ethics: evil and good, as Rolfe had said, do indeed play, braided, into one cord. Billy may be as blameless as Oedipus of any conscious evil intention, yet a malign fate, working upon his inevitable limitations as a human being, brings it about that he commits in fact a capital crime. Meanwhile, Claggart's iniquity, terrible though it is, is not the absolute and transcendent wickedness of the principle of Evil itself, the Evil of the Father of Lies. It is, as Melville insists, "a depravity according to nature," [297/298] born with him and innate, not the product of training; but it embodies some mysterious principle in human experience that "by no means involves Calvin's dogma as to total mankind." It takes chiefly the form of an instinctive hatred of the innocent and the good, but a hatred so spontaneous and so insane that it suggests a dreadful perversion of love. Claggart's glance, indeed, sometimes follows "belted Billy," moving about the deck, "with a settled meditative and melancholy expression," his eyes strangely suffused with tears. At such moments the diabolic master-at-arms looks like the man of sorrows. "Yes, and sometimes the melancholy expression would have in it a touch of soft yearning, as if Claggart could even have loved Billy but for fate and ban."

It is his miserable destiny, however, to be incapable of loving the good, indeed to be incapable of love itself, and there is no greater misery. For there is a solid reality in this incomprehensible universe, this universe of equivocations and contrarieties; it is the reality of "the heart within you." To mind "the issues there" is to know that, even in the dark midst of evil and hate, goodness exists, and that its essential reality is that of love. Neither goodness nor love can flourish in a nature "dominated by intellectuality," as Claggart's is, and certainly not in a nature like that of the ship's surgeon, with his materialistic, scientific rationalism. They attain their fairest form, perhaps, in a nature as pristine and even primitive as Billy's is, but they are not irrevocably at war with the life of the mind, and indeed they attain their highest form in association with it. Captain Vere is a man with "a marked leaning towards everything intellectual," a passion for books and learning, and a habit of abstracted meditation. Yet he is an image of the high virtue in which the sternest sense of severe and painful duty is united to a capacity for the purest and tenderest love, the love of father for son. And it was in the full imaginative realization of that love, given and received, that Melville brought his work as a writer to its serene conclusion. [298/299]

After the drumhead court has pronounced its just and inexorable sentence, Captain Vere and Billy have a final interview alone together in the stateroom where Billy is confined. What occurred there was never known, says Melville, . . . [but] whatever took place in the stateroom between the ideal father and the ideal son, its effect was indeed sacramental, an effect of the purest unction and the most complete reconcilement. When, during the night that follows, the chaplain of the vessel comes upon Billy lying asleep on the upper gundeck, he gazes down on the sleeping countenance and feels that even he, "the minister of Christ," has "no consolation to proffer which could result in a peace transcending that which he beheld." Ishmael, in the end, after so long a banishment, had been taken back to his father's heart. Billy's final words, as he stands the next morning with the noose about his neck, are an expression of rapturous surrender: "God bless Captain Vere!" [299]

The Uses of Milton

LAWRANCE THOMPSON

I HAVE SAID THAT MELVILLE'S ULTERIOR CONCEPT, IN *Billy Budd*, INVERTS Milton's ulterior concept, in *Paradise Lost*. Man's fault, says Melville, is God's fault. The many cross-references between *Billy Budd* and *Paradise Lost* are sometimes obvious and sometimes subtle; but one of the most obvious is the direct quotation which Melville uses as his title or motto for Chapter Thirteen: "Pale ire, envy and despair." Milton uses those words to describe Satan's mixed feelings when first he looks on Adam in the Garden of Eden; Melville uses those words to describe Claggart's mixed feelings when he looks on Billy. Envying Billy his innocence, Claggart yet views that innocence with disdain: ". . . to be nothing more than innocent! Yet in an aesthetic way he saw the charm of it, the courageous [379/380] free-and-easy temper of it, and fain would have shared it, but he despaired of it." Thus the reader's attention is made to concentrate on the relationship between innocence and ignorance, with many possible extensions of that relationship. Melville's handling of it recalls the remarks of Milton's Satan as he enviously soliloquizes, while watching Adam and Eve:

> Yet let me not forget what I have gain'd
> From thir own mouths; all is not theirs it seems:
> One fatal Tree there stands of Knowledge call'd,
> Forbidden them to taste: Knowledge forbidd'n?
> Suspicious, reasonless. Why should thir Lord
> Envy them that? can it be sin to know,
> Can it be death? and do they only stand
> By Ignorance, is that thir happy state,
> The proof of thir obedience and thir faith?
> O fair foundation laid whereon to build
> Thir ruin!
>
> (*Paradise Lost*, IV, 512–522)

After Melville has suggested a correlation between Milton's Satan and Claggart, he lets the narrator tuck in a more darkly significant kind of correlation:

With no power to annul the elemental evil in himself, though he could hide it readily enough; apprehending the good, but powerless to be it; what recourse is left to a nature like Claggart's surcharged with energy as such

From *Melville's Quarrel with God* (Princeton: Princeton University Press, 1952), pp. 379–381, by permission of the publisher. [Editor's title.]

natures almost invariably are, but to recoil upon itself, and, like the scorpion for which the Creator alone is responsible, act out to the end the part allotted it.

Once again the narrator has established an analogy merely for purposes of describing Claggart's specific iniquity. Melville uses this seemingly innocent remark for sinister purposes, and thus shifts the weight of meaning from Claggart to the dark allegorical concept: the fault is not Claggart's any more than the fault which ruined Satan was Satan's. Each commits actions "for which the Creator alone is responsible." In *Paradise Lost,* Satan works out ironic variations on that same theme. When God's agent Ithuriel asks who he is, Satan answers, "Not to know mee argues yourselves unknown." Later, as we have noticed, when Satan plots the corruption of Adam he speaks with unheard bitterness: "Accept your [380/381] Maker's work; he gave it me, Which I as freely give." So Claggart implies, allegorically. . . . [381]

Milton and Melville

HENRY F. POMMER

THE AUTOMATISM OF CLAGGART'S EVIL, THE SERPENT IMAGERY OF . . . the book, the allusions to Satan and the quotation from Milton, the envy aroused by Billy's beauty of body and of character, the incipient love and actual suffering in Claggart's soul, and his misleading appearance determine his position as the ultimate of Satanic villainy in Melville. . . .

With no more than the usual accuracy of epigram, one might say [89/90] that in Claggart Melville reacted classically to Satan, whereas in Ahab he reacted romantically. In the former case he condemns a man who does wrong in the eyes of the world; in the latter he sympathizes with such a man, justifies his means by referring to his ends, and makes a hero of a devil. In *Billy Budd* his attitude towards Claggart is roughly analogous to that of Christ when he told God,

> Whom thou hat'st, I hate, and can put on
> Thy terrors, as I put thy mildness on,
> Image of thee in all things; and shall soon,
> Arm'd with thy might, rid Heaven of these rebell'd;
> To their prepar'd ill mansion driven down,
> To chains of darkness, and the undying worm;

From *Milton and Melville* (Pittsburgh: University of Pittsburgh Press, 1950), pp. 89–90, by permission of the publisher.

> That from thy just obedience could revolt,
> Whom to obey is happiness entire.

. . . [90]

A Caution about Sources

NORMAN HOLMES PEARSON

THUS WHEN WE READ IN *Billy Budd* OF THE RELATIONSHIP BETWEEN BILLY, Claggart, and Vere, we are given a situation analogous to, and dependent upon, Milton's poetry and the Bible which stood behind it. This is Melville's use of the earth as the shadow of Heaven. What must be remembered is that there is only a shadow, and that Melville establishes momentary resemblances rather than complete identities. Thus Billy may without conflict be like pre-lapsarian Adam; like Christ who took the fallen Adam's place to carry out the obedience Adam denied; and like Isaac in relation to Abraham. But Billy never loses his identity as a sailor. Claggart may be like Satan, the Arch-Enemy who would attempt to rule the earth after his own fall and man's, and [107/ 108] yet retain his character as master-at-arms of the *Indomitable*. Vere, too, may bear the same relationship of ultimate command to an Adam-Christ and to a Satan, who was his renegade chevalier, that a captain of a man-of-war does to his men, in an analogy of captaincy to the authority of God which is without the blasphemous assumption of Godhead. These are simply shifting similitudes, which reënforce but do not tie down. . . . [108]

From "Billy Budd: 'The King's Yarn,'" *American Quarterly*, III (Summer 1951), 107–108, by permission of publisher and author. [Editor's title.]

Billy Budd, Antigone, and *The Winter's Tale*

RICHARD CHASE

IT IS HIGH PRAISE INDEED TO SPEAK OF A STORY AS JUST MISSING EQUALITY with the small body of great tragic literature. And that is how we

From Richard Chase's "Introduction," copyright 1950 by Richard Chase, in Herman Melville's *Selected Tales and Poems* (New York: Holt, Rinehart and Winston, 1950), pp. xiii–xvi. Reprinted by permission of Holt, Rinehart and Winston, Inc. [Editor's title.]

nowadays think of *Billy Budd*, which Melville wrote in the years between 1888 and 1891, the year of his death. A comparison of *Billy Budd* with the *Antigone* of Sophocles can, I think, be taken just literally enough to point to the decisive difference of achievement.

Both works are concerned with the defeat by abstract legality of an individual who possesses in more than usual measure certain timelessly precious human attributes. If we mean by a tragic hero a man of high estate who falls from prosperity by a flaw in his character or because he is guided by a power beyond his control or because of a mistake he makes, we may say of both *Billy Budd* and *Antigone* that the tragic hero himself is of only secondary interest. In the formal structure of these works Captain Vere and Creon are tragic heroes; yet in each instance the author's main interest, his most abundant flow of emotion, is directed toward someone else; in Sophocles, it is Antigone; in Melville, Billy Budd.

In both works, the tragic hero is personally superior to the legal ideology he believes he must enforce. The two characters are adequately conceived by their authors. But we must admit that Sophocles is more successful with his Antigone than is Melville with his Billy Budd. In Antigone's insistence on the proper burial of her dead brother we see the full lineaments of a marvelously rich and mature character and a profound commitment to certain sources of moral and spiritual health. In comparison with Antigone, we must see that Billy Budd is not quite adequately conceived for the part he is supposed to play, the part, that is, of innocence and generosity in tragic [xiii/xiv] collision with the rigid proscriptions of society. In some ways at least, Billy Budd strikes us as not quite believable. There are contradictory elements in his character; he is, for example, "innocent," yet he has had "experience." We ought to desire the tragic writer to show us innocence as it has survived or been produced by experience, by knowledge of life. The mindless innocence of Billy Budd, like that of a child, is wonderfully touching and valuable. Yet it is not quite the stuff of tragedy. Melville, as we see, was not free of the vast commitment of the American Man to the American Boy.

Captain Vere is finely portrayed. Somewhat in the manner of Captain Delano, he is an admirable if (in relation to the ultimate possibility of human character) fundamentally second-rate man. Claggart is also perfectly imagined—a man depraved by nature and by "Cain's City."

I would suggest that the relative failure of Billy Budd as a fictional character can be accounted for in a very simple manner. Melville was too personally involved with Billy Budd. Whether he was picturing his own son Malcolm (who shot and killed himself at the age of twenty) or speaking of his own youth or of Christ or making a general statement of the perpetual sacrifice of boyish innocence to law and society, the idea of Billy Budd appeared so overwhelmingly moving to the aged Melville that he was not able to express it in artistically cogent language. If the reader wishes to look into the subterranean depths of the story, its "secret mines and dubious sides," he might well begin with the large number of figures of speech having to do with the act of eating; for example, the "mesmeric glance" of Claggart at Billy Budd, which Melville compares with "the hungry lurch of the torpedo fish." These metaphors show what Melville, in his darkest vision of life, is really saying. He is saying that the "horrible vulturism" of the world, of which he had written in *Moby Dick,* is a basic principle of things. Society, law, adulthood, worldly accomplishments can sustain themselves only by feeding on youthful innocence and generosity. In this sense, the theme of *Billy Budd,* [xiv/xv] as of Melville's *Typee,* and, indeed, as of the sacrament of communion, is the ritualistic sacrifice of the hero.

But even as Melville shows us these dark and terrible ideas, we are aware that he is counterposing another range of meaning. Neither nature nor society is totally destructive of what is admirable in human life. By some genial, liberating grace, innocence and beauty are empowered to renew themselves in the very teeth of destruction. And so we are enabled to feel that *Billy Budd,* though not quite successful as tragic drama, remains immensely moving as a drama of pathos and myth. In this respect, its kinship is with the late plays of Shakespeare and with the New Testament, in its affirmation that out of the death inflicted by nature and society there issues new life. . . .

Melville is the most Shakespearean of American writers, a fact that will be brought home afresh to anyone who compares *Billy Budd* with such a play as *The Winter's Tale.** Like *Antigone* and *Billy Budd, The Winter's Tale* is concerned with the destruction of innocence and beauty by an inhumanly enforced legality. It is jealousy and suspicion which immediately cause Leontes, King of Sicilia, to bring about the death of his queen, Hermione, and his son, Mamillius. But mirrored in the jealous king we see the proscriptions of society conspiring with the destructive powers of nature—though, like Creon and Captain Vere, Leontes is personally superior to the law he lives by. In the "welkin eye" of Mamillius and of Billy Budd (Melville borrowed the phrase from Shakespeare) we see the idyllic world of eternal boyhood—described as follows by Polixenes as he recalls his boyhood friendship with Leontes:

> We were as twinn'd lambs that did frisk i' the sun
> And bleat the one at th' other. What we chang'd [xv/xvi]

* A comparison brought in detail to my attention by Professor Andrew Chiappe.

Was innocence for innocence; we knew not
The doctrine of ill-doing, nor dream'd
That any did.

The hanging of Billy Budd, at once a death and a resurrection, has the same force in Melville's story as the resurrection of Hermione at the end of Shakespeare's play, for both writers affirm that in some magical way innocence and beauty still exist in the world, that however evil nature and man may be they are still graced with a kind of minimal creative principle. Claggart's death is sudden and final. Captain Vere dies without having achieved the fame that might otherwise have come to him. But "the fresh young image of the Handsome Sailor" lives on in the heart of men. Of Melville, of Shakespeare, and of Sophocles (in *Oedipus at Colonus*) it may be said that in the works of their advanced age they took up the themes of the pathos of death, the crimes of society, the magically creative and restorative powers of nature, the myth of rebirth. . . . [xvi]

Melville's Version of Tragedy

RICHARD HARTER FOGLE

Billy Budd IS, IT SEEMS TO ME, ENTIRELY COMPREHENSIBLE AS MELVILLE'S version of tragedy. But to affirm this it is necessary to provide some definition both of tragedy and of irony as the terms are used here, though no more is attempted than an informal description sufficient for the immediate purpose. Tragedy, then, is a heightened and dignified action, intentionally so complicated as to involve its personae in the greatest conceivable difficulties, in order to elicit from them in their struggle the fullest potentialities of which they are capable. As to irony, we know that there are many notions of it, and perhaps no certain center can be found. We shall need to distinguish between different usages in order to specify the respects in which *Billy Budd* is or is not ironic. It is not ironic in the sense of irony ordinarily used by those who claim that it is; that is, a more or less complete reversal of the ostensible meaning, with, to add the words of A. R. Thompson in *The Dry Mock*, an effect of painful mockery. It is not painful, it is not sharp-edged, except by distortion of a part to misrepresent the total

From "*Billy Budd*—Acceptance or Irony," *Tulane Studies in English*, VIII (1958), 109–113, by permission of Tulane University, *Tulane Studies in English*, and the author. [Editor's title.]

effect. It is ironic in that it frequently means more—not other—than it seems to say. Correspondingly *Billy Budd* is ironic in the modern sense of irony somewhat overworked by T. S. Eliot [109/110]—who called it wit—, I. A. Richards, and the New Critics: that is, a consciousness of the difficulties which any belief or attitude must face, an awareness of complexity. Indeed, one might concede to *Billy Budd* any ironies, of character, word, situation, or general attitude, which do not impeach its essential good faith and render verbalization itself a worthless currency. But precisely this destructive irony is what the ironist critics have fixed upon.

Billy Budd can like *Moby Dick* be justly described as Melville's nineteenth century version of classical tragedy, with old form revivified by new issues. According to Aristotelian prescription it portrays men as better than they are. The principals are exceptional: Billy, Captain Vere, and Claggart stand high in the hierarchy of natural man, above the limited comprehension of the mere worldly-wise. The last meeting of Vere and Budd is too sacred for the common view. "But there is no telling the sacrament, seldom if in any case revealed to the gadding world wherever under circumstances at all akin to those here attempted to be set forth two of great Nature's nobler order embrace." As to Claggart, his evil is an object of moral and aesthetic appreciation, a quality to be savored by connoisseurs.

To heighten and dignify the tragic action Melville, as in *Moby Dick* with Ahab, magnifies his characters by investing them in heroic myth, legend, and history. The background is "a crisis for Christendom not exceeded in its undetermined momentousness at the time by any other era of which there is a record." The Handsome Sailor has mythical proportions. He is Aldebaran, a pagod, a grand Assyrian bull; at the yard-arm he is "young Alexander curbing the fiery Bucephalus. A superb figure, tossed up as by the horns of Taurus against the thunderous sky." He is Hercules refined by the influence of Venus, in him "something suggestive of a mother eminently favored by Love and the Graces." Melville thus states the problem of his modern tragedy: "Passion, and passion in its profoundest, is not a thing demanding a palatial stage whereon to play its part. Down among the groundlings, among the beggars and rakers of the garbage, profound passion is enacted. And the circumstances that provoke it, however trivial or mean, are no measure of its power. In the present instance the stage is a scrubbed gun-deck, and one of the external provocations a man-of-war's man's spilled soup." But his stage is so framed and so lighted as to display the tragic patterns to the best dramatic advantage. Antique myth, [110/111] Christian allusion at its most spacious, and finally the aesthetic distance of a more poetic age of sail are all utilized to magnify and embellish. (One may remark here in passing that it is a waste of ingenuity to prove that Billy is not the Handsome Sailor. Insofar as the Sailor is mythic hero he cannot be, for this is not a man but an archetype. Billy is as close to being the Handsome Sailor as any human, closely scanned, is likely to get. How much use was Melville able to get out of Bulkington in *Moby Dick*?) One final comment upon magnification: there is a commemorative quality about *Billy Budd* which very interestingly fuses the tragedy of hero and common man, which blends the diverse tones of *Moby Dick* and *John Marr and Other Sailors*. It is a tale at once of Lord Nelson and Greenwich pensioners, of mutiny, age-old oppression and pain, of military splendor. "To the mutineers those battles and especially Trafalgar were a plenary absolution; and a grand one; for all that goes to make up scenic naval display and heroic magnificence in arms. Those battles especially Trafalgar stand unmatched in human annals."

Like classical tragedy, *Billy Budd* makes a clear distinction between the sphere of the actual and the sphere of the ideal. True judgment of Billy lies with natural laws, here also divine, the realm of absolute justice—chronometrical, as Plotinus Plinlimmon would have it in *Pierre*. "'At the Last Assizes it shall acquit,'" says Vere. But Vere is equally clear on the distinction between a natural and a man-of-war world. The killing of Claggart is divine justice, but on the *Indomitable* it is the murder of a superior officer under wartime conditions. "'Struck dead by an angel of God. Yet the angel must hang!'" "'We proceed under the law of the Mutiny Act.'" In *Billy Budd* this tragic discrepancy is born of the dogma of the Fall of Man, which inevitably brings it into being. The law of the mutiny act is the law of a fallen world, in which an unfallen man like Billy cannot long exist. The immediate tragedy originates in a second Fall, the mutiny at the Nore, which has made any union of these worlds impossible. Age-old abuses of government, first rationally and properly protested at Spithead, have finally roused the "red meteor" of the Nore. "Reasonable discontent growing out of practical grievances in the fleet had been ignited into irrational combustion as by live cinders blown across the Channel from France in flames." The Revolution, one sees, is also a Fall. Many parallels with Melville's early writing have been suggested by critics of [111/112] *Billy Budd*. At this point one might add to the list *The Encantadas*, and most particularly Sketch Seventh, "Charles's Isle and the Dog-King." The Encantadas are a fallen world in which no rational government can flourish, in which oppression on the one hand is countered on the other by unbridled license.

In still another respect *Billy Budd* follows the classic formula of tragedy. The mainspring of the plot is a reversal, the *peripateia* defined by Aristotle as a hallmark of the complex tragic action, in which carefully laid plans produce results directly opposite to expectation, with, if well-managed, an artistic effect of combined surprise and inevitability. Thus Vere's well-planned arrangements lead to the killing of Claggart and the execution of Billy. He is not, we recall, deceived by Claggart's accusation. He brings the two men privately to his cabin, in order to confront the liar with truth in a manner as little harmful as possible to the general welfare. He fully understands Billy's inability to speak, but by his very kindness he brings on the fatal bow. "Contrary to the effect intended, these words so fatherly in tone, doubtless touching Billy's heart to the quick, prompted yet more violent efforts at utterance—efforts soon ending for the time in confirming the paralysis, and bringing to the face an expression which was as a crucifixion to behold. The next instant, quick as the flame from a discharged cannon at night, his right arm shot out, and Claggart dropped to the deck." Inevitability accompanies surprise, as Aristotle has laid down, for Melville has carefully paved the way by his references to Billy's stutter—his one connection with a fallen world—and his sudden violence once before aboard the merchantman *Rights of Man.* " 'Quick as lightning Billy let fly his arm. I dare say he never meant to do quite as much as he did, but anyhow he gave the burly fool a terrible drubbing.' "

With so many of the traits and qualities of tragedy, *Billy Budd* can claim also the final attribute of tragic reconciliation. In his defeat and passion the tragic hero yet brings about a partial redemption, he keeps alive some hope for the future, some confidence that goodness survives. So the story of Billy does not die, but is preserved and transmitted among seamen, and bits of the boom from which he was hanged are kept like pieces of the true Cross. This effect and survival of his memory might be contrasted with the effect of the announcement by Vere of Billy's impending execution, which "was listened to by the throng of standing sailors in a dumbness [112/113] like that of a seated congregation of believers in hell listening to the clergyman's announcement of his Calvinistic text."

This reconciliation is not precisely Greek, nor yet the Hebraic catharsis of *Samson Agonistes*—"nothing is here to wail, nothing for tears." There is no firm base of belief on which to ground it. The system with which we are to be reconciled is too vast and ambiguous. In one dimension of meaning Captain Vere is certainly God the Father, as Billy is God the Son; but as Nathalia Wright has well remarked Vere is not omnipotent. He acts in accordance with a law that is not of his own framing. There is something beyond him. . . .

As tragedy *Billy Budd* undoubtedly possesses tragic irony, the irony of fate. Its ironies would seem bitter to those who are inclined to view them bitterly. One might well think that Melville is presenting in *Billy Budd* a second crucifixion, which in this man-of-war world will inevitably be re-enacted whenever Christ should reassume the estate of man. His irony, however, is the natural attitude of a capacious, energetic, and subtle mind in pursuit of as much meaning as it can grasp, and its honest admission of the presence in reality of a something finally ungraspable. It magnifies and intensifies, it deepens and enriches, rather than diminishing by a mere irony of wailing mockery. Viewed in the full context of the tragedy of *Billy Budd*, this irony is neither a scream nor a sneer. [113]

Billy and Oedipus

HERBERT WEISINGER AND ADRIAN J. JAFFE

THUS MELVILLE HAS SUCCEEDED IN WRITING WHAT IS IN ESSENCE A PERFECT tragedy. Budd is the tragic hero who falls afoul of a set of circumstances which he did not cause, but which he cannot by the same token battle. Like Oedipus, Budd must suffer for the commission of a crime he did not intend to commit and which was, moreover, forced upon him. And like Oedipus, Billy Budd recognizes at the end the justice of Vere's decision and calls out before his death, "God bless you, Captain Vere," for without this understanding on Budd's part the tragedy would have no more meaning than if Othello had died without discovering that Desdemona was in fact innocent of adultery with Cassio. Thus the moral order, as in Greek tragedy, is questioned as the human being is pulled toward acquitting Billy Budd, and then in Vere's decision it is again reaffirmed and strengthened as we know that divine law still prevails on earth and that everything is in its proper place. It is a harsh and difficult acceptance that we must make, one that goes against every fiber of our human feeling, but it is of the very nature of the problem that this should be the way it is. . . . [143]

From "Billy Budd, Foretopman," in *The Laureate Fraternity: An Introduction to Literature* (Evanston: Row, Peterson & Co., 1960), p. 143, by permission of the publisher.

5. SPECIAL PROBLEMS

THE CHARACTERS

The Case for Captain Vere

MILTON R. STERN

. . . WITH PIERRE'S DEATH, THE STORY OF THE QUESTER IS COMPLETE. What remained now for Melville was to create a hero.

What would happen if there were a man who did manage to understand the proper relationship between heart and mind, a man who was not blind to history, a man who had a political or social position—say a ship's captaincy—which would allow him to translate his realizations into action? What if this man were exposed to a choice between pure ideal and "fallen" human history, with its present actuality of a crime-filled man-of-war world? Wanted: a hero.

Captain Vere is the man created to fill this position.

Billy Budd, like the early Pierre, is pictured as the childlike barbarian, the pure creature whose only experience really is just the experience of his own inner purity and ideality. His spontaneous responses preclude control by mind. This Christ figure also deceives by silence, albeit unwittingly, and finally becomes a murderer and a causer of his own death. Billy himself is the lure which Vere painfully rejects with all the insight created by an understanding of human history. Vere is educated, with the reader, to see Claggart as Satan and Baby Budd as Christ. But Vere's one overriding fact is the fact of the temporal world, the reality of his human community to which he owes his primary allegiance. He cannot choose the ideal which, by itself, is beautiful. And Claggart becomes the other facet of Budd. Budd is the ideal, Claggart is the consequence. He is the completely mad and satanized quester who has withdrawn from quest. He is Ahab, retired in his New Bedford home, staring silently and crazily out at the sea. He is Ahab who has given up the chase, but who still watches. . . . This demonized isolato seeks out and hates and yearns to believe in ideal Billy in exactly the same monomaniacal relationship which Ahab has to the white whale. Just as the reader sees that for Ahab the whale is only what Ahab thinks he is, and the whale, in a sense, becomes Ahab, so for Melville, Christ and Satan are ultimately one entity with a dual face. Like all Melvillean dualities, absolute identities are man-

From *The Fine Hammered Steel of Herman Melville* (Urbana: University of Illinois Press, 1957), pp. 26–27, by permission of the publisher and the author. [Editor's title.]

made products which unite in the flow of historical consequence in the Great God Time. The bright and the dark are the *same*. [26/27]

Vere rejects both lure and quester. His heartbroken rejection of Budd as a beautiful impossibility in favor of an ugly reality, his decision to force his position of command to operate according to what his head dictates and his heart detests, is his acceptance of this world as the only possible one. It is not, as many critics have attempted to demonstrate, an acceptance of historical necessity in a naturalistic universe. It is a consequent call for man to control his fate by controlling his actions in the historical world—and it is also Melville's statement of inability to find the way to do so. Vere decides to remain unwithdrawn, to accept the responsibility of the human community by accepting the responsibility of command. His decision to maintain order because of man's blindness is his sacrifice of self to the necessities of moral responsibility historically defined. Moreover, it is in his sacrifice of individual self to his social self that Vere finds his greatest identity, in the book as well as in the reader's mind. Vere is the polar opposite and instinctive antagonist to the quester. He offers the alternative behavior which had to be created once the quester's behavior was anatomized and rejected.

In *Billy Budd* the cast of characters changes. The quester as such drops out and the hero takes his place. And here the limitations (or perhaps the accuracy) of Melville's nineteenth-century naturalism become most apparent. For even the hero does not create a purged world. The lesson of Vere's sacrifice is lost. The lesson of Billy Budd's final realization is lost. The world gains not social insight but myth, and the cycle continues. Various studies have tried to identify Melville with his questers. But if he is to be identified with any of his characters, it must be with Captain Vere rather than with anyone else except Ishmael. (The two combined offer a very fair approximation of Melville's political, social, and metaphysical perceptions.) He is the man who turns to history for direction, yet who, when faced with the mystery of *human* nature, calls "Billy Budd! Billy Budd!" He calls for the perfection-aspiring human heart, and not in accents of remorse. . . . [27]

The Case against Captain Vere

LEONARD CASPER

Billy Budd HAS OFTEN BEEN CONSIDERED HERMAN MELVILLE'S "TESTAment of acceptance" because of Billy's unrebellious nature and because

From *Perspective,* V (Summer 1952), 146–152, by permission of the publisher and the author.

of the final blessing which he bestows on the officer who has con-demned him to hang. Such an argument depends on the assumption that Melville can be identified completely with Billy. Similarly, it de-mands the conclusion that the man who rebelled against orthodox reli-gious and political thought all his life and who, despite his unending interest, found no resolution of the tensions between good and evil, finally succumbed and accepted moral expediency and horological law. Because such a startling conversion is unprepared for by any of Melville's writings—his novels, poetry, journals, or letters—one is inevitably led to question the validity of such an interpretation of Billy Budd and to review again the case against Captain Vere. . . . [146/149]

. . . Although . . . [Captain Vere] is treated with some sym-pathy and much [149/150] understanding by Melville, it is fair to ask if the author ever accepts his reasoning.

Discussing natural depravity, Melville says

Civilization, especially if of the austerer sort, is auspicious to it. It folds itself in the mantle of respectability . . .

And he goes on to describe how irrationality often lurks behind a reasonable exterior. Although this ostensibly is an explanation of Claggart's character, is there any of it which does not apply equally to Vere? Could Melville have written this, with Vere's austere nature, doubtful sanity, and cool judgment before him, and have not intended Vere to be read into this description? Or is this indictment by indirection?

Certainly Vere's behavior demands explanation because of its unnaturalness. Although he cannot take seriously the charge that Billy is a mutineer and for a while treats the boy like a son, his attitude changes completely when Billy unwittingly kills his false accuser. The captain seems to forget the first extenuating circumstance: he himself has just warned Claggart that, in something as serious as a mutiny charge, false-witness incurs a death penalty. Not only does he forget this, but he has already reached a decision before the court-martial is summoned. Billy must hang! The trial is a pretense at deliberative justice, and is made to appear so by Melville.

Other officers are surprised at Vere's strange attitude. The surgeon is struck by Vere's implied desire for secrecy. Aware of the danger of mutiny and of all the circumstances of the event which has just occurred, still he believes that as usual the accused should be referred to the Admiral for trial. Furthermore, Melville allows the surgeon "professionally" to surmise that Vere is a victim of mental aberration—and note that just previously his "professional eyes" correctly judged that Claggart is dead. The lieutenant and captain of marines equally consider improper Vere's decision to hold a drumhead.

The court-martial itself is improperly conducted by Vere who, as a witness, should have disregarded his rank; yet he knowingly testifies from the ship's weather side. After several moments of investigation have passed, he suddenly terminates interpretation of motives and circumstances and limits the court's judgment to the death blow itself. This is tantamount to having the court-martial sit merely as a coroner's jury. They are to decide the cause and causer [150/151] of death. Punishment follows inevitably. Vere's reported strangeness of manner reveals that Melville is carefully indicating that all this is a mistrial, a miscarriage of justice. The officers are shocked at the prejudgment evident in Vere's utterances.

Having silenced the captain of marines and Billy with overruling glances, Vere proceeds to the summary of his case. His rationalizations result in "virtuous expediency" being inevitable. By refusing all natural considerations, Vere makes his verdict unnatural, a perversion as serious as Claggart's.

By shifting responsibility for his decision to the King, Vere denies that he is a free agent with an individual sense of discrimination and judgment. He assumes the attitude of freely-willed fatalism and self-determinism evident in such characters as Ahab in *Moby-Dick* and, shortly, Billy Budd himself in his acceptance of the death penalty. His decision is not to make a decision, but to hand down a prejudgment; by limiting his free will, he makes the whole seem fated.

The question of free will in *Billy Budd* is important because those who argue that this is a testament of acceptance seem to imply that the basis for resignation is a sense of real fatalism not only exhibited by Vere and Billy, but believed in by Melville.

Billy's resignation, his acceptance of the death penalty, rises directly from his uneducated sense of fatalism, a sense that inhuman forces make his death necessary, however unjust those forces may be; and his fatalism is calm and triumphant because to him death is endurable. However, despite his acceptance of necessity in this sense, he never explicitly accepts Vere's argument of expediency or necessity. He never says, "It is *right* that I die." He only implies, "I seem fated to die, right or wrong, and I am ready."

If this interpretation is correct, then Billy's final unstammered "God bless Vere" does not mean that he is accepting his fate as just or Vere's verdict as proper. Instead it is a form of absolution and Christian forgiveness (or perhaps even indifference), peculiarly ironic because it is echoed by the crew, automatically, in the more conventional sense of recognition of justice performed. Whatever the interpretation of Billy's words, obviously Melville outlives him and reflects his own opinion in the immediate murmur among the crew at the unnecessary death, in their wise revulsion and doubt.

In a post-mortem scene the implication of a conversation between the purser and the surgeon is that free will probably does exist. Among the Greeks one sense of the word euthanasia was the wilful sacrifice of one's self for one's country; the fact that the death was [151/152] willed was supposed to induce pleasure; this is obviously the sense in which the purser uses the word when he asks if Billy's death was a case of euthanasia because his limbs did not twitch. The scientist cannot refute, but can only deny, that in death Billy exhibited any will power. If this conclusion can be accepted as Melville's tentative one (all of his conclusions were open to further demonstration), then we must see that his viewpoint is much broader than Billy's self-deluding, fatalistic one; and therefore the two figures are not congruent.

Vere himself is not allowed to die such a noble death. Instead, in the description of his demise, it is intimated that he was not always wholly unselfish, but that he may have been secretly ambitious.

His death is connected with Billy's through an interesting and subtle device, an ironic newspaper report of the latter's death. The reporter says that Claggart's splendid character refutes Dr. Johnson's statement that patriotism is the last refuge of a scoundrel. Since Claggart is, actually, a depraved person, it must be obvious that Melville's opinion coincides wholly with Dr. Johnson's. And Starry Vere, of course, is the principal patriot in the story.

The story ends, not with Captain Vere, but where its center of gravity has been all the time: with the crew (the people) and their attitude toward Billy, their instinctive refusal to believe him capable of mutiny or of wilful murder (despite all the "reasons" given them). Their expression of sympathy for him, as he has become idealized in their memories, certainly is no testament of acceptance. [152]

Billy Budd

W. H. AUDEN

IF, WHEN WE FINISH READING *Billy Budd*, WE ARE LEFT WITH QUESTIONS which we feel have been raised but not answered, if so to speak the equation has not come out to a finite number, as in a work of art it should, this is not due to any lack of talent on Melville's part, but to the insolubility of the religious paradox in aesthetic terms.

For any writer who attempts a portrait of the Christ-like is faced with the following problems. His central figure

a) must be innocent of sin, yet a man like us in all things tempted as we are. If he is given any aesthetic advantages, he at once ceases to

From *The Enchaféd Flood* (New York: Random House, 1950), pp. 144–147, by W. H. Auden. Copyright 1950 by the Rector and Visitors of the University of Virginia. Reprinted by permission of Random House, Inc.

be the God-Man and becomes the Man-God, the Aesthetic Hero, Hercules, who must be admired, but cannot be imitated. His sinlessness must be the result of faith, not of fortune.

b) He must be shown as failing in a worldly sense, i.e., as coming into collision with the law of this world, otherwise there is no proof that his sinlessness is due, not to faith, but to mere worldly prudence. [144/145]

c) Failure and suffering, however, are in themselves no proof of faith, because the collision with the law may equally well be the result of pride and sin. The crucified Christ is flanked by two crucified thieves.

d) The suffering must at one and the same time be willed and not-willed. If it seems entirely against the will of the sufferer, he becomes pathetic, if it seems entirely brought about by his own actions, he becomes tragic, and it is impossible to distinguish between pride and faith as the cause of his suffering.

. . .

Melville . . . solves this problem. This Passion of Billy Budd is convincing, but fails in respects where Cervantes succeeds, and the ways in which he fails are interesting for the light they throw on the romantic conceptions of life. Like many other romantics Melville seems to hold:

1) That innocence and sinlessness are identical, or rather perhaps that only the innocent, i.e., those who have never known the law, can be sinless. Once a man becomes conscious, he becomes a sinner. As long as he is not conscious of guilt, what he does is not sin. This is to push St. Paul's remark "Except I had known the Law, I had not known sin" still further to mean that "Except I had known sin, I [145/146] would not have sinned." Thus when Billy Budd first appears he is the Prelapsarian Adam:

Billy Budd in many respects was little more than a sort of upright barbarian, much such perhaps as Adam presumably might have been ere the urbane Serpent wriggled himself into his company.

He may have done things which in a conscious person would be sin—there appears to have been a certain Bristol Molly—but he feels no guilt.

2) That the unconscious and innocent are marked by great physical beauty, and therefore that the beautiful are sinless. This is true for Billy Budd as it was for Bulkington and Queequeg.

If the story were to be simply the story of the Fall, i.e., the story of how the Devil (Claggart) tempted Adam (Budd) into the knowledge of good and evil, this would not matter, but Melville wants Budd also to be the Second Adam, the sinless victim who suffers voluntarily for the sins of the whole world. But in order to be that he must know

what sin is, or else his suffering is not redemptive, but only one more
sin on our part. Further, as long as Billy Budd is only the Prelapsarian
Adam, our nostalgic image of what we would still be if we had not
fallen, his beauty is a perfectly adequate [146/147] symbol but the
moment he becomes the Second Adam, the saving example whom we
all should follow, this beauty becomes an illegitimate aesthetic advantage. The flaw of the stammer will not quite do, for this is only an
aesthetic weakness, not a deliberate abandonment of advantages. It
succeeds in making Billy Budd the innocent who "as a sheep before
the shearer is dumb so openeth he not his mouth," but it makes his
dumbness against his will not with it. We can never look like that, any
more than, once we have become conscious, we can go back to
unconsciousness, so how can we imitate his example? He becomes an
aesthetic hero to admire from a distance. Melville seems to have been
aware that something must happen to Billy to change him from the
unconscious Adam into the conscious Christ but, in terms of his fable,
he cannot make this explicit and the decisive transition was to take
place off-stage in the final interview between Billy and Captain Vere.
[147]

Claggart–I

W. H. AUDEN

SIMILAR INSOLUBLE PARADOXES ARE RAISED BY THE DEMONIC, THE RELI-
gious passion in reverse. For the demonic must be moved solely by
pride, just as the religious must be moved solely by faith and love.
Absolute pride cannot be manifested aesthetically because it tolerates
no weakness except itself which thinks of itself as absolute strength.
[147/148]

Absolute pride denies that the six other deadly sins are its
children and despises them as weakness, being incapable of seeing
that it is the source of all weakness. The Devil, therefore, cannot
himself be lustful, gluttonous, avaricious, envious, slothful, or angry,
for his pride will not allow him to be anything less than proud. He can
only pretend in disguise to be any of these without actually feeling
them; he can only "act" them. His acts must appear to be arbitrary and
quite motiveless. No accurate aesthetic portrayal, therefore, is possible;

From *The Enchafèd Flood* (New York: Random House, 1950), pp. 147–149,
by W. H. Auden. Copyright 1950 by the Rector and Visitors of the University of
Virginia. Reprinted by permission of Random House, Inc.

Iago has to be given some motive, yet if the motive is convincing, he ceases to be demonic.

So with Claggart. Just as the bias in Melville's treatment of Billy Budd is a tendency to identify consciousness and sin, so he makes Claggart identify innocence with love; "To be nothing more than innocent," he sneers on seeing Billy Budd. This is no doubt what the serpent says to Adam, but it is not what he says to himself, which is rather "To be nothing more than loving." For the difference between God and the Devil is not that God does not know the meaning of good and evil and that the Devil does, but that God loves and the Devil will not love. That is why the motive for Claggart's behaviour, half-stated only to be withdrawn because no motive will really do, is homosexual desire.

In *Moby Dick,* where Ahab's pride revolts against lack of absolute strength, against being finite and dependent, the sexual symbolism centres round incest and the Oedipus situation, because incest is the magic act of [148/149] self-derivation, self-autonomy, with the annihilation of all rival power.

In *Billy Budd,* the opposition is not strength/weakness, but innocence/guilt-consciousness, i.e., Claggart wishes to annihilate the difference either by becoming innocent himself or by acquiring an accomplice in guilt. If this is expressed sexually, the magic act must necessarily be homosexual, for the wish is for identity in innocence or in guilt, and identity demands the same sex.

Claggart, as the Devil, cannot, of course, admit a sexual desire, for that would be an admission of loneliness which pride cannot admit. Either he must corrupt innocence through an underling or if that is not possible he must annihilate it, which he does. [149]

Claggart—II

GEOFFREY STONE

FOR THE MODERN READER, TRAINED IN A NON-MORAL CASUISTRY FOR WHICH the declared motive is never the true one, the fact that Claggart looked on "belted Billy rolling along the upper gundeck . . . with a settled, meditative, and melancholy expression, his eyes strangely suffused with incipient feverish tears" will at once suggest a key to the story's

From *Melville* (New York: Sheed & Ward, 1949), pp. 312–313, by Geoffrey Stone, copyright 1949, Sheed & Ward, Inc., New York, by permission of the publisher. [Editor's title.]

meaning. And when Melville says that "sometimes the melancholy expression would have in it a touch of soft yearning, as if Claggart could even have loved Billy but for fate and ban", it will be plain that the iniquity considered here is the one to which Sodom has given its name. There is no doubt that the story lends itself not at all implausibly to this interpretation: if Claggart entertains a perversion of love for Billy, it is psychologically quite credible that such a love should be further perverted into hate. Actually, this provides no explanation to the mystery of iniquity. Would evil cease to operate in the world if the "ban" were removed or would Billy never have been hanged had Claggart been questioned by a psychiatrist before being mustered into the King's navy?

Quite possibly Melville intended that Claggart's immediate motives—obscure even to Claggart—were to be understood for what is now called ambivalent, but if Melville sought to disguise this matter of the sexually illicit, it was a concealment [312/313] prompted by politeness, not by the belief that here was a piece of esoteric doctrine, explaining the most obscure mysteries, to be revealed only to the initiate. Each age has things it does not talk about, but they are not necessarily mysterious. Melville constantly addresses himself to the metaphysical implications of Claggart's depravity, and if these are not his chief concern with the matter, we are left with the curious spectacle of a highly intelligent old man devoting the last three years of his life to pondering a simple case of thwarted pederasty. . . . [313]

The Dansker : Archetype
of the Wise Man

JAMES BAIRD

. . . IF ONE WISHES TO SEE THE ARCHETYPE OF THE WISE MAN IN LESS DIS-tinctive guise, he has in Melville's work at least one example for study. He is the old Dansker of *Billy Budd,* known [249/250] to his shipmates as "Board-her-in-the-smoke." Among the crew of the *Indomitable,* he is the "salt seer," as Melville calls him. In the narrative he has the function of a Teiresias of the British Navy. He is the dispassionate observer of Billy's innocence and Claggart's evil. He it is who warns Billy that "Jimmy Legs" (Claggart) is "down upon him." He is

From *Ishmael* (Baltimore: Johns Hopkins Press, 1956), pp. 249–251, by permission of the publisher. [Editor's title.]

oracular, as Melville intends him; he is the "old sea-Chiron" who thinks that for the nonce "he had sufficiently warned his young Achilles." In his role as the seer, the old Dansker is the voice of fate. But this old veteran of weathered face, of a complexion like parchment, of many scars is, more particularly, a pure distillation of the ethos of the mariner's custom, of the culture of all men who go down to the sea in ships.

Now the first time that his small weasel eyes happened to light on Billy Budd, a certain grim internal merriment set all his ancient wrinkles into antic play. Was it that his eccentric unsentimental old sapience, primitive in its kind, saw, or thought it saw, something which in contrast with the warship's environment looked oddly incongruous in the Handsome Sailor?

The primitive wisdom of the ancient Dansker is the least symbolized wisdom appearing in Melville's art. It matches the primitive flowing sea beneath the *Indomitable;* it has no form save the shadowy outline of an old sailor who is dusk to the sharp light in which Billy, Claggart, and Captain Vere are shown. The Dansker is wise with the weary wisdom of the Furies and the Norns, heavy with the knowledge of human error and distorted purpose. I can think of no character in literature nearer this hoary old seer of *Billy Budd* than Shakespeare's Old Man who enters with Ross after the murder of Duncan in *Macbeth* (Act II, Sc. iv) or Marlowe's Old Man who comes to warn Faustus (Scene xiv). With either or both of these he is the seer of primordial wisdom. In the art of Melville he is the character who stands nearer to the pure archetype; he is the least symbolic sage, and the only one who may be [250/251] assigned to that area of dream content in which archetype and nothing else is seen. . . . [251]

THE DIGRESSIONS

The Digressions in *Billy Budd*

MARY FOLEY

HERMAN MELVILLE'S *Billy Budd* REPRESENTS THE CONFLICT BETWEEN two kinds of form—the metaphysical form by which an individual thing is what it is, and the external form (or pattern, or law) by which indi-

A student's paper, not heretofore published; printed with the author's permission.

vidual things exist in relation to each other. In this novel the conflict first occurs between naval law and an extraordinary malefactor, Billy Budd. Naval law, absolutely necessary to the existence of naval society, is established to deal with the "Divine average," the ninety-nine cases out of one hundred in which metaphysical form produces an "ordinary" crime. (For the sake of simplicity, "ordinary" may be here defined as meaning "that situation in which agent, intention and act correspond sufficiently to produce the same emotional and rational verdict.") Billy Budd is the one hundredth case. His metaphysical form is rare. He is unusual and, therefore, in conflict with form (or pattern, or law).

For Melville, a spirit in conflict with form might be—but is not necessarily—superior to that form. A violation of the ordinary course of things can be a Billy Budd or an "Athéiste." Either one endangers order (or law, or form) and thereby threatens the existence of society which, being by definition "the usual," functions well under law. This is the basic paradox of *Billy Budd*—that a spirit in conflict with form, whether better or worse than ordinary, cannot endure in society because that spirit is itself incapable of form.

The digressions which conclude the novel are Melville's illustration of another conflict between organic form and externally imposed form. Each of the five digressions is an attempt to apply some law or pattern to the novel's events. Since *Billy Budd* already has its own organic form, the efforts to give it form through a preconceived standard are doomed to, at best, the achievement of partial truth. But the partial truths they embody are a necessary part of the whole truth the complete tale embodies.

The first digression represents the formula by which science would handle the phenomenon of Billy Budd. The ship's doctor is doggedly empirical in rejecting what he cannot touch ("will power," for example), while defining his terms like a Schoolman. His science, predicated upon absolute laws of cause and effect, admits of no peculiarities which cannot be referred to those laws. Thus, he explains Billy Budd by restricting his singularity to the absence of muscular spasms—and explains this absence in relation to natural but undetermined causes. This scientific formularization must completely reject euthanasia ("an easy, happy death") which, while congruent with the moral rarity which Melville emphasizes throughout the novel, is unscientific and, therefore, in conflict with the doctor's law.

The second digression offers the reaction of superstition—a form in its way as rigid as science. Where pure "head"—the doctor—sees natural but unknown causes, pure "heart"—the sailors—see preternatural forces at work. Recognizing Billy's more-than-physical transcendence, they find "no prosaic significance" in the sudden convergence of sea fowl following Billy's funeral. Although Melville partially rejects the almost mythic construction which the crew places upon this event, his explanation that the birds' behavior was "dictated by mere animal greed for prey" does not totally invalidate the crew's view. By recognizing a more basic aspect of Billy's nature than the doctor does, the sailors know him better than the doctor can. Their superstitious assignment of cause and effect is, nevertheless, as much the application of external form as is the doctor's empiricism. The sailors too, therefore, attain only partial truth.

In this digression the crew's reconstruction of events is interrupted by Captain Vere's insisting upon the form of routine work. Just as at Billy's trial, however, the routine is slightly awry: the ship's schedule is carried on "at an hour prior to the customary one." At the trial, normal court-martial procedure prevailed, but earlier than usual, since the case should really have been reserved for the admiral. Captain Vere's devotion to form is here in conflict with the great foe of human order—Time. The captain perpetually imposes order upon events as rapidly as possible, lest the passage of time should make such ordering impossible. (One of his main arguments for condemning Billy is the possibility that any lapse of time will be taken by the sailors as a sign of weakness of discipline.)

In the course of this digression the ambivalence of Melville's view of Vere, the apostle of law and order, becomes apparent. In phrases like "an officer like Captain Vere, a martinet as some deemed him," the juxtaposition of "martinet" and "Vere" suggests the conflict between the author's recognition of the necessity of order and his aversion to the destruction of Billy, which is necessary to maintain that order.

The third digression is Melville's own repudiation of form, his rejection of traditional literary form in favor of the looser structure of truth. Warning the reader that "truth uncompromisingly told will always have its ragged edges," he goes on to provide ragged edges. The death of Vere has, superficially, little connection with the rest of the story. "Well-wrought" fiction would have assigned his death to some poetically just agent. Vere's destruction by the French ship *Athéiste* (formerly *St. Louis*) is, upon examination, precisely in keeping with the book's main theme. As Billy represents the "Revolutionary Spirit" in its amiable aspects, *Athéiste*, flying the flag of the French government which deliberately embodied that spirit, represents conflict with form in its positively destructive aspects.

The fourth digression applies the standard of bureaucratic morality to Billy's case. According to the journalistic syllogism: Bad men strike their superiors. Billy struck a superior. Thus, Billy was bad. The article's emphasis upon "the efficiency of his majesty's navy" and its final assurance that "Nothing amiss is now apprehended aboard HMS *Indomitable*" repeat Melville's thesis that authority will willingly sacrifice the unusual for the sake of order.

The final digression represents an effort to come to terms with the story of Billy Budd through art. The sailors' vision of Billy is based upon the false information that his death was "unavoidably inflicted from the naval point of view"; but this vision is modified by their instinctive perception of Billy's innocence. Theirs is the conflict between reason and instinct, the order of logic and the rebellion of emotion. The ballad of "Billy in the Darbies" attempts to reconcile the image of Billy as an ordinary sailor with that of Billy as a hero somehow worthy of poetic immortality. Although the poem itself does not even suggest that Billy was remarkable, its very existence implies just that, since very few sailors do become ballad heroes. The grotesqueness of images like "pendant pearl," and " 'tis me, not the sentence they'll suspend," suggests that even the form of poetry cannot capture the truth of Billy Budd.

The digressions in *Billy Budd* thus serve a dual function. First, they echo the novel's basic conflict between metaphysical and external form. Second, they demonstrate the impossibility of reducing truth to a single formal standard. Each digression captures some aspect of the story and distorts the rest. But distortions actually vindicate the novel's lack of conventional form, embodying as they do the apparent formlessness which is the necessary organic form of the whole.

Billy in the Darbies

M. L. ROSENTHAL AND A. J. M. SMITH

THE FOLLOWING DRAMATIC MONOLOGUE APPEARS IN HERMAN MELVILLE'S novel *Billy Budd*. It gives us the hero's thoughts on the eve of his execution aboard ship for the crime of killing one of the ship's officers. The crime had been an unintentional one, and it has done no discredit to the much-loved young sailor who committed it. The sympathetic quality of Billy's character can be seen in the humble way he has of putting things, in his [372/373] affectionate tone when speaking of his messmate, and in his inability to visualize his own death as being of any great importance. At the same time, there is a saintly quality to his thoughts, as though he had long ago agreed that he was dying in a good cause. . . . Notice how the slight touch of humor deepens the pathos of Melville's effect here, and how Billy's resignation to his destiny makes the pathos a minor aspect of his essentially heroic character—in which there is not a trace of whining or self-pitying

From M. L. Rosenthal and A. J. M. Smith, *Exploring Poetry* (New York: Macmillan, 1955) pp. 372–375. Copyright 1955 by The Macmillan Company and used with their permission.

bitterness. ("Darbies" are manacles. The Dansker and Taff are shipmates of Billy's: Taff is now dead.) . . . [373/374]

This monologue, in addition to what it tells us of Billy's character,
becomes, indirectly, something more—a humble, loving but fatalistic
view of the world. Through the doomed sailor's thoughts, first of all,
we receive a picture of the good life as one in which a few creature-
comforts would be available and in which men would judge each
other's motives genially and affectionately. Even if he has some "bad"
thoughts, Billy's mind does not rest with them. It passes sadly over to
details of his coming execution, halts momentarily with the all-too-
answerable question "But aren't it all sham?"—but finally moves to
calm acceptance of his lot. He knows, as a matter of fact, that it *is* "all
sham," that the laws of society have arbitrarily made him the scape-
goat in a ritual-travesty of justice which he does not quite understand.
But although he could not at first imagine his own death, he at last
comes to see himself as already, literally, dead: "I am sleepy, and the
oozy weeds about me twist."

As so often happens, in the dramatic monologue and in other
kinds of poetry as well, the "story" here involves a projection into the
future: first a recognition that a change must come about and a
parallel tension at the prospect (as in Billy's inability to get his
imagination fastened on the precise fact of his own physical death),
then the realization of its full meaning, and finally the crystallization
of an attitude or insight (in this case, Billy's complete acceptance of
his future condition).

We too must "accept." We must accept the truth of this projection
of imagination. We shall do so if we feel that we know the speaker's
essential character, if the progression of his thoughts and feelings is
credible, and if the external objects he observes and the way they enter
his consciousness are acutely enough conceived. In such case, the
"meanings" the monologue carries along with it will be seen as having
their own truth and life and will exercise a certain power over us
whether we are prepared to believe in them generally or not. Artifice
and realism move together in [374/375] Melville's poem to bring this
conviction about in us. Every reader separately will have to come to
his own conclusions, of course, about the degree of psychological
realism present in Billy's thinking. But realism is not in any case the
only consideration, for the phrasing and the balanced movements of
the poem are not always of the kind one would expect in a simple,
untutored person like Billy. There are humble picturings—"down on
his marrow-bones," "a nibble-bit o' biscuit," and "a blur's in my eyes."
And there are others with the poet's own trademark on them—"the
moon-shine astray," "a jewel-block they'll make of me," "pendant pearl
from the yard-arm-end," "his cheek . . . like the budding pink." There
is a rough correspondence between the alternation of the two kinds of

language and the swinging, up-down movements of the physical visualization in this poem. The chaplain goes *down* on his knees; the moon comes *up* and then, in forecast, *down;* Billy imagines himself *up* in the air, then *down* to the moment before he is *raised* to be hanged; and so on until the movement is quieted in his vision of himself *sinking* and, finally, rocking slowly at the *bottom* of the sea. Through much of the monologue, the sense of emotional depression grows deeper the more clearly Billy visualizes his coming death. Yet the closing lines, with their steadily downward movement until they reach a point of final rest at the ocean-bottom, actually represent a heightening of his morale as his agitation of spirit subsides and he moves into total acceptance. The poet behind the scenes—somewhat like a theatrical director—has been experimentally manipulating basic dramatic feeling toward this final impression. To do so, he has had to distort nature and add something to it. Without such distortions and additions, however, poetry and the other arts would lose their inner truthfulness to the felt meaning of experience. [375]

THE AUTHOR

Herman Melville

W. H. AUDEN

Towards the end he sailed into an extraordinary mildness,
And anchored in his home and reached his wife
And rode within the harbour of her hand,
And went across each morning to an office
As though his occupation were another island.

Goodness existed: that was the new knowledge
His terror had to blow itself quite out
To let him see it; but it was the gale had blown him
Past the Cape Horn of sensible success
Which cries: "This rock is Eden. Shipwreck here."

From *The Collected Poetry of W. H. Auden* (New York: Random House, 1945), pp. 146–147. Copyright 1940 by W. H. Auden, by permission of Random House, Inc., and Faber and Faber Ltd., Publishers.

But deafened him with thunder and confused with lightning:
—The maniac hero hunting like a jewel
The rare ambiguous monster that had maimed his sex,
Hatred for hatred ending in a scream,
The unexplained survivor breaking off the nightmare—
All that was intricate and false; the truth was simple. [146/147]

Evil is unspectacular and always human,
And shares our bed and eats at our own table,
And we are introduced to Goodness every day,
Even in drawing-rooms among a crowd of faults;
He has a name like Billy and is almost perfect
But wears a stammer like a decoration:
And every time they meet the same thing has to happen;
It is the Evil that is helpless like a lover
And has to pick a quarrel and succeeds,
And both are openly destroyed before our eyes.

For now he was awake and knew
No one is ever spared except in dreams;
But there was something else the nightmare had distorted—
Even the punishment was human and a form of love:
The howling storm had been his father's presence
And all the time he had been carried on his father's breast.

Who now had set him gently down and left him.
He stood upon the narrow balcony and listened:
And all the stars above him sang as in his childhood
"All, all is vanity," but it was not the same;
For now the words descended like the calm of mountains—
—Nathaniel had been shy because his love was selfish—
But now he cried in exultation and surrender
"The Godhead is broken like bread. We are the pieces."

And sat down at his desk and wrote a story. [147]

6. RECENT CRITICISM

Billy Budd and the Articles of War

C. B. IVES

ALLEGORY IS OFTEN SO PATENT IN *Billy Budd* THAT MANY CRITICS HAVE found in the novel not a story but Melville's philosophical generalizations about man's fate and others have read the book as a statement regarding the nature of the struggle between good and evil. It seems to me, however, that the novel contains realistic elements worth examining and that one of these is Captain Vere's appeal to the Articles of War to justify his hanging Billy.

As far as the three main characters are concerned, the reader is bound to have difficulty in seeing Billy as a human being rather than as the very type of Innocence or in finding much more in the Master-at-Arms, John Claggart, than the soul of Evil; but the other character of importance, Captain Edward Fairfax Vere, presents more doubt as to his representational function. Critics of an allegorical turn of mind have sometimes cast him in the role of God the Father and sometimes in that of Pontius Pilate;[1] and, although as God he has seemed to some critics a representative of Divine Justice,[2] to others he has been the personification of Cosmic Tyranny.[3]

This comparative lack of distinctness in any allegorical meaning of Vere's performance arose mainly, I believe, from the difficulty of his problem, which Melville based on the real and widely debated problem that had confronted Captain Mackenzie of the U.S. brig *Somers* in 1824. In using the elements of the Mackenzie Case, Melville appears not only to have retained the basic realistic problem but even, in his

[1] Nathalia Wright, *Melville's Use of the Bible* (Durham, N.C., 1949), p. 131; E. L. G. Watson, "Melville's Testament of Acceptance," *New England Quarterly,* VI, 319–327 (June, 1933).

[2] Wright, pp. 72, 132–134; Ronald Mason, *The Spirit Above the Dust* (London, 1951), pp. 254, 257; F. O. Matthiessen, *American Renaissance* (New York, 1941), p. 510; F. Barron Freeman, *Melville's Billy Budd* (London, 1948), p. 24.

[3] Lawrance Thompson, *Melville's Quarrel with God* (Princeton, 1952), pp. 356–411.

From *American Literature,* XXXIV (March 1962), 31–39. Reprinted by permission of Duke University Press, copyright owners, and of the author.

alterations of the true event, to have added tension and to have increased the captain's difficulty in choosing [31/32] between alternatives. His alterations indicate that he thought Captain Mackenzie's position to have been a weak one (though he cites it "without comment"), for he provided his fictional captain with a stronger case.

Thus, in place of an American ship in time of peace, he chose for his setting a British ship in circumstances of extraordinary pressure: Britain was at war with revolutionary France; the French Republic's Reign of Terror had recently horrified and frightened even liberal Englishmen; within the previous few months the great naval mutinies at Spithead and the Nore had threatened to destroy Britain's defenses. Furthermore, Melville designed a criminal *act* by Billy Budd instead of the mere talk and mere appearances of the sailors who were hanged by Mackenzie.[4]

Did Melville make his captain's case so strong that the problem disappeared?—so strong that every reasonable captain would have acted as he did? If so, the story has lost some of its realistic appeal. Vere's position was exactly that; he said that he had no choice and that, in fact, he was faced with no problem at all.[5] I believe that the reader is mistaken if he accepts Vere's position at face value. Let us analyze it somewhat.

Vere's argument was founded mainly on the Articles of War, a combination of enactments by Parliament and regulations by the Admiralty. He appealed also to the Mutiny Act, but the body of laws falling under that title applied only to the army[6] and were without significance to his situation.

Examine, then, that section of the Articles of War that applied to Billy's act:

If any Officer, Mariner, Soldier or other Person in the Fleet, shall strike any of his Superior Officers . . . on any Pretense whatsoever, every such Person being convicted of any such Offense, by the Sentence of a Court Martial, shall suffer Death. . . .[7] [32/33]

This provision makes it clear that Billy Budd's offense was punishable by death under the Articles, but it is equally clear that Vere was wrong in asserting that the Articles required him to hang Billy forthwith. They required no such thing. On the contrary, they provided the

---

[4] Although Billy's act was not an act of mutiny, in contrast to the words and appearances that were definitely interpreted by the captain of the *Somers* as mutinous, Billy's act was connected in Vere's statements with the danger of mutiny.

[5] Most critics agree with Vere.

[6] The Mutiny Act arose out of the loyalty of Scotch regiments to James II after the accession of William and Mary. Charles M. Clode, *The Administration of Justice under Military and Martial Law* (London, 1874), p. 20. Its application was not extended beyond the army and other land forces. *Ibid.*, pp. 31–32.

[7] 22 George II, c. 33, II, 22 (1749).

punishment of death only upon conviction by a "Court Martial," by which term was meant a general court-martial, called by the commander of a detachment, a squadron, or a fleet.[8] The Articles of War provided nowhere for such summary court-martial as was held by Captain Vere.[9]

In an emergency, however, and in the event of a mutiny, a captain might hang the mutineers as a matter of necessity, in disregard of the Articles of War.[10] In such cases it was normal to secure the advice and judgment of his officers in a summary court. That was the situation supposed to obtain on the *Somers;* and, although the acquittal of Captain Mackenzie in that case might serve as precedent only for American ships, it was based on the traditions that the American navy had inherited from England.

But Billy Budd was not a mutineer and was not hanged for mutiny. Mutiny required a "combination of two or more persons,"[11] and, besides, Vere declared emphatically, "I believe you, my man," when Billy protested his loyalty. Nor was he hanged for murder, since Vere agreed that intent was lacking. Vere's stated reasons for the hanging were that Billy had struck his superior and that there was *danger* of mutiny by some other members of the crew.

For his decision, Vere could undoubtedly find support in the British naval customs that allowed latitude to a captain's authority even in defiance of statute, the attitude of naval officers being, as one might expect, that politicians knew nothing about discipline at sea and that even the Admiralty was too much of an ivory tower [33/34] for its members to make consistently sensible regulations. Thus, for example, although printed instructions of the Admiralty limited captains of ships to imposing punishment of not more than a dozen lashes,[12]

[8] Admiralty may grant Commissions for Courts Martial to any Officer commanding in Chief any Fleet or Squadron of Ships of War. 22 George II, c. 33, VI. Commanders in Chief may impower commanders of a Squadron or Detachment ordered on separate service to hold Courts Martial. *Ibid.,* VIII.

[9] J. E. R. Stephens, C. E. Gifford, F. Harrison Smith, *Manual of Naval Law and Court Martial Procedure* (London, 1901), pp. 21, 69; formal prohibition of the power in ships' captains to give sentences of loss of life or limb were contained in official instructions as early as 1653. *Ibid.,* pp. 18–19.

[10] John Masefield, *Sea Life in Nelson's Time* (2nd ed.; London, 1920), p. 213; even J. F. Cooper, strongly critical of Mackenzie, conceded the right to hang if that was the only way a captain could save the ship, himself, or his officers. *Proceedings of the Naval Court Martial in the Case of Alexander Slidell Mackenzie . . . to which is Annexed an Elaborate Review by James Fennimore Cooper* (New York, 1844), p. 272.

[11] Stephens and others, p. 143.

[12] *Regulations and Instructions Relating to His Majesty's Service at Sea* (11th ed.; London, 1772), Article IV, p. 46; A Surgeon's-Mate of 1803, *Sketch of the Punishments to Which Common Seamen and Marines are Liable in the Royal Navy* (London, n.d.), pp. 9–10; Admiral Philip Patton, perhaps naïvely, said that custom imposed the limitation, *Strictures on Naval Discipline* (Edinburgh, n.d.), p. 86.

in practice these autocrats seldom gave less than the allowance and frequently gave several dozen more.[13]

Discretion was customarily allowed in the direction of leniency also. The faults of sailors sometimes passed without punishment at all,[14] and sometimes received lighter punishments than the Articles called for.[15] Thus, a captain might impose a minor punishment for desertion although the Articles demanded that a court-martial try the offender for his life;[16] and not only was sleeping on watch regularly overlooked (though punishable under the Articles by "Death or such other Punishment as a Court-Martial shall think fit to impose, and as the circumstances of the case shall require," 22 George II, c. 33, II, 27), but, according to at least one experienced officer of those days, it was actually encouraged.[17] Billy's offense, striking a superior officer, for which the Articles allowed no alternative to death, did not always receive that punishment.[18]

In short, a captain of a man-of-war was godlike and might exercise his disciplinary discretion or even his disciplinary whims freely with little expectation of reproof.[19] [34/35]

Was not Captain Vere aware of his broad powers? The considerable argument that he made to the officers of his drumhead court-martial implies that he was; and when he said, "one of two things we must do—condemn or let go," he explicitly recognized the power to let go that he—advised, though not bound, by his court—possessed by naval custom. His appeals at one moment to the Articles of War and at

[13] A Surgeon's-Mate of 1803, p. 10; Lieut. Thomas Hodgskin, R.N., *An Essay on Naval Discipline Shewing Part of Its Evil Effects* (London, 1813), p. 60; Graham Hewlett, "Discipline and Punishments in the Royal Navy," *United Service Magazine*, N. s., XLIV, 613 (March, 1912); T. H. Wintringham, *Mutiny* (London, 1936), pp. 68–69. However, such excessive flogging as two hundred or eight hundred lashes might, when they resulted in death, bring conviction for murder against the captain; Louis B. Davidson and Eddie Doherty, *Strange Crimes at Sea* (New York, 1954), pp. 69–90.

[14] Patton, pp. 82–83; leniency in cases involving the death penalty seems to have been the normal practice in the early days of the Articles; one authority says that, although the Articles of War of 1652 provided the death penalty for a great number of offenses, "up to the time of the Restoration there is no known instance of a death sentence pronounced under it having been carried out. Even the fomenters of mutiny escaped." Sir William Laird Clowes, *The Royal Navy* (London, 1898), II, 103. In the army, even the sentences of courts-martial were sometimes disregarded; Clode, p. 32.

[15] Patton, pp. 82–83.

[16] A Surgeon's-Mate of 1803, pp. 5–6.

[17] Hodgskin, p. 40.

[18] Masefield says (p. 213) that a man who struck an officer in Nelson's time was only "*fairly* certain to be hanged or flogged through the fleet." Italics added.

[19] ". . . they [ships' captains] are legislators, they are judges, they are juries, and they are very often parties and executioners," Hodgskin, pp. 29–30. ". . . the discipline of each ship depends upon what is called the captain's natural disposition," *ibid.*, p. 35.

the next to the "practical consequences" demonstrate his own confidence that the Articles did not control him.

In addition to the alternatives of hanging and acquittal, his officers also recognized the availability of two other lines of action: conviction with a penalty less than hanging or reference of the case to the Admiral as provided by the Articles. The first of these was called to Vere's attention by the junior lieutenant; and Vere was aware of the second,[20] though he did not discuss it at the trial.

We must, then, conclude that Captain Vere, contrary to some of his statements to his officers, had, as a matter of fact, the broadest powers in dealing with Billy. He could let him off, he could impose a minor punishment, he could refer the case to a general court-martial, or he could hang him. He chose to hang him.

Consider now some of the irregularities in the so-called trial ordered by Captain Vere. When Vere told the surgeon of his determination to call a drumhead court-martial immediately, the surgeon thought Vere was "suddenly affected in his mind." He recalled Vere's "excited exclamations so at variance with his normal manner." The lieutenants and the captain of marines "fully shared" the surgeon's "surprise and concern." The misgivings of these men were undoubtedly roused in part by the precipitancy of the "trial," the best procedure even in cases of minor crimes being to delay the decision as to punishment for at least twenty-four hours;[21] but mainly their anxiety seems to have come from Vere's decision to try Billy at all, since they saw no reason not to comply with the [35/36] provisions of the Articles of War. The "sense of the urgency of the case" that "overruled in Captain Vere every other consideration" did not possess his officers.

They also saw, no doubt, a violation of at least the spirit of the law in the secrecy with which Vere hurried on to his conviction of Billy. General courts-martial were required by the Articles of War to be held in the greatest possible publicity.[22] Since drumhead courts were not provided for by statute, only by custom, nothing explicitly required Vere to give publicity to his trial; yet the general policy was made clear by the Articles, and, after news of the hanging got abroad in the fleet, Vere was criticized for this secrecy "in the confidential talk of more than one or two gun-rooms and cabins."

[20] *Billy Budd*, Chapter xxii: "The case indeed was such that fain would the *Indomitable's* captain have deferred taking any action whatever respecting it further than to keep the foretopman a close prisoner till the ship rejoined the squadron and then submitting the matter to the judgment of his Admiral."

[21] Patton, pp. 31–32, 84–85; William N. Glascock, *Naval Sketch Book* (London, 1826), I, 243.

[22] *Regulations and Instructions Relating to His Majesty's Service at Sea* (11th ed.; London, 1772), Article III: "Courts Martial shall always be held in the Forenoon, and in the most public Place of the Ship, where all, who will, may be present. . . ."

Finally, Vere's officers must have recognized that a basic element of judicial inquiry and trial was defied by Vere's predetermination to hang Billy. It is true that they did not hear him address Billy as "Fated boy" the moment after Claggart gave his last gasp; but the surgeon had hardly confirmed Claggart's death when he heard the Captain exclaim that Billy must hang. The members of the court could not help seeing that the proceedings were sham, dominated and directed by Vere, who required them only for the sake of form—" 'With mankind' he would say 'forms, measured forms are everything. . . .' "

There is no reason for the reader to suppose that these officers of Vere's were foolish men. The surgeon not only was by profession something of a student of abnormal behavior but was also, as Melville takes pains to make clear, a man of the most matter-of-fact judgment, not given to flights of fancy or imagination. Although Melville says that Vere regarded the members of his court as "well-meaning men not intellectually mature" and had special doubts about the captain of marines (the commander of the police force on the ship, whom one might expect to know something of the demands and limitations of discipline) for being "an extremely good-natured man, an enjoyer of his dinner, a sound sleeper, and inclined to obesity," are not these strictures more revealing of Vere's own character than of the characters of his officers? [36/37]

What was there in the character of Vere that brought him to adopt his extraordinary course? Why, though appealing to the Articles of War, did he disregard them? And why did he disregard the advice of his officers, the suggestions of common sense, and the strong inclination of his own heart?

Melville gives the Captain many virtues, which need not be denied in putting emphasis on that side of his nature that seems to have been the chief cause of Billy's summary hanging.

Vere was a bachelor of "forty or thereabouts," who had "ruled out" the feminine in his personal life just as he demanded of the members of his court that they rule it out in deciding Billy's fate. He was not given to colorful talk or gestures, for when ashore "he never garnished unprofessional talk with nautical terms," and when afloat he might have been mistaken by any landsman for a civilian rather than the captain of the ship. He was undemonstrative and humorless. His bookishness was marked—"dry and bookish" some called him—and it was biased towards "actual men and events" rather than fiction or poetry. In his reading he "found confirmation" of certain "positive convictions" that he was determined never to change. So pedantic was his interest in historical fact and so stubborn his lack of interest in human nature that even with those of his fellow officers whose intellectual inclinations were thoroughly alien to his he freely alluded to his bookish research. In short, although the life he led was vigorous and dramatic, Vere turned from the enjoyment of it to books; and, although his reading might have been even more impressed with color and vitality than his adventurous life, he turned away from literary art or imagination or feeling to the dryness of recorded fact.

At Billy's trial, Vere's arguments were aimed primarily at making the decision that would be most difficult for human sympathy, most difficult for man as a living being having a natural love of life. He cited the Articles of War (which did not, in fact, support him), the Mutiny Act (which did not apply), the practicalities of the situation (which to every other judgment called for delay at least), and the necessity, as he said, of doing what no one wanted to do, of suppressing Nature, of injuring the heart—"the feminine in man"—even of violating the conscience. When he announced the court's decision to his sailors, they received his statement "like [37/38] believers in hell listening to the clergyman's announcement of his Calvinistic text."

In all this, Vere was guided not by the mind, as he professed, but by the heart turning against itself. Note well that in spite of his devotion to the facts of books, to a colorless simplicity of personal speech and appearance, to the coldest duties of his profession and rank, emotion was not always entirely concealed; for a "certain dreaminess of mood" revealed itself at times, signifying that, even before his surprising emotional outbursts in the case of Billy Budd, Vere had never been entirely as dry as dust.

Give full weight also to Melville's chapter on Nelson, inserted with no casual intent. At Trafalgar, says Melville, Nelson dressed himself out in all his decorations, advertising his identity to the enemy and suffering death in consequence. His was "a sort of priestly motive," says Melville, and the admiral "adorned himself for the altar and the sacrifice." A similar priestly motive and a similar sacrifice is declared in Melville's comparison of Vere to Abraham preparing to offer up Isaac. Although Abraham's sacrifice was not literally of himself, like Nelson's, it was of his son, whom he loved and who was, in no remote sense, a part of himself. Similarly, Vere loved Billy Budd and spoke to him in "fatherly" tone.

A review of these aspects of Vere's nature justifies the conclusion that the Captain's sudden decision to hang Billy was a sacrificial gesture, born of a kind of self-punishment that had become habitual in Vere's life, the sacrifice and denial that are involved in man's search for the comprehension of fact that destroys fancy, in man's search for the experience that gives him truth but robs him of innocence. All of his life Vere had devoted himself abnormally to this emphasis, killing repeatedly the affections that manifested themselves only in moments of dreaminess, moments that embarrassed and irritated him when they were discovered. Billy represented all of this nearly-destroyed side of him—the affectionate side, the heart, the feminine—and stirred him to such a pitch that when the innocent sailor delivered the death blow to Claggart, Vere's suppressed love for Billy and for all that Billy stood for rose suddenly to the surface. However, Vere's self-disciplinary passion for the harshness of fact-searching and heart-denial rose equally fast and dominated his will as it always had done. [38/39]

A more normal captain would never have been so eager to hang Billy Budd, and a more practical one might not have hanged him at all, in view of his great value to the morale and efficiency of the crew. Billy's destruction was doomed not only by the abnormal malevolence of Claggart but also by the abnormal "inside narrative" of Vere's personality.[23] The customs of the sea did not require it; and the Articles of War provided only a deceptive excuse for the exercise of Vere's extraordinary "priestly motive," which, as Melville suggests at the beginning of Chapter XXII, may well have contained the elements of true insanity. [39]

[23] "The struggle between Claggart and Billy is re-enacted on a wholly different plane within the nature of Vere himself," says F. O. Matthiessen (p. 509); and he seems to put the Captain on Claggart's side of the conflict when he adds, "He [the Captain] had the strength of mind and the earnestness of will to dominate his instincts."

Melville's *Billy Budd*, Chapter 1

LEONARD NATHANSON

IN CHAPTER 1 OF *Billy Budd*, CAPTAIN GRAVELING RELATES TO THE *Bellipotent's* lieutenant an anecdote concerning the young sailor just chosen for impressment and one Red Whiskers that is usually thought to serve the function of establishing Billy's trait of unreflective action and also of foreshadowing his killing of Claggart. The significance for the novel's plot of Billy's thrashing of Red Whiskers is clear enough. "Quick as lightning, Billy let fly his arm" prefigures the blow with which he strikes Claggart dead when called upon by Captain Vere to answer the Master-at-arms' accusation of intention to mutiny. "The next instant, quick as the flame from a discharged cannon at night, his right arm shot out, and Claggart dropped to the deck" (chap. 19, p. 99 in the edition by Harrison Hayford and Merton M. Sealts, Jr., Univ. of Chicago Press, 1962).

But there is also a thematic significance in the parallel of Red Whiskers and Claggart as persecutors of Billy and as "victims" of his strength. Each represents the principle of evil with which Billy comes

From *The Explicator,* XXII (May 1964), Item 75. Reprinted by permission of *The Explicator,* copyright owner, and of the author.

into conflict in the two worlds of the *Rights-of-Man* and the *Bellipotent*. What is especially interesting is that both of Billy's very different antagonists are associated with the specifically infernal. It is hardly necessary to point out that Claggart is conceived along Satanic lines, since Melville has made so much explicit reference to Milton's Satan in depicting him. In his perversion of intelligence, energy, and (as is strongly hinted) noble descent into a destructive hatred that can respond only with "Pale ire, envy, and despair" to perfect innocence and perfect beauty Claggart is perhaps the most fully developed ectype of Satan to be found in modern literature. Now Red Whiskers, it should be noted, is also delineated in infernal terms. But, of course, there is no resemblance here to the Satan after whom Claggart is modeled; there is no suggestion of fallen grandeur or of perverted capacity. Red Whiskers is conceived, instead, along the lines of the popular folk devil or the "Vice." He is not the devil as suave tempter, seriously to be feared as the agent leading man to destruction, but only the half-contemptible, half-entertaining fool, easily recognized and defeated by the protagonist.

As in medieval and Renaissance popular literary tradition, the Vice is essentially a comic figure, ranging from fool to clown to ruddy devil, embodying the spirit of troublesome misrule rather than the principle of evil. It is just this absurdity that Captain Graveling recognizes when he describes Billy's opponent as the "buffer of the gang, the big shaggy chap with the fire-red whiskers." The contrast to the intelligence, elegance of person, and self-control of Claggart could hardly be sharper. Red Whiskers, as the almost emblematic color of his hair suggests, is a noisy, obtuse mischief-maker, whose belligerence earns him a drubbing, the usual punishment of the devil-as-an-ass. He is close to the absurd kind of devil to which C. S. Lewis has attempted unsuccessfully to reduce Milton's Satan, a devil, like Claggart, to whom much more is due.

Red Whiskers is the embodiment of such evil as Billy encounters in the peaceful setting of the *Rights-of-Man*, the merchant vessel so named by its "hardheaded Dundee owner [who] was a staunch admirer of Thomas Paine. . . ." When Billy leaves this ship he moves from a world of humane and liberal regard for the individual into the implacable sphere of the *Bellipotent*, where the inflexible legalism of the Mutiny Act defines innocence, guilt, and justice according "to the frontage, the appearance," as Captain Vere insists it must. In the benign world of the *Rights-of-Man*, Red Whiskers' antipathy to the beauty and innocence of Billy is overt, harmless, and comic in its outcome. Billy clears the air of all tension by giving this bully a thrashing that everyone agrees was richly deserved, including, it would seem, Red Whiskers, who surrenders his ill-feeling and is thereafter won over. While Billy can, by virtue of his physical strength and winning manner, tame and reform the devil of the *Rights-of-Man*, no such easy victory is scored in his struggle with evil aboard the *Bellipotent.* Billy's goodness and his instinctive physical response are inadequate when set against the complex and irremediable evil incarnated in Claggart, whose malice operates furtively and tenaciously to its tragic conclusion. The parallel of Red Whiskers and Claggart as antagonists of Billy is thus constructed so as to emphasize massive and ironic contrasts pertinent to the political and ethical meaning of the novel. The incident involving the comic devil looks forward to a similar yet profoundly different clash with Satan himself.

Billy Budd and the Limits of Perception

JOHN W. RATHBUN

WITH THE PUBLICATION BY HARRISON HAYFORD AND MERTON SEALTS OF a new reading text of *Billy Budd,* accompanied by a complete transcription of the genetic text, an excellent introduction, and awesomely complete notes, we are now possessed of the most reliable text that can reasonably be expected.[1] Several changes, such as the substitution of *Bellipotent* for the British man-of-war, *Indomitable,* and the excision of the Preface, are changes to which we will become habituated only after long acquaintance, although one can recognize the force of the editors' arguments. But the primary materials included offer the first real opportunity to come to grips with the central significance of Melville's compact masterpiece. Here the genetic text compiled by Hayford and Sealts is invaluable, for it gives solid clues to Melville's increasingly sharpened purposes in writing the novel. In addition, by providing us with the chronologies of the various drafts, the editors make it possible to be conscious of inherent difficulties in the text, which, if they cannot be resolved, can at least serve as a restraint on ingenious attempts to impose an absolute order on materials that finally must remain recalcitrant.

This last point is important. Despite the vast amount of commentary on *Billy Budd,* I think there has persisted in most scholars' minds an uneasy feeling that our imaginations have failed to compre-

---

[1] Herman Melville, *Billy Budd, Sailor (An Inside Narrative),* edited by Harrison Hayford and Merton M. Sealts, Jr. (Chicago, 1962). Subsequent references to this edition will be in the body of the article.

From *Nineteenth-Century Fiction,* XX (June 1965), 19–34. © 1965 by The Regents of the University of California. Reprinted by permission of The Regents and of the author.

hend Melville's novel. The ambiguous, ranging, and habitually ironic mind of Melville, coupled with textual difficulties, defeats us. We have rendered tribute to this defeat, especially in recent [19/20] commentary, through close and intense readings of the text. These have contributed much to our understanding. But they have also encouraged fashions of analysis (such as the current preoccupation with Captain Vere) that have become increasingly narrower in focus. This article proposes to explore the novel as a whole. To achieve this, I have worked within the novel's structure as it establishes a logic of action and have analyzed the thematic imagery as it supports this action.

I would like to declare at the outset that I have avoided two sets of assumptions or expectations which I do not think especially helpful in reading *Billy Budd:* one, that the story is a tragedy; two, that the focus of the story is on any one character. I offer two alternative views. These are, first, that the story captures something of the quality and intention of a saint's play, with some modification of the term that will become apparent in the article; and second, that Melville's tale revolves about the point that social forms and conventions radically narrow the range of individual perception and response. What Melville is telling us, I think, is that society elaborates social forms and conventions to render the individual subordinate to social norms. When on occasion there emerges a man of individual nobility of heart, one who is as incapable of social "reconstruction" as Billy, it is testimony to our pathetic social condition that we intuitively recognize his superior excellence but suffer a terrible incapacity to comprehend him completely or to emulate him at all.

Social Convention, War, and the State

In the opening pages of the novel, Melville skillfully contrasts those citizens who wear the "external uniform of civilization" and the upright innocence of sailors dissociated from the land whose vices are only "frank manifestations of natural law" (pp. 52–53). The "pristine and unadulterate" virtues found in the figure of the "Handsome Sailor" are "out of keeping" with the "thoroughly civilized" man reared according to "custom and convention" (p. 53). Virtue is antecedent to culture and is a matter of individual rectitude. Therefore, no virtue can inhere in society. In the absence of virtue, society must rely on culture to induce uniform conduct. And culture is no more than the sum total of customs and conventions that encourage a kind of Pavlovian response in [20/21] men. The natural tendencies of the individual, says Melville, are transformed into a cultured crookedness of heart that leads to moral obliquity (p. 52). The free, self-determining individual simply disappears. In his place, we find man in the aggregate, unquestioning, responding mechanically to external stimuli, living in "Cain's cities" (p. 53).

This effort on the part of society to compromise innocence constitutes much of the tension of Melville's novel. Billy throughout consistently tries to correspond to the standards established by the state. On
leaving the *Rights of Man* of Captain Graveling, Billy says farewell to
his individual rights, as many commentators on the text have pointed
out. He becomes, Captain Vere later asserts, a "King's bargain." When
asked about the accusation Claggart had lodged against him, Billy
replies that he has loyally eaten the King's bread, an unwitting parody
of the Christian ritual. But for all his effort, Billy fails to become
"civilized." He suffers no deterioration of individual character despite
his various temptations. And this partially accounts for his downfall,
since it prevents him from understanding the antipathy of the "urbane"
Claggart.

Billy's inability to lose his own spontaneity of character stands in
opposition to his shipmates. More than landsmen, they possess a
residue of natural innocence. But long service aboard a man-of-war,
dedicated to the service of the state, has brought them into conformity
to the disciplined obedience that state must demand. Aboard the
Bellipotent, "usage" serves as a synonym for regulative custom or
convention. Usage standardizes action and at the same time reduces
men to the point where they are amenable to social control. It is
necessarily the official representatives of the state who must see to it
that usage is observed. Captain Vere, when acting in his official role,
habitually observes usage. He goes by the book. Following Claggart's
death, it is apparent from the thoughts of the surgeon and the
assembled officers that "usage" would allow mere confinement of Billy
until land is reached and the matter referred to the Admiral.[2] But
Vere, mindful that usage, inflexible in its particulars, must be seen in
strict relation to circumstance, and [21/22] mindful too that the
atmosphere of the time is mysterious, foreboding, and prodigious,
decrees the summary court martial as permitted in the Mutiny Acts.[3]
And it is perfectly in keeping with usage that his officers hear the case
while he reserves to himself the right to supervise the proceedings and
to intervene at need.

In all the measures taken by the ship's officers, the ultimate motive
is to exercise usage as a control over the seamen. Chapters xxiii and
xxvii are studies in depth of the social role of usage. In the former,

---

[2] The relevant passages (pp. 101–102) seem to indicate that the surgeon and
the other officers are simply inclined to postpone action in a difficult case. The
surgeon, whose doubts are given at some length, is a "prudent," politic man who
thinks confinement of Billy should be conducted as "dictated by usage." The whole
passage, however, as Hayford and Sealts point out, is ambiguous. See their comments, pp. 9–11, 35.

[3] A useful interpretation of the latitude given Captain Vere in employing the
Mutiny Acts is in C. B. Ives, *"Billy Budd* and the Articles of War," *American
Literature,* XXXIV (March, 1962), 31–39.

the crew listen to the announcement of Billy's death-sentence as Calvinist laymen might listen to a Calvinist clergyman, without protest or surprise, with full knowledge and understanding of the code. But when their "native-sense" of right becomes operative a low murmur of protest rises.[4] The officers are equal to the danger. Instantly, there is the shrill piping of whistles, piercing and imperative, and the men, who themselves are the "greatest sticklers for usage," promptly respond because of their habituation to duty.[5] Similarly, in chapter xxviii, which is concerned with events immediately following Billy's execution, the whistles and drums serve to suppress the crew's innate sense of justice and to bring them into line. And lest this point is not clear, Melville makes the point specific. "True martial discipline long continued," he says, "superinduces in average man a sort of impulse of docility whose operation at the official sound of command much resembles in its promptitude the effect of an instinct" (p. 127).[6]

Aboard the *Bellipotent*, these habituations to duty exist in the cause of war. As the story progresses, it moves from Billy's world of the yardarms and upper decks, with their sense of freedom and space, to the ghostly clutter of the upper decks at night and to the depths within. There are increasing references to shot, subterranean rooms and passages, darkness, and the heavy cumbersome guns. We move downward through various spirals of horror as we do in Dante, until we reach the heart of the matter below the luminous [22/23] surface. The *Bellipotent* is a special kind of hell in which custom and usage exist in the cause of evil. With the interview between the Chaplain and Billy, we find that even peace, ironically, is conscripted to war. Melville raises the question as to why the Chaplain did not act to save Billy and drives his point home. Sea protocol would have rendered the attempt futile. The Chaplain knew that Billy was to become a "martyr to martial discipline" (p. 121), but he occupied the "incongruous" position of being a minister of the Prince of Peace expected to obey the code of the Host of the God of War. Hence the Chaplain subserves the same cause as the cannon. We see the terrible irony of a minister who professes love and attachment serving a god who through "brute Force" would destroy those ideals. He lends the "sanction of the religion of the meek" to an abomination (p. 122).[7]

The cause of war is an enormously complicated and darksome

[4] This parallels Captain Vere's own sense of right when Claggart makes his accusation before Vere too falls back on usage.

[5] As I will indicate at various points in the article, whistles serve as a remarkable means to recall men to their habituated sense of duty and custom.

[6] Cf. Karl Zink, "Herman Melville and the Forms—Irony and Social Criticism in 'Billy Budd,'" *Accent*, XII (Summer, 1952), 136, for an effective comment on this passage. As will shortly appear, however, Mr. Zink and I disagree on the interpretation of Captain Vere's character.

[7] The attitude is persistent in Melville's writings, as Hayford and Sealts point out, pp. 185–186.

thing, reinforced by Melville's imagery of blackness and the fact that Billy's temptations, trial, and condemnation occur at night. Billy's first temptation, the incitement to mutiny, takes place on the moonless "tarry balcony" of the lee forechains. Everything is shadowily outlined, and at Billy's repulse the unknown man flees into the dark shade of the booms. The sense of mystery, intrigue, and betrayal is overwhelming. Then in close order occur Claggart's night-time accusation of Billy, the confrontation of the two below decks, the garish trial with its jail-house and dead-house so near, and the moonlight announcement of the sentence to the crew. Billy's death-vigil, muted and quiet in tone, is reinforced by a dark oppressiveness. Billy lies between two guns as if nipped in the "vice of fate." Surrounding him on the upper gun-decks are all the impedimenta of war. Everything is heavy, huge, painted black as was "customary" or tarred the same color. It all appears as an "upland cave's black mouth." Even the lantern gives off a "dirty yellow light" that stains the moonlight, and around Billy are the "obscurer bays." The white ducks worn by Billy contrast dramatically with this pervasive "funereal hue." The darkness imagery is continued in the following morning scene. The black night covers the ship. The "cavernous" decks below are like the "tiered galleries in a coal-mine." (Again the evocation is in terms of Dante.) Racks of heavy shot are everywhere. The black booms tiered on the deck cast an [23/24] eerie shadow. Then a "metallic" stroke follows the sounding of eight bells. Immediately, the preemptory whistles blow, and the men flood obediently out of the ship's bowels onto deck. The whole scene stands impressively against the exalted moment that follows, when Billy pronounces his benediction on Captain Vere and is raised to take the full rays of the sun.

Coincident with this bleak view of the state in terms of convention and war, Melville criticizes the state as a source of legal despotism over the individual.[8] As Melville develops this aspect of the novel, the principles of universal justice are seen to principally affirm man's transcendental individualism (as this is apotheosized in the upright seamen and Billy's Adamic character). The state, therefore, viewing man solely as a social creature, is impelled to set up a secular code of

[8] The context for the following paragraphs is the conflict between two concepts of government: the divine rights of kings and the Christian Commonwealth. I would argue that Melville's novel is sympathetic to the ideas of the Christian Commonwealth, which was far more liberal and far more cognizant (in theory) of the welfare of its citizens. Social and economic inequities would obviously abide in any temporal social structure, but such inequities would be held to a minimum by the Commonwealth itself as it sought to administer God's justice. With the advent of the divine right theory, the correspondence of divine and temporal justice declines, and as a matter of fact comes to be sharply discriminated. These points are admirably documented in the book of William Appleman Williams, *The Contours of American History* (New York, 1961), in the initial chapters.

justice in opposition to the divine order.[9] This has the effect of
cancelling out man's individualism and molding him into a social
pattern that assures first rank to the state. The state becomes an end in
itself, its citizens pawns in the intricate moves of statecraft. Pervasive
throughout the novel, the theme of state supremacy is clearly delineated by Melville in the trial scene. Captain Vere is the spokesman for
the new attitude. As an English sea-commander, he has committed
himself to the primacy of state policy. His "vows of allegiance" are to
"martial duty," which means in effect that he is "not authorized" to
consider abstract principles of guilt and innocence. Consequently,
prudence and rigor must be his primary attributes. Captain Vere can
look only to the external act. Scruple and compassion, which might be
operative under the terms of universal justice, are matters for "psychologic theologians" and [24/25] are outside state concerns (p. 108). In
"practical" matters (and in the world of the state all matters are
practical), one cannot afford the stance of moralist or casuist (p. 110).
As Vere tells his own officers, their allegiance is not to the natural law
but to the King. In serving under the King, no man is a free-agent. The
state pre-determines everything (pp. 110–111). A man's only duty is to
obey.

Here, of course, there is no correspondence between God's law
and state law. The very idea of correspondence, that an intimate
relationship exists between man's rage for order and the objective
world, is denied. A King's representative, Captain Vere points out,
must distinguish between the King's concerns and God's concerns.
Private conscience must yield to imperial law (p. 111). This last
statement reverses the authorities of God and King that had obtained
in past times, and it testifies to the superiority of the King in all issues
affecting the state. A new divinity has come into existence, not to shape
the best ends of man, but to secure its own interests and self-
perpetuation.[10]

The Religious Symbolism

The religious symbolism of the characters has been explored by a
number of scholars. I simply propose to examine it here in terms of
what I have already said about the state's ability to counteract man's
nature, the state's authority, and its code of justice. Much of Melville's

[9] Hayford and Sealts take a somewhat different tack in suggesting that "the
opposing positions of [Paine and Burke] concerning the doctrine of abstract
natural rights lie behind the dialectic of *Billy Budd*" (p. 138). Cf. also William
Bysshe Stein's article on the role of history in the novel: " 'Billy Budd': the Nightmare of History," *Criticism*, III (Summer, 1961), 237–250. Stein is probably too
harsh on Captain Vere, and he does not see the central significance of the Abra-
ham-Isaac analogy which I discuss later in this article.

[10] Cf. William Braswell, "Melville's *Billy Budd* as 'An Inside Narrative,' "
American Literature, XXIX (May, 1957), 133–134: "The King is a symbol of the
Deity: he does not physically appear in the story, but he is the supreme authority
under whose law the ship operates."

story is couched in Biblical and religious terms. As the novel progresses, Billy takes on in turn the characters of the pre-Fall Adam,
Isaac, and Christ, but with results radically different from the original
Biblical versions. Billy becomes the Adam who does not fall, the Isaac
who is not saved, the Christ who does not redeem. One comes away
from the book with a sense of the immense futility of Billy's death.
One comes away too with a sense of the immense sadness and
aloneness that Melville must have experienced in civilized man's
incapacity to imaginatively realize an experience of transcendental
significance to all men.

As a pre-Fall Adamite figure, Billy is primarily intended to represent unperjured innocence and guilelessness, qualities in which the
crew partially share as "upright barbarian" Adams (p. 52). Opposed
[25/26] to Billy is the depraved and deceitful Claggart. The two men
are polar exemplars of good and evil, each phenomenal in his own
way. Neither man possesses a known parentage, so that their "true
antecedents" remain obscured in mystery (pp. 51, 65). Billy, a "peacemaker" who might have "posed for a young Adam before the Fall," is a
"child-man" possessed of an "essential good nature" (pp. 86, 81).
Claggart is the "direct reverse of a saint," a man who does not have a
"normal" nature (p. 74). These differing natures lead to differing
attributes. Billy is a rosy-hued, vivacious man of "significant personal
beauty" (p. 77), while Claggart's complexion testifies to something
"defective or abnormal" in the blood (p. 64). Claggart's superior
intellectual capacity, his constitutional sobriety and ingratiating deference to superiors, his "austere" patriotism, are all the antithesis to
Billy's animal-like fatalism and "unconventional" rectitude.

In both men, the heart dictates their attitudes, but those attitudes
are put into action in different ways. The "bonfire" in Billy's heart is
heroic and innocent. He does not try to force events nor has he learned
from experience. He has not tasted of the "questionable apple of
knowledge" (p. 52). The result is that Billy's innocence does not
sharpen his faculties or enlighten his will (p. 70). Claggart's heart, on
the other hand, is filled with envy. His "innate" depravity folds itself in
the "mantle of respectability" (a "manufacturable" thing closely associated with the "moral obliquity" of the city), and he uses his reason to
effect "the irrational" (p. 76). His conscience is "lawyer to his will," so
that a fancied provocation can provide the motive for various acts
against Billy (p. 80).

Billy does not exclusively possess the qualities endowed by the
figures of Adam and the "handsome sailor," which are complementary
images. The figure of the "handsome sailor" is to be found aboard a
number of ships (p. 43). A sort of natural regality obtains in such
men. The handsome sailors, whom seamen recognize and to whom they
respond, possess a strength and beauty in excess of that of ordinary
men, and their moral natures correspond closely to their physical

beauty (p. 44). Their natural habitat is the upper deck and the shrouds, swinging airily over the decks and living in the natural sunshine of the day.

Claggart's nature is common enough to have been defined by Plato, and he enlists subordinates in his cause who share in his qualities. Claggart too belongs to a class. Where Billy's world is [26/ 27] the world of the upper decks, Claggart's world is the lower gundecks, where he serves as a sort of chief of police (p. 64). In this lower world, he controls "various converging wires of underground influence" that allow him to function as the inquisitorial arm of the state. Obviously endowed with intelligence and a good education, he displays a "ferreting genius" which is the hallmark, according to Melville, of civilized man at his worst. The "austere" civilized man is corrupt and untrustworthy. All the more reason, then, for Claggart's "austere" patriotism to employ itself in fashioning a maze of deceit for the entrapment of individuals. For this purpose, he employs subordinates like Squeak, who have the ferreting aptitude of a "rat in a cellar" (pp. 67, 79). In the dark gloom of the lower decks, such men mine their network of deceit and betrayal and work assiduously against those of the topside.

Caught between these two levels of moral experience is the world of convention. The conventional world, committed as it is to set patterns of response and pedestrian wisdom, lacks the requisite tools to comprehend either Billy's innocence or Claggart's satanism. Both men are "exceptional" creatures, moral phenomena who transcend man's ordinary way of knowing (pp. 74, 78). The world of convention "blunts that fine spiritual insight" which is needed to understand "certain exceptional characters" (p. 75). Claggart cannot be understood in terms of a knowledge of the world (p. 75), and only Vere and Claggart have any inkling of the richness of spirit possessed by Billy. This indictment of a world committed to custom and convention is harsh, and it relegates the world to the position of onlooker as the two exemplar figures clash and destroy one another.[11]

Billy's very lack of knowledge contributes to an innocence which is his blinder (p. 88). His virtues are all the more extraordinary because he is so absolutely unaware that he possesses them. Before Claggart's satanism, saintly Billy can only express blank puzzlement. Melville makes clear that Claggart's antipathy and evil are [27/28]

[11] Hayford and Sealts correctly see Billy, Claggart, and Vere as three types of men who act out of the necessity of their inner natures to affect the circumstances and action of the novel (p. 167). It seems odd, then, that they should suggest that the "theme of moral accountability and responsibility . . . is of major importance in *Billy Budd*" (p. 166). Billy, Claggart, and Vere act as they must act, and Melville does not seem so much disposed to attribute blame as to lament men's lack of perception of what actually occurs in this world. Interesting comment from a theological point of view is in James Smylie, "*Billy Budd*: the Work of Christ in Melville," *Religion in Life* (Spring, 1964), 286–296.

mysterious even while spontaneous and profound. Like Satan looking at Adam in *Paradise Lost,* Claggart knows a "soft yearning" for Billy and experiences despair, melancholy, and sadness over that unattainable station (p. 88). And so recoiling upon himself, he uses all the deceits, stratagems, and temptations he can to destroy Billy. Since culture is "auspicious" to depravity, Claggart utilizes the attributes of the landsman—his finesse, his liking for intricate moves, indirection, and obliqueness—to bring about Billy's fall.

One must be aware, however, of the complex ironies that control the fall motif. It is fairly certain that Billy does not re-experience Adam's original fall from grace. Billy does not taste of the tree of knowledge, nor does he lose his primeval innocence. This can be seen in Captain Vere's statement that at the Last Assizes Billy will be acquitted before the bar of divine justice, and seen too in the imagery attending Billy's execution, where Billy is transfigured by "the full rose of the dawn." Yet Melville is specific in attributing a human flaw to Billy in his stutter. I think the stutter serves two functions. It first establishes Billy as a finite human being and therefore no idealized "conventional" hero of romance (p. 53). His innocence is therefore "natural," just as Claggart's depravity is natural; philosophers like Rousseau and Calvin are alike wrong in plumping for one to the exclusion of the other. His stutter, secondly, is a flaw only in the eyes of man. Speech, after all, is man's method of civilized communication. To that extent, language itself is arbitrary, restricted, exclusive, deliberately regulated. Billy represents all that is uncoerced, free, and spontaneous. He transcends the reductions language must make in order to communicate. Billy must be known intuitively, not logically. His agonized attempt to talk, and his inability to do so, when Claggart makes his accusation, leads then to a fall only in the eyes of the state and its code of temporal justice. Before heaven, Billy is innocent. But in terms of the secular code Billy has fallen, and he must be punished.

With the conclusion of the trial scene, Billy's betrayal by the forces of evil is concluded and the Adam symbolism completed. Following the trial, Melville suggests a second Biblical parallel. At this point Billy acquires a father in Captain Vere, who becomes Abraham to Billy's Isaac. Again, Melville's departure from the Biblical story is as significant as his suggestion of its relevance. Captain Vere possesses many of the attributes of the established order. He [28/29] is a sailor of distinction, intrepid but not injudicious, modest and aristocratic, dreamy at times, sturdy but not brilliant in his actions (p. 60). He is inherently conservative and believes in institutionalism as a control of the social order. Of a markedly intellectual temperament, he reads history, biography, and "unconventional" (therefore honest and self-reliant) writers like Montaigne. In the process, he has come to some considered opinions on how "lasting institutions" might be established that an ordered society can live in peace (p. 63).

In his contacts with other men, Captain Vere again displays a wide range of abilities. The state recognizes his tact and initiative and gives him extra duties to perform. In the interview with Claggart, he is impatient and conscious of a "vaguely repellent distaste" for the man (p. 91). Ordinarily, he can intuitively understand other men's motives and their "essential nature" (p. 96). These are all fine qualities and certainly in Vere's favor. He is not the villain of the novel, as some recent commentators have tried to suggest. But Vere is not the hero either. He takes Claggart's measure accurately and sensibly. But he cannot fathom the guile of the man. Claggart finally perplexes Vere. In an unfamiliar situation, he resorts to the familiar position of policy and tact. He resolves to "practically" test Claggart's veracity. His learned trust in overt proof brings about the confrontation and from that the crisis ensues. Then during the trial scene Vere becomes the authoritarian representative of the state, winning out over his officers' more humane instincts (pp. 109–110).

Vere's inclinations, when he allows himself to slide away from his "formalized humanity" and to abandon his "austere" devotion to military duty, are all toward love (p. 115). In his imagined description of the private interview between Captain Vere and Billy, Melville is explicit in pointing out that both Vere and Billy are two of "Nature's nobler order" (p. 115). They share radically in the "rarer qualities of our nature," so radically, indeed, that we can hardly conjecture the extent. Vere's capacity to realize the virtue of love, although finally limited, makes the last moments between him and Billy "sacramental."

Yet there is for Vere the "exacting behest," as there was for Abraham. Vere's tragedy, finally, is that he is in the service of a dread sovereign. Abraham, in the service of a greater sovereign, was stayed in the execution of God's command: Abraham's intent was sufficient. [29/30] No such stay is granted Vere. It constitutes a failure of the only authority he knows, the state. In a society where laws are promulgated to govern the whole rather than to protect the individual, their infraction must necessarily be unquestioningly punished. No melioration is possible. Indeed, such melioration is impossible, for the state is distant and indifferent. Only the Mutiny Acts figure, and they allow (if they do not decree) the sacrifice of Billy.[12]

The suggestion of sacrifice evokes the memory of the greatest sacrificial victim of all, and with Billy's death Melville turns to the symbol of Christ. The symbol works in two ways. Just as Christ was condemned by the laws of temporal justice so Billy is condemned. The

---

[12] I think this is the only view of Vere consistent with the tone and imagery of the novel. It is a point of mediation between the position of James E. Miller, Jr., that Vere is a "Hero of Humanity" ("*Billy Budd:* the Catastrophe of Innocence," *MLN*, LXXIII [1958], 168–176) and the position of Phil Withim, who argues that Vere represents all that Melville means to attack ("*Billy Budd:* Testament of Resistance," *MLQ*, XX [June, 1959], 115–127).

injustice of what happens to Billy is accentuated through the various references to Christ's agony and execution. Second, through his death Billy achieves a spiritual father and transcendental significance. As one of "Nature's nobler order," Billy stands for all that is good, natural, and noble in mankind. He has been spiritualized by his experience. His agony is over. Resignation and peace possess him. In the final climactic moment, the darkness is dissipated, and Billy ascends to his death. But the full significance of Billy's nature and death, as the last chapters indicate, is ultimately lost on society, on Captain Vere, and on the seamen.

The Final Chapters

As Melville quite correctly points out, in terms of dramatic action the story should end with Billy's death. But if a reader has been sensitive to Melville's organization of his narrative, it soon becomes apparent that Melville has interwoven various strands which can more or less be reduced to a counterpoint of authority (the state, usage, and war) and freedom (primeval innocence, human community, and Billy's triple role as sacrificial victim.)[13] These strands [30/31] are not resolved with Billy's death. The final chapters constitute an ironic epilogue, in which in a series of tonally contrasting events we see the impact of Billy's death on the state, Captain Vere, and the seamen.

The reaction of the state occurs in the conversation of the Purser and the Surgeon and in the official version of Billy's death. In both chapters there is a deliberate downgrading of tone from the drama of Billy's death to a flat and literal level. The purser and Surgeon are utilitarian and unimaginative. They see Billy's death as a natural event, a phenomenon but not phenomenal. Their whole concern is with a "scientific" knowledge of the externals of the event, especially the absence of spasmodic movement as Billy hung at the end of the rope. Their conversation is ridiculous, pompous, and arrogant. For every natural event, a natural cause must be predicated. Here is the tell-tale clue. On the mundane level, Billy's death should *be* a natural event. But even the physical death somehow escapes definition. There is a mystery to it that resists rational explanation. Their failure to get beyond the literal is a failure of the imagination, and here no power on earth can help.

In conjunction with this scene, we have the juggling of history for the convenience of the state. At various points in the narrative,

---

[13] Hayford and Sealts note a "pattern of . . . antitheses" may be found in the novel and illustrate their point by reference to three incidents (p. 162). But they also say (p. 194) that "the deliberate juxtaposition of contrasting attitudes" in the last chapters argues against any attempt to find Melville's intent. I think precisely the opposite can be maintained. The strange sense of unreality in the last chapters is persuasive evidence for my general thesis—that social convention so clouds men's perception that imaginative insight into truth is almost totally impossible.

Melville prepares us for this eventuality. In discussing the Nore mutiny, he points out that England was chary about all reference to mutinies. The official need was to write history selectively, to avoid facts, to gloss over facts, or to ignore facts completely. Melville's sober realism acknowledges that this is sometimes necessary. He is less lenient in discussing the *Somers* incident in chapter xxi, where he is clearly out of sympathy with the Captain's procedure in an incident nearly like the one that occurred aboard the *Bellipotent*. And then there are the ambiguities of circumstance themselves, in which appearance does not always correspond to reality. The official need is to recognize only the externalities of events. This leads necessarily to changing the consideration from Billy's essential innocence to Billy's circumstantial guilt. When, therefore, the official version of Billy's execution is published, all relation to the truth is lost, even though the account is "for the most part written in good faith."[14] Billy is vilified and Claggart sanctified. And as Melville ironically comments, this is the way it has [31/32] stood "in human record" until his own reconstruction of the events. And such must be the result for the state to sustain itself. Usage, ritual, discipline, falsification, and literal adherence to political need and expediency then act in sharp contra-distinction to transcendental truth.

In the chapter on Vere's death, the mystery of Billy's character again hovers over the action. Vere's position in the narrative is ambivalent, and this ambivalence extends to his death. In terms of his native intelligence and imaginative insight, Captain Vere comes close to understanding Billy. But his habitual reliance on custom and usage finally inhibits his perception. The cause for which he fought, insofar as it was directed against the excesses of French revolutionary action, was a good cause. But in the need to preserve its own existence the state legislated away freedoms in the name of freedom, a contradiction which could only lead to tragedy for those enrolled in the service of the state. In his devotion to the state, as well as to the institutions the state elaborates for its own maintenance, Vere prepared the ground for his own untimely defeat. His capture of the *Athée* promises fulfillment of his ambition for greatness. But his mortal wound, his drugged lingering illness, and his death ashore all testify to a moral character cut short of conclusion. He realizes dimly that there was something he finally was unable to attain. His death is pathetic rather than tragic. He dies unenlightened, softly repeating Billy's name, like an invocation.[15]

14 There is a difficulty here resulting from Melville's incomplete revisions. Vere's death would likely have been reported as well as Billy's and Claggart's. Cf. Hayford and Sealts (p. 8).

15 The fact that Vere's character is developed late in the manuscript revisions (designated, X, E, F, G by Hayford and Sealts) seems to confirm the idea that Melville, as he worked out his ideas and organization, came to see Vere as a dramatic example of how even the most "exceptional" man can be so altered by habits of perception as to fail to escape their bondage.

Finally, in the reaction of the seamen to Billy's death, we have the most pathetic case of all because potentially there was great promise. Even though the seamen share in Billy's simplicity and to some extent in his innocence, they finally cannot comprehend his greatness. Chapter xxvii, which returns to events immediately following Billy's hanging, is heavy with tension, and much of the tone of the chapter on Billy's death is re-established. In the silence following the hanging, there are only the flutter of the sail and the soft wash of the sea to be heard. Then gradually a mounting murmur is heard, much as in the night announcement of Billy's sentencing. The reaction of the officers is immediate. Once again the metallic peremptory whistles are blown, and once again the men yield to [32/33] the "mechanism of discipline" and disperse. Later the men reassemble to witness Billy's burial, where the "croaked requiem" of the crying birds provokes an "uncertain movement"; immediately there is the drummed call to quarters to which the men respond instinctively. Finally, they are made to stand ritualistically by the guns they serve. During the long roll call, usage gradually removes the immediacy of Billy's death and burial, giving cogency to Captain Vere's observation that "measured forms are everything" in the control of men. Three times the crew had threatened to follow inner impulses. And three times they had yielded to the habit of discipline to which they had been conditioned by the state.

Yet, as we see in the last chapter, the seamen realize intuitively that Billy's death has some latent significance to them. Ignorant of the facts, they accept Billy's condemnation as the inevitable expression of naval authority. But they also know that he is guiltless. And so Billy becomes a sort of Christ figure to them. Billy, however, does not possess Christ's redemptive meaning in the ordinary sense. It is simply that Billy has exposed the magnificence of the primitive soul that has in it a touch of the divine, just as a touch of the divine may be in us all when not deformed by custom, usage, or austere discipline. The very simplicity of the seamen prevents them from coming to this elementary understanding. They lack the ability to link imagination with intelligence, which after all must be combined for superior understanding. Their dim perception of Billy's nobility is gradually modified into a ritualistic and fetishistic worship of pieces of wood. Such is always the case. Great men like Christ and Billy always transcend measured forms. The rest of mankind, lacking the capacity for true comprehension, progressively downgrade such greatness until it is neutralized within the folds of ordinary thurification.

These last chapters give us an ironic vision that over two-thirds of a century of living had confirmed in Melville. No one in the novel is finally able to ascertain who Billy really is. Billy's character remains enigmatic. The symbolic roles he plays as Adam, as Isaac, as Christ, become at last meaningless and futile. To the extent that we deny the existence of constituent elements in human nature and see man as simply a bundle of social habits, we impose limits to man's perception. Culture becomes simply a pattern of response. Thinking thus, it is no great step for the state to "engineer" habitual action toward some desired end. In the process, men lose their [33/34] individual capacity to realize the ultimate moment of transcendental awareness.

And yet there is at the same time something more to Melville's novel. For whatever ease it might give one, the tone of that last chapter indicates that a modicum of comfort is better than none, acceptance preferable to despair. *Moby Dick* is in many ways an angry, anguished outcry against evil and an unsuccessful exploration of its origins. *Billy Budd* accepts evil as part and parcel of the universe within which we live. This acceptance establishes a tone of wintry serenity mixed with an ironic regret that provides much of the fascination of the novel. The ballad ending is essential to Melville's purpose. "Billy in the Darbies" is the only real imaginative extension of an experience that obviously had meaning to the "artless poetic temperament" of Billy's fellow seaman. However crude in insight, it is preferable to the coldly impersonal account of Billy's death in the "authorized" naval chronicle of the time. What Melville seems to be saying is that as social creatures we fail to properly understand our saints. Our insight is clogged by forms and conventions. But fortunately for some of us our individuality is not completely buried. Our perceptions are dimmed and our aspirations limited, which is pathetic, yet occasionally we can be stirred to a muted awareness of our humanity. [34]

APPENDICES

CHRONOLOGY

1819   Herman Melville born as the third of eight children to Allan and Maria Gansevoort Melville on August 1 at No. 6 Pearl Street, New York City.

1830   Moved with family to Albany. Entered the Albany Academy.

1832   Allan Melville died.

1835   Clerked in Albany. Taught school near Pittsfield, Massachusetts.

1838   Moved with family to Lansingburgh. Took a course in the Lansingburgh Academy.

1839   Shipped in June as a sailor on the *St. Lawrence* for Liverpool; returned to New York in October. Taught school at Greenbush.

1840   Visited uncle in Galena, Illinois.

1841–   Shipped as sailor in January on the whaler *Acushnet* from Fairhaven
1844   (New Bedford); stopped at Rio de Janeiro in March; rounded the Cape in June; cruised through the Galapagos Islands in fall and winter. Arrived at Marquesas Islands in June (1842); deserted with Toby Greene to the interior of Nukahiva in July; signed on the Australian whaler *Lucy Ann* in August; left ship at Tahiti, escaped to neighboring island of Eimeo; signed on the whaler *Charles and Henry* in November. Arrived at Hawaiian Islands in April (1843); went to Honolulu in May; signed in August on the frigate *United States*, which sailed to the Marquesas, Tahiti, Valparaiso, Callao, Lima, and Mazatlan. Arrived at Rio in August (1844) and at Boston in October. Rejoined family at Lansingburgh.

1846   *Typee* published in London and New York. *Omoo* completed.

1847   *Omoo* published in London and New York. Married Elizabeth Shaw in Boston on August 4; moved to New York.

1849   *Mardi* published in London and New York. *Redburn* published in London and New York. Completed *White-Jacket*. Visited London, Paris, Brussels, Cologne, and the Rhineland. Son, Malcolm, born.

1850   Returned to New York, began book on whaling. *White-Jacket* published in London and New York. Moved to "Arrowhead," near Pittsfield, Massachusetts; there met Hawthorne, who was his neighbor until November, 1851.

    With the aid of Jay Leyda's excellent *The Melville Log: A Documentary Life of Herman Melville: 1819–1891*, 2 Vols. (New York: Harcourt, Brace and Co., 1951)

1851   *Moby-Dick* published in London (as *The Whale*) and in New York. Began *Pierre*. Second son, Stanwix, born.

1852   *Pierre* published in London and New York.

1853   Began to contribute stories and essays to *Putnam's* and *Harper's* monthlies. Daughter, Elizabeth, born.

1854   *Israel Potter* serialized in *Putnam's*.

1855   *Israel Potter* published in book form. Second daughter, Frances, born.

1856   *The Piazza Tales* published in U.S. and England. Completed *The Confidence-Man*. Sailed to England and the Mediterranean, visiting Malta, Syria, Salonica, Constantinople, Alexandria, Cairo.

1857   *The Confidence-Man* published in U.S. and England. Traveled through Palestine, Italy, Switzerland, Germany, the Netherlands, and (again) England. Returned to America.

1858–   Lectured in South and Middle West. Worked on poems. Sailed to
1860   California and returned to New York (1860).

1863   Moved family to 104 East 26th Street, New York City.

1866   Volume of poems, *Battle-Pieces and Aspects of War,* published. Appointed Inspector of Customs at the Port of New York.

1867   Son Malcolm died of a self-inflicted pistol shot.

1869   Surviving son, Stanwix, went to sea on the *Yokohama,* sailing for China.

1870   Began work on *Clarel*.

1876   Published *Clarel* with a subsidy from uncle, Peter Gansevoort.

1886   Son Stanwix died in San Francisco.

1888   Voyaged to Bermuda, returning by way of Florida. Printed *John Marr and Other Sailors* privately. Began *Billy Budd*.

1891   Completed *Billy Budd*. Printed *Timoleon* privately. Died September 28.

1924   *Billy Budd* published.

STUDY QUESTIONS

1. What are the esthetic advantages, or disadvantages, of Melville's having conceived of a ship for his locale?

2. In what different way is *Claggart* as appropriate a name as the names of Billy, Vere, and the three ships: *Rights-of-Man, Bellipotent,* and *Athéiste?*

3. The three major characters, Billy, Claggart, and Vere, all die. What do their deaths have in common? In what ways are they different? How are they related? In what sense are the deaths "comments" on one another? Do they collectively embody a single comment? If so, what is it?

4. Compare Braswell's reading of the story as "spiritual autobiography" with Auden's poem. In what ways are they similar? In what ways dissimilar?

5. Observe the color symbolism in the tale, the use of *rose* in connection with Billy and of *pallor* with Claggart. How closely may we associate them, respectively, with "heart" and "head"? How is the opposition between dark and light used generally? In what other ways does Melville assign symbolic values to his characters?

6. What differing esthetic premises appear to lie behind the five essays in Section III? Are the premises mutually exclusive? Which approach seems best to take into account the complete tale? What kind of comment do the authors collectively make about the nature of the tale? Much criticism of *Billy Budd* is dominated by a consideration of Melville's attitude toward Vere. How crucial is this question to these five critics? Is it a necessary critical problem of the tale?

7. How far are we to press the Christian parallels? "Are we to regard them as overtones and images," as Bruce Harkness and Royal Gettman have asked, "or are we to regard them as echoes and counterparts?" Can Billy effectively be the "upright barbarian," Adam, *and* Christ? Can Vere be God, father to Billy, *and* the ideal temporal Governor? Are Auden's objections to the characterization of Billy and Claggart valid ones?

8. Is the function of the early digressions similar to that of the ending ones? Does Melville intend them as comments on one another?

9. How convincing is Melville's understanding and depiction of the *psychological* motivations behind the actions of Billy, Claggart, Vere, and the Dansker? Do their symbolic functions reduce or strengthen their worth as believable human characters? Discuss each character in this connection.

10. Is it a serious limitation to read the story simply as a conflict between a natural world and a civilized one? Stallman and Watters see the following additional antitheses suggested by the story: depravity versus innocence, intuition versus "knowledge of the world," the earthly versus the heavenly, head versus heart, military duty versus private conscience, war

versus religion, landsmen versus seamen, society versus the individual. Does one of these more accurately reflect that conflict? Does one of your own?

11. Examine carefully the background information given about Billy, Claggart, and Vere. What considerations seem to have determined the kind and amount of information Melville provides about these three characters? Take into consideration theme, characterization, and technique.

12. Is the uncertainty about the meaning of *Billy Budd* a reflection on the esthetic achievement of the tale? What are, finally, its strengths and weaknesses as a story, as a unified work of art?

13. Over forty additional articles (in journals and in books) on *Billy Budd* have been published since the first edition of this book in 1961. Discuss those aspects of the tale that seem *to you* to foster this increased critical attention. Are these the aspects that critics have been most concerned with in recent years?

14. Few works of literature have been as variously adapted to other genres as has *Billy Budd*—a play, an opera, a movie, a television drama. Discuss those elements in the story that seem to you to account for this eclectic adaptability. Do those elements appear to you to come from weaknesses or strengths in the story? You might well begin with a list of the specific differences between the happenings in the story and those in the play.

15. Read carefully the editor's essay-review of the new Chicago text of the story and discuss the whole problem of how various texts of *Billy Budd* have affected critical reactions to it. What have been the critical results of the fact that Melville himself did not finally complete the story?

THEME TOPICS

1. Following is a list of authors referred to in *Billy Budd:* Sir William Blackstone, Edmund Burke, John Calvin, Camoëns, Sir Edward Coke, Charles Dibdin, Diderot, Oliver Goldsmith, Hawthorne, G. P. R. James, Samuel Johnson, Martial, Andrew Marvell, Milton, Montaigne, Thomas Paine, Plato, Ann Radcliffe, Tennyson, Voltaire.* Discover where in *Billy Budd* the reference or references are made to each. Find out what you can about each author and his works; then explain Melville's purpose in thus referring to him. What contribution is thereby made to the tale?

2. State explicitly the central theses in the two articles under the section "*Billy Budd* as Testament." Then support that thesis which most nearly parallels your own reading of the story. (The same can be done with each of the sections, or with selected essays from different ones—the case for or against Captain Vere, for example, or Auden's doubts about the characterization of Billy and Claggart.)

3. Select one of the following episodes from the tale: Billy's last words, Vere's last words, the moment of Claggart's death, "Billy in the Darbies," Vere's speech to the court-martial, the conversation between the purser and the surgeon, the dedication to Jack Chase, Billy's hanging, the spilt soup episode, the unreported conversation between Vere and Billy as Vere reports the court-martial's verdict, the newspaper account of Billy's death, the Nelson digression, the function of the Dansker or of the Chaplain, the reference to the *Somers*, and so on. Then examine and evaluate the function performed by the episode, the contribution it makes to the meaning of the whole.

4. Explicate Auden's poem, using as model the technique and method Rosenthal and Smith employ in their examination of "Billy in the Darbies." In what way is the poem an interpretation of *Billy Budd?* Is it in any sense also an evaluation of it?

5. Reread the Biblical account of Adam's expulsion from Eden and make your own analysis of Melville's intention in that regard in *Billy Budd.* Compare your results with Arvin's. Do the same with the Biblical accounts of Christ (or with Milton's *Paradise Lost*) and test your findings against the findings of the appropriate critics. Do the allusions work, as Tindall suggests, in a fashion similar to the mythical parallels in Joyce's *Ulysses* or Eliot's *The Waste Land?*

6. Compare Billy with Othello, Vere with Hamlet, or Claggart with Iago. For more recent parallels, compare and contrast Billy with Huck Finn, or with Maisie Farange (from James's *What Maisie Knew*), Morgan Moreen

* Suggested to me by Gordon Roper's useful "An Index of Herman Melville's *Mardi, Moby-Dick, Pierre,* and *Billy Budd*" (Unpublished Ph.D. dissertation, University of Chicago, 1944), pp. 255–257.

257

(from James's "The Pupil"), Holden Caulfield (from Salinger's *Catcher in the Rye*), George Willard (from Anderson's *Winesburg, Ohio*), Ike McCaslin (from Faulkner's *The Bear*), or Tommo (from Melville's first novel, *Typee*).

7. One might also make comparative studies of the tale as a whole with the works listed above or with *Antigone, Oedipus Rex,* or *Oedipus at Colonus;* or with Hawthorne's "The Birthmark," specifically referred to in the tale.

8. Analyze, specify, and evaluate the varying critical methods employed by Braswell, Glick, Chase, West, and Tindall in order to define what literary criticism should be.

9. Take what you consider to be Melville's resolution of the central moral issue in *Billy Budd;* examine it, test it, and evaluate it in the light of your own beliefs regarding the basic nature of goodness, evil, justice, or fate.

10. Examine carefully the imagery and sentence rhythm of Chapter 25, the hanging scene. What commitment does the style itself here make to the conflict between Billy and Vere?

11. What transpired between Vere and Billy at their meeting the night before the hanging is not given in the story; it is in the play. Examine the advantages and disadvantages of the omission and inclusion of that scene in, respectively, the story and the play.

12. Compare and contrast the functions performed by the digression chapters (26–30) according to Mary Foley with those they perform according to John Rathbun. What is lost and gained in the dramatic version, which excludes them altogether?

13. Develop other conclusions that might be reached from the remarkable historical research accomplished by C. B. Ives in his *"Billy Budd* and the Articles of War."

14. Does the omission of the "Preface" from *Billy Budd* (deleted from the Chicago text but reprinted in this volume from the Freeman text) strengthen or weaken the tale as a whole?

15. Why do you think Melville finally chose the name *Bellipotent,* instead of *Indomitable,* for the ship on which the major action occurs? List as many reasons as occur to you.

TOPICS FOR LONGER ESSAYS
AND TERM PAPERS

1. Trace the critical reputation of *Billy Budd* from Weaver's brief remarks in 1921 through the comments of the critics in 1966. Does this also become a brief history of American critical thought over the same four decades, its strengths, weaknesses, and variety? Compare and contrast the British and American reactions to the story.

2. Place *Billy Budd* in its proper perspective as the culmination of a development begun in Melville's *Mardi* and continued through *Moby-Dick* and *Pierre*. Or take another track and trace Melville's development through his sea stories, beginning with *Typee* and *Omoo*, through *Redburn*, *White-Jacket*, *Moby-Dick*, and his short tales of the sea, on to *Billy Budd*. Or, more simply, take an early novel, a middle one, and *Billy Budd*. Such studies could be focused on major themes, major characters, major moral resolutions, and so on. The possibilities are many. One might also trace Melville's development from *The Confidence-Man* to *Billy Budd* by way of the considerable amount of poetry he wrote in between.

3. Trace the history of the *Somers* affair and its relation to Melville and his family. Begin with the items by Anderson, Freeman, Arvin, and Harrison (see checklist). In what ways does knowledge of the affair affect one's understanding and evaluation of Melville's tale?

4. Compare and contrast *Billy Budd* with late tales by other major nineteenth-century American novelists—for example, Hawthorne's *The Marble Faun*, Twain's *The Mysterious Stranger*, and James's "The Beast in the Jungle" or "The Jolly Corner." Do they throw light on one another in any meaningful way? Do they allow you to make any generalizations about American fiction?

5. At least one critic (Jean Jacques Mayoux) approaches the problem of Melville's treatment of innocence in *Billy Budd* by pointing to Kafka's *The Trial* as a contrasting treatment of essentially the same problem. In what ways are the two views alike? In what ways different? Or contrast *Billy Budd* with Camus's *The Fall*.

6. Contrast Melville's treatment of innocence in *Billy Budd* with one of James's American innocents—with Christopher Newman, say, or Daisy Miller. In what ways is Twain's view of innocence (in *The Innocents Abroad*, for example) essentially different from Melville's and James's? How about Twain's view in *Huckleberry Finn*?

7. In *The American Novel and Its Tradition* (Garden City: Doubleday Anchor Books, 1957), pp. 5–7, Richard Chase says this:

The American novel has usually seemed content to explore, rather than to appropriate and civilize, the remarkable and in some ways unexampled territories of life

259

in the New World and to reflect its anomalies and dilemmas. It has not wanted to build an imperium but merely to discover a new place and a new state of mind. Explorers see more deeply, darkly, privately and disinterestedly than imperialists, who must perforce be circumspect and prudential. The American novel is more profound and clairvoyant than the English novel, but by the same token it is narrower and more arbitrary, and it tends to carve out of experience brilliant, highly wrought fragments rather than massive unities.

In fact, he continues, "many of the best American novels achieve their very being, their energy and their form, from the perception and acceptance not of unities but of radical disunities." In what ways does *Billy Budd* fit this generic definition of the American novel? In what ways does it *not* fit the definition?

8. Tindall says that the "teller" of *Billy Budd* "is not unlike the Marlow of Conrad's *Heart of Darkness*"; that Melville's thought-process, like that of Marlow, "is the heart of this darkness and its shape the objective correlative, a form for something at once imperfectly understood and demanding understanding." Reread the latter part of Tindall's essay and then Conrad's *Heart of Darkness* and compare the technique of the two tales. See also Thompson, Freeman, Braswell, and Rathbun on the narrative technique in *Billy Budd*. In what ways does Conrad's depiction of the center of experience parallel Melville's depiction in *Billy Budd*? Tindall also suggests that the narrative technique in Faulkner's *Absalom, Absalom!* is essentially the same. Test it in relation to *Billy Budd*.

9. In Conrad's *Lord Jim* the character Stein makes this well-known statement:

A man that is born falls into a dream like a man who falls into the sea. If he tries to climb out into the air as inexperienced people endeavour to do, he drowns. . . . No! I tell you! The way is to the destructive element submit yourself, and with the exertions of your hands and feet in the water make the deep, deep sea keep you up.

Does this passage throw any light on *Billy Budd*? Compare the two novels.

10. McElderry, the Gollins, Cameron, and Sutton (see checklist) have all found what they describe as earlier treatments of the *Billy Budd* theme. Read the various works they cite and discover your own parallels. Test your readings against Withim's use of their findings.

11. Provide annotations for some or all of the allusions in *Billy Budd*. What is their collective contribution to the meaning and worth of the tale? (See Pearson, in checklist.)

12. Study the genetic text of *Billy Budd* (see Hayford and Sealts) and apply its account of how the tale was written, how it grew, to the major interpretive problems of the reading text. Pay specific attention to the developing role of Captain Vere.

13. Make a detailed study of the differences in the various adaptations of the tale to other genres—the dramatic version, the movie version, the operatic versions. Then discuss the extent to which the differences are appropriate to the varying needs of the differing adaptations. In what ways do they individually and collectively "interpret" the story?

14. Compare the criticism of the tale written after 1962 that uses the Hayford and Sealts edition of the text with that of earlier years that uses the Freeman edition. What specific interpretive differences have resulted from the new text?

15. What, finally, are the appeals of *Billy Budd*—to readers, to critics, to adaptors? What specifically are the *qualities* in Melville's tale that seem to you best to account for this continued and varied appeal?

BIBLIOGRAPHY
An Annotated Checklist of Studies
of *Billy Budd*

NOTE: I have provided brief descriptive annotations only for those important studies whose titles are either misleading or unspecific. The entries preceded by an asterisk (*) are printed in complete or nearly complete form in this collection; those preceded by a dagger (†) are excerpted in this collection and carry annotations only when the unexcerpted portions are of major importance.

Abel, Darrel. *American Literature.* Great Neck: Barron's Educational Series, 1963. Vol. 2, pp. 449–451.

Anderson, Charles Roberts. "The Genesis of *Billy Budd,*" *American Literature,* XII (Nov. 1940), 328–346. Important first extensive treatment of sources.

Anderson, Quentin. "Second Trip to Byzantium," *Kenyon Review,* XI (Summer 1949), 516–520. An essay-review of the Freeman text.

Arvin, Newton. "A Note on the Background of *Billy Budd,*" *American Literature,* XX (March 1948), 51–55. Additional evidence on the *Somers* affair.

*———. *Herman Melville.* New York: William Sloane Associates, Inc., 1950. Pp. 292–299. Reprinted as a Compass Book (New York: The Viking Press, 1957).

*Auden, W. H. *The Enchafèd Flood or The Romantic Iconography of the Sea.* New York: Random House, 1950. Pp. 144–149.

*———. "Herman Melville," *Collected Poems of W. H. Auden.* New York: Random House, 1945. Pp. 146–147.

† Baird, James. *Ishmael: A Study of the Symbolic Mode in Primitivism.* Baltimore: Johns Hopkins Press, 1956. Pp. 249–251, 272–273, 426–427. Reprinted as a Harper Torchbook (New York: Harper & Brothers, 1960).

Baritz, Loren. *City on a Hill: A History of Ideas and Myths in America.* New York: John Wiley and Sons, 1964. Pp. 329–330. Brief statement on *BB* as a "condemnation of a life that must make war . . . on the Baby Budds" of this world.

Barnet, Sylvan. "The Execution in *Billy Budd,*" *American Literature,* XXXIII (Jan. 1962), 517–519.

Bercovitch, Sacvan: "Melville's Search for National Identity: Son and Father in *Redburn, Pierre,* and *Billy Budd,*" *College Language Association Journal,* X (March 1967), 217–218.

Bernstein, John. "Billy Budd: The Testament of Rebellion," in *Pacifism and Rebellion in the Writings of Herman Melville.* The Hague: Mouton, 1964. Pp. 202–213.

Berthoff, Warner. " 'Certain Phenomenal Men': The Example of *Billy Budd*," *ELH*, XXVII (Dec. 1960), 334–351. Billy and Vere represent complementary "motions of magnanimity under the most agonizing worldly duress . . ." Reprinted in *The Example of Melville* (Princeton: Princeton Univ. Press, 1962), pp. 183–203.

Blackmur, R. P. "Introduction," *American Short Novels*. New York: Thomas Y. Crowell Co., 1960. p. 5–8. Views *BB* as Melville's "continuing allegory of how it is that we seek what we must shun."

Bonheim, Helmut. "The Vocabulary of *Billy Budd*," *Exercise Exchange*, X (March 1963), 13–14.

Bowen, Merlin. *The Long Encounter: Self and Experience in the Writings of Herman Melville*. Chicago: University of Chicago Press, 1960. Pp. 216–233. Views *BB* as a study of moral blindness: anti-Vere.

*Braswell, William. "Melville's *Billy Budd* as 'An Inside Narrative,' " *American Literature*, XXIX (May 1957), 133–146.

———. *Melville's Religious Thought: An Essay in Interpretation*. Durham: Duke University Press, 1943. Pp. 122–124. Reprinted (New York: Pageant Books, Inc., 1959).

Brown, John Mason. "Hanged from the Yardarm," in *As They Appear*. New York: McGraw Hill, 1952. Pp. 186–192. Compares the tale with the play.

Browne, Ray B. "*Billy Budd:* Gospel of Democracy," *Nineteenth-Century Fiction*, XVII (March 1963), 321–337. Sees *BB* as political allegory.

Brumm, Ursula. "The Figure of Christ in American Literature," *Partisan Review*, XXIV (Summer 1957), 403–412, *passim*.

Callan, Richard J. "The Burden of Innocence in Melville and Twain," *Renascence*, XVII (Summer 1965), 191–194. On Billy and Huck.

Cameron, Kenneth W. "*Billy Budd* and *An Execution at Sea*," *Emerson Society Quarterly*, No. 2 (First Quarter 1956), 13–15. Reprints an earlier treatment of the *BB* theme.

Campbell, H. M. "The Hanging Scene in Melville's 'Billy Budd,' " *Modern Language Notes*, LXVI (June 1951), 378–381.

———. "The Hanging Scene in Melville's 'Billy Budd': A Reply to Mr. Giovannini," *Modern Language Notes*, LXX (Nov. 1955), 497–500.

Cannon, Agnes Dicken. "Melville's Use of Sea Ballads and Songs," *Western Folklore*, XXIII (Jan. 1964), 13–16. Sees "Billy in the Darbies" as an account of "Christ in Chains."

Carpenter, Frederic I. *American Literature and the Dream*. New York: Philosophical Library, Inc., 1955. Pp. 79–82, 203–205. *BB* as an expression of the problem of liberty and authority; compares *BB* with Wouk's *The Caine Mutiny*. First appeared as "Melville: The World in a Man of War," *University of Kansas City Review*, XIX (Summer 1953), 257–264.

*Casper, Leonard. "The Case against Captain Vere," *Perspective*, V (Summer 1952), 145–152.

Chandler, Alice. "The Name Symbolism of Captain Vere," *Nineteenth-Century Fiction*, XII (June 1967), 86–89.

Chase, Richard. "A Note on *Billy Budd*," in *The American Novel and Its Tradition.* Garden City, N.Y.: Doubleday Anchor Books, 1957. Pp. 113–115. A reply to R. W. B. Lewis (see below) and a "political" reading of *BB.*

———. "Dissent on Billy Budd," *Partisan Review,* XV (Nov. 1948), 1212–1218. Expanded in Chase, *Herman Melville* (see below).

† ———. *Herman Melville: A Critical Study.* New York: The Macmillan Co., 1949. Pp. 258–277, 298. Questions the conscious esthetic achievement of *BB.*

° ———. "Introduction," *Selected Tales and Poems* of Herman Melville. New York: Rinehart Editions, 1950. Pp. xiii–xvi.

Clive, Geoffrey. *The Romantic Enlightenment.* New York: Meridian Books, 1960. Pp. 161–165. *BB,* Kierkegaard's *Fear and Trembling,* and *Crime and Punishment.* Originally appeared as "The Teleological Suspense of the Ethical in Nineteenth Century Literature," *Journal of Religion,* XXXIV (April 1954), 75–87.

Cowie, Alexander. "Herman Melville," in *The Rise of the American Novel.* New York: American Book Co., 1948. Pp. 394–395.

°Coxe, Louis O., and Robert Chapman. *Billy Budd,* with "Foreword" by Brooks Atkinson. New York: Hill and Wang, 1962. The dramatic version of the tale. The "Foreword" is Atkinson's review of the play, *New York Times,* Feb. 11, 1951.

° ———. "Notes on the Play." See above, pp. 88–90.

Cramer, Maurice B. " 'Billy Budd' and 'Billy Budd,' " *Journal of General Education,* X (April 1957), 78–91. Compares play with tale.

Cunliffe, Marcus. *The Literature of the United States.* London: Pelican, 1954. Pp. 118–119.

Dillistone, F. W. "The Angel Must Hang," in *The Novelist and the Passion Story.* New York: Sheed and Ward, 1961. Pp. 45–68. Melville is here "feeling after a way of reconciliation which he can accept with his mind as well as with his heart."

Doubleday, Neal F. "Jack Easy and Billy Budd," *English Language Notes,* II (Sept. 1964), 39–41.

Duerksen, Roland A. *"Caleb Williams, Political Justice,* and *Billy Budd,"* *American Literature,* XXXVIII (Nov. 1966), 372–376.

Feidelson, Charles N. *Symbolism and American Literature.* Chicago: University of Chicago Press, 1953. Reprinted as a Phoenix Book. Chicago: University of Chicago Press, 1959. Pp. 212, 344–345. Questions the "acceptance" thesis.

Fiedler, Leslie. *Love and Death in the American Novel.* New York: Criterion Books, 1960. Pp. 359, 362, 434–435.

°Fogle, Richard Harter. "*Billy Budd*—Acceptance or Irony," *Tulane Studies in English,* VIII (1958), 107–113.

———. "*Billy Budd:* the Order of the Fall," *Nineteenth-Century Fiction,* XV (Dec. 1960), 189–205. Defends Vere.

*Foley, Mary. "The Digressions in *Billy Budd*," in *Melville's Billy Budd and the Critics*, ed. William T. Stafford. 2nd ed. Belmont, Calif.: Wadsworth Publishing Company, Inc., 1968. Pp. 220–223.

Forster, E. M. *Aspects of the Novel*. New York: Harcourt, Brace and Co., 1927. Pp. 204–206.

————. "Letter," *The Griffin*, I (1951), 4–6. Explains his treatment of Vere as villain in his libretto (see below) for the Benjamin Britten opera of *BB*.

————, and Eric Crozier. "Libretto" for Benjamin Britten's *Billy Budd: Opera in Four Acts*. London: Boosey & Hawkes, Ltd., 1951.

Freeman, F. Barron. "Introduction," *Herman Melville's Billy Budd*. Cambridge: Harvard University Press, 1948. Pp. 1–126. Extended analysis of the biographical background, sources, composition, text, style, technique, and significance of *BB*.

* Freeman, John. *Herman Melville*. New York: The Macmillan Co., 1926. Pp. 131–136.

Freimarck, Vincent. "Mainmast as Crucifix in *Billy Budd*," *Modern Language Notes*, LXXII (Nov. 1957), 496–497.

Freund, Philip. "Sea and Sky: Herman Melville," in *The Art of Reading the Novel*. Rev. ed. New York: Collier Books, 1965. Pp. 71–78, *passim*. *BB* "is idealism's most complete document."

Gerould, Gordon Hall. *The Patterns of English and American Fiction: A History*. Boston: Little, Brown and Co., 1942. Pp. 354, 358. *BB* "predicts" Conrad.

Gettmann, Royal A., and Bruce Harkness. "Billy Budd, Foretopman," in *Teacher's Manual for A Book of Stories*. New York: Rinehart & Co., Inc., 1955. Pp. 71–74.

Giovannini, G. "The Hanging Scene in Melville's *Billy Budd*," *Modern Language Notes*, LXX (Nov. 1955), 491–497. Retort to H. M. Campbell (see above).

*Glick, Wendell. "Expediency and Absolute Morality in 'Billy Budd,'" *PMLA*, LXVIII (March 1953), 103–110.

Goldsmith, Arnold L. "'The Discovery Scene' in *Billy Budd*," *Modern Drama*, III (Feb. 1961). Defends the discovery scene in the dramatic version.

Gollin, Richard and Rita. "Justice in an Earlier Treatment of the *Billy Budd* Theme," *American Literature*, XXVIII (Jan. 1957), 513–515.

Gross, John J. "Melville, Dostoevsky, and the People," *Pacific Spectator*, X (Spring 1956), 160–170. Sees parallels between the two writers.

Hagopian, John V., and Martin Dolch, with the assistance of W. Gordon Cunliffe and Arvin R. Wells. *Insight I: Analyses of American Literature*. Frankfurt am Main: Hirschgraben-Verlag, 1962. Pp. 155–165. Anti-Vere, with good discussion questions at the end.

Hall, Joan Joffe. "The Historical Chapters in *Billy Budd*," *University Review*, XXX (Oct. 1963), 35–40. Primarily on Vere and Nelson.

Hayford, Harrison, ed. *The Somers Mutiny Affair.* Englewood Cliffs: Prentice-Hall, Inc., 1959.

°————, and Merton M. Sealts, Jr., eds. Melville's *Billy Budd, Sailor (An Inside Narrative): Reading Text and Genetic Text.* Chicago: University of Chicago Press, 1962. The single most important book on *BB* to date, with important "Editors' Introduction," "Notes and Commentary," "Bibliography," and "Textual Notes" (to both reading and genetic texts).

Heilman, Robert. *Magic in the Web: Action and Language in Othello.* Lexington: University of Kentucky Press, 1956. Pp. 37, 43, 113, 116, 247–248. Compares Iago with Claggart.

Hillway, Tyrus. *"Billy Budd: Melville's Human Sacrifice," Pacific Spectator,* VI (Summer 1952), 342–347.

————. *Herman Melville.* New York: Twayne, 1963. Pp. 138–144. *BB* "comes close to being Melville's 'Everlasting Yea,' though the affirmation is oblique, not positive."

————. "Melville's *Billy Budd,*" *Explicator,* IV (1945), Item 12. Defends Vere.

Howard, Leon. *Herman Melville.* University of Minnesota Pamphlets on American Writers, No. 13. Minneapolis: University of Minnesota Press, 1961. Pp. 42–44. "Man's relationship to his private self and to the society in which he dwells is still the greatest source of tension of modern times."

————. *Herman Melville: A Biography.* Berkeley: University of California Press, 1951. Pp. 324–328. About sources and conditions under which *BB* was written and a view of its meaning as "The best thing possible 'in this comprehensible world.' "

Hudson, H. E., IV. "Billy Budd: Adam or Christ?" *Crane Review,* VII (1965), 62–67.

Humphreys, A. R. "Billy Budd," in *Herman Melville.* New York: The Grove Press, 1962. Pp. 111–114. Brief lyrical praise of the tale's power.

°Ives, C. B. *"Billy Budd and the Articles of War," American Literature,* XXXIV (March 1962), 31–39.

Karl, A. N. *The American Vision: Actual and Ideal Society in Nineteenth-Century Fiction.* New Haven, Conn.: Yale University Press, 1963. Pp. 277–279.

Kazin, Alfred. "Ishmael in His Academic Heaven," *New Yorker,* Feb. 12, 1949, pp. 88–89. Review-essay of Freeman's edition.

Kilbourne, W. G., Jr. "Montaigne and Captain Vere," *American Literature,* XXXIII (Jan. 1962), 514–517.

Krieger, Murray. *The Tragic Vision.* New York: Holt, Rinehart and Winston, Inc., 1960. Pp. 256, 260, 263–264. Questions the tragic achievement of the tale.

Ledbetter, Kenneth. "The Ambiguity of *Billy Budd,*" *Texas Studies in Literature and Language,* IV (Spring 1962), 130–134.

Lemon, Lee T. *"Billy Budd:* The Plot against the Story," *Studies in Short Fiction,* II (Fall 1964), 32–43.

Lesser, Simon. *Fiction and the Unconscious.* Boston: Beacon Press, 1957. Pp. 92–93. A psychological reading.

Levin, Harry. *The Power of Blackness.* New York: Alfred A. Knopf, Inc., 1958. Pp. 194–197. *BB* is at best "a truce."

Lewis, R. W. B. *The American Adam: Innocence, Tragedy, and Tradition in the Nineteenth Century.* Chicago: University of Chicago Press, 1955. Pp. 146–152. Billy Budd as an "American" Adam.

London, Philip W. "The Military Necessity: *Billy Budd* and Vigny," *Comparative Literature,* XIV (Spring 1962), 174–186.

Malbone, Raymond G. "How Shall We Teach the New *Billy Budd, Sailor?*" *College English,* XXVII (March 1966), 499–500.

Mary Ellen, Sister. "Parallels in Contrast: A Study of Melville's Imagery in *Moby-Dick* and *Billy Budd," Studies in Short Fiction,* II (Spring 1965), 284–290.

Mason, Ronald. *"Billy Budd* and the Victory of Innocence," in *The Spirit above the Dust: A Study of Herman Melville.* London: John Lehmann, Ltd., 1951. Pp. 245–260. Also on *BB* and *The Tempest.*

Matthiessen, F. O. "Billy Budd, Foretopman," in *American Renaissance: Art and Expression in the Age of Emerson and Whitman.* New York: Oxford University Press, 1941. Pp. 500–514. Proposes the "acceptance of necessity" theme and sees parallels with Jonathan Edwards, Shakespeare, Keats, and other Melville works.

Mayoux, Jean Jacques. *Melville,* trans. John Ashbery. New York: Grove Press, 1960. Pp. 125–128. Contrasts *BB* with Kafka's *The Trial.*

McCarthy, Paul. "Character and Structure in *Billy Budd," Discourse,* IX (Spring 1966), 201–217.

McElderry, B. R., Jr. "Three Earlier Treatments of the *Billy Budd* Theme," *American Literature,* XXVII (May 1955), 251–257.

McNamara, Anne. "Melville's *Billy Budd," Explicator,* XXI (October 1962), Item 11. Examines the many classical allusions in *BB.*

Miller, James E., Jr. *"Billy Budd:* The Catastrophe of Innocence," in *Reader's Guide to Herman Melville.* New York: Farrar, Straus and Cudahy, 1962. Pp. 218–228. Originally appeared in *Modern Language Notes,* LXXIII (March 1958), 168–176.

———. "Melville's Search for Form," *Bucknell Review,* VIII (Dec. 1959), 275–276. Melville turns to Christian myth in *BB* to demonstrate ". . . its weakness and final inefficacy."

Montale, Eugenio. "An Introduction to *Billy Budd* (1942)," *Sewanee Review,* LXVIII (Summer 1960), 419–422. English translation of an introduction to an Italian edition of *BB.*

Monteiro, George. "Melville and Keats," *Emerson Society Quarterly,* No. 31 (Second Quarter 1963), 55. The term *Jemmy Legs* may have come from a Keats letter.

*Mumford, Lewis. *Herman Melville.* New York: Harcourt, Brace and Co., 1929. Pp. 353–357.

†Murry, John Middleton. "Herman Melville's Silence," *Times Literary Supplement,* No. 1173, July 10, 1924. Reprinted in *John Clare and Other Studies.* London: Peter Neville, 1950. Pp. 209–212.

*Nathanson, Leonard. "Melville's *Billy Budd,* Chapter 1," *Explicator,* XXII (May 1964), Item 75.

Noone, John B., Jr. "*Billy Budd:* Two Concepts of Nature," *American Literature,* XXIX (Nov. 1957), 249–262. Ideological reading in terms of Hobbes, Locke, and Rousseau.

Oates, J. E. "Melville and the Manichean Illusion," *Texas Studies in Literature and Language,* IV (Spring 1962), 117–129. By the time of writing *BB,* Melville had drifted into a sort of "Nihilism."

†Pearson, Norman Holmes. "Billy Budd: 'The King's Yarn,'" *American Quarterly,* III (Summer 1951), 99–114. Shows that literary associations (especially Milton), sources, and parallels enrich and are necessary to a reading of *BB.*

Phelps, Leland R. "The Reaction to *Benito Cereno* and *Billy Budd* in Germany," *Symposium,* XIII (Fall 1959), 294–299. Includes important discussion of Thomas Mann's reaction to *BB.*

Plomer, William. "Introduction," *Billy Budd, Foretopman.* London: John Lehmann, Ltd., 1947. Pp. 7–10. *BB* as "final protest against the nature of things."

†Pommer, Henry F. *Milton and Melville.* Pittsburgh: University of Pittsburgh Press, 1950. Pp. 83–85, 87–90.

*Rathbun, John W. "*Billy Budd* and the Limits of Perception," *Nineteenth-Century Fiction,* XX (June 1965), 19–34.

Reed, Henry. "Books in General," *New Statesman and Nation,* May 31, 1947, p. 397. Melville cherished his "ambiguities" to the end.

Reich, Charles A. "The Tragedy of Justice in *Billy Budd,*" *Yale Review,* LVI (Spring 1967), 368–369. Important examination of the conflict between the "natural" element in man and justice.

Rogers, Robert. "The 'Ineludible Gripe' of *Billy Budd,*" *Literature and Psychology,* XIV (Winter 1964), 9–22. Psychological reading of Billy as unconscious rebel.

Rosenberry, Edward H. "The Problem of *Billy Budd,*" *PMLA,* LXXX (Dec. 1965), 489–498.

*Rosenthal, M. L., and A. J. M. Smith. *Exploring Poetry.* New York: The Macmillan Co., 1955. Pp. 372–375.

Roudiez, Leon S. "Strangers in Melville and Camus," *French Review,* XXXI (Jan. 1958), 223–225. Compares *L'Étranger* with *BB.*

Sale, Arthur. "Captain Vere's Reasons," *Cambridge Journal,* V (Oct. 1951), 3–18. Couples Claggart and Vere and views *BB*'s death as ironic.

Schiffman, Joseph. "Melville's Final Stage, Irony: A Re-examination of 'Billy Budd' Criticism," *American Literature,* XXII (May 1950), 128–136.

Sealts, Merton M., Jr. "The Ghost of Major Melville," *New England Quarterly*, XXX (Sept. 1957), 291–306. Melville's uncle may have been one of the many prototypes for some aspects of *BB*.

Sedgwick, William E. *Herman Melville: The Tragedy of Mind.* Cambridge: Harvard University Press, 1944. Pp. 231–249. *BB* as acceptance in contrast to *Typee, Redburn,* and *Pierre.*

Shattuck, Roger. "Two Inside Narratives: *Billy Budd* and *L'Étranger,*" Texas *Studies in Literature and Language,* IV (Autumn 1962), 314–320.

Sherwood, John C. "Vere as Collingwood: A Key to *Billy Budd,*" *American Literature,* XXXV (Jan. 1964), 476–484.

Short, Raymond W. "Introduction," *Four Great American Novels.* New York: Henry Holt and Co., 1946. Pp. xxxi–xxxii. Brief comparisons with Shakespeare.

Shulman, Robert. "Montaigne and the Techniques of Melville's *Billy Budd,*" *Comparative Literature,* XVI (Fall 1964), 322–330.

Smylie, James. *"Billy Budd:* The Work of Christ in Melville," *Religion in Life,* XXXIII (Spring 1964), 286–296. Sees "dominant theological lines of the Nineteenth Century" represented in *BB.*

Snell, G. P. *Shapers of American Fiction, 1798–1947.* New York: E. P. Dutton & Co., Inc., 1947. Pp. 77–78.

Snyder, Oliver. "A Note on 'Billy Budd,' " *Accent,* XI (Winter 1951), 58–60. *BB* as "a great political Mystery drama."

Spilka, Mark, Kingsley Widmer, and Arthur Efron. "Controversy on Lawrence and the Academy," *Paunch,* No. 27 (Oct. 1966), pp. 83–96. A series of public letters on institutionalism vs. individualism with a long digression about *BB.*

Spiller, Robert E. *The Cycle of American Literature.* New York: New American Library, 1957. P. 83.

*Stafford, William T. "The New *Billy Budd* and the Novelistic Fallacy: An Essay-Review," *Modern Fiction Studies,* VIII (Autumn 1962), 306–311.

Stallman, R. W., and R. E. Watters. *The Creative Reader.* New York: The Ronald Press, 1954. Pp. 334–338. Notes and questions for discussion.

Stein, William Bysshe. " 'Billy Budd': The Nightmare of History," *Criticism,* III (Summer 1961), 237–250. On the "tone" of the narrator and the conflict between fact (history) and fable (myth) in the tale.

———. "The Motif of the Wise Old Man in *Billy Budd,*" *Western Humanities Review,* XIV (Winter 1960), 99–101.

†Stern, Milton R. *The Fine Hammered Steel of Herman Melville.* Urbana: University of Illinois Press, 1957. Pp. 26–27, 206–239.

———. "Introduction," *Typee and Billy Budd.* New York: E. P. Dutton & Co., 1958. Pp. xx–xxv; "A Note about the Text," pp. 269–274.

Stewart, Randall. *American Literature and Christian Doctrine.* Baton Rouge: Louisiana State University Press, 1958. Pp. 98–102. Compares *BB* with Hawthorne's "The Birthmark," Claggart with Iago. Appeared earlier in *The Tragic Vision and the Christian Faith,* ed. Nathan A. Scott, Jr. New York: Association Press, 1957. Pp. 257–262.

†Stone, Geoffrey. *Melville*. New York: Sheed & Ward, Inc., 1949. Pp. 306–319. *BB* reveals Melville's continued ambiguity.

———. "Herman Melville: Loyalty to the Heart," *American Classics Reconsidered*, ed. Harold C. Gardiner, S. J. New York: Charles Scribner's Sons, 1958. Pp. 227–228.

Strandberg, Victor H. "God and the Critics of Melville," *Texas Studies in Literature and Language*, VI (Autumn 1964), 322–333. Attacks Lawrance Thompson's *Melville's Quarrel with God*, especially as it relates to *Moby-Dick* and *BB*.

Suits, Bernard. "*Billy Budd* and Historical Evidence," *Nineteenth-Century Fiction*, XVIII (Dec. 1963), 288–291. See Browne (above).

Sutton, Walter. "Melville and the Great God Budd," *Prairie Schooner*, XXXIV (Summer 1960), 128–133. *BB* read in terms of Schopenhauer.

†Thompson, Lawrance. "Divine Depravity," *Melville's Quarrel with God.* Princeton: Princeton University Press, 1952. Pp. 331–332, 355–414. Extensive analysis, viewing *BB* as irony, Claggart as agent of Vere, Vere as agent of God.

Thorp, Willard. "Foreword," *Billy Budd, Foretopman and Other Tales.* New York: Signet Classics, 1961.

———. "Herman Melville," in *Literary History of the United States*, ed. Robert E. Spiller, et al. New York: The Macmillan Co., 1948. Pp. 469–471.

———. "Introduction," *Herman Melville: Representative Selections*. Cincinnati: American Book Co., 1938. P. lxxxiv.

°Tindall, William York. "The Ceremony of Innocence," in *Great Moral Dilemmas in Literature, Past and Present*, ed. R. M. McIver. New York: Harper & Brothers, 1956. Pp. 73–81.

Tyler, Parker. "Milly and Billy as Proto-Finnegans," *Every Artist His Own Scandal: A Study of Real and Fictive Heroes*. New York: Horizon Press, 1964. Pp. 239–255. On James's Milly Theale and BB.

Van Doren, Carl. *The American Novel 1789–1939*. Rev. ed. New York: The Macmillan Co., 1940. Pp. 101–102.

———. "Foreword," *Billy Budd, Benito Cereno and the Enchanted Isles.* New York: The Readers Club, Inc., 1942. Pp. viii–ix.

———. "A Note of Confession," *Nation*, CXXVII (Dec. 5, 1928), 622.

Von Abele, Rudolph. "Melville and the Problem of Evil," *American Mercury*, LXV (Nov. 1947), 592–598. A general survey of Melville's works.

Wagner, Vern. "Billy Budd as Moby Dick: An Alternate Reading," in *Studies in Honor of John Wilcox*, ed. A. Dayle Wallace and Woodburn O. Ross. Detroit: Wayne State University Press, 1958. Pp. 157–174. And Claggart as Ahab!

Warner, Rex. "Introduction," *Billy Budd and Other Stories.* London: John Lehmann, Ltd., 1951. Pp. vii–xi.

°Watson, E. L. Grant. "Melville's Testament of Acceptance," *New England Quarterly*, VI (June 1933), 319–327.

Watters, R. E. "Melville's 'Sociality,'" *American Literature*, XVII (March 1945), 33–49. Acceptance of an "embracing sociality."

*Weaver, Raymond M. "Introduction," *The Shorter Novels of Herman Melville.* New York: Liveright Publishing Corp., 1928. Pp. xlix–li.

*———. *Herman Melville: Mariner and Mystic.* New York: George H. Doran Co., 1921. P. 318. Reprinted as a Pageant Book. New York: Pageant Books, Inc., 1960.

Weir, Charles, Jr. "Malice Reconciled: A Note on Herman Melville's 'Billy Budd,'" *University of Toronto Quarterly*, XIII (April 1944), 276–285.

†Weisinger, Herbert, and Adrian H. Jaffe: "Herman Melville," in *The Laureate Fraternity: An Introduction to Literature.* Evanston: Row, Peterson and Co., 1960. Pp. 142–143; "Study Questions," p. 177.

West, Ray B., Jr. "Primitivism in Melville," *Prairie Schooner*, XXX (Winter 1956), 379–385.

*———. "The Unity of 'Billy Budd,'" *Hudson Review*, V (Spring 1952), 120–127.

White, Edgar Walter. "Billy Budd," *Adelphi*, XXVIII (First Quarter 1952), 492–498. Compares the tale with the Britten opera.

Willett, Ralph W. "Nelson and Vere: Hero and Victim in *Billy Budd, Sailor,*" *PMLA*, LXXXII (October 1967), 370–376.

Wilson, G. R., Jr. "*Billy Budd* and Melville's Use of Dramatic Technique," *Studies in Short Fiction*, IV (Winter 1967), 105–111. The "multiple meaning" of the story would not have been possible had Melville "further dramatized any important action."

Winters, Yvor. *Maule's Curse: Seven Studies in the History of American Obscurantism.* Norfolk: New Directions, 1938. Pp. 86–87. Reprinted in *In Defense of Reason.* Denver: Alan Swallow, 1947. Pp. 230–231.

*Withim, Phil. "*Billy Budd:* Testament of Resistance," *Modern Language Quarterly*, XX (June 1959), 115–127.

*Wright, Nathalia. *Melville's Use of the Bible.* Durham: Duke University Press, 1949. Pp. 126–136.

Zink, Karl E. "Herman Melville and the Forms—Irony and Social Criticism in 'Billy Budd,'" *Accent*, XII (Summer 1952), 131–139.

For continuing studies of *Billy Budd*, see the annual bibliographies (May issues) of *PMLA*, the quarterly issues of *American Literature*, and the monthly issues of *Abstracts of English Studies.*